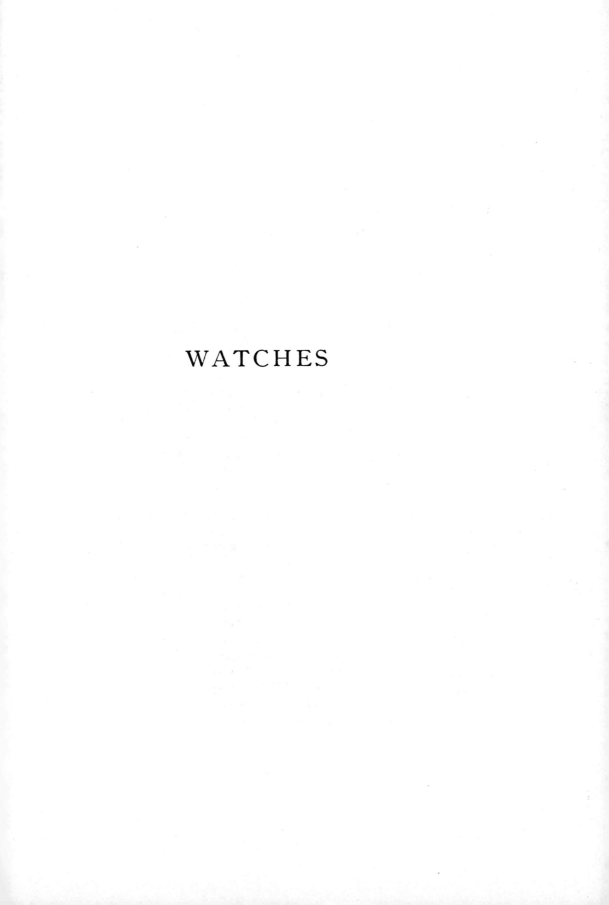

WATCHES

L'expérience a fait connoistre, depuis notre heureux retour en nostre bonne Ville de Paris, que l'art d'orlogerie est infiniment au delà de ceux que nous avons bien voulu gratiffier ; que par l'application d'un mouvement inconnu, il fait découvrir les degrez du Soleil, le cours de la Lune, les effets des Astres, la disposition des secondes, des minutes, des momens, des heures, des jours, des sepmaines, des mois et des années, les productions des métaux, les qualités des minéraux, et que toutes les sciences contribuent unaniment au succeds favorable de ses objets ; que le coup d'un orloge addroitement disposé préserve la personne d'un malade des attaques funestes de ses douleurs, quand le remède lui est proportionnement donné à l'heure prescrite par le Médecin ; qu'une bataille se trouve ordinairement au point de sa gloire par le secours d'un juste réveille-matin ; et que l'invention de la montre doit effectivement passer pour le principal mobile du repos, de la douceur et de la tranquillité des hommes.

Lettre patente de Louis XIV., 1652.

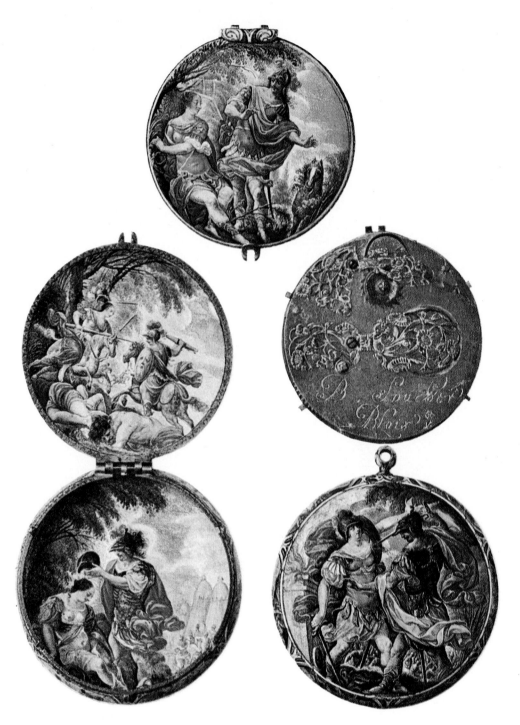

WATCH BY BLAISE FOUCHER

WATCHES

THEIR HISTORY, DECORATION
AND MECHANISM

BY

G. H. BAILLIE

N.A.G. PRESS LTD.
LONDON EC1V 7QA

First Published in 1929

* Facsimile Reprint 1979

* This Edition published by N.A.G. Press Ltd, London,
in conjuction with Northwood Publications Ltd.

*This facsimile edition is published to mark the jubilee of
the original work, and the publishers wish to acknowledge
the assistance given in its preparation by Messrs T & A
Constable Ltd, who also printed and made that edition.*

ISBN 7198 0140 0

PRINTED AND BOUND IN GREAT BRITAIN BY
T & A CONSTABLE LTD, EDINBURGH, SCOTLAND

PREFACE

'C'est un métier de faire un livre comme de faire une pendule.'

LA BRUYÈRE.

MY own métier is neither book- nor watch-making, and, if anything fits me to write about watches, it is that I have been attracted with equal force by all their three aspects—their history, their decoration, and their mechanism. No book has yet been published dealing adequately with these three aspects, and I have realized that through neglecting one or other of them nearly all the collectors and lovers of watches miss much of the pleasure their pursuit could yield.

I have endeavoured to apportion this book fairly as between history, decoration, and movement, in the hope of giving a wider interest to those who are already under the spell of the watch, and attracting under it some of those who have not yet appreciated its wonderful variety.

It is the variety that gives the watch its peculiar interest. Its history has so many obscure periods that there is still ample scope for conjecture and research. It became common—as a jewel of price—early enough to benefit by the fine decorative work of the seventeenth century, and no one thing has been beautified by so many different craftsmen. It, with its parent the clock, was the first automatic mechanism made, and four centuries of science and ingenuity have made it the physical measuring instrument that measures its quantity with the greatest accuracy.

Old watches are plentiful, but few have cases worth a second glance ; rather more, but still few, have movements of interest ; but the collector who looks at both case and movement finds twice as many worthy specimens as he who cares for one or the other only.

There is little difficulty in interesting the mechanically minded in the work of art that encloses his bit of mechanism, though true appreciation comes only with study. There is far more difficulty in awaking in the student of the arts with no mechanical instincts any enthusiasm for 'wheels.' Those to whom mechanism is an offence will find the more complex parts tactfully relegated to the end of the book. Those who are willing to venture into strange regions of wheels, pinions, and levers will find the descriptions written and the drawings prepared on the assumption that the reader has no technical knowledge. Those to whom mechanism, but not a watch, is familiar will discover some beautiful mechanical devices. Those who know the watch movement may find one or two things of interest.

Chapter III. may seem irrelevant to the title of the book. A reason for it is that the early history of clocks is the pre-natal history of watches. An excuse is that much in the chapter has never been published in English.

The last chapter, 'The Chronology of Watches,' recapitulates very shortly the more important features of watch-cases and movements at different periods. It is intended for reference only and as a help in judging the date of a watch.

The most difficult part of the book was choosing the watches for illustration. My aim was to show types to serve as illustrations to the text. My constant temptation was to collect beautiful and interesting watches, forgetting the text. I have succumbed to the temptation to a considerable extent, with the result that many of the illustrations show great treasures and rarities of the world of watches.

For these illustrations and for facilities for examining and taking apart many of the watches, I owe a great debt to many people. I have given infinite trouble to the

PREFACE

authorities of the British Museum, the Victoria and Albert Museum, and the Fitzwilliam Museum, and they have shown the perfect courtesy of appearing to like it. I am grateful for special facilities to those in charge of the Guildhall Museum, the Science Museum, South Kensington, the Wallace Collection, the Louvre, the Kunsthistorische Museum and the Uhren Museum, Vienna, and the Palais du Cinquantenaire, Brussels. Mr. Francis Mallett has been most kind in granting me frequent access to his watches and in giving me photographs of a number of his treasures. To Mr. Percy Webster I am greatly indebted, not only for letting me choose examples for reproduction from his wonderful collection, but also for revising the chapter on 'The Chronology of Watches.' A chapter with so many possibilities of error needed the stamp of his authority to give it value.

Acknowledgement of the great assistance I have had in compiling the list of watch- and clock-makers of the world, forming the companion volume, is made in its special preface.

> 'Ce discours ennuyeux enfin termina
> Le bonhomme partit quand ma montre sonna.'
> CORNEILLE. *Le Menteur.*

NOTE.—The Victoria and Albert Museum is referred to by the name by which it is generally known—The South Kensington Museum.

Britten's invaluable book, *Old Clocks and Watches and their Makers*, is referred to as 'Britten.'

G. H. BAILLIE

August 1928

CONTENTS

WATCHES

LIST OF ILLUSTRATIONS

WATCHES

xii

LIST OF ILLUSTRATIONS

WATCHES

xiv

LIST OF ILLUSTRATIONS

A SHORT BIBLIOGRAPHY
MAINLY OF BOOKS TREATING OF WATCHES
FOLLOWED BY A SUBJECT CLASSIFICATION

The figures before the place of publication indicate the size of the book in inches.

ABBOTT, HENRY G. *The Watch Factories of America, Past and Present.* 145 pp. 9×6. Chicago, 1888.
A good account of the start and struggles of the early American factories.

ALLEXANDRE, R. P. DOM JACQUES. *Traité générale des Horloges.* 388 pp. 26 plates. 7½×5. Paris, 1734. German editions 1738 and 1763, with additions.
A famous book in the eighteenth century.

ANDRADE, JULES. *Horlogerie et Chronométrie.* 582 pp. 9×6. Paris, 1924.
A fine treatise on the theoretical side of horology.

ATKINS AND OVERALL. *Some Account of the Worshipful Company of Clock-makers of the City of London.* 346 pp. 10×6½. London, 1881.
A most interesting account compiled from the Company's records, 1632 to date.

BABEL, ANTONY. *Histoire Corporative de l'Horlogerie et de l'Orfèvrerie et des industries annexes.* 600 pp. 9½×6½. Geneva, 1916.
A history of watchmaking and the watchmakers' corporation in Geneva.

BALET, LEO. *Führer durch die Uhrensammlung.* Kgl. Württemberg-isches Landes-Gewerbemuseums, Stuttgart. 108 pp. 8×5½. Stuttgart, 1913.
An excellent short history of watches and clocks written round the Stuttgart Museum collection.

BASSERMANN-JORDAN, ERNST VON. *Die Geschichte der Räderuhr, unter besonderer Berücksichtigung der Uhren des Bayerischen National Museums.* 112 pp. 15×11. Munich, 1905.
One of the best histories of early watches and clocks.

——. *Uhren.* Bibliothek für Kunst- und Antiquitäten-Sammler. 174 pp. 9×6. Berlin, 1920 and 1922.
A handbook containing an immense amount of valuable and accurate information.

——. *Alte Uhren und ihre Meister.* 179 pp. 11×8½. Leipzig, 1926.
A collection of interesting articles on horological subjects.

A SHORT BIBLIOGRAPHY

BERNER, P. *Historique du Réglage de Précision depuis son origine jusqu'au commencement du xxe siècle.* 20 pp. Bienne, *c.* 1910.

The best account of the development of the art of adjusting watches.

BERTHOUD, FERDINAND. *Essai sur l'Horlogerie.* 2 vols. 477 and 452 pp. 38 plates. Paris, 1763. 2nd edition in 3 vols., Paris, 1786. German edition, shortened, 1790.

Berthoud was one of the foremost makers of his day, and an indefatigable experimenter. This is a valuable work in giving, in great technical detail, the construction of the most accurate timekeepers of the mid-eighteenth century. Many of the books published during the following half-century are compilations from this book.

——. *Histoire de la Mesure du Temps par les Horloges.* 2 vols. 373 and 447 pp. 23 plates. $10\frac{1}{2} \times 8$. Paris, 1802.

Most valuable for contemporary and eighteenth-century history, though much of the earlier history is inaccurate.

BILFINGER, GUSTAV. *Die Mittelalterlichen Horen und die Modernen Stunden.* Ein Beitrag zur Kulturgeschichte. 279 pp. $8 \times 5\frac{1}{2}$. Stuttgart, 1892.

A most interesting history of the canonical hours and of the gradual change to the modern system of time-reckoning. Contains an account of the earliest clocks known.

BOLTON, L. *Time Measurement: An introduction to means and ways of reckoning physical and civil time.* 166 pp. $7\frac{1}{2} \times 5$. London, 1924.

An excellent account of time-reckoning and measurement.

BREGUET. 'Le Centenaire de Breguet.' Special number of the *Journal Suisse de l'Horlogerie et de Bijouterie.* 40 pp. $10\frac{1}{2} \times 8$. Neuchâtel, 1923.

Articles on Breguet's life and work.

BRITTEN, F. J. *Old Clocks and Watches and their Makers.* 3rd edition. 790 pp. $8\frac{1}{2} \times 5\frac{1}{2}$. London, 1911. 5th edition, 1922.

The best general work, non-technical, on watches and clocks, with a very large number of illustrations. The early history, however, is incomplete and contains many inaccuracies. It includes a valuable list of makers, mainly English.

——. *Watch and Clockmakers' Handbook, Dictionary, and Guide.* 10th edition. 492 pp. $8\frac{1}{2} \times 5\frac{1}{2}$. London, 1902.

Contains a mass of useful information, mainly technical.

BUFFAT, EUGÈNE. *Historique et Technique de la Montre Roskopf.* 98 pp. 7 plates. $9\frac{1}{2} \times 6$. Geneva, 1914.

The only account of Roskopf and his great work in producing a good, cheap watch.

WATCHES

CHAMBERLAIN, PAUL. *Watches.* The Paul M. Chamberlain Collection at the Art Institute of Chicago. 64 pp. $9\frac{1}{2} \times 6\frac{1}{2}$. Chicago, 1921.
  A catalogue with excellent descriptions of technical details.

CHAPUIS, ALFRED. 'Montres et Bijoux suisses pour l'Inde.' Special number of the *Journal Suisse d'Horlogerie.* pp. 17-27. $10\frac{1}{2} \times 8$. Geneva, 1920.
  The only account of the rich and gaudy watches made for India at the end of the eighteenth and beginning of the nineteenth century.

——. *La Montre Chinoise.* 272 pp. 33 plates. $11 \times 8\frac{1}{2}$. Neuchâtel, *c.* 1923.
  The only account of the watches made with special forms of decoration for China.

DA CAPRIGLIA, GIUSEPPE. *Misura del Tempo, cioè Trattato d'Horologii da Ruota di tre ordine, da Campanile, da Camera e da Petto.* Padua, 1665. Also later French translation.
  The first book written about clocks.

DEVELLE, E. *Les Horlogers Blésois au xvie et au xviie siècle.* 1st edition, Blois, 1913. 2nd edition. 459 pp. 30 plates. 11×9. Blois, 1917.
  Most valuable in giving many details of the customs of the earliest corporation of watchmakers of importance and of the lives of the members, obtained by research in the archives of Blois.

DIETZSCHOLD, C. *Die Hemmungen der Uhren, ihre Entwicklung, Konstruktion, Reparatur und Behandlung vor der Reglage.* 244 pp. 9×6. Krems a. Donau, 1905.
  One of the best technical works on the escapements now in use.

DONDI DALL' OROLOGIO, MARCHESE FRANCESCO SCIPIONE DE. *Notizie sopra Jacopo e Giovanni Dondi dall' Orologio.* Padua, 1782 and 1844.
  The first accurate account of Giovanni Dondi dall' Orologio's work, correcting the generally accepted version given by Falconet.

DUBOIS, PIERRE. *Histoire de l'Horlogerie, depuis son origine jusqu'à nos jours, précédée de recherches sur la mesure du temps dans l'antiquité et suivie de la biographie des Horlogers les plus célèbres de l'Europe.* 406 pp. 36 plates. $10\frac{1}{2} \times 8\frac{1}{2}$. Paris, 1849.
  A beautiful and finely illustrated book, but the earlier history is most unreliable.

——. *Collection Archéologique du Prince Soltykoff. Horlogerie . . . Précédée d'un abrégé historique de l'horlogerie au Moyen Age.* 214 pp. 20 plates. $10\frac{1}{2} \times 8\frac{1}{2}$. Paris, 1858.
  The engravings of the Soltykoff watches and clocks, some coloured, are exceptionally good, but the history and descriptions contain many inaccuracies.

ENGELMANN, MAX. *Leben und Wirken des Württembergischen Pfarrers und Feintechnikers, Philipp Matthäus Hahn.* 273 pp. 9×6. Berlin, 1923.
  An interesting account of the life and work of the greatest German horologist.

xviii

A SHORT BIBLIOGRAPHY

FALLET-SCHEURER, MARIUS. *Geschichte der Uhrmacherkunst in Basel, 1370-1874.* Ein Beitrag zur Entwicklungsgeschichte der Uhrmacherkunst im Allgemeinen, sowie zur Wirtschafts- und Kulturgeschichte Basels. Beiträge zur Schweizerischen Wirtschaftskunde, Heft 9. 284 pp. $9\frac{1}{2} \times 6\frac{1}{2}$. Bern, 1917.

FRÄNKEL. *N. R. Fränkel's Uhrensammlung.* Herausgegeben von Heinrich Frauberger. 59 pp. 44 plates with 309 reproductions. $15\frac{1}{2} \times 12$. Düsseldorf, 1913.
   Good reproductions and descriptions, with a great deal of useful information.

FRANKLIN, A. *La vie privée d'autrefois : La mesure du temps.* 240 pp. 15 plates. $7 \times 4\frac{1}{2}$. Paris, 1888.
   A good account of early time-reckoning and timekeepers, mainly with reference to Paris.

GELCICH, E. *Geschichte der Uhrmacherkunst.* 5th edition of *Barfuss' History.* 208 pp. and folio atlas. $9 \times 5\frac{1}{2}$. Weimar, 1892.
   The main history is of no great value, but the later editions contain many interesting details of advances in horology in the first half of the nineteenth century.

GIERSBERG, JOSEPH. *Kölner Uhrmacher im 15 bis 19 Jahrhundert.* Beiträge zur Kölnischen Geschichte, Sprache, Eigenart. Mai 1915. pp. 274-291. $9 \times 5\frac{1}{2}$. Cologne, 1915.

GOULD, R. T. *The Marine Chronometer.* 287 pp. 40 plates. $9\frac{1}{2} \times 6$. London, 1923.
   An exceptionally good book on the history of the development of the chronometer.

GROS, CHARLES. *Échappements d'Horloges et de Montres.* Exposé technique, descriptif et historique des échappements d'horlogerie. 267 pp. 9×6. Paris, 1913.
   Not really a history of escapements, but a most valuable collection of the mass of devices that have been invented.

GROSSMANN, JULES AND HERMAN. *Horlogerie Théorique.* 2 vols. 408 and 426 pp. 20 plates. 9×6. Paris, 1911.
   Quite the best work treating of the theoretical side of the organs of timekeepers.

GROSSMANN, M. *Horological Dictionary, English-French-German. Dictionnaire, Français-Allemand-Anglais. Taschen-Wörterbuch für Uhrmacher, Deutsch-Englisch-Französisch.* 3 vols. 168, 162, and 178 pp. $6\frac{1}{2} \times 5$. Bienne, 1920.

HELWIG, ALFRED. *Drehganguhren (Tourbillons und Karusseluhren).* Ihr Bau, ihre Eigenarten ; Vorzüge und Nachteile der verschiedenen Konstruktionen. 99 pp. $9\frac{1}{2} \times 6$. Berlin, 1927.
   The only full account of this type of watch.

HOWGRAVE-GRAHAM, R. P. *Peter Lightfoot, Monk of Glastonbury, and the Old Clock of Wells.* 56 pp. 7 plates. $8\frac{1}{2}\times5\frac{1}{2}$. Glastonbury, 1922.

An interesting little book, in which, for the first time, legends have been distinguished from facts.

——. 'Some Clocks and Jacks, with notes on the History of Horology,' *Archæologia,* vol. lxxvii. 312 pp. 12 plates. $11\frac{1}{2}\times9\frac{1}{2}$. Oxford, 1928.

A most valuable contribution to the history of early clocks.

JAMES, ÉMILE. *Les Sonneries de Montres, Pendules et Horloges: Pratique et Théorie.* 93 pp. $7\frac{1}{2}\times5$. Bienne, 1927.

The best account of striking mechanism.

KENDAL, F. J. *A History of Watches and other Timekeepers.* 258 pp. 7×5. London, 1892.

Contains interesting details about watches and clocks in England.

LEBON, E. *Histoire de la fondation de la fabrication de la montre à Besançon en 1793 par une colonie d'horlogers suisses émigrés.*

LE NORMAND, JANVIER ET MAGNIER. *Nouveau Manuel complet de l'Horloger.* 7th edition. 464 pp. 12 plates. $6\times3\frac{1}{2}$. Paris, 1863.

A largely extended edition of the original work by the great maker Antide Janvier. Mainly a workshop handbook, but containing a great deal of information about early nineteenth-century watchmaking.

LEPAUTE, J. A. *Traité d'Horlogerie, contenant tout ce qui est nécessaire pour bien connoître et pour régler les pendules et les montres.* 308 pp. 17 folding plates. $9\frac{1}{2}\times7\frac{1}{2}$. Paris, 1755. 2nd edition, with supplement, Paris, 1767.

A fine work by an eminent maker, but treats more of clocks than of watches.

LEUTMANN, JOHANN GEORG. *Vollständige Nachricht von den Uhren, . . .* Erste Continuation oder Zweyter Theil, in welcher die Probir- auch Repetir- Uhren und Viatoria mit den vornehmsten Instrumenten, so zu ihrer accuraten Ausarbeitung und Stellung gehören, beschrieben . . . sind. Two parts. 109 and 132 pp. 22 folding plates. $6\frac{1}{2}\times4$. Halle, 1717-21.

The earliest treatise giving details of watch- and clock-making.

LIISBERG, BERING. *Urmagere og Ure i Danmark, med en kort fremstilling af urets og tidsforkyndelsens historie.* 290 pp. 12 plates. 10×8. Copenhagen, 1908.

The only book dealing with Danish horology, and a very good book.

LOESKE, M. *Die gesammte Literatur über Uhrmacherei und Zeitmesskunde.* Bautzen, 1897.

The best bibliography, though one is now appearing in *L'Horloger.*

XX

A SHORT BIBLIOGRAPHY

MARTINELLI, DOMENICO. *Horologi Elementari*. Divisi in quattro parti. Nella Prima Parte fatti con l'Acqua. Nella Seconda con la Terra. Nella Terza con l'Aria. Nella Quarta col Fuoco. Alcuni muti, ed alcuni col Suono. Tutti facili e molto commodi. 159 pp. 8×6. Venice, 1669.
> The second book written about clocks.

MIGEON, GASTON. *Collection Paul Garnier*. Musée du Louvre. Horloges et Montres. 112 pp. 48 plates. 7½×5. Paris, 1917.
> A catalogue, with good reproductions, of the choice collection of watches in the Louvre. The descriptions and historical notes are excellent.

MILHAM, WILLIS J. *Time and Timekeepers*. 609 pp. 8½×5½. New York, 1923.
> Especially good in technical particulars.

MOINET, H. L. *Nouveau Traité Générale Astronomique et Civil d'Horlogerie : Théorique et Pratique*. 2 vols. 444 and 544 pp. 51 plates. Paris, 1848. Third edition, with appendix, 1875.
> The best work dealing with the construction of watches and clocks of the first half of the nineteenth century.

MORGAN, OCTAVIUS. 'Observations on the History and Progress of the Art of Watchmaking, from the earliest period to modern times,' *Archæologia*, vol. xxxiii. London, 1849.
> Morgan's collection of watches, now in the British Museum, served as the text for this article.

NORDMANN, CHARLES. *Notre Maître le Temps*. 223 pp. Paris, 1924.
> A most interesting account of time and its reckoning.

OTTEMA, NANNE. *De Uurwerkmakerskunst in Friesland*. 38 pp. 4 plates. 9×6. Leeuwarden, 1923.
> The only account of Friesland watch- and clock-makers.

OVERTON, G. L. *Clocks and Watches*. 126 pp. London, 1922.
> An excellent little book, serving as an introduction to the study of horology.

PFLEGHART, A. *Die Schweizerische Uhrenindustrie, ihre geschichtliche Entwicklung und Organisation*. 203 pp. Leipzig, 1908.

PHILIPPE, ADRIEN. *Les Montres sans Clef*. 306 pp. 2 folding plates. Paris, 1863.

PHILLIPS, EDOUARD. *Mémoire sur le spiral réglant des Chronomètres et des Montres*. Mém. de l'Acad. des Sci., Tome 18, pp. 129-229. 4 folding plates. 11×9. Paris, 1868.
> This memoir, first published in 1861, forms the foundation on which rests the art of adjusting watches and chronometers.

RIGG, EDWARD. *Watchmaking.* Cantor Lecture of the Society of Arts. 39 pp. 10×6½. London, 1881.

A remarkable review of English watchmaking in its decline.

SALOMONS, D. L. *Breguet, 1747-1823.* 156 pp. 230 plates. 9×6. London, 1923. Also in French.

A catalogue, with fine reproductions of Sir David Salomon's collection of Breguet watches, with biographical notes.

SAUNIER, CLAUDIUS. *Die Geschichte der Zeitmesskunst.* Translated, with many additions, by Speckhart. 3 vols. 1096 pp. 8½×6. Bautzen, 1903.

A most valuable historical work.

——. *Treatise on Modern Horology.* Translated by Tripplin and Rigg. 2nd edition. 844 pp. 21 plates. 10½×7. London, 1880. First French edition, Paris, 1869.

A famous but much overrated work, verbose and weak in its theory, but useful in giving many results of experience.

——. *The Watchmaker's Handbook.* Translated by Tripplin and Rigg. 5th edition. 498 pp. 14 plates. 7×4½. London, 1912.

A valuable workshop handbook.

SIDENBLADH, ELIS. *Urmakare i Sverige under äldre Tider.* 173 pp. 43 plates. 9½×6. Stockholm, 1918.

The only account of the Swedish makers and their corporation.

SMITH, JOHN. *Old Scottish Clockmakers.* 2nd edition. 436 pp. 25 plates. 9×6. Edinburgh, 1921.

A valuable work, containing a list of Scottish makers, with details of their lives and works, and an account of the Incorporation of Hammermen.

THIOUT, L'AÎNÉ. *Traité de l'Horlogerie, méchanique et pratique.* 2 vols. Paris, 1741.

The best book of the eighteenth century.

VIAL, EUGÈNE, and CÔTE, CLAUDIUS. *Les Horlogers Lyonnais de 1550 à 1650.* 255 pp. 12 plates. 10×8. Lyons, 1927.

An account of the lives and works of the makers of Lyons, with many beautiful reproductions.

VIGNIAUX, P. *Horlogerie Pratique, à l'usage des Apprentis et des Amateurs.* 1st edition. 342 pp. 12 plates. 8½×5½. Toulouse, 1788. 2nd edition, 1802.

Interesting in giving practical working details of watch construction.

WOOD, EDWARD J. *Curiosities of Clocks and Watches.* 443 pp. 8×5. London, 1866.

A wonderful collection of interesting historical facts and stories of clocks and watches.

xxii

A SHORT BIBLIOGRAPHY

SUBJECT CLASSIFICATION, IN ORDER OF DATE

GENERAL TREATISES.—Da Capriglia, 1665. Martinelli, 1669. Leutmann, 1717. Allexandre, 1734. Thiout, 1741. Lepaute, 1755. Berthoud, 1763. Moinet, 1848. Saunier, 1869. Overton, 1922. Milham, 1923. Bolton, 1924.

HISTORICAL, GENERAL.—Allexandre, 1734. Berthoud, 1802. Dubois, 1849. Morgan, 1849. Wood, 1866. Gelcich, 1887. Kendal, 1892. Saunier, 1903. Bassermann-Jordan, 1905, 1920, and 1926. Balet, 1913. Britten, 1922.

EARLY CLOCKS.—Dondi dall' Orologio, 1782. Franklin, 1888. Bassermann-Jordan, 1905. Howgrave-Graham, 1922 and 1928.

NINETEENTH-CENTURY WATCHMAKING.—Rigg, 1881. Abbott, 1888.

TIME-RECKONING.—Franklin, 1888. Bilfinger, 1892. Nordmann, 1924.

SPECIAL COUNTRIES AND TOWNS.—*America*, Abbott. *Basle*, Fallet-Scheurer. *Besançon*, Lebon. *Blois*, Develle. *Cologne*, Giersberg. *Denmark*, Liisberg. *Friesland*, Ottema. *Geneva*, Babel. *London*, Atkins and Overall. *Lyons*, Vial and Côte. *Scotland*, Smith. *Sweden*, Sidenbladh. *Switzerland*, Pfleghart.

INDIVIDUAL MAKERS.—*Breguet*, Breguet and Salomons. *Dondi dall' Orologio*, q.v. *Hahn*, Engelmann.

TYPES OF WATCHES.—*Chinese watch*, Chapuis. *Chronometers*, Gould. *Indian watches*, Chapuis. *Keyless watches*, Philippe. *Roskopf watch*, Buffat. *Tourbillons*, Helwig.

CATALOGUES OF WATCHES.—Dubois, 1858. Balet, 1913. Fränkel, 1913. Migeon, 1917. Chamberlain, 1921.

TECHNICAL, GENERAL.—Leutmann, 1717. Thiout, 1741. Lepaute, 1753. Berthoud, 1763. Vigniaux, 1788. Moinet, 1848. Le Normand and Janvier, 1850. Saunier, 1880. Britten, 1902. Grossmann, 1911. Saunier, 1911. Andrade, 1924.

ESCAPEMENTS.—Dietzschold, 1905. Gros, 1913.

STRIKING MECHANISM.—James, 1927.

KEYLESS MECHANISM.—Philippe, 1863.

TOURBILLONS.—Helwig, 1927.

ROSKOPF WATCHES.—Buffat, 1914.

ADJUSTING.—Phillips, 1868. Berner, *c.* 1910.

DICTIONARY, ENGLISH–FRENCH–GERMAN.—Grossmann, 1926.

BIBLIOGRAPHY.—Loeske.

CHAPTER I

TIME

'Solem quis dicere falsum audeat?'—VIRGIL.
'Solem audet dicere falsum.'—*Engraved on dial of 17th-century watch by* JEAN VIET.

SINCE Einstein showed that time depends on the speed of the observer, the definitions of time given by philosophers from Aristotle onwards have become obsolete. We must be content with possessing the conception of time as a quantity existing between two events which we regard as successive. Granted this conception, there is no difficulty in defining the quantity measured by old timekeepers, but it is far from easy to define accurately the different quantity measured by modern timekeepers.

Three natural periods of time have been recognized in every country, from the earliest times of which there is record :—

The day, marked by the succession of day and night or the apparent motion of the sun.

The month, marked by the successive phases of the moon.

The year, marked by the succession of seasons, or by some annual occurrence such as a rainy season or the rising of the Nile.

The day-and-night period, which has always regulated the life of man, is the most important of the three, and has been taken as the unit of time in all countries. There are, though, various ways of measuring this period, and there are now in use three kinds of time which differ because the rotation of the earth is measured by different criteria. These are :—

(1) Apparent Solar Time, sometimes called True-

I

Time, which is the time measured by sundials and was in general use until the fifteenth century.

(2) Mean Solar Time, which is the time now in general use. Its unit cannot be measured, but has to be calculated.

(3) Sidereal Time, the time used by astronomers and measured daily in all observatories, when stars are visible. It is from this time that mean solar time is calculated.

There are three kinds of mean solar time—Local time, Standard time and Summer time, but these differ, not in the length of the day, but only in the time of its beginning.

It is worth while taking the trouble to gain a clear idea of the main relations of the sun and the earth, in order to appreciate the differences between the sidereal, the solar and the mean solar days, and also to understand the 'equation of time' mechanism which was fitted to many clocks and watches of the eighteenth century.

First, the axis on which the earth spins is inclined to the plane of its orbit round the sun. To appreciate what this means, it is simplest to imagine the heavens as a hollow sphere, studded with the stars, and the solar system at its centre. If the plane of the earth's equator were extended in all directions to meet this hollow sphere, it would trace on it a circle which is called the Celestial Equator. Next, if the plane of the earth's orbit were also extended to meet the sphere, it would trace on it another circle which is called the Ecliptic.[1] If the stars were visible in the daytime, so that the sun were seen in front of the background of stars, its apparent position among the stars would change from day to day as the earth moved along its orbit, and the Ecliptic is the course the sun would appear to take among the stars.

The earth's axis being inclined to its orbit, it follows that its equator (and the celestial equator) is inclined to

---

[1] The moon has to be in this plane to be eclipsed or to eclipse the sun ; hence the name.

the ecliptic, and the two circles traced on the sphere of the heavens cross each other. Half of the ecliptic is above or North of the equator and half below or South of it. While the sun is following the Northern half of the ecliptic, the Northern hemisphere of the earth receives the greater share of the sun's rays, and the days there are longer than the nights. This period corresponds to the seasons of spring and summer for the Northern hemisphere. During autumn and winter the sun is following the Southern half of the ecliptic, so the Northern hemisphere receives the smaller share of sunlight and the days are shorter than the nights. Twice in the year, when the sun crosses the celestial equator in passing from North to South of it and again from South to North of it, the two hemispheres are equally illuminated and the days are of the same length as the nights. These two occasions are the spring and autumn equinoxes. The spring equinox is the all-important moment in time measurement.[1]

Turning now to another feature of the earth's motion, it travels round the sun, following, not a circle, but an ellipse, and the sun is not at the centre of the ellipse but about one and a-half million miles off it, along the larger diameter of the ellipse (at one of its foci). Plate I, I shows the orbit, but with the ellipse greatly exaggerated. If the orbit were correctly drawn it would be indistinguishable by eye from a circle with the sun at its centre. Two consequences follow from the orbit being elliptical: first, the earth's distance from the sun varies throughout the year, and, secondly, its rate of travel varies, being greater the nearer the earth is to the sun. The earth is nearest to the sun (at perihelion) at the point P about January 1, and farthest from it (at aphelion) at A,

[1] It is not quite correct to say that day and night are equal at the equinoxes; they would be equal if the earth had no atmosphere, but actually the atmosphere refracts the sun's rays, so that the sun is seen after it has sunk below the horizon and the day is a little longer—less than a minute—than the night. This, though, is pedantic, because the day has no abrupt beginning or ending, thanks to the twilight caused by reflection of the sun's light by particles in the atmosphere.

about July 1, nearly half a year later. It is not always realized that the sun is some three million miles nearer to the earth in winter than in summer, and gives it in consequence about ten per cent. more heat. In England this effect is so much overshadowed by the effect of the inclination of the earth's axis that the extra heat is not noticed or appreciated, but it makes summer and winter more equable in the Northern hemisphere than at corresponding latitudes in the Southern hemisphere.

The four seasons are determined by the sun's position on the ecliptic. Two of the seasonal points, dividing winter from spring and summer from autumn, are the crossing points of the equator, at the spring and autumn equinoxes; these divide the ecliptic into two halves, and each half is divided into quarters at points called the winter and summer solstices. In Plate 1, 1 the position of the earth at these four points is indicated by the letters SE., SS., AE., WS. (Spring Equinox, Summer Solstice, etc.), and the approximate date of its arrival at each point is given. It is evident from the figure that the division of the ecliptic by these four seasonal points allocates different lengths of the earth's orbit to the four seasons. Combining with this the greater speed of travel of the earth the nearer it is to the sun, it follows that the four seasons are of different durations, which are, on the average :—

Spring	.	.	. 92 days 20 hours.
Summer	.	.	. 93 days 15 hours.
Autumn	.	.	. 89 days 19 hours.
Winter	.	.	. 89 days 0 hours.

Another irregularity is in the length of the apparent solar day. The solar day of any particular place on the earth is the time from the sun's passage across the meridian of that place to its next passage across it.[1]

---

[1] The meridian of a place is the plane through it and the earth's axis, and, in the Northern hemisphere, one generally says that the sun is due South when it crosses the meridian. This definition is not quite accurate, because the earth is not a homogeneous sphere, but the inaccuracy is negligible.

4

PLATE I

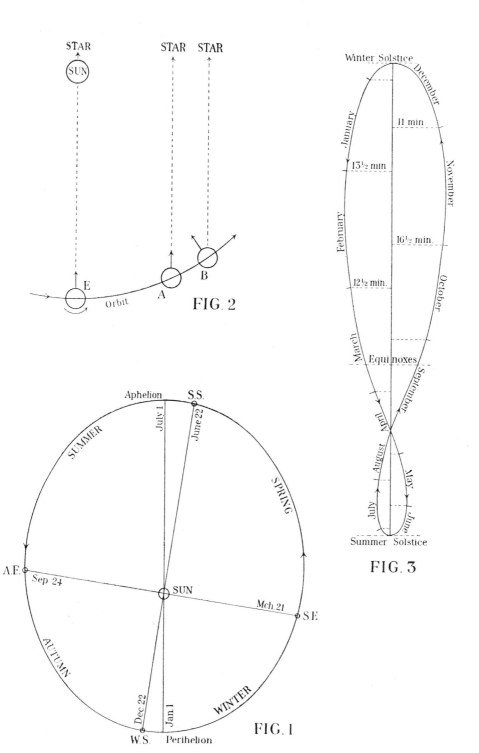

FIG. 2

FIG. 3

FIG. 1

SOLAR AND SIDEREAL TIME

TIME

This time varies from day to day, being about forty-eight seconds longer near the winter solstice than near the equinoxes. Clearly, so variable a day is quite unsuitable as the unit of time. The variation, however, is due to the earth's changing speed of travel and to the inclination of its axis to its orbit, and not to any irregularity in the rate at which it spins on its axis. To get a constant time unit, the time of rotation of the earth must be measured by some criterion which is unaffected by the earth's motion in its orbit. The stars serve as this criterion. The nearest star is so far off, about 260,000 times the distance of the sun, that the earth's travel is, in comparison, negligibly small.

Sidereal Time.—The rotation of the earth with reference to the stars gives sidereal time; it is now the only time that is measured, and is the time actually used in astronomical work. The astronomical unit of time is the sidereal day, measured as the time between two successive passages of the same star across the meridian.[1] It would, though, be most inconvenient as a unit of time for general use, because it is about four minutes shorter than the solar day, and four minutes daily, in six months, makes sidereal midnight occur at solar midday.

The reason for this difference of four minutes between the solar and sidereal days may be seen from Plate I, 2. The sun is shown at S and the earth at E, arrows indicating the direction of travel of the earth in its orbit and the direction of its spin. The arrow protruding from the earth represents an observer looking in the direction

[1] This is not quite accurate. Instead of an actual star, the point of the heavens at which the ecliptic crosses the equator when the earth is at the spring equinox is taken as the point of reference by which the earth's rotation is measured. This point is not quite stationary, but moves round the celestial equator at the rate of one revolution in about 26,000 years. It is called the First Point of Aries, though actually it is in the neighbouring constellation of Pisces. Hipparchus discovered the motion of the point, or the Precession of the Equinoxes, about 150 B.C., and it was then in Aries and nominally has remained there. The difference in the length of the sidereal day as measured with reference to the stars and with reference to the First Point of Aries is less than one-hundredth of a second.

5

of his meridian at the sun and at a star beyond the sun. On the scale of the diagram, in which the earth is about two and a half inches from the sun, this star would be at least ten miles off. When the earth has travelled to position A, it has turned on its axis enough to bring the observer into position again to see the star in his meridian. The earth then has made one revolution with reference to the star, and a sidereal day has passed. But the sun has not yet come to the observer's meridian; the earth must turn more and travel farther, to B, before he sees the sun; before, therefore, a solar day has passed. The time of the earth's travel from A to B represents the difference of four minutes between the sidereal and solar days. After a year, when the earth has returned to its original position, the observer will have seen the star cross his meridian once more than the sun, because he has made a circuit round the sun but not round the star, so the year contains one more sidereal day than it contains solar days.

Clocks which have a hand indicating sidereal time are not uncommon; watches giving both ordinary and sidereal time are rare.

Reverting to the unit of time, the sidereal day is the only measurable period which is constant enough to serve as a unit.[1] For convenience, however, the unit must be such that the midday determined by it is never far off

---

[1] It is not quite constant. The earth spins like a top that is wobbling, and the wobble is double. If there were a single steady wobble, the pole of the earth would describe a circle, as does the end of every top, at some moment during its spinning career. Actually, it describes a path which is a wavy line in the general shape of a circle. The motion is regarded as being made up of the two wobbles: the main wobble, which would make the pole describe a circle, and gives rise to *the Precession of the Equinoxes*, and the secondary wobble, which turns the circle into a wavy circular line, and is called the *Nutation*. The Precession of the Equinoxes has a period of about 26,000 years, this being the time taken for the pole to describe its circle. The Nutation has a period of about nineteen years. In reckoning the length of a sidereal day, the Precession is allowed for, as has been explained, by taking the Spring Equinox as a datum point instead of a star; but the Nutation is too rapid to be allowed for in this way. If the Spring Equinox, as affected by the Nutation, were really taken as the datum point, the length of the sidereal day would be continually varying over the period of nineteen years.

the midday of the sun's crossing the meridian. The problem has been solved by the invention of an imaginary sun, which is supposed to move at constant speed along the celestial equator instead of along the ecliptic, completing its circuit round the equator in the same time that the real sun takes to go round the ecliptic. The result is the same as if the earth travelled round the sun at constant speed in a circle. This imaginary sun is called the 'mean sun,' and the day it would determine, as the period between two successive crossings of the meridian, is called the 'mean solar day,' and is the present unit of time.[1]

The Equation of Time.—The equation of time can now be defined as the correction which has to be applied to apparent solar time, or, to use a more expressive term, sundial time, to give mean time.[2] It varies erratically throughout the year, because it depends on two causes, one the varying speed of the earth and the other the inclination of the earth's axis to its orbit. If only the

The effect of the Nutation is, therefore, averaged, and the datum point actually taken as the basis of time determination is the average position of the Spring Equinox over a period of nineteen years. For astronomers, Precession and Nutation are real troubles ; for every one else they have only a theoretical interest, because they affect the length of the sidereal day by only a small fraction of a second. Astronomers have a further difficulty to face. The stars used nightly to determine the time are not stationary ; they have what are termed proper motions, and these have to be allowed for. Finally, when all corrections have been applied, and the length of the sidereal day determined, the question arises, Is it constant ? In other words, Does the earth spin at a constant rate ? Two distinct investigations have shown that its rate of spin is not constant ; it is diminishing, and, therefore, the length of the sidereal day is increasing. The reason is that the tides cause a waste of energy in friction of the water. Power can be, and is, obtained from the tides, but only at an expense of the earth's rotation. The effect is not serious. One century, as measured by the sidereal day, will be one-tenth of a second longer than the previous century. One disturbing suggestion has been made : the moon will not keep to the position reckoned for her by astronomers, and it has been suggested that it is not the fault of the moon or of the reckoning, but is the fault of our timekeeping ; that, in fact, the rotation of the earth, as measured by the stars, is subject to irregularities of which nothing is known.

[1] The legal unit of time is the mean solar second. It is obtained by multiplying the sidereal second by a certain number, and there is some doubt about the accuracy of this number.

[2] Theoretically, a sundial does not measure apparent solar time accurately, but practically it does, because the error is too small to be seen on a sundial.

7

former were acting, the sundial would be fast between July and January and slow between January and July. If only the latter were acting, the sundial would be fast from each equinox to the following solstice (autumn and spring) and slow from each solstice to the following equinox (summer and winter). When the two effects are combined, the result is that the sundial time is correct on April 16, June 15, September 1 and December 25, and alternatively fast and slow in the intervals. On November 3 it reaches its maximum of about sixteen and a half minutes fast. Plate 1, 3 shows the equation of time throughout the year. This diagram forms the 'face' of a number of dials of the type called 'meridian dials' because they indicate only when the sun is on or near the meridian. The diagram is on a wall facing south, with a stile or gnomon in the meridian and parallel to the earth's axis. The stile ends in a small disc with a hole, and a shadow of the disc with a central bright spot is cast on the diagram. When the bright spot is on the central line of the diagram it is midday of apparent solar time; when it is on the curved line bounding the diagram, it is midday of mean solar time.

Before clocks were invented, and for four centuries afterwards, the sundial was the standard timekeeper. Clocks and watches were so erratic that they were useful only if constantly set by a sundial, and the equation of time was then an important article of everyday use. The meridian dial just described carried its own equation, but showed the time only at midday. The ordinary sundial, though it indicated whenever the sun shone, needed a table of corrections. By far the best was the watch or clock with an equation of time mechanism, showing on a dial either solar time or the number of minutes the sun was fast or slow. A watch with this mechanism was very expensive, but the fortunate possessor could set his watch whenever he saw a sundial in the sun.

It remains to note the conventions adopted for fixing

8

the moment of midday throughout the world. Sundial time and mean time have their own local times for any given longitude, and for every degree of longitude the local time differs by four minutes, making twenty-four hours for the 360 degrees round the world. In the latitude of London this means a difference of one minute for every eleven and a half miles east or west.

By an International Convention, local time at Greenwich Observatory is taken as the basis of what is termed 'Standard Time,' and the world is divided up into zones of longitude of 15 degrees each, corresponding to one hour of time. The time is the same over each zone, but differs by an hour from one zone to the next. The boundaries of some zones deviate slightly from their meridians of longitude in order to follow the frontiers or seacoasts of countries. Thus, all France and Ireland are regarded as being in the zone of Greenwich Mean Time (abbreviated to G.M.T.), though the western coast of France and about half of Ireland are properly in the next zone, with time one hour slow. The meridian of Greenwich is in the centre of the G.M.T. zone, so that, except for these deviations, Standard Time never differs from local time by more than 30 minutes. At the meridian 180 degrees from Greenwich there is a discontinuity of twenty-four hours, and ships crossing this meridian have to change their date, those sailing eastwards counting two days of the same date, and those sailing westwards missing a day. Jules Verne's traveller round the world forgot this when he reached home thinking he had failed.

When comparing a watch with a sundial, therefore, allowance must be made not only for the equation of time but also for the difference between G.M.T. (or the Standard Time in any zone other than that of Greenwich) and local time, reckoning that the sundial is slow by four minutes for every degree it is west of Greenwich (or the centre of the zone).

Summer Time is the time of the next zone to the

9

west. Some opponents of Summer Time base their objections on its differing from 'God's time.' Apparent solar time is the only possible meaning of this phrase, and it is interesting to note that the inhabitants of the western half of Ireland enjoy a time, during the period of Summer Time, which is nearer to 'God's time' than the time during the rest of the year. Opponents on this ground are mostly in Ireland.

'Keep time like the sun.'
—*London advertisement of watches.*

CHAPTER II

TIME MEASUREMENT BEFORE CLOCKS

'Horam non possum certam tibi dicere,
facilius inter philosophos convenit,
quam inter horologia.'—SENECA.

THE duty of early timekeepers was to divide the solar day into hours, twelve day-hours between sunrise and sunset and twelve night-hours between sunset and sunrise. The hours consequently varied in length with the time of year, and the day- and night-hours differed except at the equinoxes. The variation was considerable, the day-hour being forty-four and a-half of our minutes on December 23 and seventy-five and a-half on June 25 in the latitude of Rome. These hours were called *Temporal* (Horæ temporales), and were in use almost to the end of the Middle Ages. The modern division of the day-and-night period into twenty-four *equal* hours (Horæ æquales), though it was used by astronomers from very early times, was brought into general use only when public clocks became common. The change was spread over a full century (1350-1450), and what was regarded as a natural division of the day was given up reluctantly.

The Canonical Hours.—In the Roman Empire the temporal hours were recognized, but not commonly used. At this period, and ever since, the time divisions in general use were those marked by public signals. In Rome signals were given at three-hourly intervals, as their names indicate:—*mane, tertia (pars diei), sexta* (midday), *nona* and *vespera*. The Christian Church, in providing Offices at fixed hours, had necessarily to adopt the times of the signals, and eventually these times

11

became known, under their original Roman names, as the Canonical hours. Churches and monasteries continued to give bell signals at the Canonical hours, and these regulated daily life up to about the end of the fourteenth century. Guido Panciroli, writing his 'Rerum memorabilium jam olim deperditarum' at the end of the sixteenth century, starts his chapter on Bells :—

They are of very great use, in regard they give us at a distance the Hour of the Day or Night when we cannot see the sun.[1]

This gives a good idea of the value attached to public time signals even three centuries after the invention of clocks.

The history of the Canonical hours is given in an erudite work by Bilfinger,[2] who traces the change in different countries from Canonical to modern hours. In the fifth century the original Roman hours had been increased to seven, and further additions to the bell signals, notably the Ave Maria bell, were made later. Also the times of the Canonical hours gradually became earlier, until *nona*, which originally was three P.M., came to be midday, the English *noon* and the French *nonne*.

Cocks.—The first timekeepers were the cock and the sundial. The cock has a right to be classed as a timekeeper because in Roman times, and as late as the fifteenth century, cocks were taken with armies to serve as alarums, and there are references to their use at sea and in monasteries ; the Rule of St. Benoît, for example, enjoins the monks to rise at the 'song' of the cocks,[3] and the term *Gallicinium* was used for the time of their song. The mediæval cock crew at midnight and at earliest dawn ; he was evidently a bird of different habits from the modern cock.

---

[1] Translation. London, 1727. The book is said to have been written in Italian, but the earliest edition in the British Museum is in Latin of 1599.

[2] *Die Mittelalterlichen Horen und die modernen Stunden.* Stuttgart, 1892.

[3] 'In verni vel æstatis tempore, a pullorum cantu nocturni inchoentur.' Dom Calmet, *Commentaire sur la règle de Saint Benoît.*

TIME MEASUREMENT BEFORE CLOCKS

Sundials.—The earliest form of sundial was a vertical rod or pillar which indicated time by the length of its shadow.

A 'Gnomon' is the name generally accepted for the vertical rod, but some writers apply it also to the inclined stile of the modern sundial. It would be preferable, even though not justified by derivation, to confine the word 'gnomon' to a vertical rod of which the tip, or a hole near the tip, is the indicating point, and to use the word 'stile' for the rod or plate of which the straight edge is the indicating line. The origin of the gnomon is uncertain. The Babylonians used it, and probably the Egyptian obelisks served as gnomons; there is, too, some evidence that the Chinese gained a knowledge of astronomy as early as the eleventh century B.C. by the use of the gnomon.

The Greeks expressed a time as 'when the shadow was so many feet long' (ὅταν ᾖ δεκάπουν τὸ στοιχεῖον—Aristophanes), meaning, when the man's shadow was so many of his own feet long. This assumed a constant relationship between a man's height and the length of his feet, so that an unduly long-footed man was liable to arrive late for an afternoon appointment and early for a morning one.

The length of the shadow cast by a gnomon varies with the sun's altitude, being least at midday. The direction of the shadow also varies, and can serve as a time-indicator instead of the length. Speaking quite generally, the earlier dials used the length of the shadow and the later the position of the shadow of the tip of the gnomon. Both length and position, however, vary with the time of the year, and, on any particular day, the shadow of the tip of the gnomon traces out a curve on the ground or dial, and this curve can be divided up by marks indicating the hours. It was usual to mark out on the dial three such curves, one for each solstice and one for the equinoxes, and to join the hour divisions on the three curves by hour lines, which, on small dials on a flat surface, were generally assumed to be straight.

13

This was the type of sundial in common use until about 1400. In form there were many variants, because almost any surface, curved or flat, at any inclination, lends itself to the construction of a dial. As an instance, portable dials were frequently made with the markings on a small cylinder, sometimes a walking-stick. A complexity of markings, like a spider's web, though not unknown in early dials, became more common towards the Middle Ages, but otherwise the dials of the fourteenth century were the same as those of Egypt and Arabia.

The discovery which converted the old into the modern sundial was made probably about 1400, and consisted in fixing the stile of the dial parallel to the earth's axis. This gave the result that the time in 'equal' hours, as indicated by the stile or one of its edges, was independent of the time of year. There is little doubt that the discovery would have been made earlier had it been wanted, but, for showing temporal hours, it offered no advantages over the gnomon, and only astronomers reckoned by 'equal' hours. The earliest mention in Europe of a stile parallel to the earth's axis, or a 'polos' as it was then called, is found in a manuscript written by Theodoricum Ruffi in 1447,[1] and the earliest in existence appears to be a portable dial with a thread 'polos,' dated 1451, in the Ferdinandeum Museum in Innsbruck. Recently K. Schoy[2] discovered the description of a dial made with both a gnomon and a 'polos' by Sibt-al-Mâridîni,[3] an Arabian astronomer who lived 1423-95, and a similar dial made by an Egyptian astronomer, Ibn-al-Mâgdi,[4] 1359-1447.

By the end of the fifteenth century the modern type of sundial had become common, about a century after

[1] Munich Hof- und Staatsbibliothek. Cod. Cat. 11067. Quoted by Joseph Drecker, 'Die Theorie der Sonnenuhren,' in vol. i. of *Die Geschichte der Zeitmessung und der Uhren.* Von Bassermann-Jordan. Berlin and Leipzig, 1925.
[2] 'Sonnenuhren der spätarabischen Astronomie.' *Isis*, No. 18, Bd. vi. (3). 1924.
[3] MS. in Bodleian.
[4] MSS. in Leiden and Berlin.

14

the 'equal' hours had come into fairly general use. Then the next three centuries saw an immense development in dialling. The mathematicians and geometers of every country studied it and poured out a stream of treatises, characterized by most complex explanations of the simplest things. Now that the sundial is regarded merely as a garden ornament, it is difficult to realize its importance as the only timekeeper of the general public for many centuries. The water-clocks that existed from Grecian times were possessed only by wealthy individuals and communities, and were so inaccurate as to be useless without a sundial by which to set them. The same may be said of clocks up to the middle of the seventeenth century; they served only those who lived within sound of public clocks. The use of sundials extended with the development of clocks, following, no doubt, the need of better timekeeping as life became more civilized, and they were not ousted by clocks and watches until comparatively recently.

Watches with sundials were not uncommon in the sixteenth and early seventeenth centuries. Examples are illustrated on Plates XXVIII, XXX and XXXIX.

Water-clocks.—Water-clocks of the simplest type, in which time was indicated by a varying water-level, were used in all civilized countries before Christ. Ctesibius (second century B.C.) and Hero of Alexandria (first or second century A.D.) appear to have been the first to study their construction, devising means to render the rate of flow of water independent of the head of water in the supply cistern, and means of varying the rate of flow or the scale of hours, so as to show the temporal hours. Hero wrote books on Clepsydra which have been lost, but a very elaborate clock attributed to Ctesibius and many others are described in Vitruvius' ten books of Architecture, and were probably taken from Hero's works. Ctesibius' clock contained toothed wheels which actuated a column making one revolution a year. This is the earliest known mechanical clock, and in ingenuity of

15

design fully equals any of the later water-clocks. The Arabs developed the water-clock mainly by adding automata, and a number of clocks constructed by them are recorded as wonders of the age. Hours were struck by metal balls falling into a basin, or piped by a bird by air compressed in a vessel which was filled quickly by a siphon. The more elaborate clocks had twelve doors which opened in turn to show figures representing the twelve hours. The mechanism consisted of floats, siphons, pulleys and cords, and occasionally a toothed wheel. There was even a public striking water-clock, the only one known, on the Great Mosque in Damascus, early in the thirteenth century. A great variety of water-clocks, both ancient and contemporary, is shown in Gaspar Schott's book *Mechanica Hidraulica-Pneumatica*, published in 1657. Several of them could never work, and probably only a few were ever constructed. It is an interesting collection of seventeenth-century and earlier mechanics, and shows how little progress in water-clocks had been made since Ctesibius and the Arab makers.

Ecclesiastical communities generally possessed a water-clock and a sundial by which to set it. Timekeeping was an essential part of their duties, both for regulating their own offices and for giving out the canonical hours to the public on their bells. The rules and constitutions of monastical orders made frequent references to the importance of accurate timekeeping and the duties of the sacristan in regulating the clock. Cassiodorus (died *c.* 570) tells the brethren [1] :—

As you know, I have erected for you a clock which indicates by the rays of the sun ; and, too, another clock working by water, which, in flowing, indicates the passage of the hours by day and night ; because on many days the sun's rays are known to fail.

Even with a water-clock the sacristan's duty was far from easy :—

---

[1] *De Institutione Divinarum Litterarum*, c. xxx.

He shall look after the clock and regulate it diligently ; since however it may happen that it goes wrong, he shall estimate the time by a candle, or by the positions of the stars or of the moon, so that he may be able to wake the brethren at the proper time.[1]

The most complete record of monastery timekeeping has been found at the Cistercian Abbey of Villers, engraved on slate and dated 1267. A recent study of the text[2] has disclosed the system of timekeeping by means of a water-clock. Its dial had the twenty-four letters of the alphabet repeated four times, the space from one letter to the next indicating a time of twenty minutes. The water-clock was set by the position of the sun's rays on the choir windows.

Early water-clocks are extremely rare. Planchon[3] reproduces a photograph of a Chinese water-clock of elementary form attributed to the fourteenth century, and illustrates a mechanical striking water-clock dated 1754 in private possession in France. The Cluny Museum has a pottery water-clock of the seventeenth century, but it is more a sand-glass, using water instead of sand, than a water-clock ; and the Deutsche Museum in Munich has a sixteenth-century example of the drum type. English water-clocks of simple type with sixteenth- and seventeenth-century dates are plentiful, but the Author has not seen a genuine example.

Oil, Lamp and Candle Clocks.—These form quite an interesting subject, but they are not links in the chain of events in the history of timekeeping. They are only pendants to the chain and here deserve only a passing mention.

Sand-glasses.—Sand-glasses would appear hardly to merit the title of timekeepers, as they can measure only short intervals of time. An hour was the longest time for which they were currently made, but a four-hour glass

---

[1] *Vetus Disciplina Monastica.* Edit. Herrgott. *De Majori Sacrista Ecclesiae,* chap. 51 (tenth and eleventh centuries).
[2] Paul Sheridan. 'Les instructions sur ardoise de l'abbaye de Villers,' *Ann. de la Soc. Arch. de Bruxelles*, t. ix. p. 360, t. x. pp. 206-435.
[3] *L'Horloge.* Paris, 1912.

was not uncommon, and glasses are said to have been made for twenty-four hours. They have, though, played a very important part in timekeeping, and were in common use on board ship. Von Bassermann-Jordan quotes the *Mercure Galant* of 1678 as saying that there were few rooms in which a sand-glass was not in use.

Their origin is unknown. The Greeks have been credited with the invention on the ground that a sand-glass can be seen—with the help of imagination—in the bas-relief of the marriage of Peleus and Thetis, but there is no real evidence that sand-glasses existed before clocks. Only one book has been devoted to sand-glasses: *Nuova Scienza di Horologi a polvere, che mostrano, e suonano distintamente tutte l'hore*, by Archangelo Maria Radi, published in Rome in 1665.

The book describes an attempt to turn a sand-glass into a clock by fixing twelve sand-glasses radially to a wheel which is turned round by a weight. The weight is able to turn the wheel only as the sand in the glasses on the rising side flows towards the centre of the wheel and that in the glasses on the falling side flows towards the periphery. The device could be made to work in a sort of way, but could not have been of the slightest use.

Domenico Martinelli, in 1669, published a book, *Horologi Elementari*, treating of Water-clocks, Earth-clocks, Air-clocks and Fire-clocks. The 'Earth-clocks' are sand-glasses, and Martinelli writes that, after a long and diligent search made in Italy and Germany to ascertain whether anyone had written about sand-glasses, he found the book by Radi. His chapter on sand-glasses and the accompanying drawings are based on Radi's work.

The only other reference to sand-glasses of any importance is a chapter devoted to them by Christoph Weigel in his *Abbildung der Gemein-nützlichen Haupt-stände*. (Regensburg, 1698.) Weigel deals mainly with the industry of sand-glass making, of which Nürnberg was the most important centre.

18

TIME MEASUREMENT BEFORE CLOCKS

The sixteenth and seventeenth centuries produced many men filled with ideas and devoid of practical knowledge, eager to theorize and reluctant to experiment. The result in mechanics was a crop of absurdities, many horological. One of the more picturesque absurd clocks, designed by Athanasius Kircher (*Magnes sive de Arte Magnetica*: Rome, 1641), is a sunflower with a long spike projecting horizontally from its centre and showing the hour on a circular band surrounding the flower and conveniently supported by cherubs.

'Ma il piu giusto horologio del mondo è quello de' villani, che mai falla, perche si sentano al ventro l' hora di pranso, di colatione e della cena mirabilmente.'

TOMASO GARZONI. *La Piazza Universale di Tutte le Professioni del Mondo.* Venice, 1585.

CHAPTER III

THE INVENTION OF CLOCKS

' L'orloge est, au vrai considérer,
Un instrument très-bel et très notable,
Et s'est aussy plaisant et pourfitable.'

FROISSART. *Le Orloge amoureus.* (*c.* 1365.)

THE *New English Dictionary* defines a clock as an instrument for the measurement of time. The definition agrees with the old use of the word, and its equivalent in all languages, to include sundials, sand-glasses and water-clocks; it does not really define what is now meant by the word.

The French have their modern words *pendule* and *montre*, which were never applied to sundials or water-clocks. The Germans, on the other hand, have only the single word *Uhr* (the Italians, too, the single word *Orologio*) for clocks and watches, and can distinguish them only by calling the latter pocket-clocks. Latterly, however, the word *Räder-Uhr* (wheel-clock) has been used to distinguish the clock proper from the sundial and water-clock, but the distinction is incomplete, because many water-clocks had wheels.

The Author regards the *escapement* as the characteristic of the timekeeper now called a clock, and defines a clock or watch as a timekeeper having a motive power applied to turn a train of wheels, the speed of which is regulated by an escapement or device permitting only a step by step motion of the wheels. It is not a perfect definition, but it covers all timekeepers that are commonly known as clocks or watches, with the sole exception of the conical-pendulum clocks used by astronomers for driving telescopes. It will, at any rate, serve to define

20

the words *clock* and *watch* when used in this book without attribute.

It may seem that there is little real difference between timekeepers in which the speed of the wheels is regulated, on the one hand by water escaping through a hole, and on the other hand by an escapement. Results show how great the difference is. The water-clock, in the course of many centuries, made practically no progress and was too unreliable to effect any improvement in the primitive methods of time-reckoning. The escapement clock, within a century of its invention, gave hourly time-signals in every town of importance, indicating *equal* instead of *temporal* hours, and introduced the modern system of time-reckoning.

The mechanism of the timekeeping part of clocks is so simple that the least mechanically-minded need not shrink from the trouble of following it. It remained essentially the same up to the middle of the seventeenth century, and the mechanism of early watches differs only in form.

Plates II and III are drawings of the clock that was erected at Dover Castle about the end of the fourteenth century, and the upper view in Plate V is a photograph of it. The clock is in the Science Museum at South Kensington, and is kept going. Plate II is a view of the clock looking at the right-hand end of Plate III. The left-hand portion of Plate III is the striking mechanism, and is more complicated than the timekeeping mechanism, which consists of only three moving parts. The driving weight is hung on the cord wrapped round the drum A; this is connected with the large toothed wheel B, which engages with the small toothed wheel C on the shaft D′ (the smaller of a pair of toothed wheels is called a pinion, and its teeth are generally called *leaves* by clock-makers, but not by engineers). Also fixed on the shaft D′ is the escape wheel D, which has teeth cut on its face (Plate III). The wheel B has 96 teeth and the pinion C 9, so that the pinion and escape wheel make over ten turns for every turn of the drum A. Now comes the escapement, the essential organ of the clock, the part that prevents the escape wheel being whizzed round by the fall of the weight and compels it to turn at a more or less regular and at only a very slow rate. A rod E (Plate III) passes across the face of the escape wheel, and has attached to it two small plates F, F, called *pallets*, which engage with the teeth of the escape wheel. The rod with its pallets is shown in Plate II in dotted lines; it is called a *verge*, from its Latin or Italian equivalent. The verge is mounted to turn in holes in two brackets H and G, and just below the upper bracket H a large cross-arm J is attached to the verge and has, hung on its ends, two lead blocks K, K.

The pallets F, F prevent the escape wheel being whizzed round; they permit it, though, to turn slowly, because a tooth of the escape wheel, which is trying to turn to the right, as seen in Plate II, presses against the upper pallet and slowly turns the verge—slowly, because of the great mass of the cross-arm J with its weights. At a certain point the tooth is able to slip past the pallet, but then the escape wheel is brought to rest by another tooth coming against the lower pallet. To escape past this pallet the tooth must first stop the swing that was given to the cross arm, and then turn it in the opposite direction; and so on alternately.

The exact action of the verge escapement can be seen in the figures of Plate IV, which show it in the different stages of its operation. It is worth following out, because the verge is the escapement of practically all watches made up to 1750 and of many later; it was being made even up to 1850. The Plate shows an escape wheel and verge of more modern proportions, the pallets being larger and the body of the verge thinner than in the Dover Castle clock. The view of the escapement shown is looking down on it from above the clock in Plates II and III, the cross-arm and brackets being omitted to let the pallets be seen. The left-hand pallet

22

PLATE II

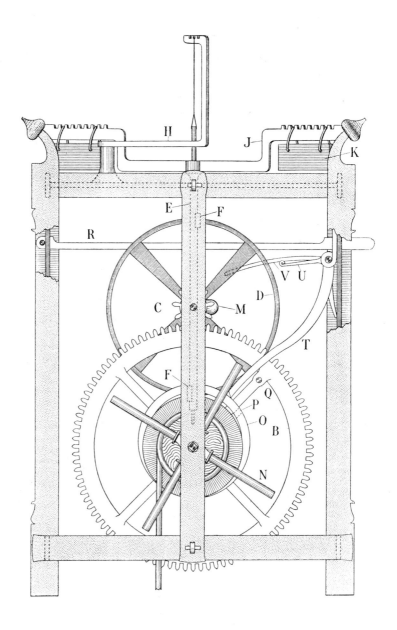

THE DOVER CASTLE CLOCK. END VIEW

PLATE III

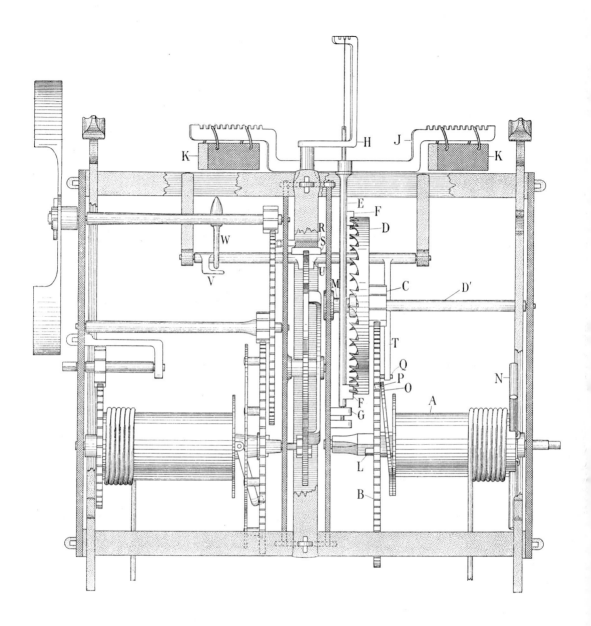

THE DOVER CASTLE CLOCK. SIDE VIEW

is the upper and the right-hand the lower, engaging with the dark-shaded teeth, which are on the lower side of the escape wheel. The escape wheel tends to turn to the left, with the points of its teeth forward.

In Fig. 1 of this Plate, a tooth is seen escaping from the lowest pallet; when it escapes, the wheel moves on suddenly till the upper tooth drops on the upper pallet, and the position is then that of Fig. 2. This motion is called the *drop*. Now the verge was given a swing in the direction of the arrow by the action of the tooth on the lower pallet, and its momentum is enough to overcome the pressure of the tooth on the upper pallet and to turn the escape wheel backwards for a short distance until the momentum is exhausted; the whole clock, in fact, turns backwards, and the weight is wound up by a minute amount. Fig. 3 shows the position when this backward movement has come to an end and the verge is stationary. The arc through which the verge turns in pushing the escape wheel backwards is called the *supplementary arc*, because it is supplementary to the arc through which it has to turn to let the teeth of the wheel escape.

As soon as the verge has been brought to rest, the tooth, which is steadily pressing on the upper pallet, begins to swing the verge in the opposite direction. Fig. 4 shows the position when this action is in progress, and Fig. 5 when it is at an end and the tooth is just escaping from the upper pallet. The arc through which the verge turns, from the position of Fig. 3 to that of Fig. 5, under the pressure of the tooth, is called the *impulse arc*, because the escape wheel is then giving impulse to the verge. When the tooth escapes from the upper pallet, the tooth on the other side of the wheel drops on to the lower pallet, as in Fig. 6. This tooth and the lower pallet then go through the same action, but in the reverse direction; the escape wheel is first driven backwards while the verge makes its supplementary arc, and the tooth then gives the verge its impulse in the opposite direction until it escapes from the pallet; the position is then once more as in Fig. 1.

23

The result of the action which has been described in detail is that the escape wheel can turn only by oscillating the verge with its weighted cross-arm back and forth, and it turns through the distance of one tooth for every pair of oscillations, once back and once forth. The cross-arm is called a *foliot*. The word, possibly derived from the Old French *folier*—to dance madly—was used by Froissart in his poem *Le orloge amoureus*, written about 1365. The poem gives quite a good technical description of a clock, and probably the various technical words in it were those in use by clockmakers. The Author knows of no other use of the word *foliot* until comparatively modern times, but it is now the accepted word for the weighted cross-arm by English and French writers. The copy of a Latin manuscript of 1364 in the Bodleian uses the term *frenum* (brake) for the escapement and *corona freni* for the foliot, which was, in the clock described, in the form of a crown, instead of the usual bar. A German name for it, ungallantly expressing its oscillating motion, is found in instructions left by the maker of the Lucerne clock, Heinrich Halder, in 1385, *Frowen gemuete* (*Frauen Gemüthe*—Woman's mind). In modern German, *Waage* is the usual word.

The construction of the Dover Castle clock is typical of work of the period. There are no screws; they were not used in clocks in England until nearly two centuries later. Parts that could be permanently fixed together were riveted, as, for instance, were the top and bottom cross-bars of the frame (seen in Plate II) to the side uprights. Parts that had to be dismountable were held by taper wedges. The central upright bar, in which the pivots of the wheels run, is fixed in this way to the cross-bars; a loop is riveted to the cross-bar and passes through a slot in the central bar, and then a wedge is driven through the loop. Another wedge, holding the wheel B on to its square shaft, is seen at L in Plate III.

The wheel B with the weight drum turns once an

24

PLATE IV

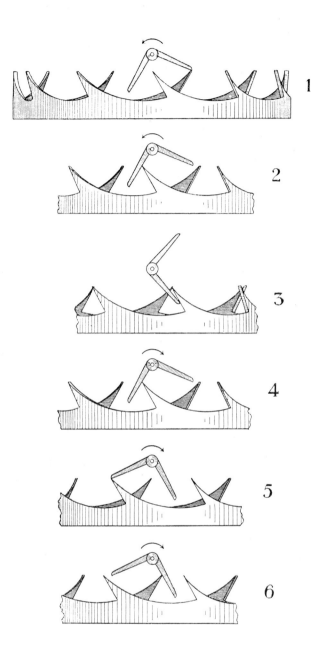

1

2

3

4

5

6

VERGE ESCAPEMENT

hour; the escape wheel once in a little under six minutes, and, since the wheel has thirty-three teeth, the foliot takes about ten seconds to make its double swing. The weight falls at the rate of twenty-six feet in twelve hours; probably the clock was wound every eight hours. The wheels of the clock, and of all early clocks, are mounted between two narrow upright bars, in which their pivots turn, but the verge escapement introduces a difficulty in mounting the escape wheel, because the verge has to pass across the face of the wheel and so gets in the way of its shaft. One pivot of the escape wheel shaft has, therefore, to be in a bracket M, which curves round the verge and supports the shaft between the wheel and the verge. The same constructional difficulty is found in watches with a verge escapement.

The clock is wound by turning the weight drum by the four arms N. For winding, however, provision must be made to enable the drum to turn backwards without turning the wheels of the clock; the drum is loose on its shaft, but a narrow iron ring O is fixed to the flange of the drum at one point (Plate III), and the ring is bent so that it springs against the arms of the wheel B. Where it touches the arms, a projection P (Plates II and III) is fixed to it, which acts as a ratchet with the wheel-arms; that is to say, when the drum is turned by the weight the projection catches on an arm of the wheel and turns the wheel, but, when the drum is turned backwards in winding, the sloping face of the projection rides over the arms and permits the drum to turn alone.

On the end of the shaft of wheel B that protrudes outside the frame there must have been a pinion, engaging with a wheel carrying the hour hand. The pair of wheels is missing, but there are indications of its attachment to the frame.

It will be noticed that the verge is hung on a cord tied to an upward extension of the upper bracket H. This is to relieve the lower bearing of the verge of the great weight of the foliot and avoid the friction that

25

would result. All later foliot clocks adopted this device.[1]

The clock illustrated in nearly all books on horology as an early example is one that was erected on the Palais de Justice in Paris by Charles v. and made by Henry de Vic (Vic in Lorraine) in 1370. The clock no longer exists, but a detailed drawing of it was made by Julien Le Roy about 1700 and published in Moinet's *Traité générale d'Horlogerie*. (Paris, 1848.) The drawings indicate that the clock must have been largely reconstructed, leaving little of the original work. The general construction of the two clocks is the same, the only essential difference being that the lighter verge in Henry de Vic's clock made its double swing in two seconds instead of ten, and, to compensate for this quicker beat, the train had an extra wheel and pinion. The Dover Castle clock, which may have been of about the same date, or only a little later, affords a better illustration

[1] The following brief description of the striking mechanism of the Dover Castle clock may be of interest to students of early clockwork. The great wheel on the winding drum has seventy-two teeth, and drives a pinion of nine on the intermediate wheel. This has seventy-two teeth, and drives a pinion of eight on the shaft of the fly, which is driven through a ratchet. The shaft of the great wheel protrudes through the vertical bar in which it is pivoted near the centre of the frame, and carries a pinion of eight leaves driving the count wheel by an internal gear of seventy-eight teeth. This wheel and the other wheels of the striking mechanism are not shown in Plate II, but this figure shows the bar R, which carries the detent S for the count wheel and also a detent for the pin on the intermediate wheel. A pin Q on one arm of the wheel B once an hour lifts the pawl T, which is attached to a shaft carrying a pawl U and a detent V. When the pawl T is lifted by the pin Q, the pawl U raises the bar R and so frees the count wheel and the intermediate wheel, and the striking train begins to turn. At the same time, however, the detent V is raised and catches the projection W on the shaft of the fly, so stopping the train. This is the *warning*. When the pawl T slips off the pin Q, the detent V falls and releases the striking train, but the bar R is prevented from falling with it because the count wheel has turned enough to move its notch from under the detent S. The striking train therefore turns until the detent S falls into the next notch in the count wheel and brings the detent into the path of the pin on the intermediate wheel. The lever working the bell hammers is pivoted on a bracket on the frame, and its tail is worked by the eight pins on the great wheel. A special winding pinion and wheel are provided for the striking drum ; no doubt want of space prevented a similar provision for the drum of the going train. A form of ratchet different from that of the going drum may be noted. The wheel shafts are all forged roughly octagonal excepting the escape wheel shaft, which is a later turned shaft.

PLATE V

DOVER CASTLE CLOCK

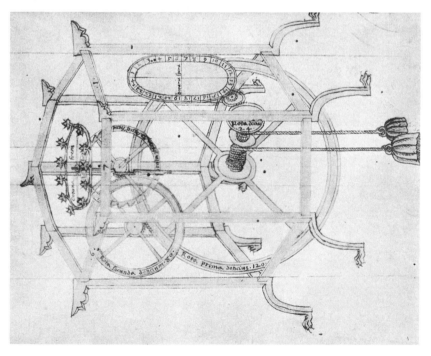

DONDI'S CLOCK

THE INVENTION OF CLOCKS

because it exists and is nearly in its original condition. The escape wheel shaft has certainly been renewed and also, probably, the escape wheel and verge, but all the other parts appear to be as originally made.

The lower view of Plate v is interesting in illustrating the earliest clock of which any details are known. It is reproduced from a manuscript in the Bodleian,[1] a copy of a work written in 1364 by Giovanni Dondi, the maker of the clock. The clock will be referred to later, but the illustration is worth noting in connection with the Dover Castle clock, because it shows the same elements of mechanism, though with an extra wheel and pinion as in Henry de Vic's clock.

The inventor of the clock and the date of its invention are unknown. The date is probably near the end of the thirteenth century. The use of the same word—Horologium, Orlogio, Reloge, Uhr, etc.—for sundial, water-clock, sand-glass, hour-bell and clock makes it difficult to interpret the records, and has led many writers to attribute the invention of the clock to various periods, going back as far as the ninth century.

Each of eleven horologia has, or has had, some claim to be regarded as the earliest clock known :—

(1) A horologium erected in 1306 on the Campanile of Sant' Eustorgio, Milan.
(2) The clock now existing in Beauvais Cathedral.
(3) A horologium made by Richard de Walingford, Abbot of St. Albans, 1326-35.
(4) A horologium made by Peter Lightfoot about 1325 for Glastonbury Abbey.
(5) A horologium erected in 1335 on the church of San Gottardo, Milan.
(6) The Dover Castle clock, now in the Science Museum, South Kensington, said to have been erected in 1348.

[1] Laud Misc. No. 620.

27

(7) The Wells Cathedral clock, now in the Science Museum, South Kensington, to which various dates, from the thirteenth century onwards, have been attributed.

(8) Giovanni Dondi's planetarium clock, completed in 1364 and placed in the library of the Castello di Pavia.

(9) A clock in Exeter Cathedral in 1284.

(10) A horologium in Canterbury Cathedral in 1292.

(11) An orloge in St. Paul's Cathedral in 1286 and a new orloge in 1344.

The evidence for and against the claims of these horologia to be clocks of the dates mentioned will be examined.

The evidence for the horologium of Sant' Eustorgio, Milan, is derived from a chronicle of Galvano Fiamma, which has been wrongly quoted in all books on horology mentioning it. The quotation always made is *horologium ferreum multiplicatur*, which could only mean that a previously erected horologium was enlarged. The correct quotation is, under date 1306 :—

Benignus tercia vice prior efficitur. Iste fecit ampliari celles infirmatorii et cameras, stella aurea super campanile ponitur, horologium ferreum fabricatur.[1]

An iron horologium was constructed. There is no indication here that *horologium* was anything but a sundial. Fiamma certainly wastes no words in his chronicles, but he would hardly have dismissed in three words the construction of the first clock of Milan. Caffi,[2] writing of this horologium, refers to a manuscript of Bugati ('Istoria del Convento di Sant' Eustorgio'), saying that it was restored in 1333, 1555 and 1572. The Author has not been able to find a copy of this manuscript, but, unless it contains evidence in favour of a clock and not a sundial, the horologium of Sant' Eustorgio

---

[1] Fratris Galuagni de la Fiamma. Cronica ordinis praedicatorum ab anno 1170 usque ad 1333. Recensuit Fr. B. M. Reichert. Rome and Stuttgart, 1897.
[2] *Della Chiesa di Sant' Eustorgio in Milano.* Michele Caffi. Milano, 1841.

has no real claim to be the earliest clock. Fiamma's chronicles extend to 1333, and make no mention of any restoration of the horologium.

The clock existing and kept going in Beauvais Cathedral was brought into prominence in 1913 by a pamphlet written by Paul Miclet, a local horologist.[1] The clock strikes on a bell with no clapper and no signs of there ever having been a clapper, and it is argued that the bell must therefore have been cast for the clock and must be contemporary with the clock. The bell has an inscription, and from this and other evidence it is fairly well established that the bell dates from 1300 or a little earlier. The argument has no real weight. The fact that the bell had no clapper does not prove that it was made for a clock; Beauvais was a conventual church, and the bell may have been struck by hand for giving hour signals to the brothers. The Author has examined the clock and, making all allowances for reconstruction, found none of the characteristics of fourteenth-century work. Judging from the work, the date is in the sixteenth century.

The horologium made by Richard de Walingford, Abbot of St. Albans from 1326 to 1335, has been generally accepted as a clock, and the references relied on afford quite good grounds for the belief. The following are free translations of extracts from *Gesta Abbatum Monasterii Sancti Albani* :—

He [Walingford] produced many books and instruments relating to Astronomy, Geometry and other sciences, in which he excelled above all others of his time. Among these was a remarkable astronomical instrument, the like of which had never before been seen, called ' Albion,' meaning All by one.

A later passage reads :—

He erected a magnificent horologium in the church at great cost of money and work ; nor did he abandon finishing it because of its disparagement by the brethren, who, wise in their own eyes, regarded it as foolishness. He had, however, the

[1] *L'Horloge de la Cathédrale de Beauvais.* Beauvais, 1913.

excuse that he originally intended to construct the horologium less expensively, in view of the great and generally recognized need for repair of the church, but that, in his absence, and as a result of interference by some brethren and the greed of the workmen, it was begun on a costly scale and it would have been indecent and shameful not to have finished what had been put in hand. Indeed, when King Edward III. came to the Monastery and saw so sumptuous a work undertaken while the church was still not rebuilt since the ruin it suffered in Abbot Hugo's time, he discreetly rebuked Abbot Richard in that he neglected the fabric of the church and wasted so much money on a quite unnecessary work, namely the horologium in question. To which the Abbot replied, with all due respect, that many Abbots would succeed him who could find workmen for the fabric of the monastery, but that there would be no one who, after his death, could finish this work he had begun. And, indeed, he spoke the truth, because in that art nothing of the kind remains or was discovered in his lifetime.

It appears that the remonstrances of the king and the brethren had the result that the horologium was left indecently and shamefully unfinished, because towards the end of the rule of the next but one following Abbot, Thomas de la Mare, 1349 to 1396, there is found the following :—

The great dial and wheel, originally laid down by that master of all such things, the Abbot Richard, but meanwhile set aside by reason of his early death and other more urgent expenditure, was splendidly completed, at the charge and by the exertions of this Abbot, and by the work of Master Laurentius de Stokes, an eminent *horologiarius* and of a certain brother monk called William Walsham, who, in the work of their hands and in skill of fashioning, almost surpassed all the craftsmen of the district. The cost of this work, on account of its size and complexity, was estimated at a hundred marks and over.

One other reference to the horologium is found in Leland (*Apud Tannerum Biblioth. brit. hibern.*, p. 629) :—

He constructed this horologium with great labour, at greater cost and with still greater skill, and, in my opinion, it has not its equal in all Europe ; one may look at the course of the sun and moon or the fixed stars, or again one may regard the rise and fall of the tide or the lines with their almost infinite variety of figures and indications.

So far, the records show that Richard de Walingford, a man of great ability in science, designed an astronomical instrument which he called *Albion*; that he started to make a complex and costly horologium in the Abbey but failed to finish it, and that it was finished about 1390. The two have generally been regarded as one and the same clock, and the punning name has been taken to mean that all its motions were worked by a single weight. The Abbot, however, left a manuscript describing his Albion[1] in a small octavo of forty-four folios, well written but much abbreviated. The Author, on a cursory examination, could find no indication that Albion was anything but an astronomical instrument, showing the course of the sun, moon and stars by rotating discs; an instrument, indeed, to which Leland's description is applicable.[2] Instruments of this type had long been known, though they remained sufficiently rare to be regarded as marvels. A real clock, showing the hours and the celestial motions automatically, would have been a far greater achievement, and it is improbable that Walingford would have omitted to describe what he must have known to be the greater novelty and the greater triumph. Whatever it was that was erected in the Abbey was finished about 1390, but was then called, not a clock, but *superius diale et rota fortuna*, an obscure phrase that tells little. The fact that a *horologiarius* was employed to finish it is the only connection with a clock.

Later will be mentioned evidence of quite a different kind, pointing to the existence of a clock in the Abbey of St. Albans in 1394, but this evidence is equally against the existence of a clock in England before about 1370.

[1] Bodleian. Laud Misc. No. 657.
[2] Mr. Gunther, father and curator of the splendid collection of early scientific instruments in the Old Ashmolean Museum, Oxford, has since made a thorough examination of the MS., and has told the Author that Albion is not a clock.

Walingford certainly did not produce a clock that worked, but he may have designed one and started to make it. The Author inclines to the view that he did not, and that *Albion* and the *Horologium* started in the Abbey were one and the same thing, a complex astronomical instrument, worked manually as the canonical hours were given out by the Abbey bell. A horologium of some kind, sundial, water-clock, or both, was essential to the timekeeping system of the Abbey.

The monk Peter Lightfoot would not deserve consideration as a claimant clockmaker were it not that clocks at Glastonbury, Wimborne, Wells and Exeter have been attributed to him by many English writers. Everything known of this monk is given in Howgrave-Graham's book, *Peter Lightfoot, Monk of Glastonbury, and the Old Clock of Wells.* (Glastonbury, 1922.) It is little more than Leland's reference to Glastonbury Abbey, *Horologium Petrus Lightfote Monachus fecit hoc opus,* and the confirmation that a *horologium* was provided for the Abbey by Lightfoot's Abbot. There is no evidence that this *horologium* was a clock.

The evidence for the horologium erected in 1335 on the church of the Beata Vergine, later San Gottardo, in Milan, is found in Fiamma's chronicles :—

There is there a wonderful clock, because there is a very large clapper which strikes a bell twenty-four times according to the XXIV. hours of the day and night, and thus at the first hour of the night gives one sound, at the second two strokes, at the third three, and at the fourth four ; and so distinguishes one hour from another, which is of the greatest use to men of every degree.[1]

The description makes it clear that a clock making strokes corresponding in number to the hour was a

[1] 'Est ibi unum horologium admirabile, quia est unum tintinabulum grossum valde, quod percutit unam campanam vigintiquatuor vicibus, secundum numerum XXIV. horarum diei et noctis, ita quod in prima hora noctis dat unum tonum, in secunda duos ictus, in tertia tres, et in quarta quatuor ; et sic distinguit horas ab horis quod est summe necessarium pro omni statu hominum.' Gualvanei Flammae, Gesta Azonis Luchini et Joann. Vicecom. Med. 1328-42. Muratori Italicarum Rerum Scriptores.

novelty to Fiamma. It does not, though, rule out an earlier non-striking clock, or a clock striking one at each hour. In the absence of any record in Europe of a water-clock with full striking mechanism on the scale of a public clock, it may be assumed that this was an escapement clock.

The Dover Castle clock, which has been described in detail above, has been for many years in the Science Museum at South Kensington, and had a label stating that the clock was of Swiss origin and was erected in Dover Castle in 1348. The present officials of the Museum, recognizing that origin and date were purely legendary, have altered the label. Unfortunately, no facts were known to substitute for the legend. The clock was found in Dover Castle, was brought to the Patent Office Museum, and, when this was abolished, transferred to its present house. The work shows it to be a very early clock, and it seemed worth while investigating the possibility of its being the earliest clock now existing. The Author, having failed to find any mention of the clock in any published work, had a search made in the Pipe and Foreign Rolls and the Exchequer Accounts in the Record Office. The result was meagre, but showed the origin of the legendary date and proved the existence of a clock about 1405. The relevant extracts are as follows :—

Exchequer Accounts E. 101/16, 19-22 Edward III. (1345-8). Under the heading *Nove Campane* are a number of expenses incurred in casting and hanging two large bells and one small bell. A later account (E. 101. 462/23, 40-49 Edw. III.) for ropes states that they are for the bells in the chapel of the Castle, and refers to plumbing work above the chapel tower room.

In 1345-8, therefore, three new bells were installed in the bell-tower over the chapel of the castle, and there is little doubt that the frequent confusion between bells and clocks is responsible for the date of 1348 having been attributed to the Dover Castle clock.

The first reference to a clock is in Exchequer Account 462/26, 3-6 Henry v. (1415-18) :—

And paid to a certain man for his work in keeping the Cloke, for his time per annum 13s. 4d., for the said time £7, 7s. 8d.

This sum probably should be £7, 6s. 8d., which amounts to eleven years' wages at 13s. 4d. per annum, and there was therefore a keeper of the clock at a date between 1404 and 1407. The Exchequer Accounts and Rolls in existence prior to this date cover only a small proportion of the years, and consequently the absence of any earlier reference to the clock does not indicate that the clock was not installed earlier. It is, however, most probable that it was not in existence much before 1400, because references to the bells are found in the Pipe Roll for 1364, the Exchequer Accounts for 1366-76, and the Foreign Rolls for 1377, 1379, 1381, 1389, 1391, and 1403, without a single reference to the clock.

There remains the question whether the existing clock is the original clock. Without a continuous series of accounts, which do not exist, this can never be settled ; the clock itself is the only evidence available. In its construction, the clock appears earlier than any other clock the Author has examined, but early appearance is not conclusive evidence, because a skilled craftsman can do work that appears to be half a century later than that of a less skilled man. Dr. Von Bassermann-Jordan, Director of the National Museum, Munich, bases his opinion that the clock is of much later date on the bent-out form of the finials on the uprights. He knows the clock, however, from photographs, and the Author thinks that no great weight should be attached to the bent form of the finials, because these may have been bent out-wardly to give room for a longer foliot ; the actual foliot would just miss the finials, if straight, but the builder may well have allowed for some margin. Major Bailey, of the Victoria and Albert Museum, South Kensington, who has made a special study of early ironwork, has

34

examined the clock critically, as a piece of ironwork, and tells the Author that the work appears to him quite consonant with a date of 1400.

The internal evidence of the clock is strongly in favour of its not being later than 1450, so it is probable that the clock is the original one of 1390-1400.

The Wells Cathedral clock, which is kept regularly going and striking in the Science Museum, South Kensington, is considerably larger than the Dover Castle clock, but has undergone far more reconstruction, including the substitution of a pendulum for the foliot. It used to bear a label attributing to it a date in the thirteenth century, but so early a date has been disproved by Howgrave-Graham, who, in the book already mentioned, gives 1380 as the earliest probable date.

The earliest reference to the clock is found in the Accounts of the Dean and Chapter of Wells.[1] Church expenses are extant for the years 1343-4, 1392-5, 1400-1 and 1407-9, and the wages of the clock-keeper is an item of the expenses in 1392-3 and each of the subsequent years. Here again evidence is lacking to decide the date of erection, but it may be put between 1380 and 1392.

Giovanni Dondi's planetarium clock has been wrongly attributed to Jacopo Dondi, father of Giovanni, and, with this authorship, has been put forward as the first clock made. It is, though, the first clock of which details are extant, and the first house clock known. It was a remarkable achievement and, as a piece of mechanism, fully a century ahead of its time. How great a stir it created may be gathered from the account of Philippe de Mezières :—

All its movements are controlled by a single weight, and it is so great a marvel that the famous astronomers of distant countries come with all reverence to visit Maître Jehan and his work ; and all the great students of astronomy, of philosophy and medicine declare that, within the memory of man, as recorded in writing or otherwise, there has never been made so

---

[1] Historical Manuscripts Commission. *Calendar of the Manuscripts of the Dean and Chapter of Wells*, vol. ii. London, 1914.

ingenious and so marvellous a planetarium as this clock ; such was the genius and skill of Maître Jehan that, with his own hands and without assistance, he forged the clock all of brass and copper ; and he did nothing else for sixteen years.[1]

Giovanni Dondi, born in 1318, was a man of great attainments, and had been, in different universities, professor of astronomy, medicine and logic ; the clock gained for him the title of *Horologius* or *dall' Orologio*, a title which his descendants still retain. Falconet, in 1745, read a paper before the Académie des Belles-lettres on ancient clocks,[2] in which he attributed Dondi's clock to his father, Jacopo Dondi, to whom also he attributed the clock erected in Padua in 1344. The error was corrected in a paper by Francesco Scipione, Marchese de Dondi dall' Orologio,[3] who had access to original documents possessed by the family. There is no evidence that Jacopo Dondi, who was one of the most famous doctors of his time, ever interested himself in clocks. In spite of this correction, Falconet's mistake has been perpetuated in nearly every work on horology which mentions this clock.

The manuscript written by Giovanni Dondi to describe his clock, and already referred to, fully bears out the contemporary accounts of the man and his work ; it is one of the few mechanical treatises of the fourteenth or fifteenth centuries written with the clearness that indicates a full grasp of the subject. The clock showed the courses of the sun, moon and planets among the stars ; to show the courses of the sun and moon to the accuracy then known presented no great difficulties, but the planets were quite another matter. At that time the earth was the centre of the universe ; this made no difference to the apparent motions of sun and moon, but the planets

---

[1] Lebeuf. *Actes de l'Acad. des Inscriptions et Belles-lettres*, t. xvi. p. 227.

[2] 'Dissertation sur les anciennes horloges et sur Jacques de Dondis, surnommé *Horologius*,' lue à l'Académie des Belles-lettres, 1745, par Falconet. *Collection Leber de Pièces relatives à l'Histoire de France*, t. xvi. pp. 384-409. Paris, 1838.

[3] 'Notizie sopra Jacopo e Giovanni Dondi dall' Orologio.' *Atti dell' Accademia di Padova*, 1782. Reprinted Padova, 1844.

moved in looped circular curves called *epicycles* or *episti-cules*, and the mechanical reproduction of these complex curves in the light of the fourteenth-century knowledge was a very great feat.

The lower view on Plate v (half the size of the original drawing) shows the timekeeping part of the clock, the astronomical part being supported on this in a separate framework. It will be seen that this clock has an extra pair of wheels in its train, as compared with the Dover Castle clock. The large toothed wheel fixed to the rope drum drives the escape wheel, not directly as in the Dover Castle clock, but through a wheel and pinion to the left of the escape wheel. The verge, with its pallets, is clearly shown, and this drawing gives the earliest information existing of the verge escapement. An ornamental crown takes the place of the bar foliot of the Dover Castle clock.

There are three later references to this planetarium. Pier Candido Decembrio, about 1470, mentions it as

A famous clock, memorable above all those of our time.[1]

Michele Savonarola, in 1440, says :—

Such was the wonderful complexity of this clock that, when it had gone out of order, there was no astrologer capable of adjusting it. However, a great astrologer and mechanician came from France to Pavia, attracted by the fame of the machine, and worked very many days in putting the wheels together ; finally he succeeded in giving the machine its correct motion.[2]

Finally, Bernardo Sacco, writing of the coronation of Charles v. in 1529, says :—

When Charles v. received the imperial crown in Bologna, this clock was shown to him, as it was, all corroded with rust. Charles admired it immensely, and summoned clever men from all parts to repair it. These having worked on it without result, finally a certain Giovanni de Cremona, surnamed Gianello, presented himself, deformed in appearance but of brilliant

---

[1] *Ital. Rerum Script.*, xx. p. 1017.
[2] *Commentariolus de laudibus Patavii.* Apud Muratori, *Ital. Rerum Script.*, xxiv. 1164.

genius. He, after examining the machine, said that he could put it in order, but that those iron pieces that were corroded with rust could not serve, and that a new instrument like it would have to be made. Setting himself to work and either imitating the old work or improving on it or carrying it out more skilfully, he completed the great machine, which the illustrious Emperor then desired to take with him to Spain, together with its craftsman Maestro Gianello.[1]

It is a testimony to Giovanni Dondi's genius that, a century and a half after he had made his clock, an exceptional man was needed to repair it.

There now remain for consideration the three English clocks of the thirteenth century. There exists the copy of an agreement[2] made in 1344 between the Dean and Chapter of St. Paul's and Walter 'Lorgoner' of Southwark for making a 'dyal en lorloge' to replace one already existing at the cathedral. The more important portions of this read, in translation, as follows :—

The said Walter shall make a dyal for the clock of the same church with roofs and all manner of apparatus appertaining to the said dyal and for turning the Angel in front of the clock[3] so that the said clock may be good and suitable and profitable to show the hours of the day and night. The said clock is to remain without defects, and in case defects shall be found afterwards in the said clock the said Walter binds himself by this indenture to make the repairs whenever he shall be summoned by the ministers of the church. And for this work well and duly done and completed the aforesaid Dean and Chapter shall pay him six pounds sterling. . . . And the said Walter shall find at his own cost the iron, brass and all manner of other things for carrying out the said work: and shall have for himself the old apparatus which will no longer serve.

The sentence of which the original is given in the footnote is not very clear, but the agreement, with its reference to iron and brass, seems to be good evidence that the *orloge* was a clock ; and the reference to the old

---

[1] *De Italicarum Rerum varietate et elegantia*, lib. vii. cap. 151. Ticino, 1587.

[2] *Cottonian Charter*, xxi. 24.

[3] '. . . une dyal en lorloge de mesme leglise od roofs et totes maneres de ustimentz appartenantz al dit Dyal et au tourner del Angel par amunt lorloge. . . .'

38

apparatus which will no longer serve indicates that it replaced a similar existing *orloge*, no doubt the *orloge* looked after by Bartholomew the Orologius, mentioned in 1286.[1]

Records of Exeter and Canterbury Cathedrals are, in themselves, no real evidence of clocks, but are mentioned because their dates strengthen the evidence of St. Paul's clock. In Canterbury there was a 'Novum Orologium Magnum in Ecclesia' in 1292.[2] At Exeter there was a bell-founder repairing organs and clocks in 1284. The former may have been a sundial and the latter a bell for giving out the canonical hours.

It might certainly be concluded that there was a new clock at St. Paul's in 1344, replacing an older clock existing in 1286, if there were not strong evidence that there was no clock in England till nearly a century later.

First there are Bilfinger's researches on the change from canonical to modern hours, referred to above, which serve as a sound check on the records of public clocks. In the early part of the fourteenth century all chroniclers used the canonical hours. Later, modern hours were occasionally used in recording times; towards the end of the century their use became frequent, and by the middle of the fifteenth century they had almost entirely displaced the canonical hours. The date of change varies with the country. In Milan the first use of modern hours found by Bilfinger is in 1339, four years after the date of erection of the San Gottardo clock.

Froissart's chronicles yield valuable evidence, because

---

[1] Bartholomew the Orologius received an allowance of beer in 1286. (Extract from Dean Baldock's Statutes in Simpson's *Registrum Statutorum*.) Also, from Hale's *Domesday of St. Paul's*, Bartholomo Orologiario, the clock-keeper, had a loaf a day. The Author is indebted for this and the following reference to Mr. Howgrave-Graham, who has done more than any one in searching the records of early English clocks and separating truth from legend. Besides his book on the clock of Wells, mentioned above, Mr. Howgrave-Graham has read a paper before the Society of Antiquaries embodying some results of his researches; this paper, published in May 1928, with many excellent illustrations, marks a real advance in the history of early clocks.

[2] List of Prior Henry of Eastry's works in Register I., Cant. MSS.

times of day are recorded so frequently. Up to 1377 canonical hours are used exclusively. In the account of the return of the Count of Flanders to Ghent in December 1379 or January 1380, there are, however, many uses of modern hours ; and, turning to the records of clocks, the archives of Ghent record payments for a clock on the belfry, which appears to have been finished in 1376-7, while the years 1372-7 include the probable dates of erection of a number of clocks in Flanders, at Courtrai, Mons, Maestricht, Malines, Ypres and Termonde. In recording events in Spain and Portugal, from 1382 to 1386, Froissart uses modern hours but once, and in these countries the only clock before 1400 for which there is any evidence was erected in Toledo in 1366. Finally, in the chronicles of the period 1389-1400 the canonical hours are gradually ousted by the modern time-reckoning, and there can be no doubt that this was the result of the erection of public clocks during or before this period in all the more important towns of France and Flanders.

Turning now to England, in the St. Albans chronicles the first use of modern hours is in 1394, two years before the death of the Abbot Thomas de la Mare who finished Walingford's horologium. In all the English chronicles Bilfinger finds no reference to modern hours before 1377. This is nine years after Edward III. issued letters-patent allowing three Dutch clockmakers—John Lietuyt, John Uneman and William Uneman—to enter the kingdom and exercise their profession, and four years after a Malmesbury monk wrote that in this year (1373) clocks indicating twenty-four hours were invented.[1] One can only guess at the clock of which the monk was thinking. It may have been the clock of the neighbouring cathedral of Wells. There was, almost certainly, a clock erected on the tower of the Palace of Westminster

---

[1] 'Hoc anno horologia distinguentia 24 horas primo inventa sunt.' *Rerum Britannicarum Medii Aevi scriptores. Eulogio (Continuatio). A Monacho quodam Malmesburiensi exaratum.* Ed. Haydon. Vol. iii. p. 336. London, 1863.

some years previously, but the date of erection is uncertain. The tower for the clock was built in 1365-1366, and there is a record of a clock-keeper in 1371.

From the review of the records about early clocks, the Milan clock of 1335 emerges as the earliest known, apart from the possible English clocks of fifty years earlier. Fiamma's brief account is the only record of it, but his wording makes it clear that it was the first striking clock of which he had knowledge; probably, therefore, it was the first in northern Italy. From Italy's leading position in arts and sciences, it would be natural for the birthplace of clocks to be in Italy, and there is confirmation of this in the fact that the three public clocks next in order of date, of which there are fairly reliable records, are all Italian :—Modena 1343, Padua 1344, and Monza 1347. Omitting a doubtful record of a clock at Bruges 1345, the first clock known on the Continent outside Italy is the Strasbourg clock of 1352. Then between 1354 and 1360 come clocks at Geneva, Florence, Bologna, Siena, Frankenburg and Nürnberg. Not until 1362 does any clock appear in the North, at Brussels, but then appear a number in rapid succession in Flanders, and, in natural geographical and date sequence, there follows the evidence of clocks in England afforded by the Westminster Palace clock, the coming of the Dutchmen to England in 1368, the statement of the Malmesbury monk in 1373, and the use of modern hours in 1377.

In the face of this orderly sequence of events, it is highly improbable that St. Paul's had a clock in 1286. The Author holds the view that the Milan clock of 1335 is the first public clock of which there is record, and was, quite possibly, the first erected.[1]

---

[1] A quotation showing the existence of a clock on the Cathedral of Cambrai appears under the date 1318 in *Les Accessoires du Costume et du Mobilier*, by d'Allemagne (Paris, 1928). The date, however, is an error. The source (*Histoire artistique de la Cathédrale de Cambrai*. Houdoy. Paris, 1880) gives the reference under the date 1408. There is mention of payment in 1318 to the keeper of a *horologium*, but there is evidence that Cambrai first had a real clock in 1395.

It is difficult enough to fix with any certainty the date of introduction of public clocks, but it is far more difficult to discover when house clocks were invented. They are more likely to escape the notice of chroniclers, and they could have no influence on the methods of time-reckoning. Probably the fourteenth-century house clocks differed little from the public clocks in construction or in size; they must have been what would now be called monumental clocks, and, as monasteries would not have welcomed a timekeeper showing equal hours, only princes could have afforded or housed them. Giovanni Dondi's clock of 1364 is the first house clock known, but there are a few references to clocks of earlier date. The first and most important references are in Dante's *Paradiso*, Cantos X. and XXIV. The latter, in Longfellow's translation, is :—

> And as the wheels in works of horloges
> Revolve so that the first to the beholder
> Motionless seems, and the last one to fly.[1]

This is a puzzling allusion. In an ordinary clock, though the first wheels certainly appear motionless, the last, the escape wheel, cannot be said to fly; it moves visibly, but with a slow intermittent motion. If the lines referred to the striking movement of a clock the simile is clear, but it seems unlikely that Dante would take as characteristic of a clock a part which works for only a few seconds in the hour. A possible interpretation is that *l' ultimo che voli* refers to the swinging foliot which, in all early clocks, was in a prominent position at the top. It does not turn as do the wheels of the clock, but the word *cerchio* would apply to the earliest foliot known—that of Dondi's clock—and it certainly gives the appearance of flying.

[1] ' E come cerchi in tempra d' oriuoli
si giran siche il primo, a chi pon mente,
quieto pare, e l' ultimo che voli.'

The passage in Canto x. is :—

> Then, as a horloge that calleth us
>   What time the Bride of God is rising up
>   With matins to her Spouse that he may love her,
> Wherein one part the other draws and urges,
>   Ting ! Ting ! resounding with so sweet a note,
>   That swells with love the spirit well disposed.[1]

Here the reference is not so clearly to a clock, but, taking the two passages together, there can be little doubt that Dante had a clock in mind. He wrote the *Paradiso* between 1316 and 1321, and so has given a date for the invention of the clock some twenty years before that of the first clock known.

An earlier mention of an *orloge* that has frequently been quoted is found in the *Roman de la Rose*,[2] written (mainly) by Jean de Meun *dit* Clopinal between 1300 and 1305 :—

> Et refait sonner ses orloges
> Par ses sales et par ses loges,
> A roës trop sotivement
> De pardurable movement.

Taken without their context, these lines point to a clock, but they come in the middle of a long list of musical instruments, and orloge clearly has here its occasional meaning of a carillon of small bells.

The *Libros del Saber de Astronomia del Rey D. Alfonso X. de Castilla* affords an indication that clocks were not in existence much before the king's death in 1284. Vol. IV. of this book is on timekeepers, and describes in detail a sundial, a water-clock, a mercury-clock and a candle-clock. It is probable that any new type of clock would soon have reached the court of a ruler so deeply interested in astronomy and mechanism.

---

[1] ' Indi, come orologio, che ne chiami
        nell' ora che la sposa di Dio surge
        a mattinar lo sposo perchè l' ami.
        che l' una parte l' altra tira ed urge,
        tin tin sonando con si dolce nota
        che il ben disposto spirito d' amor turge.'
[2] Line 21,289 or 22,022, according to the edition.

43

The inventory of the possessions of Charles v. of France (1364-80)[1] contains the following items :—

Ung grant orloge de mer, de deux grans fiolles plains de sablon ; ung reloge d'argent tout entièrement, sans fer, avec deux contrepoix d'argent empliz de plomb ; ung reloge en façon d'un timbre ; ung reloge d'argent blanc qui se met sur ung pillier.

The first is described as a sand-glass, but the second, which had belonged to Philippe le Bel (1285-1314), has generally been assumed to have been a clock, on account of its two weights. Being entirely of silver, it must have been small and must be compared with the portable clock made for Louis XI. in 1481,[2] which was packed in a case and carried on the back of a horse, Martin Guerier, the driver, receiving five sous a day for himself and his horse.[3] The size of the clock indicated by this account is quite in accord with the rough and heavy work to which clockmakers were restricted by their tools, at any rate in the fourteenth century, though it is surprising that so late as 1481 Louis XI. was unable to obtain a clock that did not need a horse and driver of its own. It shows the extreme improbability of a clock small enough to be made entirely of silver so early as 1314, and makes it far more likely that Philippe le Bel's *reloge* was a sand-glass and that the weights were used with a device for turning the glass over. Another light is thrown on Charles the Fifth's *reloges* by Christina de Pisan :—

He had in his chapel a burning candle, which was divided into twenty-four parts, and men were appointed to come and tell him the mark to which the candle had burned, so warning him of what he had to do.[4]

[1] *Inventaire du Mobilier de Charles V., Roi de France.*   Labarte.   Paris, 1879.

[2] 'A Jean de Paris, orlogeur, pour une orloge où il y a un cadran, et sonne les heures, garnie de tout ce qui luy appartient ; laquelle le Roy a fait prandre et achecter de luy pour porter avec luy par tous les lieux où il yra.'   Douet-d'Arcq, *Comptes de l'hôtel des rois de France*, p. 388.

[3] Jal, *Dictionnaire de biographie et d'histoire.*

[4] *Le livre des fais et bonnes meurs du sage roi Charles.*   Ed. Michaud.   Ire partie, ch. xxi. t. i. p. 609.

Though there is nothing improbable in Charles having possessed a house clock, the *reloges* of his inventory are more likely to have been sand-glasses. Better evidence of a house clock in his reign is the payment made for a case for the Dauphin's clock which struck the hours at the Louvre.[1]

The Author can trace no other reference to a house clock till 1389, when the Duchesse de Bourgogne had her chamber clock repaired. After this date the purchase of clocks by kings and princes is fairly frequent, but the first private person to possess a clock appears to have been the Nürnberg astronomer, Bernard Walther, in 1484.

The records of early clocks lead to no satisfactory conclusion. The inventor of the clock is unknown, and the date of its invention is obscure. All that can be said is, that the evidence so far available points to the clock on San Gottardo, Milan, as being the first public clock, and to the existence of earlier house clocks, starting, perhaps, in the last decade of the thirteenth century. Public clocks became common only in the last quarter of the fourteenth century; house clocks not until much later.

No example exists of the first century of clockmaking. The earliest clocks still in existence are, probably, the clocks of Dover Castle, Wells and Rouen, and a clock now in the Germanische Museum in Nürnberg, which was in the tower of the S. Sebaldus Church. Speckhart gives the date as probably 1392, if not earlier; von Bassermann-Jordan as about 1400. The clock is only sixteen inches high, without striking mechanism, but with a device to release an alarum at the hour. It was used to warn the watchman of the tower, whose duty was to strike the hour on the bell. This use of a clock to give the hour to the watchman instead of striking the bell directly was quite common.

The construction of house clocks of the fifteenth

---

[1] 'Un estuy pour hébergier l'orloge de M. le Dalphin qui sonne les oeures audit Louvre.' Compte des dépenses faites par Charles v. au château du Louvre.

century was exactly the same as that of the large public clocks, only on a smaller scale. The open framework was enclosed at the front, though sometimes only by a large dial, and the other sides were generally open, so that the whole mechanism was visible. From the four upper corners arched bars formed a skeleton cupola, and the bell hung from its centre. Later, the sides were enclosed by pierced or engraved plates, and sometimes the spandrels between the arched bars were filled in.

As time went on, clocks were improved in design by making them go for a longer period after winding. In most very early clocks the drum round which the cord of the weight was coiled made one turn in the hour. The time of going was therefore limited to the number of turns of cord which the drum would hold, generally eight to twelve, and the clocks required winding two or three times in the twenty-four hours. The amount of the weight and the distance through which it can fall are limited by the size and position of the clock. Together they represent the work expended on the clock, and in every clock all this work is wasted in friction. Increasing the time of going of the clock means, therefore, diminishing the rate at which the work is wasted in friction, and this can be done only by improving the design and workmanship. The improvement was very slow. Even at the end of the fifteenth century, clocks more commonly required winding twice in the twenty-four hours. Then technical skill developed more rapidly, and within the next two centuries Tompion had made grandfather clocks which went for a year with one winding—a triumph of perfect workmanship.

'Confusion to the black-faced clock that awoke me. May its head, its tongue, its pair of ropes and its wheels moulder, likewise its dullard balls, its orefices, its hammer, its ducks quacking as if anticipating day, and its ever restless works! This turbulent clock clacks ridiculous sounds like to a drunken cobbler . . . the yelping of a dog in pain echoed! the ceaseless clatter of a cloister! a gloomy mill grinding away the night.'
DAFYDD AP GWILYM, 1343-1400.

CHAPTER IV

THE INVENTION OF WATCHES

'There are also imperfect clocks called Watches that do not strike but only have a Dyall with a hand turning round.'

SYMON PATRICK, 1662.

THE step which had to be taken to turn the clock of the fourteenth and fifteenth centuries into a watch or portable clock was, essentially, to change the motive power from a weight to a spring. It was no easy step, because the manufacture of a long thin strip of steel, sufficiently uniform in quality and temper to withstand repeated coiling and uncoiling, presented great technical difficulties.

Peter Henlein of Nürnberg.—It has generally been accepted that watchmaking, as an industry, started in Nürnberg between 1500 and 1510, and there is no doubt that Peter Henlein, a locksmith, was the first maker there. As will be seen later, however, there is evidence of the existence of French watches very soon after 1510, and it cannot be said with certainty that Henlein made the first watch. In Nürnberg, however, he was regarded as the inventor. Johannes Cocclaeus wrote as follows in 1511 :—

From day to day more ingenious discoveries are made ; for Petrus Hele, a young man, makes things which astonish the most learned mathematicians, for he makes out of a small quantity of iron horologia devised with very many wheels, and these horologia, in any position and without any weight, both indicate and strike [*pulsant*] for 40 hours, even when they are carried on the breast or in the purse.

It is probable that the Latin word *pulsant* means strike, though it might refer merely to the tick of the watch.

47

Johann Neudörfer, writing in 1547 of the Nürnberg craftsmen, mentions Andreas Heinlein, a locksmith, as being almost the first to discover how to make small watches in musk-balls.[1] Dopplmayr, a later Nürnberg chronicler, writing in 1730, mentions a Petrus Hele (died about 1540) and an Andreas Heinlein (died about 1545), having evidently copied from Cocclaeus and Neudörfer.[2] A former Archiv-Sekretär of Nürnberg, M. M. Mayer, in a search through the archives, found no trace of Peter Hele or Andreas Heinlein, but found a number of references to Peter Henlein.   He was accepted as master locksmith in 1509, several times got into trouble with the magistrates, and died in 1542 ; in the notice of his death he was called *vrmacher*.   Both Neudörfer and Dopplmayr are known to have been inaccurate in giving names, and there can be no doubt that the Petrus Hele and Andreas Heinlein mentioned in their chronicles were one and the same man, Peter Henlein.   He must have been about thirty years old when he became master in 1509, and probably produced his first watch about the same time. The only other watchmaker mentioned by Dopplmayr, of about the same date, is Caspar Werner, who died about 1545 and

devoted himself with especial industry to the making of watches, which he brought into great popularity as the result of continual study and the introduction of various new inventions, though he injured his memory and health thereby.

Some further light has been thrown on Peter Henlein by Albert Gümbel, Staatsoberarchivar in Nürnberg, who recently published (1924) a pamphlet in which he recounts some discoveries in the Nürnberg archives. The Rats of Nürnberg (Mayors is the nearest equivalent) had the custom of sending presents of considerable value to important foreigners who were in a position to help or

[1] Johann Neudörfer, *Nachrichten von Künstlern und Werkleuten daselbst aus dem Jahre 1547.* Hrsn. von Dr. G. W. K. Lochner. Wien, 1875.
[2] Johann Gabriel Dopplmayr, *Historische Nachricht von den Nürnbergischen Mathematicis und Künstlern.* Nürnberg, 1730.

hinder the interests of the city. An examination of the lists of these presents showed that in 1521 a self-acting horologium in a silver case[1] was sent to the Graf von Lombecke at Worms. In 1522 a similar present was sent to the chaplain of the Duke of Saxony,[2] and in 1523 two horologia were sent as presents to the Spanish Chancellor.[3] Altogether, between 1521 and 1525, seven horologia were sent as presents, and in reference to three of them there exist the statements of payments made to Peter Henlein for his work. In every case the horologium is called self-acting, which can only mean spring-driven as opposed to weight-driven. Gümbel argues, with good ground, that these horologia were Peter Henlein's watches, and that, judging from the high value of the Nürnberg presents, they were at that period regarded as rare and curious treasures. In the next fifteen years only two or three watches were sent, and it is concluded that after 1525 watches became too well known to serve as princely presents.

No watch exists which can be dated with any probability earlier than 1540, and the only mention of a Nürnberg watch, beyond those found by Gümbel, is in the letter written by Martin Luther in 1527 to thank the Abbot Fredericus Pistorius of Nürnberg for a brass horologium sent to him. He adds that he has never before seen such a thing.[4] Beyond this remark, there is nothing in the letter to indicate that the horologium was a watch, but its provenance from Nürnberg, and the fact that Luther must have been acquainted with recent developments in clocks, associating as he did with all the important personages of the time, indicates that it was a spring-driven table clock, if not a watch. Luther's letter and Gümbel's discoveries show that watches were extremely rare, even fifteen years after their first production.

[1] 'Ein selbgeent oralogium mit einem silberen geheus.'
[2] 'Ein aroligium selbgeend.'
[3] 'Zwey selbgeende oralgia.'
[4] Enders, *Dr. Martin Luthers sämtliche Werke. Briefwechsel.* Vol. vi. p. 41. Stuttgart, 1895.

The First Spring Clocks.—Though it is quite likely that watchmaking was started in Nürnberg by Peter Henlein, it does not follow that he was the first to replace a weight by a spring in a timepiece. There are two spring-driven clocks in existence which may be of an earlier date, and there are two references indicating earlier spring clocks. One of the existing clocks is in the possession of Carl Marfels of Berlin. It is a large table clock of Gothic form, bearing the lion and the arms of Burgundy. It has going and striking trains, each driven by a spring through a fuzee, an ingenious device for equalizing the force of the spring, which will be described later. The former owner, Von Leber, after making a historical research into its origin, came to the conclusion that it formed part of the wedding treasure of Maria of Burgundy, and was of a date between 1429 and 1435.[1]

The clock was examined by von Bassermann-Jordan, Director of the Bayerische National Museum in Munich, and pronounced by him to be original throughout and of about the date claimed by von Leber. With this date, it would probably have been made by Pierret Lombart of Mons, the duke's clockmaker. On the other hand, while there is nothing improbable in finding a spring at this date, it is somewhat improbable that a spring, which must then have been a novelty, should be found combined with a fuzee, in itself a remarkable invention for the period. The Nürnberg watches of the sixteenth century had a very crude substitute for the fuzee, which is not found, apart from this clock, before the end of the fifteenth century, in Leonardo da Vinci's sketches.

The second spring clock is one in the Germanische Museum, Nürnberg, illustrated by Speckhart[2] and Albrecht.[3] It also has going and striking trains, each with a spring in a barrel and a fuzee. Speckhart attri-

---

[1] *Notice sur l'Horloge Gothique construite vers 1430 pour Philippe III., dit le Bon, Duc de Bourgogne.* M. de Leber. Vienna, 1877.
[2] *Die Geschichte der Zeitmesskunst,* by Saunier. Trs. and ed. Speckhart. Bautzen, 1903.
[3] *Die Räder-Uhr.* Rud. Albrecht. Rothenburg ob der Tauber.

butes it to the first decades of the sixteenth century, and Albrecht, judging by the decoration of the case, to 1480 to 1500.

A reference indicating a small spring clock of some-what earlier date is the tale of a gentleman at the court of Louis XI. (1461-83) who, being in financial difficulties, concealed a clock belonging to the king in his pocket ; whereupon the clock disclosed the theft by striking. The story is given in the *Encyclopédie* without quoting its source, and the article on clocks in the *Encyclopédie* is so unreliable that little weight can be given to the tale. A better authenticated reference to spring clocks is found in the *Historia Literario-Typographica Mediolanensis*,[1] which quotes a sonnet written by Gaspare Visconti in 1493, with the prefatory title :—

There are made certain small portable clocks which, though with little mechanism, keep going, indicating the hours and the courses of many planets and the feast-days, striking at the proper times. This sonnet is put in the mouth of a lover who, looking at one of these clocks, compares himself to it.

Octavius Morgan[2] says that Gaspare Visconti died in 1499 and left his collection of sonnets in an illuminated MS. to the library of St. Barnabas in Milan. The Author has not been able to obtain any information about this MS.

The most probable conclusion to be drawn from the evidence about early watches and spring-driven clocks is that springs were applied to clocks in the fifteenth century, but, except possibly in a few isolated instances, only at the end of the century ; that the spring-driven clock was made small enough to be worn—became, in fact, a watch—about 1510, Peter Henlein being the first maker in Nürnberg and, so far as is known, the first man to make a watch.

It is uncertain what the watches were like that were

[1] Philippi Argelati. *Bibliotheca Scriptorum Mediolanensium*, vol. i. cols. 357-361. Praemittitur Josephi Antonii Saxi. Mediolani, 1745.
[2] *Archæologia*, vol. xxxiii. 1849.

PLATE VI

1

German striking watch ; first half of sixteenth century.
Gilt metal engraved case.   Iron plates and wheels ;
no spring barrels.
Mallett coll.   pp. 55, 93.

2

French striking watch by Jacques de la Garde of
Blois, dated 1551, the earliest French watch known.
Gilt metal engraved case.   Brass movement with
fuzee and spring barrels.

   Jacques de la Garde, 1551-65, was one of the most
famous makers of Blois.   Another watch and a small
clock by him are known.
Louvre.   pp. 55, 63, 93.

PLATE VI

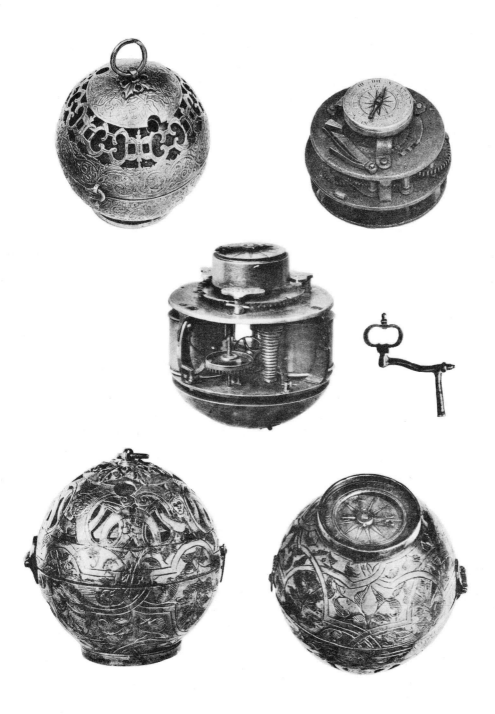

made at the beginning of the sixteenth century. The British Museum has one of the finest collections in existence of sixteenth-century watches, but none can be dated with any certainty before 1550. Von Bassermann-Jordan says definitely that no existing watch is known of an earlier date than 1535-45, and intimates that this date is by no means certain.

There are table clocks of slightly earlier date. Holbein, in his picture of the merchant Gisse, painted about 1530, shows on the table a clock of the most usual type. It is a plain cylindrical box about two and a half inches in diameter and about the same high. Most of the early watches known are like this clock, but of half the height. In Germany this *drum* type was retained, with much the same mechanism, to the end of the sixteenth century, and it has generally been supposed that it was the type of Peter Henlein's watches. Plate VII shows three views of a watch of the drum type with exceptionally fine piercing and chiselling in the Mallett collection.

The First Watches.—There is, though, some possibility that the first watches were more of a spherical shape. Dopplmayr writes under Andreas Heinlein (Peter Henlein) :—

A locksmith artist, who gained renown through the small watchworks which he was one of the first to make in the form of the musk-balls [*Bisam-Knöpffe*] at that time in use.

And now Gümbel has recently discovered an entry in the Nürnberg archives of a payment in 1524 of fifteen florins to H. Henlein for a gilt musk-apple with a watch.[1] The musk-balls or musk-apples, the scent bottles of that day, were small pierced hollow balls, hinged to open, and were often worn hanging on a neck chain or on a rosary. Five or six watches of this form are known. One, to which a date of 1540 is assigned, is, with a larger and later one, in the Koch collection[2]; one is in the Louvre,

---

[1] 'Fur 1 vergulten pysn Appfel fur all Ding mit einem Oaiologium.'

[2] Illustrated and described in *Alte Uhren und ihre Meister*. Von Bassermann-Jordan. Leipzig, 1916.

PLATE VII

Case with dial of a late sixteenth-century German watch, showing exceptionally fine piercing and chiselling.
Mallett coll.   pp. 55, 57, 94.

PLATE VII

in the Paul Garnier collection, of French make and dated
1551 (Plate VI, the three lower views); one in the
Mallett collection (the two upper views on the same plate);
and one in the Schloss Museum, Berlin.

All are very early examples, and the spherical watch
of this type must have gone out of fashion in the second
half of the sixteenth century, when the drum was the
general shape. The natural conclusion would be that
the first watches were table clocks in miniature, that is, of
the drum type; but there is the possibility that they were
of the type of the very rare spherical watch.

The cases of all known early watches are of gilt
bronze. That silver and gold were used is known from
the Nürnberg archives and from Robertet's inventory of
1532, to be mentioned later; but other inventories of
sixteenth-century watches indicate that gilt cases were
the rule and silver and gold cases rare. This use of base
metal is strange, because the cost of a gold case would
have been small in comparison with the cost of the watch,
which was a luxury only the very wealthy could afford.
Possibly the reason lay in guild restrictions. The early
watchmakers all belonged to the guild of locksmiths, and
their use of gold and silver might have been an infringe-
ment of the rights of the gold- and silver-smiths. At
Blois, early in the seventeenth century, the rights of the
Orfèvres were guarded by the proviso that any gold or
silver used by the watchmakers had to be purchased from
them and marked by them. There is no doubt that we
owe the survival of so many early watches to the use
of a metal of no value for melting down, and it is not
surprising that no gold-cased watch survives.

Nearly all the existing sixteenth-century watches
were provided with either an alarum or a mechanism for
striking the hours, and some had both. The cases in
consequence were pierced round the edge and often on the
bottom, as in the watch on Plate VII. Generally there
was a hinged cover pierced and chiselled in a pattern
giving openings over the hour figures on the dial.

55

PLATE VIII

1

Oval German striking watch, early seventeenth century. Gilt metal case with two hinged covers. Silver dial with central incised star filled with translucent enamel; steel hand. Movement with brass plates and steel wheels. Stackfreed and wheel balance.
British Museum.　　pp. 57, 61, 94.

2

Case of German watch, *c.* 1600. Gilt metal.
British Museum.　　pp. 57, 61, 94.

3

Circular German striking watch, late sixteenth century. Gilt metal case, pierced and engraved. Movement with brass plates and steel wheels ; stackfreed and early type of striking mechanism.
British Museum.　　pp. 57, 61, 94.

4

Octagonal German striking and alarum watch, *c.* 1575. Gilt metal case with two hinged covers and pierced baluster edge. Silver dial with gilt alarum disk within band incised and filled with translucent enamel. Gilt hand. Movement on Plate XVI, 3. Signed G. H. with shield between letters.
British Museum.　　pp. 57, 61, 94, 131.

56

PLATE VIII

Watch Dials, Bells and Hands.—The dial throws an interesting light on the two systems then in use of reckoning the hours. In Italy, Bohemia and parts of Germany the hours were reckoned from 1 to 24, starting at sunset ; this was known as the *Italian hour.* In the rest of Europe the hours were reckoned from 1 to 12, starting from midnight and midday. Nürnberg and Augsburg lay on the borderland between countries using the two systems, and their watch dials in consequence were adapted to both. The more common form of dial had an outer ring of figures I to XII and an inner ring of figures 13 to 24. The cover then was often pierced in a pattern of twelve outer and twelve inner holes. All the dials of the German watches illustrated on Plates VI, VII, VIII, IX and XXVIII have the two circles of hour figures. Two of these watches have their covers pierced with a single circle of twelve large holes (Plates VII and VIII), and three with two circles (Plates VIII and IX). There was also the dial with a single ring of twenty-four figures I to XII and again I to XII, the hand going once round the dial in twenty-four hours. This led to a pattern of twenty-four holes in the cover (Plate VIII). More rarely, the piercing bore no relation to the figures.

The dial of the book-watch on Plate XXVIII is particularly interesting because, inside the main circle of roman figures I to XII and I to XII is a circle of arabic figures 1 to 24 which can be turned round for setting to sunset, so as to read the Italian hour. As shown, the circle is set for sunset at 7.30.

A few watches of the third quarter of the sixteenth century were without cover to the dial, and later solid covers, engraved with Biblical or mythical scenes or patterns, became common. In non-circular watches a small circular cover was often fitted, as in the watch in the centre of Plate XVII.

The bell for the alarum or striking mechanism was usually fixed to the bottom of the case, and the movement was then hinged to the case and had to be turned out of

PLATE IX

Circular German striking and alarum watch, late
sixteenth century. Gilt metal edge. Silver dial,
dark blue enamel figures. Steel hand. Dumb-
bell foliot with bristle regulator operated by hand
on dial.
Mallett coll.   pp. 57, 61, 94.

PLATE IX

it for winding. Occasionally the bell was fixed to a
bottom hinged cover, and then the movement dropped
into the case from the top and was held in it by a latch.
Balet, in the exceptionally well-planned guide to the
Stuttgart collection,[1] says that a pierced back holding
the bell is a characteristic feature of the period 1670-
1720, but the Author has found sixteenth- and early
seventeenth-century watches with this feature.   There is
a type of watch, generally called a *canister* watch, in
which the covers are not hinged but pressed on ; the
type, however, is comparatively rare and is confined to
the sixteenth century.

There was, of course, only one hand ; a century and a
half had to pass before the timekeeping of watches was
good enough to make a minute hand useful.   Hands
were always steel and carefully shaped with the chisel ;
the rough, flat hands often seen may be regarded as later
additions.   They were sometimes rather clumsy, but had
to be strong enough to withstand pushing round for
setting to the hour

A ring of small knobs, one at each hour, was usual to
enable the time to be read in the dark by feeling the
position of the hand.   These feeling knobs were common
until the middle of the seventeenth century, and are seen
on the dials of all the early German watches illustrated.
Franklin quotes an amusing passage from *Les lois de
la galanterie* of 1644, where they are hailed as a new
invention :—

Those who wear a watch showing the hours, half-hours and
quarters can sometimes use it to time the length of their visit.
But it smacks too much of the business man to look at your
watch in company ; it is impolite to your hosts because it looks
as if you had another engagement and were in a hurry to keep
it. As for striking watches, they are very tiresome, because
they interrupt conversation. That is why one should adopt
the new kind of watch in which the hour and half-hour marks
are raised enough to enable one to feel them with the finger and

[1] *Führer durch die Uhrensammlung.* Leo Balet. Stuttgart, 1913.

so tell the time without having to take out the watch and look at it.[1]

A ring was fixed to the edge of the case, opposite to the XII, generally balanced by a finial ornament opposite to the VI. Hanging the watch on a neck chain was the original fashion of wearing a watch ; pride of possession must have been great to outweigh the discomfort of a sixteenth-century watch on the breast.

Nürnberg Eggs.—The drum watch continued to be made in Germany until the end of the sixteenth century, but soon after the middle of the century the cases began to change in the direction of the Nürnberg egg. This term has been much abused. It is often supposed that the Nürnberg egg was the type of the earliest watches made, whereas the egg shape is almost unknown in the sixteenth century and did not become common until after 1625. The term is almost certainly an eighteenth-century corruption. Its first use known to the Author is in Dopplmayr, the Nürnberg historian of 1730. In a footnote to his account of Peter Hele (Henlein) he says :—

This kind of timekeeper has for a long time been called the Nürnberg (living) egg,[2] because at first it used to be made in the shape of a small egg, and this name also occurs in chapter 26 of the German translation of a book of adventures left by Fr. Rabelais.

The last book of Rabelais' *Gargantua-Pantagruel* was published in 1564, and a number of German editions (translations with many changes) were published in Strasbourg in the years 1575, 1590 and later. The French editions contain no reference to Nürnberg eggs, nor does the first German edition, but in the 1590 and later editions there was inserted, after a paragraph about observations of the heavens :—

Unnd solche ohn die Nörnbergischen lebendigen Ueurlein, unnd ohn ein Uhrwerck in Mönster zu Strassburg.

[1] *Recueil des pièces en prose les plus agréables de ce temps.* Quoted by Franklin, *La vie privée d'autrefois :* 'La mesure du temps.' Paris, 1888.
[2] 'Die Nürnbergische (lebendige) Eyerlein.'

Dopplmayr's ' Eyerlein ' (little egg) was therefore a mis-reading of ' Ueurlein ' or ' Uürleinn ' (1631 edition), which means ' little clock,' and his mistake is no doubt responsible for the present-day use of the term Nürnberg egg for the early German watches, a term that is quite inappropriate, because the early watches were not like eggs and the real egg shape was never common enough to be regarded as the standard form of watch.

The first departure from the drum lay in rounding the edges, and rounded edges were nearly always accompanied by domed covers, as in the watches on Plate IX and Plate VIII, 2 and 3. This is, perhaps, the most usual form of the German watch in the last quarter of the sixteenth century. During the same period the circular form gave place to the oval or octagonal, but the oval did not become common before 1600. The octagonal form with equal sides (Plate VIII, 4) and the elongated octagon (centre of Plate XVII) were both common towards the end of the sixteenth century and continued throughout the seventeenth century. The oval watch was often ungainly, especially when it departed only slightly from circular form. The watch shown in Plate VIII, 1 is a typical egg, with the oval pronounced and with sharply domed covers. There are several engravings of seventeenth-century ladies wearing watches of this type hung by a short chain from their girdles.

A German watch of quite exceptional form is on Plate LI, 2. It belongs to the first quarter of the seventeenth century, and is one of the small but choice collection of watches in the Kunsthistorische Museum, Vienna.

Watchmaking in France.—Watchmaking started in France possibly about the same time as Nürnberg, and in the course of the sixteenth century developed at Blois into a considerable industry. French watches before the end of the sixteenth century are, however, very rare. The earliest in existence is the spherical watch in the Louvre, mentioned above, dated 1551, and made by

PLATE X

German rapier and dagger with watches on hilts,
c. 1610. The larger watch has a striking movement. Both signed with monogram TR. Gilt
metal cases with two hinged covers. Movement
with stackfreed and wheel balance, and an
unusual amount of decoration. The maker of
these watches is almost certainly Tobias Reichel,
Court clockmaker in Dresden, 1603-10. A table
clock with automata and an automaton spider
by him are in the Grüne Gewölbe, Dresden.
The Johanneum, Dresden. p. 63.

PLATE X

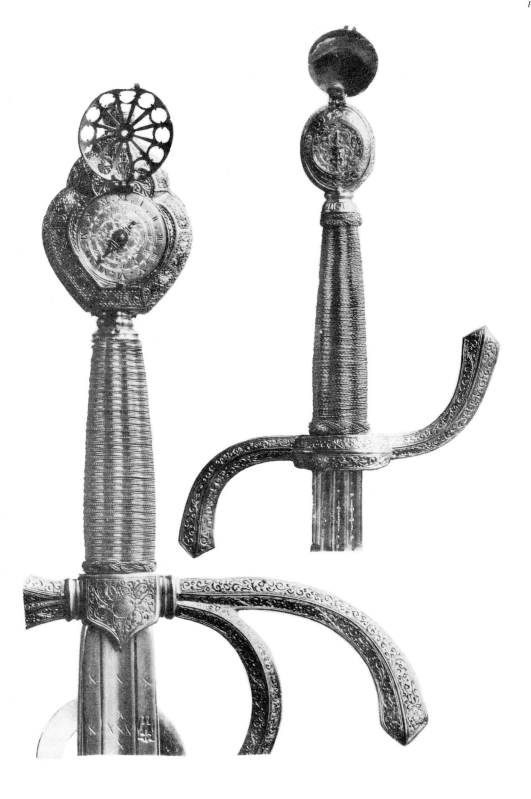

Jacques de la Garde of Blois (Plate VI, three lower views); and there exists another by the same maker dated 1565.

Julien Coudray of Blois, clockmaker to Louis XII. and François I., is perhaps the first French watchmaker known. His claim to have made watches is based on an order by François I. in 1518:—

Order to Jean Sapin, receveur général de Languedoil et Guyenne, to pay to Julien Couldray clockmaker at Blois the sum of 200 gold écus: as payment for two fine daggers, their hilts containing two gilt orloges destined for the King's service.[1]

It is a question whether these *orloges* were sundials or watches. Watches in dagger hilts are known, but rare. Plate X shows a rapier and a dagger with watches made by Tobias Reichel of Dresden about 1610. They are in the Dresden Johanneum. On the other hand, portable dials were common, and, though the Author knows of no dagger with a dial, it is a combination quite as probable as a dagger with a watch. Perhaps the fact most in favour of the *orloges* being watches is that they were made by Coudray. Coudray, who died 1530, figures in the royal accounts from 1504 to 1529, and was a clock-maker of great repute. He made a clock for the church of St. Gatien at Tours with carillon and automata, show-ing the day of the week and month, the moon's phases, the fixed and movable feast-days, the Sunday letter, the golden number and the indiction. It is not therefore improbable that the *orloges* of the order quoted were really watches, and that he was the first watchmaker in France.

Although no French watch of the first half of the sixteenth century survives, many must have been made in France. Florimond Robertet, trésorier des finances

---

[1] *Archives Nationales*, k.k. 289, fol. 444. Quoted by Develle, *Les Horlogers Blesois du XVIme et XVIIme siècles.* Blois, 1913 and 1917.

under Charles VIII., Louis XII., and François I., left at his death in 1532—

Twelve watches, of which seven are striking and the other five silent, in cases of gold, silver, and brass of different sizes ; but of these I [the widow] attach value only to the large one, merely of gilt copper, that my husband had made ; it shows all the stars and the celestial signs and motions, which he understood perfectly.[1]

Robertet was a collector of *objets d'art* of all kinds and a wealthy man, but, even so, his possession of twelve watches in 1532 is surprising, and shows that our knowledge of the beginnings of watchmaking is far from complete. In the inventory is the first use known to the Author of the word *montre*, as applied to a timepiece, and the evidence of early watchmaking in France turns on its meaning. There is no doubt that weight clocks are excluded, but *montre* may include spring-driven table clocks. In the early seventeenth-century inventories of the Blois watchmakers quoted by Develle, the word *orloge* is nearly always used for table clocks, but there are a few entries of *montres à mettre sur table*. This suggests that *montre à mettre sur table* was a smaller thing than the table clock called *orloge*, and that *montre* by itself meant watch.[2] It is probable, then, that Robertet's *montres* were watches, and, though some may have been small table clocks, it is almost certain that those in cases of gold and silver were watches.

[1] 'Douze montres, dont sept sont sonnantes et les cinq autres muettes à boëstes d'or, d'argent et de leton de differentes grandeures : mais entre ce nombre je ne fais estat que de la grosse qui n'est que de cuivre doré, que mon mary fit faire, laquelle marque tous les astres, les signes et mouvemens celestes, qu'il entendoit fort bien.' *Mém. de la Soc. Nat. des Antiquaires de France*, 3ᵉ Série, t. x. 1868.

[2] The French Académie did not till 1694 define the word *monstre* as a pocket timepiece. In its earliest use, the word meant the dial of a clock (*monstre d'orloge*). The Author is indebted for this note to Monsieur Damourette of Paris, author of *Essai de Grammaire de la langue française*, who has kindly signified his agreement with the meaning attributed by the Author to the word *montres* in Robertet's inventory.

It is interesting to compare this inventory with Martin Luther's statement, referred to above, that in 1527 he had never seen such a thing as a watch. The comparison indicates that watchmaking had made fully as much progress in France as in Germany, and that Cocclaeus' account of Peter Henlein's watches is not sufficient evidence to prove the generally accepted view that the watch industry started in Nürnberg. There is, too, an essential difference between the mechanisms of the German and French watches, which is evidence that the French did not copy from the Germans but made an independent start.

After Julien Coudray, five clock- or watch-makers are known in Blois belonging to the first half of the sixteenth century, including Guillaume Coudray and Jehan du Jardin, who were Horlogers du roi. Before the end of the century the number known reaches forty-five, and there were others in Autun, Rouen, Paris, Lyons, Sedan, Angoulême, Loches, Dijon and Grenoble. Their work is very rare; the only sixteenth-century French watch in the British Museum is one by Augustin Forfaict of Sedan, who died in 1586. This watch, with its movement, is shown at the bottom of Plate XVI. The Pierpont Morgan collection, now in the Metropolitan Museum of Art in New York, had two of the last quarter of the sixteenth century, one by F. Vallier of Lyons and the other by Nicolas Gaillard of Lyons, and the Paul Garnier collection in the Louvre has the watch of 1551 already mentioned. Besides these, and two or three in private collections, there is no French watch which can be assigned to a date before the last decade of the sixteenth century. None of these is of the circular drum type; one is spherical, another in the form of a tulip, and the others oval.

From 1590 to 1625, French watches are comparatively numerous. The most common form is an oval, with straight sides and moderately domed covers, and the case is generally of gilt metal, covered with engravings of scenes, figures and foliage patterns. Another common

65

PLATE XI

Oval French watch by Jean Vallier, Lyons, *c.* 1610, showing hours, minutes, days of the week and month, months and seasons, and age and phase of moon. Silver engraved case. Silver engraved dial with steel hands. Striking and alarum movements. Jean Baptiste Vallier is known in Lyons in 1596; he became master in 1602, and died in 1649. He was one of the finest makers of his time, and this watch is regarded as his *chef-d'œuvre*. Another watch by him on Plate XXIV, 5. Thirteen watches by him are known.

British Museum.   pp. 67, 95.

PLATE XI

form is an elongated octagon, never an equal-sided one. The covers are not pierced, as in the German watches; piercing required for striking or alarum watches was confined to the sides. The Author knows of only one exception to this: an octagonal watch with small cover, similar to the German watch shown in the centre of Plate XVII.

One of the finest watches of this period is by Jean Vallier of Lyons in the British Museum, and is illustrated in Plate XI. Its rather unattractive shape is redeemed by the exquisite engraving covering the whole case. The movement, which shows most beautiful workmanship and decoration, contains striking, alarum and calendar mechanisms which are all in perfect order. The lowest dial on the face is the hour dial; the dial on the right has a minute hand, an extremely rare addition to a watch before the second half of the seventeenth century; four quarters are indicated by figures with intermediate five-minute divisions. The dial on the left shows through the opening the engraved figure emblematic of the day of the week, and the top dial indicates by its hand the age of the moon in days, while the moon's phase is shown in the opening of the central disc. The month is shown in the sector-shaped opening to the right of the top dial, and the day of the month in the opening above the top dial. The calendar mechanism of this watch is described later.

Jean Vallier was a maker of great repute in Lyons, and all his watches have beautiful work, both in the decoration and movement; thirteen are known, of which one is in the South Kensington Museum, two in the Fitzwilliam Museum, Cambridge, and three in the Louvre.

The author of the Louvre catalogue says that the watch just described is certainly his *chef-d'œuvre*. The first record of Jean Vallier in the Lyons archives is in 1596, and he died in 1649. His father, F. Vallier, was the maker of one of the early French watches referred to, in the Metropolitan Museum of Art, New York.

67

PLATE XII

1

English watch by Jacob Cornelius, London, *c.* 1650.
Gold case enamelled turquoise blue, with flowers in
white in relief and black markings. Dial champlevé
and enamelled with white ground and translucent
coloured flowers. Steel hand.
Webster coll.   p. 139.

2

English watch by François Nawe, London, late sixteenth century. Gilt metal engraved case. Gilt
engraved dial. Steel hand. François Nawe is
probably the same as Francis Noway, who was born
in Brabant and is known of in London from 1580-3.
A second watch by him is in the same collection.
Webster coll.   pp. 71, 92, 97, 117.

PLATE XII

Watchmaking in England.—England appears to have been much behind Germany and France in producing watches. No English watch is known of a date earlier than 1590, or possibly 1580, and only a short time before this is there any record of a watchmaker. Yet Queen Elizabeth possessed a number of watches, one small enough to form part of a bracelet. Kendal[1] gives an interesting list of jewelled clocks and watches presented to the Queen from 1571 to 1580; this is quoted by Britten, who adds a list of the clocks and watches mentioned in the inventory of her possessions.

A watche of golde sett with small rubies, small diamondes and small emerodes, with a pearle in the toppe called a buckett,

is the first item in the inventory, which described twelve clocks and ten watches, all of great richness. It is more probable that these watches came from Blois than that they were the work of English makers, of whom we have no record.

Our knowledge of early English makers is due mainly to the work of Atkins and Overall, who published in 1881 an account of the Company of Clockmakers of London, compiled from the Company's and other records. To this Britten has added much from his own researches, and his book contains nearly all that is known of London makers. Scottish makers may be found in the exhaustive work by John Smith,[2] and several lists of local provincial makers have been compiled.

The Author, through the courtesy of the Court and Secretary of the Blacksmiths' Company, was enabled to examine the minute- and account-books of this Company, which harboured the clockmakers of London before the Clockmakers' Company was formed in 1632. Some records of early makers were found, but little that threw any clearer light on the beginning of watchmaking in England. Certain material found by the Author in

[1] *A History of Watches and other Timekeepers.* London, 1892.
[2] *Old Scottish Clockmakers, 1453 to 1850.* 2nd ed. Edinburgh, 1921.

PLATE XIII

English striking watch by Randolf Bull, London, *c.* 1600.   Gilt metal pierced and engraved case. Silver dial.   Steel hand.   Movement with fuzee and steel wheels.   Randolf or Rainulph Bull is known from 1590 to 1617.   He was clockmaker to the King and keeper of Westminster Palace clock.   A table clock by him is known. *Mallett coll.*   pp. 72, 117.

PLATE XIII

the State Papers shows that there is room for further investigation of sixteenth-century documents, but the reward is likely to be scanty.

Queen Elizabeth had two, or possibly three, clock-makers: Nicholas Urseau, who is mentioned in 1553, 1556 and 1572, and died in 1590 (Britten suggests that there were two of this name), and Bartholomew Newsam, who was working as a clockmaker in 1568 and died in 1593. There is no record of Urseau as a watchmaker, but Bartholomew Newsam almost certainly made watches as well as the small table clocks of which examples survive. The Metropolitan Museum of Art has a large striking watch, four inches across, with a mark B x N, which is most probably by him. It is illustrated in Britten's book. Also his will mentions

One cristall jewell with a watche in it, garnished with goulde.

The English watch of the end of the sixteenth century appears to have been copied both from German and French types, though in mechanism it is essentially French. Probably there was no settled English type till about 1610, when French forms were followed. A little later, though, comes a type of plain watch which is characteristic of England, a smooth oval with a small circular glass, generally of silver without engraving or any decoration. The type resembles an egg more than does any German watch.

The two lower views on Plate XII show one of the very rare sixteenth-century English watches in Mr. Percy Webster's collection. It is by François Nawe of London, almost certainly the same man as a Francis Noway who, born in Brabant, came to London in 1580 and is known until 1583, and a relation of the Michael Nouwen who, in the early years of the seventeenth century, made watches of great beauty in case and workmanship. Nawe's watch may be compared with that of Augustin Forfaict (Plate XVI, 2). The latter is typical of the ordinary plain watch of the late sixteenth and early seventeenth centuries.

71

Nawe's is the same type of watch enriched by engraving of fine quality; it is essentially a French watch, quite distinct from the contemporary German type.

Plate XIII, on the other hand, shows an English watch which, in its case and dial, has many characteristics of the German watch. It is by Randolf Bull, clockmaker to the king, known from 1590-1617. Bull's origin is unknown, and one can presume that he was an Englishman only from his name. He is referred to as an alien, but this proves merely that he was not a Londoner. This watch is the only one known to the Author, of English and French origin, that has the circle of Arabic figures 13-24 on the dial. A 24-hour day was not in use in England in 1600, so the dial, as well as the general form of the case, points to the watch having been copied from a German example. The movement, on the contrary, is of French type.

Two English watches are known with pierced covers similar to those of the two German watches on the left-hand side of Plate VIII, one the watch, probably by Bartholomew Newsam, already mentioned, and the other by Richard Crayle; both of these are illustrated in Britten.

In the first quarter of the seventeenth century, England made up the time lost in watchmaking and began to found its reputation of the foremost watchmaking country of the world, though, in regard to decoration, the French always had the advantage of their school of enamel painters. The decoration of the sixteenth-century watch-case will, however, be reserved for a later chapter, after completing the description of the early watch by examining its mechanism.

This chapter will be concluded by quoting the verses written by Hans Sachs under the heading of *The Clock-maker* in Jost Amman's book on craftsmen, published in 1568.[1] The drawing shows a clockmaker's shop, but the

---

[1] *Stände und Handwerker.* Frankfurt a/M., 1568. Facsimile reproduction in *Liebhaber-Bibliothek Alter Illustratoren.* Munich, 1884.

verses refer to a sand-glass in a frame with four glasses, giving the hour and the three quarters. It is interesting in showing how little the clock and the watch were known, even in 1568.

> ' Ich mache die reysenden Uhr,
> Gerecht und Glatt nach der Mensur,
> Von hellem glass und klein Uhrsant,
> Gut, dass sie haben langen bestandt,
> Mach auch darzu Hülssen Geheuss,
> Dareyn ich sie fleissig beschleuss,
> Ferb die gheuss Grün, Grau, rot und blaw
> Drinn man die Stund und vierteil hab.'

CHAPTER V

THE MOVEMENT OF THE EARLY WATCH

'Wer hat nichts zu schaffen
Der kaufe eine Uhr
Oder nehme eine Hur
Oder schlage einen Pfaffen
Dann kriegt er was zu schaffen.'
Eighteenth Century.

THE early German watch movement is shown in Plate XIV, not as it is arranged in a watch, but spread out for clearness. The mainspring is coiled round the arbor A (*arbor* is the watchmaker's term for a rotating spindle or axle), its coils being broken away on the right-hand side to show the parts below it. Its inner end has a hole through which passes a hook on the arbor A ; its outer end is looped round one of the pillars B, which hold together the two plates which constitute the framework of the movement. The upper end of the arbor A is square and takes the winding key, and, when this is turned to the left, the spring is coiled up round the arbor and tends to uncoil by turning the arbor to the right. The arbor is attached to the ratchet-wheel C, which lies in a depression in the toothed wheel D. The ratchet-wheel C, when turned to the right by the mainspring, turns the wheel D with it, because its teeth engage with the small finger E (called a *pawl* or *click*), which is pivoted to the wheel D. This arrangement enables the arbor and ratchet-wheel to be turned to the left in winding, without turning the wheel D. The mainspring arbor therefore corresponds exactly with the rope drum of the early weight clock.

The train of wheels which is driven by the wheel D consists of three arbors, F, G and H, each having a

74

PLATE XIV

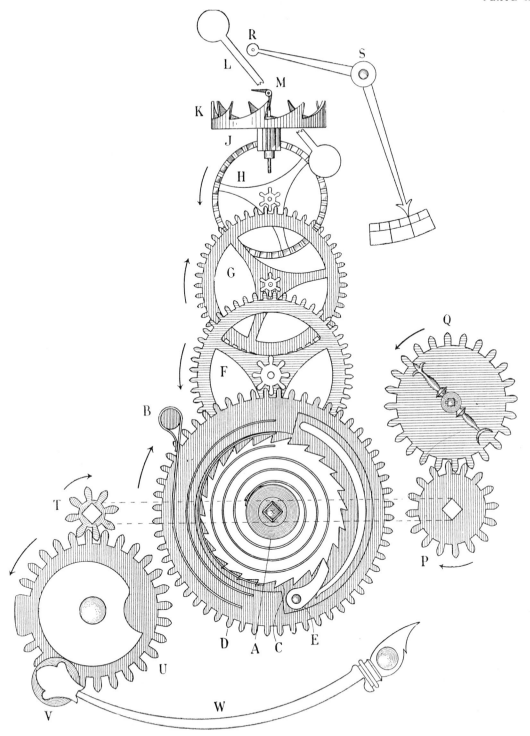

THE EARLY GERMAN WATCH MOVEMENT

pinion and a toothed wheel. The watch *pinion* is a toothed wheel with a small number of teeth or *leaves*, generally from five to eight, while the wheels in watch trains have, generally, from thirty to sixty-four teeth. The wheel D has fifty-six teeth, and it engages with the pinion of eight leaves on the arbor F, so that this makes seven turns to each turn of the wheel D. The wheel on F engages with the pinion on G, and the wheel on G with the pinion on H. Now the wheel on H is a *crown* wheel, or a *contrate* wheel as watchmakers frequently call it; that is to say, the teeth stand up from the face of the wheel instead of being formed on its edge. This type of wheel is used when the arbor to be turned by it is perpendicular to its own arbor. Here the arbor is J, and it carries the escape wheel K. The teeth on the wheels and pinions are in such ratios that the escape wheel makes 2100 turns for one turn of the wheel D.

The same type of movement is drawn in side view in Fig. 1 of Plate XLIII, where the parts, arranged slightly differently, are seen in place between the two plates of the watch, which are drawn in section. Plate XXXIX, 3 is a photograph of this type of movement in a German watch of about 1600.

The balance or foliot L is on the arbor M (watchmakers call the arbor of a balance the *staff*), with its two pallets. This escapement is exactly the same as that described in connection with the Dover Castle clock, the foliot making two swings in permitting one tooth of the escape wheel to pass. Here, again, watchmakers have their peculiar nomenclature; they call the movement of a foliot or balance or pendulum from right to left a swing or oscillation, and the return movement from left to right another swing. Engineers and physicists, on the other hand, mean by a swing or oscillation the complete movement from right to left and back again. In this book, the watchmaker's definition of a swing will be adopted.

The foliot is well seen on the watch movements on Plates IX, XXIX and XXXIX.

The escape wheel has nine teeth, so that the foliot makes 37,800 (18 times 2100) swings for each turn of the wheel D. It oscillates much more slowly than the balance of a modern watch, and, in this case, at the rate of about eighty swings a minute; this allows the wheel D to make one turn in eight hours or three turns in twenty-four hours.

In the early watches the mainsprings were wound up a little over three turns, so that this watch movement would run for about twenty-six hours. This is the usual time of running for the larger German watches of the sixteenth century, though French and English watches, and the later German watches, more usually went for only sixteen hours at one winding. It may be recalled that Cocclaeus wrote that Peter Henlein's watches went for forty hours. If this was not a mistake by Cocclaeus, it was a wise provision on the part of Henlein, because a watch that could go for forty hours, but was wound up every twenty-four hours, would go far more regularly than one that would go only twenty-six hours.

It remains to show how the hour hand is worked. In the drawing, the watch is being looked at from below, so that the hand mechanism would be hidden from the train of wheels. The drawing shows it moved to a position clear of the train, and its first wheel P must be imagined as fixed on the lower end of the arbor of the wheel D. The mechanism is seen in position in Plate XLIII, 1. The wheel P engages with the wheel Q, which has one and a-half times as many teeth, and carries the hand. Two turns of the hand, representing twenty-four hours, correspond therefore to three turns of P or D, that is, to three turns of the mainspring. In watches which have a hand going round once in twenty-four hours, the only difference is that Q has three times as many teeth as the wheel P.

The majority of watches of this type, though not the earliest, have a bristle regulator which consists in a bristle interposed in the path of one arm of the foliot, so as to limit its swing. It will be recalled that the foliot continues its swing beyond the point at which it permits an escape wheel tooth to pass, and it is the amount of this extra swing, or *supplementary arc*, which is regulated by moving the bristle to different positions. The less the supplementary arc, the faster the watch goes. The drawing shows a common form of this regulator; the bristle R is fixed upright on the end of one arm of a lever pivoted at S, while the other arm serves as an index. By turning the lever, the bristle is struck by the arm of the foliot at an earlier or later moment of its swing.

The Stackfreed.—The watch has one other accessory part, the curious device called a *Stackfreed*, designed to equalize the varying force of the mainspring. The great defect of the foliot is that its rate of oscillation depends on the force with which the escape wheel acts on it. In clocks driven by a weight the defect is not so serious, because the force due to the weight remains constant. It will vary in the course of months, because the friction of the train of wheels will vary, depending on the condition of the oil, but it will not vary in the course of one winding of the clock. In a watch, however, or in a clock driven by a mainspring, the force transmitted to the escape wheel when the mainspring is fully wound up is about twice that when it is nearly run down. With twice the force, the foliot will oscillate about one-third faster, with a bristle regulator keeping its swing the same, and this means that a watch regulated to keep time over twenty-four hours will gain about three-quarters of an hour in the first twelve hours after winding and lose the three-quarters in the second twelve hours. The need for an equalizing device is clear, and every watch had one, either the most inefficient stackfreed or the perfect bit of mechanism called a fuzee.

The stackfreed is shown in the drawing, removed from its normal position to the left hand of the watch movement, and the wheel T must be imagined as fixed on the arbor of the mainspring and turning with it as the watch goes. (See also Plate XLIII, I.) The wheel T

77

has eight teeth and engages with a wheel U which has twenty-eight teeth and a portion not cut into teeth. In winding up the watch, the wheel T turns the wheel U until its teeth come against the uncut portion, and this serves as a stop beyond which the mainspring cannot be wound. Similarly, when the mainspring unwinds, the wheel T turns in the opposite direction (indicated by arrows) until its teeth come against the other side of the uncut portion of wheel U, and the watch then stops. So far, this mechanism of two wheels, one with a portion not cut into teeth, is what is termed a *stop-work*, and is fitted to the mainspring arbor of the striking train of many early watches, quite apart from a stackfreed, and merely for the purpose of preventing the mainspring being wound up too far.

On the wheel U is fixed an irregularly shaped piece, called by engineers a *cam* and by watchmakers, more appropriately, a *snail*. A roller V is pressed against the edge of the snail by a stiff spring W. With the parts in the position shown, which corresponds to the watch being about three-quarters wound up, the roller is at a point of the snail where the radius of the snail is greatest; in this position the spring W is bent to its farthest and so exerts its maximum pressure against the snail. This pressure causes considerable friction in the pivot of the wheel U and the pivot of the roller V, and part of the force of the mainspring is employed in overcoming this friction, leaving less force available for driving the escapement. As the watch runs down, the snail, in turning, brings against the roller portions of its edge which have shorter and shorter radii; this permits the spring W to relax gradually and to exert less and less force on the snail, so that the friction due to it diminishes. Finally, when the watch is nearly run down, the roller begins to enter the semicircular notch in the snail and, in doing so, presses against the rounded corner of the notch and tends to turn the snail in the direction in which the mainspring is turning it. Here, therefore,

78

when the mainspring is at its weakest, the spring W, for a very short time, tends to assist it.

The mechanism can be seen on the watches on Plates IX, XVI, XXIX, XXXIX.[1]

The word *stackfreed* is as curious as the mechanism. No reasonable derivation of it has ever been suggested, and the Author has not found any use of the word before the nineteenth century.

The stackfreed is found only in watches made in Germany and never in a French or an English watch, and it is strange that its use continued in Germany into the seventeenth century, while watches of all other countries had the immeasurably superior fuzee.

The Framework.—In Plate XIV all the framework of the watch has been omitted to show more clearly the moving parts. The framework or cage of a German watch of about 1600 can be seen on Plate XXXIX, and of a French-type watch of about 1620 on Plate XXX, 1, and the two types are shown in the drawings on Plate XLIII.

The cage consists, mainly, of two plates held apart by pillars. The pillars are permanently fixed, by riveting, to the plate immediately below the dial, which is called

---

[1] Writers on the stackfreed have not agreed on its action, so the Author has examined carefully and taken drawings of a considerable number of examples. On the average, the snail is circular for a little less than half its course, very gradually diminishes in radius for a further quarter of its course, then diminishes more rapidly in radius until, during the final sixteenth or smaller fraction of its course, the roller bears on the corner of the notch and exercises some pressure tending to turn the snail in the direction in which the mainspring is turning it. In a 26-hour watch, therefore, the action of the stackfreed spring is to cause a constant high friction for the first 12 hours after winding, a slowly diminishing friction for the next 6 hours, a more rapidly diminishing friction for the next $6\frac{1}{2}$ hours, and, approximately, no friction during the last $1\frac{1}{2}$ hours, the tendency to assist probably balancing the friction then caused. This action agrees, roughly, with the variation in force of a coiled spring. Its force falls slowly at first, then more rapidly, and, when nearly unwound, very rapidly. The Author has seen snails which are circular for over three-quarters of their course, and others which diminish in radius from the start, and there is every intermediate form. The roller always starts from the highest point and finishes in the notch; it never starts by pressing against the high corner of the notch as has been suggested. The action is purely by introducing friction; the work which the roller spring can do by its movement is quite negligible compared with the work done by the mainspring in uncoiling.

79

the bottom plate or pillar plate. The top plate has holes through which the ends of the pillars project, and it is fixed to them by tapering pins that pass through the projecting ends of the pillars above the plate and wedge the plate down on to the shoulders of the pillars. All the wheels of the watch train, except the escape wheel and balance, are held between the two plates ; the arbors of the wheels are pivoted at each end, as seen in the drawing of a wheel and pinion in Plate XLII, 1, which shows the pivots running in holes in the two plates shown in section. The escape wheel, with its horizontal arbor, runs between two blocks fixed to the under side of the top plate, and the edge of the escape wheel just projects through a rectangular hole in the top plate. The balance and its verge, in all later watches, was supported below on a bracket fixed to the top plate, but, in some of the very early watches, its lower pivot ran in the bottom plate. The balance itself was above the top plate, and the upper pivot was held by a bracket fixed to the top plate and called the *cock* or, more properly, the *balance cock*, because all brackets of this shape are termed cocks.

In early watches the dial was attached to a separate plate which had short pillars riveted on, by which it was held to the bottom plate, thus imitating the construction in the ordinary clock. Frequently the removal of this dial plate was made more easy by having hinged latches instead of taper pins to fix the pillars to the bottom plate.

The movement of the earliest known German watches was entirely of iron and steel. Their makers being all locksmiths, it was natural that they should continue to use the metal with which they were familiar. These movements were usually without any decoration, except for cutting the fixed end of the stackfreed spring and the foot of the cock into a more or less graceful shape. A rare example of decoration is found on the top plate of the watch by Hans Gruber of Nürnberg in the South

80

Kensington Museum; the iron plate is etched in a pattern of foliage, and the etched portions are gilt. The stackfreed spring in Plate XIV is copied from this watch, and this and a similarly shaped cock are the only other features with any claim to ornament.

Soon after the middle of the sixteenth century, brass began to be used in the movement, first for the cocks, plates and pillars and later for the wheels. One cannot, though, say that one watch is early because its movement is all iron and another later because its movement is mainly of brass, but, speaking quite generally, the iron movement is probably before 1575 and the brass probably after. The iron movement of the Hans Gruber watch must be, from the records of the maker's life, about 1575, and it is a late example. Most movements of this date have at least some parts of brass.

Decoration.—Simultaneously with the use of brass began the practice of decorating the parts of the move-ment which were visible when the case was opened. The balance cock and the ratchet for the mainspring arbor were the first parts to be decorated (Frontispiece Plate); when the ratchet gave place to the worm-wheel and screw, two bearing pieces, always of steel, were needed for the screw, and, in French watches of the first quarter of the seventeenth century, these often had a wide spread over the plate but were pierced to leave only a slender tracery.

Later, the decoration spread to the pillars and all visible parts, though the top plate itself generally remained plain. Only in rare cases was any considerable amount of engraving done on the plate itself.

At first the parts were designed for the purpose they had to serve, but were given a pleasing form and, where suitable, were pierced and chiselled; but, in the seven-teenth century, the desire for ornament went beyond this and parts were designed for decoration and extended in size far beyond their mechanical needs, solely to give scope for piercing and chiselling. There was a tendency

81

to hide the movement as much as possible by providing ornamented covers for wheels on the top plate and filling up the space between the top plates by decorated screw-heads and detents.

Screws.—Screws for holding parts together are said to have come into use for watches in Germany about 1540 and about fifty years later in England, though screws for presses and other machines and endless screws for driving worm-wheels were known at a much earlier date. Watches with no screw at all are extremely rare, but most sixteenth-century watches and many later English watches had only one or two. Parts that could be fixed together permanently were riveted; those that had to be removable were fixed by a mortice and tenon and wedge, in the style of the carpenter. The fixing of the balance cock is a good example of this method. All later balance cocks are made of a single stepped piece of brass, held to the top plate by one or two screws. The earlier cocks were made in two parts, one riveted permanently to the top plate, with an upstanding tenon at one end, and the other, in which was the pivot hole for the verge, with a mortice that slipped over the tenon and was wedged on to it by a tapering pin (see Plates XLIII, 2, and XXX, 1). This construction is found in French and English watches well into the first quarter of the seventeenth century.

All French and English watches, apart from a few without any screw, have either one screw serving as a pivot for the ratchet of the mainspring arbor, or two screws fixing the bearing pieces of the screw of the worm-wheel. It is, though, impossible to be sure whether or not a screw is original. Early screws had an imperfectly formed thread of coarse pitch and a sharply rounded head, but their character changed only quite gradually.

The Foliot.—Another part of the first watches that changed, at any rate in German watches, towards the end of the sixteenth century was the foliot. In clocks this was a bar with leaden weights hung on the ends, the

82

position of the weights being adjustable for regulating the rate of the clock. The bar form was copied in German watches, but it was not practicable to make the weights adjustable in position, so the foliot took a dumb-bell shape. In the third quarter of the sixteenth century the foliot became a ring with a pair of arms (Plate XVI, 3). The date of the change is doubtful, because dumb-bell foliots are so rare; in most sixteenth-century watches the original foliot is missing or has been replaced by a later one. No French or English watch with an original dumb-bell foliot is known; all, including the spherical watch of 1557, have the steel ring which is generally called a *balance*, though there is no real reason to change the name merely because the shape of the weights is changed from two disks to an annulus. It would be better to speak of a *dumb-bell foliot* and a *wheel foliot*, and restrict the word *balance* to the wheel used with a spring. Probably it will never be known whether the French started putting a wheel foliot in their watches or copied the German dumb-bell foliot.

The Fuzee.—The most important change in German watches was that from stackfreed to fuzee. The change was made, on the whole, near the end of the sixteenth century, though there were earlier German watches with fuzees and many seventeenth-century watches with stackfreed. Plate xv shows the fuzee with its accompanying spring barrel. It was used in all French and English watches from the earliest known and in all watches from about 1600 to 1800, and is still used in chronometers and in all good spring-driven clocks. In the upper drawing the fuzee and the spring barrel are shown mounted between the two plates of the watch, which are drawn in section. In the lower drawing they are seen, without the plates, looking down on them from above. The fuzee consists of a conical drum with a spiral groove cut round it; at its lower end is a ratchet-wheel, which drives the toothed wheel in exactly the same way as the mainspring drives the toothed wheel D

83

in the watch movement of Plate XIV already described, the toothed wheel driving the watch movement as does the toothed wheel D. The ratchet-wheel is not seen in the upper drawing because it is sunk in a recess in the toothed wheel. The mainspring, however, works differently; in the watch movement of Plate XIV the outer end of the spring is fixed and the inner end turns its arbor to drive the watch. With the fuzee the inner end of the spring, attached to its arbor, is held stationary and the outer end is attached to the barrel, which contains the spring and is turned by it to drive the watch. The barrel drives the watch through the fuzee by means of the chain, one end of which is hooked into the barrel at A, and after (in the drawing) making two turns round the barrel, passes to the spiral groove of the fuzee, makes two turns round the fuzee, and is then hooked to it at B. The spring tends to turn the barrel in the direction of the arrow and, by pulling on the chain, tends to turn the fuzee in the same direction. In the position shown, the spring is about half wound up. To wind it up fully, a key is put on the end of the fuzee arbor and is turned to the left, so winding the chain from the barrel on to the spiral groove of the fuzee and turning the spring barrel in doing so. When the spring is fully wound up, the chain passes nearly directly from the point where it is hooked into the barrel to the groove in the upper small end of the fuzee. The spring is then exerting its greatest force, but the chain, in pulling round the fuzee at its small end, is acting with only a small leverage. As the spring runs down, the chain coils up on the barrel and uncoils from the groove of the fuzee, and, in doing so, reaches points where the fuzee is of continually increasing diameter; where, therefore, the chain is acting with greater and greater leverage. In this way the fuzee equalizes the varying force exerted by the spring. As the spring, in running down, pulls on the chain with less and less force, so this diminishing force is made more and more effective in driving the watch, because it acts

84

PLATE XV

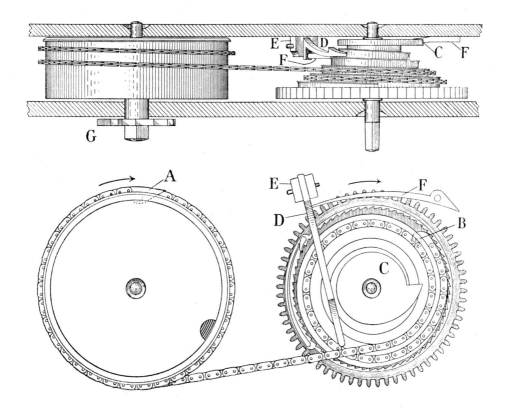

THE FUZEE

at an increasing leverage. It is only a matter of shaping the fuzee correctly to suit the mainspring to make the force on the watch movement constant from the time when the spring is fully wound to when it is nearly run down.

The fuzee was a very wonderful invention. It was invented at a time when mechanism hardly existed, apart from clocks, and yet perhaps no problem in mechanics has ever been solved so simply and so perfectly. Apart from the possibility of the fuzee in Philip of Burgundy's clock dating from about 1440, the earliest fuzees known are in Leonardo da Vinci's sketches, about 1490, in the standing clock of about the same date in the Germanische Museum in Nürnberg, and in a table clock in the possession of the Society of Antiquaries, made by Jacob Zech (Jacob the Czech) of Prague and dated 1525. The fuzees in da Vinci's sketches, the earliest that can be definitely dated, were not for clockwork.

For about a century a gut cord was used instead of a chain, the chain being first introduced by Gruet, a Swiss, in 1625. When made for a gut cord the grooves in the fuzee were round, and it is not uncommon to find fuzees of this type fitted later with a chain, which has badly worn the round grooves to which it could not adapt itself. The drawing shows the proper shape of groove for a chain. Early chains had links about twice as long as those of a modern chain, but are rarely seen ; only one of the watches in the British Museum has an early chain of this kind.

The fuzee was fitted from the beginning with a stop-motion to prevent the fuzee being turned beyond a point when the mainspring is nearly fully wound up. A stop-motion is always advisable in a watch, to save the mainspring from the undue force which can be applied by the key in winding, but in the fuzee the main function of the stop-motion is to save the chain or gut from this undue force. A disk C, fixed to the upper end of the fuzee, has a projection which comes against the side of

85

a notch in an arm D, which is pivoted to a block E on the watch plate. A spring F presses this arm downwards out of reach of the projection on the disk C, but the arm is lifted up by the chain as it mounts up the fuzee in winding, until, when the chain is wound round the uppermost turn of the spiral, it has lifted the arm up to the level of the disk C, so that the projection on the disk comes against the side of the notch on the arm and stops any further turning of the fuzee.

There is a point of difference that is worth noting between the direct-acting spring of the stackfreed watches and the fuzee ; in the former the outer end of the spring was always acting to drive the watch movement, and the turning of the spring arbor, in winding, did not hinder this action ; in the fuzee watch, however, when the fuzee is turned to wind the watch, the force of the mainspring, which had been acting through the fuzee on the watch movement, is now taken by the hand on the key, and the watch is no longer driven. The stopping of the watch for some seconds during winding was of no consequence to early watches, but later, and more especially in chronometers, it became a serious defect, and in the eighteenth century a *maintaining device* was invented which provided an auxiliary spring to keep the watch going during winding.

The Regulator.—The regulator of the stackfreed watches—the bristle which limited the swing of the foliot—has already been described. It was used occasionally with fuzee watches, but these were always fitted with another form of regulator that acted on the mainspring. In describing the fuzee, it was explained that the inner end of the mainspring, attached to its arbor, was held stationary. It was held by means of a ratchet-wheel, shown at G, fixed on the arbor, and a ratchet engaging the teeth of the wheel and preventing its turning. By putting a key on the end of the arbor, however, the arbor can be turned to wind up the spring from the inside or, by releasing the ratchet, to let it unwind. In this way

86

the force of the spring can be altered, and, with a foliot, this alters the rate of swing and the going of the watch It is a bad method of regulation, because it destroys the proper action of the fuzee in equalizing the force of the mainspring, but it was quite good enough for a foliot watch. The ratchet and wheel are clearly seen on Plate XVII, 1. Exactly the same arrangement is found in all modern fuzee clocks, but here the adjustment is used to adapt the mainspring to the fuzee; a particular position of the ratchet-wheel can be found which enables the fuzee to be most effective in equalizing the force of the spring.

Later, about 1610, the ratchet-wheel and ratchet began to be discarded for a worm-wheel and tangent screw, to make the regulation more easy; the tangent screw could be turned in either direction by a key, to wind up or unwind the spring. In many watches a disk with figures was mounted above the worm-wheel as a guide in regulating (Plate XXIII, 1). Both the ratchet and the tangent screw devices were generally mounted on the top plate of the watch, but occasionally the ratchet was mounted on the pillar plate, between this and the mainspring barrel.

In Leutmann's book on Watches and Clocks,[1] which is the earliest book to give any useful particulars of watch and clock mechanism, there is a chapter on how to tell the age of a watch. It is particularly interesting in mentioning some forms of mechanism which are not found in any existing watch, and also in omitting any mention of the stackfreed. The following is a translation of Leutmann's characteristics of old watches in chronological order, with comments by the Author in brackets :—

(1) Watches in which the balance strikes against two pig's bristles and has a dumb-bell foliot (*Leffel-Unruhe*), but no fuzee; these are the oldest.

(2) Then came the circular balance, still without fuzee or chain.

---

[1] J. G. Leutmann, *Vollständige Nachricht von den Uhren.* First part, Halle, 1717; second part, Halle, 1722.

87

(3) Next, the watches were so made that one could let down or set up the mainspring; they had, though, still no fuzee. [This is a type of watch of which no example exists, so far as the Author knows. Where there is no fuzee there is a stackfreed, and the construction of a stackfreed requires the outer end of the mainspring to be fixed. It would have been quite simple to make this fixed end adjustable in its position by attaching it to a barrel with ratchet-wheel and holding this stationary by a ratchet. This would give the type of watch described, which quite probably did exist.]

(4) At last the fuzees were invented, but one retained the small balance.

(5) Fuzees were made with a large balance about sixty years ago [i.e. *c.* 1657, rather too early].

(6) Watches were made with fuzees and a long slender spring formed as a pendulum, and fixed on one arm or else on the arbor of the round balance, so that it controlled the swings (*so derselben Schwung coercirte*). [A few watches exist in which a long bristle or spring is fixed to the plate and is bent back and forth by the balance. An illustration of one in the British Museum is on Plate XVII, 1. The Author knows of no example in which such a spring is fixed on the arbor, and does not see how any but a spiral spring could be so fixed.]

(7) Then Huygens discovered the spiral spring for the balance; for the past fifty years this has been a very good thing.

(8) About thirty years ago [i.e. *c.* 1687] one began to make large crown wheels. [There was an increase in the size of the crown wheel, but not the marked change here suggested.]

88

(9) At the end of the previous sixteenth century the large round balance was made with two weights on the two arms of the balance, whereas up to then the balances were made with three arms, and this is till now the latest fashion. [These weights must be the little round disks fixed on the balance of 'pendulum' watches, to imitate the pendulum bob.]

CHAPTER VI

WATCH-CASES TO 1675

'Ah, by my troth, sir ; besides a jewel and a jewel's fellow
A good fair watch, that hung about my neck.'

Mad World, my Masters.

SEVENTEENTH-CENTURY watches were execrable timekeepers. The workmanship of their movements was often good—more than good when the tools available are considered—and was bettered only as tools became better. It was the principle of their working that was bad, so bad that the watch could be useful only if set daily by a sundial. They were really the toys of the wealthy and regarded more as articles of jewellery than of use.

From the beginning they were worn as jewels, hanging on a chain either from the neck or the girdle. Early in the seventeenth century they were carried in a fob pocket, but the fashion of wearing them exposed to view continued right through the century and recurred at intervals throughout the eighteenth century. Probably those possessing only plain-cased watches and the puritanically inclined wore them in the pocket and the owners of decorative cases displayed them.

Both in France and England it became fashionable to wear two watches. Develle quotes from a contemporary record that Marie de Médicis 'détacha de son côté deux montres d'or pour les offrir à l'ambassadeur de Venise,' and Kendal quotes a rhyme from the *Universal Magazine* for 1777 about a fop :—

A lofty cane, a sword with silver hilt,
A ring, two watches and a snuff-box gilt,

showing the same fashion at an interval of a century and

90

a half. At the later period, at any rate, fashion and economy were combined by carrying one real and one imitation watch; and another way of acquiring, with economy, the one watch necessary to a well-dressed man is shown by :—

> And I had lent my watch last night, to one
> That dines to-day at the sheriff's.
>
> *Alchemist,* Act i. 2.

The displayed watch of 1600 was a fresh field for the work of the goldsmith, the engraver, the lapidary and the enameller, at a period when the craftsman had acquired a high degree of technical skill and before he had ceased to be an artist. These craftsmen gave to the watch-cases of the first half of the seventeenth century nearly every form of decoration applied to watches, and in a degree of perfection which, in later times, has never been surpassed and seldom equalled. There are six main types of decoration, which will provide convenient subject-heads for this chapter; they are :—

(1) Engraved scenes, landscapes and patterns on the covers and dial.
(2) The piercing of covers and edges, and sometimes dials, in conventional and other patterns, always combined in good work with chiselling and engraving.
(3) Chased and repoussé work. This was not common until the end of the seventeenth century, but was fashionable in the eighteenth century.
(4) Inlay, including damascening and niello work. This is rare.
(5) Lapidaries' work of all kinds, varying from cases formed of rock-crystal, agate, etc., to cases set with pearls and precious stones.
(6) Enamel, including enamels translucent and opaque and paintings on enamel.

Besides these, there are the varieties of decoration applied almost exclusively to outer cases, such as filigree, piqué tortoiseshell, and leather and shagreen. There is also engine-turning, the mechanical form of decoration used on watches at the end of the eighteenth century and becoming popular to-day.

The watches illustrated in the coloured and collotype plates have been chosen as typical examples of these different forms of decoration, and in the following pages are described in groups falling under the six types enumerated. Notes on the history and technique of the decorative art are added where likely to be helpful in appreciating the results.

Engraving and Piercing.—The two kinds of engraving are well shown on the cover and dial of the watch on Plate XII, 2. The figure scene on the cover is produced by *line engraving*, and is composed entirely of fine V-grooves cut in the metal by a graver and appearing as dark lines. The pattern on the dial, however, is an example of *champlevé engraving*, though combined with line engraving to give shading. Here the elements of the pattern stand out, literally, from the background, which is sunk by cutting to a common level and covered with fine grooves to give it a dark appearance. The butterfly, for example, close to the figure V stands up as a whole from the background, while the shading on its wings and body is given by line engraving. Generally, the landscape and figure scenes on watches are done by line engraving and the patterns mainly by champlevé engraving.

In the earlier years of watchmaking, engraving was often done by the watchmaker himself, and at Blois, a noted centre of engraving, the contract for a watchmaker's apprentice sometimes provided that he should go to a painter or engraver for two hours a day for the first six months, to learn *portraicture, nécessaire aud* [au dit] *estat d'orloger*, while some boys passed through a complete apprenticeship of one or two years with an engraver before starting watchwork. The majority of watchmakers, however, left the decoration of their cases to professed

engravers. Some of these were probably more craftsmen than artists, copying their designs from *livres de
portraicture* by Étienne Delaune, Théodore de Bry,
J. Berain, Toutin and other *graveurs d'estampes*. Usually,
designs made for other objects were adapted to the watch-
cases, but a number of artists designed specially for
watches, and it is not uncommon to find designs for
watch covers and edge bands in books and collections
of prints dating from the first half of the seventeenth
century. In the Garnier collection in the Louvre is a
watch by Jehan Flant of La Rochelle engraved after
plaques by Valerio Belli, a rare example of Italian design
on a watch.

Later in the century Blois had its own artist engravers,
two of whom, Jacques, born 1621, and Jean, later,
belonged to a family including several watchmakers,
calling themselves indifferently Vauquer, Vautier or
Vauthyer, and the famous painter on enamel Robert
Vauquer.

Engraving is so frequently combined in early watch-
cases with piercing and chiselling that these types of
work cannot be conveniently considered separately.
Piercing of the case was required when the watch had
alarum or striking mechanism. This laid open to view
the thickness of the case, and then chiselling came in to
give the metal form and shape. The great majority of
watches had cases of sheet metal, hammered to shape
and built up by soldering, and here the thin metal offered
little scope for chiselling. Some cases, however, were
of cast metal, and then the whole surface had to be
worked over by the chisel to give the finish of fine work.
Cases cast *à jour* were fairly common among the early
German watches, where brass was the metal and weight
less considered. After 1600 they are not so common,
but cast silver cases are not rare.

In the spherical watches of the middle and first half
of the sixteenth century (Plate VI), the cases are of sheet
metal, pierced in a pattern without any chiselling, but

93

with line-engraved ornament covering the whole surface. The French watch of 1551 (lower views) has the strapwork pattern introduced in the second quarter of the sixteenth century and frequently found on the sides of the tower-shaped table clocks of the second half of the century. The ornament on the German spherical watch in the upper views indicates a rather earlier date.

The circular and octagonal German watches of later date, shown at the bottom of Plate VIII, also have sheet-metal cases with line engraving but no chiselling, and cases of this kind continued to the end of the century and into the seventeenth century, though it was then usual to give the pierced ornament an appearance of solidity by shallow chiselling, as in the egg-type watch in Plate VIII, 1, and on the cover of the watch in the centre of Plate XVII. At the same time, in the third quarter of the sixteenth century, there are heavier sheet-metal cases in which the pierced ornament is fully shaped by the chisel (Plates IX and VIII, 2, and also still thicker cast-metal cases which give opportunity for deeper cutting. Two good examples are illustrated, the German watch of Plate VII, which has exceptionally fine chiselling of the figures, animals and grotesques, and the German book-watch of Plates XXVIII and XXIX, both in the Mallett collection. Another good example is the watch by Hans Gruber in the South Kensington Museum, of about 1575, with a finely chiselled St. George on horseback and the dragon forming the centre of the cover.

In the centre of the dial of the early German watches the commonest engraved forms are the pointed star, seen on the dials of the two spherical watches (Plate VI), and the rose (Plate VIII, 3). The star, often with alternate straight and wavy points, is the early form, but continues into the seventeenth century. A leaf ornament, as in Plates XXVIII and IX and in Plate VIII, 4, is less common, and a complex pattern as in Plate VII is rare. The dial of the German watch at the bottom of Plate XXXIX is particularly interesting in having a sundial on the dial

94

plate. Though common in the cover, especially in French watches, a sundial on the dial plate is extremely rare. The time dial has the ordinary engraved star.

Engraved landscapes and figures are rarely found on German watches in the sixteenth century, and are not usual in the later watches. The watch on Plate XIX, 2 is a fine example of an early seventeenth-century watch, engraved with scenes from the history of Esther. The watch is probably German, though there are indications of French influence; possibly it was made at Strasbourg. It has four scenes—on the back, on the dial, and on both sides of the cover. The engraving on the dial shows Esther kneeling before Ahasuerus, with Mordecai in the background and, through the window, a tiny Haman hanging on a gibbet. The engraving seen on the cover represents Esther's banquet to Ahasuerus and Haman.

The inner side of the cover is generally left without engraving, or with the rather perfunctory work seen on the watches in Plate IX and in the bottom left hand of Plate VIII. Occasionally, the pattern or scene on the outside of the cover is repeated on the inside, as in a fine watch by Thomas Chamberlin of Chelmsford in the South Kensington Museum, of the first quarter of the seventeenth century, but the engraving of an independent scene, as in the watch under discussion, is uncommon. The movement of the watch is essentially German, with stack-freed and dumb-bell foliot, brass plates and iron wheels.

In French and English watches of the early seventeenth century, with engraved metal cases, scenes and figures were usual and ornament the exception. Ornament was freely used in spaces that did not admit of scenes, but figures, human or animal, were nearly always worked into the design.

The watch by Jean Vallier of Lyons, of about 1610, illustrated in Plate XI, has already been described; it has, probably, the finest example of engraving work on a watch. The scene on the back represents Apollo surrounded by the Muses, each with her emblem and name,

95

PLATE XVI

1

French striking and alarum watch by Jehan
Flant, La Rochelle, 1610. Showing days of
week and age and phases of moon. Gilt metal
case with silver chased cover. Silver engraved
dial with gilt alarum disk. Cover engraved with
calendar for years 1610-65. Bottom cover replaced. Top plate of movement engraved in
foliage design. Wheels of striking train pierced
with six holes instead of with usual arms. Jehan
Flant was apprenticed in Geneva in 1584.
Watches by him in the Louvre and Gelis coll.
British Museum.   pp. 97, 99, 119.

2

French watch by Augustin Forfaict,
Sedan, before 1586, when he died.
Gilt metal case. Gilt dial plate with
silver hour ring.
British Museum.

pp. 65, 71, 99, 114.

3

Movement of German striking
and alarum watch on Plate VIII,
4. Brass plates, steel wheels,
no barrels. Wheel balance with
bristle regulator operated by
hand on dial.
British Museum.

PLATE XVI

on a background of floral scrolls. The delicacy of the work is extraordinary; it gains in beauty when examined with a strong lens, and this reveals no imperfection. The reproduction will bear the use of a glass until the grain of the plate becomes too apparent. The spaces surrounding the four dials on the dial plate are filled with figures and scroll-work, but these are rather more than a pure pattern, because the figures are to some extent related. The edge of the watch is a fine example of carefully chiselled and engraved pierced work, and the cable and ribbon moulding is a feature that the Author has not seen on any other watch.

It is interesting to turn to the somewhat similar dial plate of the same date on the watch shown on the upper part of Plate XVI. Here the engraving is a symmetrical pattern of scroll-work with two figures and a mask. It is fine work, but has not the delicacy and freedom of the Vallier watch.

Another exquisite example of engraved ornament, also on a watch by Jean Vallier, is on Plate XXIV, 5. In this the sunken background is filled in with a soft, black enamel, giving more contrast than a background darkened only by shading lines. Unfortunately, the cover of the watch, originally solid and engraved, has been cut to take a glass, and its movement has been spoilt by work of about a century later. The Fitzwilliam Museum has another watch by this great maker, in an octagonal crystal case, cut in facets.

The watch shown at the bottom of Plate XII, mentioned above in describing the two types of engraving and in Chapter IV, is of particular interest as one of the very few English sixteenth-century watches in existence. The finely engraved dial has a type of ornament very rare in watches, and the figure on the cover is on a larger scale than is usual. The more typical engraving is seen on the watches on Plate XVIII and on Plate XVII, 2. This last is an English watch of about 1620 by David Ramsay, who was born in Dundee about 1585, went to France, and

PLATE XVII

1a

French watch by N. Lemaindre, Blois, *c.* 1600. Gilt metal case, with single cover. Gilt dial plate with engraved hour ring. Steel hand. Movement with later addition of bristle regulator; no screws. This maker is almost certainly Nicolas, who is known in 1598 and died in 1652, and was clockmaker to Marie de Médicis. A large watch by him is in the South Kensington Museum.
British Museum. pp. 99, 114.

2a

English alarum watch by David Ramsay, *c.* 1620. Gilt metal case engraved on cover and back with biblical scenes. Gilt dial plate with silver hour ring. Pierced gilt alarum disk on blued steel ground. Signed 'David Remsay Scotus Me fecit.' David Ramsay was born in Dundee about 1585, went to France, and came to London within a year or two of 1610, being appointed clockmaker to the King in 1613.
British Museum.

pp. 97, 99, 115, 122.

3

German watch, late sixteenth century. Gilt metal case. Silver dial sunk in gilt dial plate, champlevé and filled with translucent enamel. Hour figures I-XII and 13-24. Movement with brass plates and steel wheels. Some engraving on top plate and signature L. P.
British Museum. pp. 57, 61, 94.

1b

2b

PLATE XVII

came to London within a year or two of 1610, being appointed clockmaker to the King in 1613. The two gilt-metal covers are engraved with biblical scenes, with their references on the plaques below.

The watch shown in three views at the top of Plate XVIII is a particularly fine example of the engraved cross watch with faceted silver covers, the cross, with its double arms, making one of the most graceful shapes given to watches. The covers and dial plate are engraved with scenes representing the Visit of the Magi, the Nativity, the Annunciation, the Baptism, and the meeting of the Marys, with floral scroll ornament on the inclined facets. The watch has an English movement of later date than the case, which is probably French work of an early date in the seventeenth century. The small watch on the same plate, in the form of an elongated octagon, is typical of many French and English watches of the first quarter of the seventeenth century. A figure scene is engraved in the centre of each cover, with foliage and scroll-work, frequently combined with figures of animals, on each of the facets.

The most common form of French watch, in the earliest period in which watches are at all common, say 1590 to 1625, is the rather long oval. The watches by Augustin Forfaict of Sedan, before 1586, and by Nicholas Lemaindre of Blois, c. 1600, shown on Plates XVI, 2 and XVII, 1, are examples of the plain, undecorated watch of this type. Probably the great majority of the watches made were like these. The Garnier collection in the Louvre, which is particularly rich in French watches of this period, has nine watches of this shape with engraved covers. The oval form that departs only slightly from a circle—certainly a less pleasing form—is not often found in French watches, though the watch by Flant on Plate XVI is an example. In England the oval form is not so common, and the slightly oval form is as frequent as the long oval. The watch on Plate XVII, 2, by David Ramsay, is of this shape, and there is a similar

PLATE XVIII

1

Cross watch, probably French, early seventeenth century. Gilt metal case with silver covers, dial plate and side band. Covers and dial engraved with scenes representing the Visit of the Magi, the Nativity, the Annunciation, the Baptism and the Meeting of the Marys. Movement of later date by Jeremie Gregory, *c.* 1660. *Mallett coll.*   pp. 97, 99, 103, 115.

2a

French watch by J. Chesneau, Orléans, *c.* 1610. Silver case and dial. The centre panels of the two covers are engraved with female figures emblematic of Hope and Charity. *Mallett coll.*

pp. 97, 99, 115.

3

French watch by C. Phelizot, Dijon, *c.* 1620. Gilt metal case, set white pastes. Another watch by this maker is on Plate XXXVI, 5. *Mallett coll.*

pp. 97, 113, 115.

2b

PLATE XVIII

watch in the Louvre by Richard Morgan, one of the subscribers to the incorporation of the Clockmakers' Company. The long oval watch in the centre of Plate XLVI is of particular interest as a rare example of an early English provincial watch.

Next after the oval, the elongated octagonal form of watch is the most common, and then follow circular, cruciform, shell, lobed, and other forms; the circular watch, common enough in Germany, is rare in France and England at the beginning of the seventeenth century.

A form of watch found only in England is more like an egg than any made in Nürnberg. It has a perfectly plain and smooth silver case without any break, and generally has a small opening over the dial, fitted with a crystal or glass. The diminutive watch on Plate LI shows the type, though in this the dial is engraved on the somewhat flattened front of the case. Its maker, Richard Crayle, was a petitioner for the incorporation of the Clockmakers' Company in 1631. The key is shown below.

On Plate XIX are three views of a particularly interesting circular watch covered with engraving of fine quality. The back is pierced in the form of a true lover's knot, engraved with the words of a madrigal in *Britannia's Pastorals* by William Brown of Tavistock :—

> This is Love and worth Commending,
> Still beginning, never ending,
> Like a withy net insnaring,
> In a round shuts up all squaring,
> In and out whose every angle
> More and more doth still intangle,
> Keepes a measure still in moveing,
> And is never light but loving,
> Twineing arms, exchanging kisses,
> Each partaking other's blisses ;
> Laughing, weeping, still together,
> Bliss in one is mirth in either,
> Never breaking, ever bending—
> This is Love and worth Commending.

PLATE XIX

1a   1b

English 'Love' watch by Edmund Gilpin, London,
c. 1625. Silver case with cover engraved inside and
out, with Adam and Eve on a ground of floral
arabesques. The back is pierced with a winged
cherub above a true lover's knot engraved with a 14-
line poem. The dial has a central alarum disk and
a turning day-of-the-month ring outside the hour ring.
The silver balance-cock has the form of a cupid
holding a heart. Edmund Gilpin, 1630-77, was a
petitioner for the incorporation of the Clockmakers'
Company. Three other watches by him are known,
one illustrated on Plate XXX, 2.
Mallett coll.   pp. 101, 115, 122.

2

1c

Watch, probably German or near the
Rhine, *c.* 1610. Silver case engraved
with five scenes from the history of
Esther. The movement has brass plates,
steel wheels and stackfreed with dumb-
bell foliot and dial for regulator.
Mallett coll.   p. 95.

PLATE XIX

The space available appears at first sight far too little to contain these fourteen lines. The emblems engraved on the watch bear on the Love theme; the cover is pierced and engraved with figures of Adam and Eve and Mars and Venus on a groundwork of flowers and foliage, and the balance-cock, of silver, is fashioned in the form of a cupid holding a heart.

The cruciform watch, in its ordinary form of a Latin cross with single arms, as in the watch on Plate XXII, 2, generally has the inclined facets wide, leaving a flat central portion only just large enough to contain a representation of the Crucifixion, whether engraved or, as in the watch on Plate XXII, chased. The less common and more graceful form, with double arms, as in the watch on Plate XVIII, always has small inclined facets and a large flat portion. The Louvre has a crystal watch in this shape. Cross watches with the ends of the arms rounded or with the corners bevelled are found, but are rare; one with rounded arms is in the Louvre, and one with the corners bevelled in the Metropolitan Museum, New York. Cross watches generally bear representations of the Passion or of incidents in the life of Christ, as would be appropriate if they really were what their French name, *Montres d'Abbesse*, indicates. There are, though, many exceptions; of the two cross watches in the Louvre, shown on Plate XXXVI, that on the right has a female figure below and a winged cherub above the dial, with scrolls at the sides, while the Maltese cross is engraved with large flowers. Nor is it rare to find a mixture of sacred and profane subjects in the same watch.

Lapidary's Work. — Lapidary's work covers an enormous variety of cases dating from the latter part of the sixteenth century as well as from the seventeenth. The rock-crystal case is common in Germany, France and England, two kinds of rock-crystal being used, the ordinary clear crystal and the comparatively rare 'smoky' kind, which has a brown tinge.

Plate XX shows a variety of forms taken by the crystal

103

PLATE XX

1a

English watch by Edward East, London, *c.* 1630. Crystal case. Silver dial plate. Steel hand. Movement has 3-wheel train going 26 hours.
British Museum.

pp. 103, 104, 115, 117, 194.

1b

Edward East, a founder member of the Clockmakers' Company in 1632, and Master in 1645 and 1652, died *c.* 1693. He was watchmaker to the King, and the most celebrated of early English makers. Many fine watches and clocks by him are known. An enamelled watch is on Plate xxxv.

2

English watch by Michael Nouwen, London, *c.* 1600. Case and cover of smoke crystal without frames. Dial of gold with red and green enamel. Gold enamelled plate on top plate of movement. Four-wheel train. Steel barrel cover. Michael Nouwen, 1582-1613, probably of Flemish origin, was an exceptionally fine maker. Four other watches by him are known.
British Museum. pp. 103, 104, 114, 131, 194.

3

Watch, probably French, early seventeenth century. Case and cover of reddish-brown agate. Gilt dial plate with raised gilt hour circle. Steel hand.
British Museum.

pp. 103, 109, 114.

4

Watch by Conrad Kreizer, *c.* 1620. Gilt metal case set with plates of crystal, and crystal covers. Gilt dial plate with silver hour disk and gilt hand. Leather-covered wooden outer case. Movement of brass, with fuzee. Seven fine watches and a clock by Conrad Kreizer are known. His place of work is not known; it was probably Strasbourg or Augsburg.
British Museum. pp. 103, 113.

5

Watch, probably French, 1600-10. Case of agate with agate cover. Gilt dial plate guilloché with remains of translucent enamel, and raised gilt hour ring. Steel hand.
British Museum.

pp. 103, 109, 149.

6

French watch by P. Croymarie, *c.* 1620. Cut crystal case. Gilt dial plate with silver hour disk and engraved landscape. Steel hand.
British Museum. pp. 103, 109.

PLATE XX

case. In the most usual for
block of crystal hollowed ou
metal frame is fixed to the u
the movement, with dial pla
while the cover, which is a s
also set in a frame, is attach
beautiful little watch by Ed
good example of this constr
the most famous maker of his
of the century—and was wa
was one of the original assi
Company, named in its Chart
and must therefore have beer
date. The last record of hi
thinks that there may have be
name. His watches, sometin
had a great reputation, and v
prizes at tennis, East being f
established near the tennis-cou

The watch shown on Plate
a crystal case without the cu
the only metal parts in the case
with the pendant ring, and the
the crystal. This construction
the four examples known to t
In the watch of Plate xx,
crystal is transparent but slig
the case is very deep, width ar
and length $1\frac{3}{8}$ inches. There
Nowan, clockmaker, born in
England in 1568, and attende
records in 1582 and 1583 of M
de Nowe; also of Andrewe No
Nowethe), who was born in Flar
'for religion' in 1571, and of
François Nawe, referred to ab
watch shown at the bottom of
belonged to the Dutch Church a

PLATE XXI

1

Swiss watch by Jean Baptiste Duboule, Geneva, early seventeenth century. Cast silver gilt chiselled case. Silver disk dial on gilt dial plate. Duboule, *c.* 1610-40, was a maker of 'form' watches.
Webster coll.   p. 122.

2

French watch by A. Fremin, *c.* 1600. 8-lobed crystal case cut in pattern of lines. Silver disk dial on gilt dial plate.
Webster coll.   pp. 111, 114.

German striking watch by Nicolaus Rugendas, Augsburg, early seventeenth century. Crystal case in form of shell, without frame. Bell between dial and movement, covered by gilt pierced and engraved frame. Gilt dial with engraved landscape. Steel hand.
Webster coll.   p. 107.

PLATE XXI

Ward,[1] and there is little doubt that they were of the same family, and that Michael Nowan or Michel de Nowe is the same as Michael Nouwen, the maker of the watch. He is not mentioned in connexion with the Clockmakers' Company, so it may be presumed that he died or ceased business before 1632. There is an oval gilt watch by him, dated 1613, in the Ashmolean Museum, Oxford, and a circular gilt watch in the Guildhall Museum. This crystal watch shows exceptionally fine work, both in the case and the movement.

The watch from the Louvre in the centre of Plate XXXVI bears no signature, but is so like the watch by Michael Nouwen as to make it probable that the two are by the same hand. The shape is hexagonal instead of octagonal, but the crystal, with faceted base and cover, is of similar smoky quality. The dials of both watches are of gold, cut out with the graver and filled with translucent enamel of different colours, in a star pattern in one case and in a garland in the other. The most striking point of resemblance is that a similar gold enamelled plate is affixed to the top plate of the movement in both cases; this is an extremely rare feature.

The third watch of this type is that on Plate XXXVI, 4, in the rare shape of a Maltese cross. It also is in the Louvre, but not in the main Garnier collection, and is by Josias Jolly of Paris, dating from about 1640. The fourth watch is an octagonal crystal watch by Nicolas Bernard of Paris, in the Metropolitan Museum, New York. It is of slightly smoky crystal, and dates from about 1620.

Another rare type of watch is similar to these four in having the bottom part of the case of crystal without frame. Instead of a crystal case, however, a metal plate is hinged to the crystal case, carrying on one side the movement, and on the other a bell and dial with pierced edging between dial and plate, covering the bell. A very fine German watch of this type in the Webster collection is shown on Plate XXI; its signature 'N. R.' shows

[1] Cecil MS., and S. P. Dom. Eliz.

PLATE XXII

1

French or Swiss cross watch by David Rousseau, early seventeenth century. Crystal case. Gilt dial plate engraved with emblems of the Passion and the Crucifixion. Silver hour disk. Hand not original. *British Museum.* pp. 111, 114.

2a

French watch by C. Tinelly, Aix, *c.* 1635. Gilt metal case with plates of repoussé gold on covers and silver side band. Gilt dial plate with silver hour ring. The front cover shows the Crucifixion, and the back the Virgin and Child. The side band has symbols of the Passion. *British Museum.* pp. 103, 119.

3

Swiss watch by Jacques Sermand, Geneva, early seventeenth century. Crystal case and cover. Gilt dial plate with silver hour ring, engraved in the centre with Jupiter and other gods and goddesses in the rays. Steel hand. Many crystal and other watches by this maker are known. *British Museum.* pp. 113, 115.

2b

4

German watch by Wilhelm Peffenhauser, Augsburg, *c.* 1660. Crystal case in form of a snail, with crystal cover. Silver hour disk on engraved gilt plate. Movement with fuzee. Three watches and a clock are known by this maker, who married in 1647 and is known till 1676. *British Museum.* p. 113.

5

Watch by Aymé Noel, probably French, *c.* 1640. Twelve-lobed crystal case and cover. Silver outer case. Silver dial plate with plain centre. Steel hand. *British Museum.* p. 111.

PLATE XXII

it to be by the famous Augsburg maker Nicolaus Rugendas, who became a master in 1610. It is a most unusual watch, and is of the finest workmanship in the engraving, piercing and movement. A crystal watch in the Louvre is of the same construction in having the bell under the dial with a domed pierced cover, but is of four-lobed form, with triangular projections between the lobes. It is by Conrad Kreizer, and most probably is German work. The Metropolitan Museum, New York, has a crystal cross watch, with double arms, by this maker, which has a frame to its cover but not to its base, and also two octagonal crystal watches, like the watch by Nicolaus Rugendas in having the bell under the dial. These are by Marc Girard of Blois and Timothée Hubert of Rouen, both about 1620.

A most remarkable crystal-case watch, probably the earliest in existence, is in the collection of M. Olivier of Paris. The case is a crystal barrel, and the movement, rather higher than it is in diameter, is pushed into the barrel, its dial and a back plate closing the ends of the barrel.

In crystal and stone watches, the elongated octagonal form is by far the most common in France, England and Germany. The lobed circular and oval forms come, perhaps, next, and then the crystal cross watches; then follow an immense variety of shell, star and other forms. The plain circular or oval crystal watch does not exist, as far as the Author knows. The two watches Nos. 3 and 5 on Plate xx are in cases of agate, and in the black-and-white reproduction do not look so attractive as they are in reality. Neither is signed, but the work is probably French. The watch No. 6 of the same plate is an example of an oval with eight lobes, the crystal being cut in a pattern of lines and small circular facets. It is French, signed P. Croymarie, without name of place. About the same date, early seventeenth century, there was a Jehan Croymarie at Le Puy, and a Guillaume Croymarie at Lyons. Another eight-lobed watch, with

PLATE XXIII

1

French cross watch by Didier Lalemand, Paris, *c.* 1630. Crystal case and cover. Enamel dial painted with emblems of the Passion; a very early example of enamel painting. This maker became master in 1606. *Mallett coll.* pp. 111, 148.

2

Octagonal watch, probably French, *c.* 1620. Crystal case and cover with gold mounts, enamelled black. Gold dial enamelled with coloured floral scrolls. *Mallett coll.* p. 131.

3

French watch by Estienne Hubert, Rouen, early seventeenth century. Gilt metal case with silver side band and cut crystal covers. *Mallett coll.* p. 113.

PLATE XXIII

the crystal similarly cut but of circular form, is on Plate XXI, 2. The maker, A. Fremin, is unknown from any record.

A circular watch with twelve lobes is shown on Plate XXII, the lobes being continued on the cover and base to meet at central points. This watch is by Aymé Noel, a maker of whom nothing is known ; most probably he was a relative of the Rouen maker Étienne Noel, who became master in 1660. It has a silver outer case which is not illustrated. A watch closely resembling it, in the Louvre, is by J. Silleman of Leeuwarden, both dating from about 1640. On Plate XXVI, 4 is a four-lobed watch of unusual shape, with crystal base and cover cut deeply into lobes, and on each lobe a three-branched figure. Bold cutting of this character is quite common on crystal covers, but the Wallace collection has a watch with the very rare feature of fine engraving on the crystal. The watch is octagonal and the covers are cut in facets ; the central facet of each cover is occupied by a figure and each side facet by a pattern of flowers and birds. The watch is signed Lemaindre, Blois, probably the Nicolas Lemaindre who made the exquisite watch on Plate XXVI, 1.

On Plate XXII, 1 is shown a typical crystal cross watch. The case and cover are formed from blocks of crystal set in gilt-metal frames, and a gilt dial plate, carrying the movement, is hinged with the cover to the frame in which the base is set. Its maker, David Rousseau, is not known by any records, but is probably related to a family of watchmakers of which one member, Jean of Paris, born 1606, is known by many works, and another, David of Geneva, was grandfather of Jean Jacques Rousseau. Another cross watch with similar case is illustrated at the top of Plate XXIII, one view showing the arrangement of the movement ; it will be mentioned in discussing enamel work as being a very early example, about 1630, of painting on enamel. A third crystal cross watch of about the same date is on Plate XXXVI, 5, and is by Phelizot of Dijon, the maker of the watch on Plate XVIII, 3.

PLATE XXIV

1

French watch by Nicolas Cuisinier, Paris, mid seventeenth century. Cast silver case, chiselled in figure scenes on cover and on back. Silver pierced and engraved plate on top plate.
Fitzwilliam Museum. pp. 119, 121.

2

Heptagonal watch, probably French, *c.* 1640. Crystal case and cover.
Fitzwilliam Museum. p. 113.

3

Pod-shaped watch signed U. Klötz, Augsburg. Cast silver case, gilt and chiselled on both covers with biblical scenes and foliage scrolls. For dial, see Plate XXV, 2.
Fitzwilliam Museum. pp. 119, 121.

4

English vegetable-marrow watch by John Midnall, London, *c.* 1625. Gilt silver case. John Midnall, one of the first assistants of the Clockmakers' Company, is known from 1620-35. Two other watches by him are known.
Fitzwilliam Museum. p. 115.

5

French alarum watch by Jean Vallier, Lyons, early seventeenth century. Gilt metal case; champlevé engraving filled with black enamel. Sides pierced and engraved in birds and foliage. Gilt engraved dial with silver hour ring, and outer ring of minutes, figures filled with dark blue enamel. Steel hand. Another watch by J. Vallier on Plate XI.
Fitzwilliam Museum. p. 97.

6

English watch by Robert Grinkin, London, *c.* 1640. Silver case, ribbed and engraved. Grinkin became master under the Blacksmiths' Company in 1609, was Master of the Clockmakers' Company in 1648, and died 1660. Six other watches by him are known.
Fitzwilliam Museum.

PLATE XXIV

On the left of Plate XXII are two crystal-case watches of unusual forms, one an attractive little star watch, with its key, by Jaques Sermand of Geneva, of the first quarter of the seventeenth century, and the other the less attractive but curious watch in the form of a snail by Wilhelm Peffenhauser of Augsburg, son-in-law of the Nicolaus Rugendas who made the shell watch at the bottom of Plate XXI; this watch is of later date, about 1660. There were two Sermands of about the same date, one signing 'J. Sermand,' the maker of the watch, and the other signing 'Sermand,' who was a Paris maker.

Then there are many watches which, though their cases are not formed from blocks of crystal, have a good deal of crystal in their composition. The shell watch at the bottom of Plate XXIII is an example. The case of this is really a band of metal engraved with floral scrolls, while two plates of crystal, cut in shell-like ribs, form the back and front covers. The watch is signed 'Estienne Hubert à Rouen,' and is of fine quality, both in movement and engraving. It would appear to be of a date early in the seventeenth century, but no Estienne Hubert of this date is known. The Huberts were a family of watch-makers in Rouen of which the best-known members are Noel, 1612-50, and an Estienne who was received master in 1656, a date too late for the maker of this watch. Another example of a watch in crystal front and back covers is shown on Plate XXIV, 2. It is the only seven-sided watch known to the Author.

Watches of this type, with the side band set with crystals or stones, are not uncommon. Examples are illustrated on Plate XX, 4 and on Plate XVIII, 3. The former is by Conrad Kreizer, a fine maker of the early seventeenth century, known by many watches in the principal museums but unknown from any record. Dubois, unreliable as a historian, said that he worked at Strasbourg, but Ungerer's recent researches into the Strasbourg makers have revealed no trace of him; on the other hand, Kreizer is a name found at Augsburg.

The other watch, by C. Phelizot of Dijon, is unusual both in its form and in the setting of the crystals round the edge. There is a watch in the Cluny Museum in Paris with crystals in similar hobnail settings, not only round the edge but on back and front covers; it is by Duboule, probably of Geneva, and is more curious than beautiful.

Dials.—The two main types of early seventeenth-century watches, with engraved metal cases and with crystal or other stone cases, have the same type of dial. The plain watch has a plain gilt-metal dial plate, and the hour ring, with its roman figures and marks at the half-hours, is either engraved in the metal of the plate, as in the watch by Nicolas Lemaindre (Plate xvii, 1), or as a separate ring, generally of silver, attached to the plate, as in the watch by Augustin Forfaict (Plate xvi, 2). The same two types of hour ring are found in the engraved crystal watches, and are about equally common. There is also the less common type with a silver disk instead of a ring, as in the agate watch on Plate xx, 3, the cross watch on Plate xxii, 1, and the crystal watch on Plate xxi, 2.

The hour ring is generally considerably smaller than the dial plate would allow, as in the watches at the bottom of Plate xviii and on Plate xxi, 2, and in many of the other watches illustrated, and the space surrounding the hour ring is filled with floral scrolls, figures at the top and bottom being more common than not; a reclining female figure, as in the watch by East (Plate xx, 2), is frequently found. In cross watches only a small hour ring is possible, and the larger spaces in the arms usually have engraved scenes or figures. In the watch on the left of Plate xxii there is a representation of the Crucifixion below the dial, with emblems of the Passion in the three other arms and the centre. In the watch on the right there is, below the dial, the Virgin and Child, an angel in each side arm, and what is, perhaps, the Holy Spirit above; within the hour ring is a pattern formed of four winged cherubs' heads. The double arms of the cross

114

watch on Plate XVIII allow a larger hour ring, leaving only quite small spaces in the three short arms, which have floral scrolls at the sides and, possibly, Jehovah above, while figure scenes are engraved in a medallion below and within the hour ring. The two watches at the bottom of Plate XXXVI have already been mentioned as instances of cross watches with profane engravings. The star watch on Plate XXII is unusual in having engravings of the gods in the six triangular spaces outside the hour ring and of Jupiter inside.

Inside the hour ring, a scene with buildings, often a river and one or two figures, is the general rule. The watches at the bottom of Plates XVIII, XXI and XXIII show charming engravings of this kind. The floral pattern of the watch by East (Plate XX, 1) is much less common. When, however, an alarum is fitted, the central disk inside the hour circle turns, either acting as the hour hand or serving to set the alarum, and an engraved scene therefore is unsuitable. A most effective form of decoration then often adopted is a pierced and gilt central disk over a ground of contrasting colour, such as blued steel. This may be seen in the watch by David Ramsay on Plate XVII, 2, the watch by Edmund Gilpin on Plate XIX, 1, and the rather later watch by Josias Jenti at the bottom of Plate XLVI. In the curious vegetable-marrow watch on Plate XXIV, 4 the centre of the hour ring has a scene with the figure of a man walking in the foreground and buildings in the background, and the space above has a second scene of buildings and trees.

The roman figures on the hour ring are always very broad and stumpy in comparison with the figures of a modern watch. The XII figure of the early seventeenth-century watch is rarely higher than it is broad, and often, as in the watch by East (Plate XX, 1) and the watch by David Ramsay (Plate XVII, 2), it is much broader than it is high. There is a certain tendency for an earlier watch to have more stumpy figures, but to this there are many exceptions.

PLATE XXV

1

English 3-case watch signed on movement J. Grantham and on dial Faver, both London, *c.* 1750. Gold outer case repoussé in very high relief.
Fitzwilliam Museum.   pp. 119, 215.

2

Pod-shaped watch signed U. Klötz, Augsburg.   Silver-gilt dial plate chiselled in scene of the Annunciation, with winged cherubs.   Steel hand. Bottom cover on Plate XXIV, 3.
Fitzwilliam Museum.   pp. 119, 121.

3

French watch by Vauché, Paris, *c.* 1780.   Gold case, guilloché and covered translucent orange enamel, with appliqué sprays of flowers in four-colour gold and garlands in diamonds.   Small enamel painting in centre with border of diamonds.   Bezel with circle of diamonds and four-colour gold band.   Enamel dial with silver hands set diamonds.   Daniel Vauché, Vaucher or Vauchez, master in 1767, was an eminent maker.   Many watches by him are known.
Fitzwilliam Museum.   p. 220.

4

English watch by Henricus Jones, London, *c.* 1650.   Gold case enamelled alternately blue and white in melon-seed pattern with black markings. Henry Jones, apprenticed 1654, master of the Clockmakers' Company 1695 and died 1695, was a famous maker. Many watches by him are known.
Fitzwilliam Museum.   p. 135.

5

French watch by F. L. Meybom, Paris, *c.* 1660.   Case of blued steel covered with pierced and chiselled gold, on back and sides.   Two other square watches by him are known.
Fitzwilliam Museum.   p. 121.

PLATE XXV

Between the hour figures there is, with rare exceptions, a point, star, fleur-de-lis or other mark to indicate the half-hour. Generally, there is a small mark at the hour on a very narrow band inside the hour ring, as in the watch by Nicolas Lemaindre (Plate XVII, 1). The division of this band into quarter-hours, which is usual in sixteenth- and early seventeenth-century German watches, is not so common in French and English, but is often found; an example is on the watch by East on Plate XX.

Hands are of steel. The gilt or brass hands occasionally seen on watches before 1630 are, nearly always, later additions. The tail is generally as long as the pointer, which is distinguished by an end shaped more or less like a fleur-de-lis, though arrow-head and pointed ends are frequent. The hand of the watch by Lemaindre on Plate XVII, 1 is typical, with the length of its oval centre across the length of the hand. The hand is always well finished, carefully rounded above and flat below, and its centre conceals the square end of the arbor on which it is fixed. The rather rough flat hands often seen may be assumed to be later replacements. The hands of German watches are often flat, as in the watch on Plate VIII, 4, but are always shaped to some extent. The hand of the English watch by François Nawe, at the bottom of Plate XII, is a German-type hand, and is an example of the rare hand with little or no tail; the early English watch on Plate XIII affords another example, but these are two exceptional watches. The hand on the cross watch on Plate XXII, 1 is a late addition.

Hands of special forms are rare. The cross watch by Phelizot (Plate XXXVI) has a dove enamelled in white, and a watch in the original Marfels collection had a more conventional dove hand also enamelled in white. Three watches are known having lizards as hands; one in the Louvre, but not in the main Garnier collection, has the lizard enamelled in translucent green enamel.

Chasing and Repoussé Work.—Chasing and repoussé

117

PLATE XXVI

1

Square French watch by Nicolas Lemaindre, Blois, *c.* 1650. Gold case champlevé to leave a chiselled ornament in relief, on a ground of translucent green enamel on a guilloché ground. Painted enamel medallions, with cupids and mottoes on back and on each side and in the centre of the dial. Steel hand. This maker was the nephew of the Nicolas Lemaindre who made the watch on Plate XVII, 1. He was born in 1600 and was clockmaker to Louis XIV. and the Duc d'Orléans. Three other watches by him are known.
Louvre. p. 121.

2

Square French watch by Baltazar Martinot, Paris, *c.* 1675. Blued steel case, covered outside with pierced and chiselled gold ornament and inside with gold plates. Gold dial enamelled in centre with translucent blue on guilloché ground. White enamel hour circle and flowers and foliage in red enamel on white ground in corners. Steel hand. Baltazar Martinot, 1637-95, was clockmaker to Louis XIV. and a celebrated maker. Several watches and clocks by him are known.
Louvre. p. 121.

3

Square French watch by Pierre de Baufre, Paris, *c.* 1675. Gold case champlevé to leave a chiselled ornament of flowers in relief, on a ground of translucent red enamel, set with small diamonds. Painted enamel dial. Gilt hand. See Plates XXXVI, 2 and XLVIII, 2 for other watches by this maker.
Cluny Museum. p. 148.

4

French watch, unsigned, early seventeenth century. Crystal 4-lobed case with crystal cover, the crystals cut in branched figures. Gilt dial plate and silver hour disk.
Cluny Museum. p. 111.

PLATE XXVI

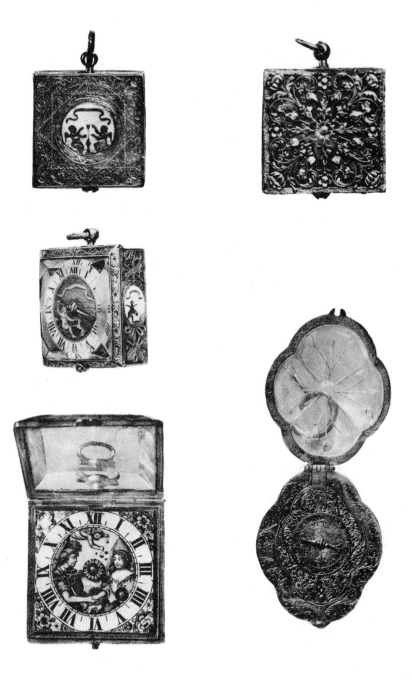

are done by a hammer and punch, without removing any metal by cutting. In chasing, the metal is worked on from the front, and in repoussé from the back. Works in higher relief are generally done by repoussé, and sometimes, to secure a higher relief than the metal would stand without becoming too thin, the parts in relief are soldered on. It is perhaps a mistake to distinguish between the two; in earlier examples there is no doubt that the metal was worked from both sides.

This work is rare early in the seventeenth century, but became a fashionable form of decoration for gold cases in the eighteenth century. Two examples of the early seventeenth century are illustrated. One, of 1610, is on the cover of the watch by Flant (Plate XVI), which has a charming group of the Judgement of Paris. This is worked on a silver plate soldered on to a metal cover engraved inside with a calendar and gilt. A most beautiful example of slightly later date is the cross watch by Tinelly of Aix (Plate XXII, 2) with a representation of the Crucifixion and Mary and St. John standing by the side of the Cross. The angels supporting the arms depart from their usual custom of wearing clothes. On the back cover is the Virgin and Child with surrounding figures. The repoussé work is done on plates of gold soldered on to gilt-metal covers. The watch has a silver side band engraved with symbols of the Passion. The cross watch is in good condition, but the other has suffered somewhat by rubbing of the parts in higher relief. It is interesting to compare these with two fine examples of mid eighteenth century repoussé work on Plates XXV and LI. The technique of the work on these is marvellous, far beyond that on the early watches, but the eighteenth-century watches seem to lack the charm of the early work.

Chiselled Work.—Chiselling in high relief is a rare form of decoration, apart from the chisel work found on early German watches. Plates XXIV and XXV show two examples from the Fitzwilliam Museum, Cambridge.

119

PLATE XXVII

1

German skull watch by Johann Maurer,
Füssen, Bavaria, *c.* 1660.   Silver case.
Lower jaw opens to disclose dial.
British Museum.   p. 123.

2

German watch by Hans John, Königsberg, *c.* 1660.   Case of gilt metal in
form of an acorn, with flint-lock pistol
fired by watch at 1 o'clock.
British Museum.   p. 123.

3

French or Swiss watch in form of a
dog by Jacques Joly, *c.* 1640.   Silver
case.
British Museum.   p. 123.

4

Square German watch by Johann
Michael Kheller, *c.* 1640.   Silver gilt
case covered with silver pierced and
chiselled ornament.
British Museum.   p. 121.

5

German watch by Georg Glück, Berlin,
c. 1640.   Silver case in form of a
book.
British Museum.   p. 123.

PLATE XXVII

One is a most unusual pod-shaped watch, illustrated on both Plates. The watch is of silver, with case and covers cast and finely chiselled in figure scenes and foliage scrolls. The back cover, shown on Plate xxiv, has a scene of the Magi bringing gifts, with an angel below. The dial on Plate xxv has, below the hour circle, the Annunciation and, above it, three winged cherubs and, in a circular frame, a figure of Jehovah. The hour circle is formed out of the plate, and has foliage ornament inside. The upper cover has a scene of the Adoration by Shepherds. The work is very good, but, judging by the character of the signature and the movement, the authenticity is doubtful The other watch, by Nicolas Cuisinier, and probably a little later, is shown on Plate xxiv, 1. In this, the case with sides is cast in one, with a cast cover. The case and cover are finely chiselled in relief, the cover showing a battle scene full of action and the back a group of figures.

Open pierced work, when well chiselled and put on a ground of contrasting colour, can give a singularly beautiful effect. Four square watches with this form of ornament are shown on Plates xxv, xxvi and xxvii. That on Plate xxvi, 2 has a case of blued steel covered on back and sides with plates of gold pierced and chiselled with great delicacy. This watch, with its exquisite pattern in bright gold on a deep blue ground, is most attractive. The second watch, on Plate xxv, is constructed in exactly the same way, though the pierced and chiselled ornament does not quite reach the perfection of that on the former.

The third watch, on Plate xxvii, is quite different, having a gilt case with the pierced ornament of silver. The chiselling is not nearly so fine as in the other two watches, but the design is attractive. The fourth (Plate xxvi, 1), in the Louvre, is an exceptionally beautiful watch by Nicolas Lemaindre of Blois, the nephew of the Nicolas who made the plain oval watch on Plate xvii and a large circular watch in the South Kensington

Museum. The reproduction, in omitting the colours, does not do it justice. The pierced gold plates on the back and sides are on a background of translucent emerald-green enamel, itself on a guilloché ground. The centre of the back and of each side is occupied by a medallion of painted enamel with one or two cupids, and four of the medallions have bands with mottoes :—
Poinct ne me touche. Je le trève. Il se trouver uni [sic]. *Je ne crains rien.*

This type of ornament is, without any apparent reason, almost confined to square watches and to the second half of the seventeenth century. In an incomplete form, though, it is often found in the centre of the dial of earlier alarum watches, the pierced plates having no chiselling to form and only more or less engraving on the flat surface (Plates XVII, XIX and XLVI).

Cast cases always needed working over with the graver and chisel to give a properly finished surface. An example of such a case is the silver watch by Edmund Gilpin in the form of a seeded rose on Plate XXX. The same pattern is found on a silver watch by Benjamin Lysle of Rotterdam in the South Kensington Museum, and in the same collection is another, rather larger, watch with the same pattern, but in this case of gold, champlevé and filled in with cream enamel; it is by Du Hamel of Paris, and is illustrated in Britten. Another Paris maker, J. Anisse, also copied the pattern in gold, and a fifth example, in cast silver, by Daniel Gom of Lyons, is in the Fränkel collection. This use of the same pattern in London, Rotterdam, Paris and Lyons must be due to its publication in some book of design, and is a good example of the extent to which watchmakers relied on these books and how far afield the books were carried.

An eight-lobed watch in cast case of earlier date, about 1600-25, is shown on Plate XXI, 1, and is by Jean Baptiste Duboule of Geneva, a maker who specialized in 'form' watches, or watches imitating other things. There are by him a tulip watch in the Wallace collection,

122

death's-head watches in the Louvre and the Olivier collections, a tulip watch in the Cluny Museum, a lion watch illustrated in Britten and a large astronomical watch in the British Museum.

Form Watches.—Form watches, when they depart too far from the watch form, are frequently poor in execution and unworthy of their period. Plate XXVII has some examples : a silver skull watch by Johann Maurer of Füssen, near Augsburg, a silver dog by Jacques Joly of Paris or Geneva, a silver book watch by George Glück of Berlin and a very curious acorn watch by Hans John of Königsberg, with a pistol alarum. The case is carefully finished and gilt ; the watch is contained in the upper, smaller part, while the lower part has a flint-lock pistol firing through a hole at the small end of the case. The trigger can be seen protruding from the plate facing the watch dial ; it is actuated by the hand of the watch at one o'clock, and there is no means for varying the time of firing. These four watches are all about the middle of the seventeenth century, the lion and book a little before and the skull and acorn a little after.

German watches in book form are not uncommon of dates before and after 1600. An exceptionally fine example in the Mallett collection is on Plates XXVIII and XXIX, and dates, probably, from the third quarter of the sixteenth century. The case is of gilt cast metal, finely pierced and chiselled. The dial, with its circle of arabic figures, adjustable for setting to the Italian hour, was mentioned in Chapter IV. Within this circle again is a central disk with figures 1 to 12 and 1 to 12, also adjustable for setting the alarum. Unlike the modern alarum, this watch could be set to ring at a time more than twelve hours ahead. Two sundials, with a compass, are provided. One is ingeniously made a meridian dial, because this is the only form of dial with a 'face' that would fit into the space to the right of the watch dial ; the stile is missing and was probably attached by means of the hole on the '6' line, but how it was arranged is not clear, as

123

German striking and alarum watch in the form of a book, signed HK, *c.* 1575. The hour dial marked I-XII and I-XII with inner rotatable ring marked 1-24, and alarum disk in centre. Adjoining this is a meridian sundial, with stile missing. On the inside of the cover is a horizontal sundial with folding stile and compass and figures for four different latitudes. Adjoining this is a dial relating the age and phase of the moon. Case of gilt cast metal, pierced and chiselled in a design of flowers and foliage. The dial plates are gilt and engraved in a foliage pattern, with the signs of the zodiac on each side of the meridian dial. The movement has stackfreed and dumb-bell foliot, with bristle regulator operated by hand on dial. The striking movement is to one side of the going movement. The maker is probably Hans Kiening of Füssen in Bavaria, the maker of an astronomical clock. *Mallett coll.* pp. 57, 9ᵃ, 123.

PLATE XXVIII

PLATE XXIX

the stile should rise from the intersection of the '6' line with the midday line marked AEQVATOR DIEI. This type of dial has to be held in a vertical plane and with its midday line tilted to an angle depending on the latitude, and no provision is apparent for holding the watch at this angle. The other sundial, on the cover, is an ordinary horizontal dial with folding stile, but it has four circles of hour figures for four different latitudes. The dial to the left of it is a moon dial for setting by hand.

Another form watch of great interest is the silver sphere engraved with a map of the world, on Plate xxx. The map is signed 'Franciscus Demoncent 1552,' and is evidently copied from a globe by François De Mongenet, a map- and globe-maker of the Vosges, the signature being copied with the map. Several globes or gores by him, with the date 1552, are known. The watch itself dates from about 1620. The lower view shows the watch open, with sundial and compass in the cover. The engraving on the dial plate is most unusual, as the subject in the centre of the hour ring is continued outside it; the plate is gilt, with a silver hour ring and steel hand. The movement, with good piercing and engraving, is shown removed from the case, and the workmanship throughout, in engraving and movement, is particularly good. The maker, Henry Sebert of Strasbourg, has not been found by Ungerer in the Strasbourg records.

The tulip watch on Plate xxxix, 5 shows a type of chiselled decoration occasionally found on a cast case; the alternate squares of the chequer pattern are sunk and cut with fine cross-hatching, so as to make them appear dark in contrast to the bright surface squares. It may be intended as an imitation of the niello inlay of the watch on its left. The watch is signed Thomas Sande, a maker unknown from any record; its date is in the first quarter of the seventeenth century.

Enamel.—Enamel has been used for decorating watch-cases from the sixteenth century to the present day. Enamel is a form of glass, its basis being a transparent,

125

PLATE XXX

1

Strasbourg watch by Henry Sebert, *c.* 1620. Spherical silver case engraved with a map of the world signed Franciscus Demoncent, 1552, no doubt copied from a globe or gores by François De Mongenet, who made several of this date. Dial plate gilt and engraved in a landscape scene with buildings and figures, extending within and without the silver hour circle. Steel hand. The cover contains a horizontal dial with folding stile and a compass.
Staats Museum, Amsterdam. p. 125.

3

English watch by N. Massy, London, *c.* 1690. Gold case enamelled on back with white floral scrolls on a lilac blue ground, surrounding a painted medallion with a cupid. Edge and inside of case enamelled with flowers on a white ground. Dial enamelled with a cupid. The movement has a blued steel balance-cock. Nicolas Massy of Blois went to London about 1680.
Mallett coll.

2

English watch by Edmund Gilpin, London, *c.* 1635. Cast silver chiselled case. Another watch by this maker is on Plate xix, 1.
Mallett coll. p. 122.

PLATE XXX

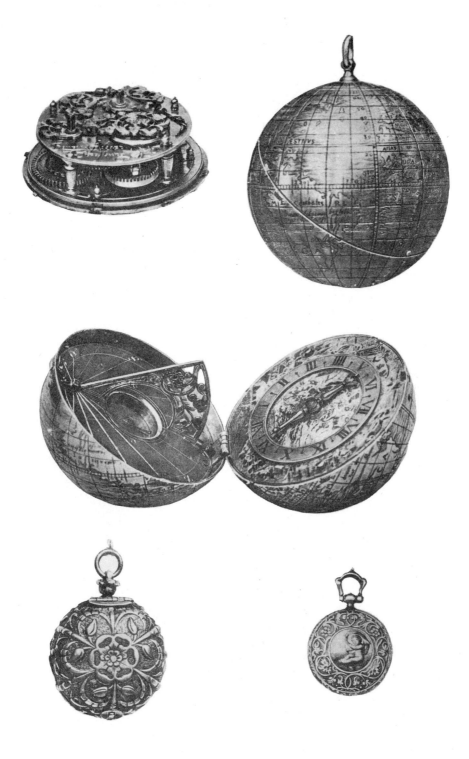

colourless compound called 'flux' (*fondant*), which is coloured by the addition of oxides of metals while fused. The flux is composed of silica, red lead and potash, and, by varying the proportions of the constituents, the temperature of fusion may be made high, giving a 'hard' enamel, or low, giving a 'soft' enamel. The harder the enamel, the less liable it is to suffer decomposition on the surface by exposure to the atmosphere. On the other hand, the harder enamels, fusing at a higher temperature, are more liable to crack and flake off their metal backing as a result of strains caused by the different expansions of the metal and the enamel.

Enamelling is done on gold, platinum, silver, copper and their alloys, but the melting-point of silver and most alloys is too low for the hard enamels. The enamelling on seventeenth-century watch-cases is nearly always on gold of a high standard of purity. Many transparent enamels suffer changes in colour or transparency when applied to silver or copper, alone or in alloys, and the early enamellers had a more restricted range of colours applicable to the baser metals and alloys than are available now.

There are three methods of decoration by enamel: enamelling proper, painting in enamel and painting on enamel. In the first, which is a very old art, metal cells are formed and filled with enamel, a single colour in each cell. The cells are formed in two ways. In champlevé work, the metal plate is cut away with a graver to form a design in which walls of metal are left standing, up to the original surface of the metal. In cloisonné work, the design is formed by thin strips of metal fixed to the metal plate or ground. The strips or cloisons, when bent to shape, are attached to the plate by solder or to a preliminary layer of enamel by flux.

The process of applying the enamel is the same in the two cases. Finely ground enamel, made into a paste with water, is filled into the cells and, after drying, is fired. Several coats are applied until the enamel is above

127

the level of the metal partitions. The enamel is then ground down to the level of the partitions, and the whole is either polished or glazed on the surface by a short firing.

Champlevé work requires a thick plate, and generally substantial portions of the plate are left to form the walls of the cells. In cloisonné work the amount of metal used can be reduced to a minimum, and the process is more common when the cost of the precious metal is a consideration. Cloisonné enamel, though, is not by any means confined to cheaper work ; some designs are suited to champlevé and others to cloisonné, and a combination of the two in the same work is not unusual. When translucent enamel is used, champlevé has the advantage over cloisonné that variations in depth in the cells give variations in the tint of the enamel, and this shows up engraving on the ground to very good effect.

When translucent enamel is fused on an engraved plate, the work is known as *basse-taille*. At the present day it is the most common form of enamelling, the ground being cut by engine-turning to geometric patterns or by engraving machines to other patterns. It is not frequently found in seventeenth-century watch-cases except on a small scale in combination with champlevé work. An accessory form of decoration used with champlevé and cloisonné enamel is in the use of *paillons*, which are small pieces of gold or silver foil cut to the shape of some portions of the design and covered with translucent enamel.

In Limoges enamel, which was started soon after 1500, enamels of different colours are used without cells, so that it is a process of painting in enamels. Pierpont Morgan collected four watch-cases, now in the Metropolitan Museum, New York, which are said to be Limoges enamel. There is no example, as far as the Author knows, in any British, French, German or Dutch museum. As Limoges enamel had fallen into complete decadence by 1600, and anyhow was unsuited

128

to the small scale of watch-cases, the lack of examples is not surprising.

Painting in enamel of quite a different kind is, however, used extensively in decorating watch-cases, and is most effective. Enamel is applied to a gold or plain enamel surface in the form of threads or little blobs which, on fusing, take a rounded shape and remain in low relief.

The last enamelling process is painting on enamel. In this the colours are not true enamels but oxides of metal, mixed with sufficient flux to make them vitrifiable. A uniform layer of enamel, generally white, is fused on the metal plate and is used as a ground for a miniature painting. The colours are made to adhere to the enamel ground, sinking into it to some extent, by firing the plate until the surface is fused. The whole is then covered with a protective layer of transparent flux.

There is little doubt that the process was discovered by Jean Toutin, a goldsmith, who was born in Châteaudun in 1578 and died at Paris in 1644. Félibien des Avaux wrote in 1676 that Toutin had made the invention in 1632, but there is a royal order for *sept boistes d'or émaillées à figures* in 1630, and this is a more probable date in view of the extent to which the process had developed in Blois by 1635. The discovery has been attributed to Jean Petitot, born in Geneva in 1607, no doubt because he acquired so much fame in England and France from his portraits painted on enamel. He was, however, a pupil of either Jean Toutin or one of his immediate followers at Blois.

Early paintings on enamel are rare and are seldom signed. No work by Jean Toutin is known, but watches enamelled by his sons, Henri and Jean, exist. Other enamellers of Blois who are known to have decorated watches are:—Isaac Gribelin, master before 1634; Dubié, said to have been one of the first taught by Toutin; Pierre Chartier, born 1618 and master 1638, who specialized in flowers (there is a plaque in the Grüne

PLATE XXXI

1

Watch - case, probably French, early seventeenth century. Gold. Back, sides and cover pierced and chiselled in pattern of flowers and foliage, enamelled in translucent and opaque colours. Dial enamelled in a green and white foliage pattern on a white ground. Silver outer case with the royal arms. *S. Kensington Museum.*

p. 137.

2

Watch, probably French, in form of a bud, by J. H. Ester, early seventeenth century. Gold case, enamelled white and set with four large garnets and paste brilliants. The cover inside is champlevé and enamelled in blue, green and red. Gold dial champlevé and enamelled in translucent blue and red. Steel hand. *S. Kensington Museum.*

p. 133.

3

Swiss watch by Henriot, Geneva, early nineteenth century. Four - colour gold case set with rubies and turquoises. *S. Kensington Museum.*

p. 219.

4

Watch, probably French, *c.* 1670, with later movement. Gold case, champlevé and enamelled on back and edges in flowers and foliage with translucent and opaque enamels. Dial similarly enamelled is shown on Plate XXXV, 1. *S. Kensington Museum.*

p. 135.

5

Watch-case, probably French, mid seventeenth century. Back and edges chiselled in high relief in flowers and leaves, which are enamelled with opaque and translucent enamel. Dial with gold hour circle on a white enamel ground with flowers and leaves in red, blue and green. Gold outer case engraved with scenes of Joseph and his brethren. *S. Kensington Museum.*

p. 137.

6

French watch by Julien Le Roy, Paris, *c.* 1745. Gold case with painted enamel of Danaë and the shower of gold. Julien Le Roy, one of the greatest French makers, was born 1686 and died 1759. *S. Kensington Museum.*

p. 217.

7

French watch by Pierre Gregson, Paris, *c.* 1785. Gold case with central painted enamel of a cupid, surrounded by a broad band of translucent blue enamel on an engine-turned ground and border of white enamel with blue-green circles. Pierre Gregson was clockmaker to Louis XVI. *S. Kensington Museum.*

pp. 219, 224.

PLATE XXXI

Gewölbe attributed to him); Jean Grillié, 1652. Christophe Morlière, who was born in Orléans 1604, came to Blois in 1628, and was an enameller of great repute. In 1643, the year of his death, the town of Blois ordered an enamelled watch from him as a present to Monsieur Frère du roi. Robert Vauquer, son of the watchmaker and engraver Michel Vauquer, born in 1625, inherited Morlière's vogue and is said to have surpassed him in ability. Two watches by Vauquer are known, of which one is in the Louvre, but of Morlière there is only one very fine watch in Vienna which is attributed to him with fair certainty. It is illustrated on Plate LVI, 3.

Blois was the first centre of painting in enamel and the home of the best work. The art spread to different countries, but soon settled in Geneva, and remains there to this day.

After this review of the processes of enamelling, their application to watches will be described.

Early Enamelling.—A simple form of enamelling is often found in German watches of the latter part of the sixteenth century and later, the sun or star commonly engraved in the centre of the dial, having its rays sunk and filled with translucent enamel. The watch by Nouwen at the top of Plate xx is an example, though on an English watch. The German watch on Plate VIII, 4 has a little enamel decoration of this elementary kind, just inside the circle of arabic figures; the short bands and the circles separating them are sunk by the graver and filled with translucent enamel.

A splendid example of the type of champlevé enamelling in German watches is that on the silver dial plate of the watch by Johannes Buz on Plate XXXIII, 2. The work on the dial contrasts with that of a rather roughly pierced case. The small crystal watch in the centre of Plate XXIII is of about the same date, and shows similar enamelling work on the gold dial and the gold frame of the crystal; on the frame is the same ornament of bands alternating with circles as in the German octagonal watch

131

PLATE XXXII

1

German watch by Johan Sigmund Schloer, Regensburg, *c.* 1645. Gold case enamelled in high relief with a winged cupid in white surrounded by flowers and foliage. On the other side is a grotesque female figure. Dial enamelled in centre with a pattern in pink on a green ground. Two other watches by this maker are known.
Louvre. p. 142.

2

French watch in form of tulip by J. Jolly, Paris, *c.* 1625. Gold case champlevé and enamelled in green and purple on a white ground. One petal opens to disclose the dial, similarly enamelled. Josias Jolly became master in 1609. Four other watches by him are known, of which one is on Plate XXXVI, 4.
Louvre. p. 133.

3

French watch by I. Ballart, Bourges, *c.* 1600. Silver case with straight sides; back champlevé and enamelled with translucent coloured enamels.
Louvre. p. 133.

4

Watch in form of poppy-head, perhaps German, early seventeenth century. Case of amber with gilt edging held on by gold threads passing between the lobes and fixed to the pendant. Silver dial champlevé and enamelled in blue-green and yellow. The only amber watch known.
Louvre. p. 151.

PLATE XXXII

of Plate VIII. The watch on Plate XXXI, 2 has a gold case shaped like a bud and set with four large garnets, one being on the cover. The settings are enamelled white, and the gold dial plate and the inside of the cover have translucent coloured enamels. The watch, of about 1620, is by J. H. Ester, who may be the same as a Henry Ester, the maker of many fine watches, one in the South Kensington Museum, in the form of a swan, two in the British Museum, a crystal cross watch with double arms in the Louvre, and one in the Kunsthistorische Museum, Vienna, and several in private collections; his signature has never been accompanied by the name of a place, and it is curious that nothing should be known of so fine and prolific a maker. His country was probably France or Strasbourg. An early example of champlevé enamel on a French watch, dating from about 1600, is illustrated in the centre of Plate XXXII. It shows more definite composition than the watches just mentioned, but the work is rather rough.

These examples are typical of the enamel work found on English, French and German watches at the end of the sixteenth and beginning of the seventeenth centuries. It is rather primitive, generally without much attempt at composition, bits of enamel in the form of birds, flowers, etc., being dotted about the available surface. Some watches of 1600 and earlier with enamelling of a high order are known, and, judging from contemporary goldsmith's work, are possible, but any watch of this kind should be examined with care.

Champlevé and Cloisonné Enamel.—The graceful tulip watch on Plate XXXII, 2 shows champlevé enamel work in perfection. The flowers are of green and purple enamel on a white ground, while the edges of the petals and the flower-stalks are gold. One of the petals hinges open to disclose the dial, which is decorated in the same way, the hour figures being gold on a black enamel circle. The watch, dating from about 1630, is by Josias Jolly of Paris, the maker of the crystal Maltese cross watch of

133

PLATE XXXIII

1

French or Swiss watch by Pierre Duhamel, Paris and Geneva, mid seventeenth century. Gold case enamelled on back with a half figure of an Amazon surrounded by a band of translucent blue enamel on a guilloché ground, within a garland of red, pink, yellow and green flowers. The bezel is enamelled with a similar garland. The dial has a translucent blue enamel centre with a narrow garland of flowers. Silver hand, set brilliants.
South Kensington Museum.

2

German striking watch by Johannes Buz, Augsburg, *c.* 1625. Gilt metal case pierced and engraved with a female figure and large flowers and foliage. Sides pierced in floral scrolls. Dial of silver showing days of the week and month and the phases of the moon. Gilt hands. The dial plate is champlevé and enamelled with translucent enamels in birds, flowers and leaves. Bezel with glass held by tags.
South Kensington Museum.   p. 131.

3

French watch by Jacques Huon, Paris, mid-seventeenth century. Gold case, enamelled on back and edge with white flowers, shaded pink, on a black ground, with stems, pistils and other parts left in gold. The centre of the dial is similarly enamelled. The bezel is enamelled in a black and white pattern. Outer case of shagreen. One other watch by this maker is known.
South Kensington Museum.   p. 135.

4

Octagonal French watch, made at Blois, but unsigned, early seventeenth century. The back and cover have a thick layer of translucent blue enamel, and embedded in it is a floral pattern formed by cloisons and paillons enamelled in colours. Gilt dial plate with silver hour ring and central engraved landscape scene.
South Kensington Museum.   p. 148.

PLATE XXXIII

Plate XXXVI.   Several other watches by him are known—
an octagonal watch in the British Museum, two in
Vienna, and another enamelled watch in the Olivier
collection.   He is to be distinguished from Jacques Jolly
or Joly, who signed without the name of a place, and
may be a Geneva maker.   Another watch with fine
champlevé work is on Plates XXXI, 4 and XXXV, 1 ; it is
unsigned but is probably French, dating from about the
middle of the seventeenth century.   This is an example
of the combined use of champlevé and cloisonné work,
the main design being formed by champlevé cutting,
while the petals of the central daisy and other details
are, most probably, formed by cloisons.

Probably the most beautiful watch with cloisonné
enamel is that by Jacques Huon of Paris, shown on
Plate XXXIII, 3.   The cloisons are so fine as to be hardly
visible.   The work, however, is not pure cloisonné where
each cell is filled with enamel of one colour, but the
white flowers and leaves, each in its cloison, are shaded
in pink by painting on the enamel.   The central rose,
for instance, is composed of white enamel in a single
cloison and then has its petals indicated by painting.

Enamel in Relief.—In the enamel work described so
far, the surface of the work is smooth, and the cells,
whether champlevé or cloisonné, are overfilled with
enamel and the surplus ground down to the level of the
gold.   When, however, enamel is used in relief, an
immense variety of effect becomes possible, and some or
the watches decorated in this way are most beautiful.

Starting with the simpler forms of work, the watch
on Plate XXV, 4 has its back enamelled in cloisons, but
each cell is filled well above the walls, so that the enamel
lies in blobs, alternating turquoise blue and white, each
with black markings.

A similar treatment of the enamel is seen on the
watch at the bottom of Plate XLVI, but here it is combined with piercing of the gold case, the cells for the
enamel being formed by hammering and chiselling.

135

PLATE XXXIV

1

English watch by David Bouquet, London, mid seventeenth century. Gold case enamelled on back, edges and cover with a ground of black enamel on which are flowers and foliage enamelled in relief in many opaque colours. The cover has two circles of paste brilliants and a centre cluster. Inside the cover is a river scene and house painted in black on light blue enamel, and inside the case is a similar scene of ruins. The dial has a white enamel hour ring and, in the centre, an enamel landscape scene in colours. Gilt hand. David Bouquet was admitted to the Blacksmiths' Company in 1628 and died 1665. Four other watches by him are known.
British Museum. p. 139.

2

Dutch watch by Hans Conraet Elchinger, Amsterdam, *c.* 1645. Gold case with enamel paintings by Jean Toutin, son of the Jean who invented the process of painting on enamel. The two illustrations show the paintings on the back of the case and the outside of the cover. Scenes with figures and ruins are painted on the insides of the case and cover. The edge has six landscape scenes, with figures and ruins.
British Museum. p. 143.

3a

3b

French watch by Louys Vautier, Blois, early seventeenth century. Gold case enamelled white, the whole covered with an open framework of gold, of hexagonal form, composed of flowers and foliage enamelled in many translucent colours. The dial has a cloisonné enamelled centre of flowers on a white ground, with an hour ring of translucent blue enamel. Vautier was born 1591 and died 1638.
British Museum. p. 137.

4

Dutch watch by Steven Tracy, Rotterdam, *c.* 1690. Gold case with enamel paintings by Huaud le puisné. Inside the case is a river scene with castle, and the edge bears four landscapes. The dial has a central painting of a woman seated with a basket of flowers. Silver hand set paste brilliants.
British Museum. p. 145.

5

Watch-case of metal, with enamel painting of Battersea type, *c.* 1760.
British Museum. p. 217.

PLATE XXXIV

This enamel also is turquoise blue and white. The same combination of enamel and pierced and chiselled work is seen in the beautiful watch on Plate XXXI, 1. The pattern of flowers and foliage is most skilfully formed and delicately chiselled, with little cells for each flower petal, leaf and bud, filled with translucent enamel. Unfortunately, the enamel has cracked off in many places.

The watch of which front and back are shown in the centre of Plate XXXIV is another splendid example of delicate piercing and enamelling. The case proper is enamelled plain white, and the whole is covered with a gold framework fashioned as flowers and foliage and enamelled in many colours, the framework being attached by solder to the gold edging round the dial. There were two Blois makers called Louys Vautyer, one who died in 1623, while the other was born in 1591 and died in 1638 and probably is the maker of this watch.

A watch with similar work but without piercing is the lower of the two centre watches on Plate XXXI. The gold case is hammered and chiselled in high relief in a pattern of flowers and leaves, and these are enamelled, some with opaque and some with translucent enamel of many colours, the pattern extending round the edge of the case. A gold disk below and to the left of the centre is a shutter covering the winding hole. The dial, not illustrated, is of champlevé enamel, with flowers and leaves in colour on a white ground within the hour circle; this is left in the gold with the figures engraved and filled with black enamel. The watch has an outer case of gold with two engraved scenes, one of Joseph being let down into the well by his brethren, and the other of the brethren giving the news to Abraham.

Painting in Enamel.—In the next type of enamel decoration — painting in enamel — enamel is applied, always in small blobs or thin threads, to a smooth enamelled surface. This kind of work is shown in its perfection on the watch by Edward East at the bottom of Plate XXXV, one of the most attractive watches there

137

PLATE XXXV

1

Watch, probably French, *c.* 1670. Gold case. Centre of dial and bezel champlevé and enamelled with translucent and opaque colours. Back shown on Plate XXXI, 4.
S. Kensington Museum. p. 135.

2

Swiss watch by Henri Colomby, Hüningen, *c.* 1690. Case enamelled with white flowers, picked out in pink, in relief on a blue ground with black markings.
S. Kensington Museum. p. 142.

3

Dutch watch by Pieter Visbach, The Hague, *c.* 1660. Back of case covered with translucent blue enamel, with wreath of white flowers, shaded pink, in relief. Central painted bust. Dial with centre of translucent blue enamel and wreath in white.
S. Kensington Museum. p. 139.

4

Dutch watch by Claude Pascal, The Hague, *c.* 1650. Back and cover pierced and formed with flowers and foliage in high relief, enamelled with opaque enamel and shaded by painting.
S. Kensington Museum. p. 141.

5

English watch by Edward East, *c.* 1650. Gold case with cover enamelled with a smooth layer of turquoise-blue, with flowers formed by specks of white enamel in relief, picked out in pink, and foliage indicated by black markings. Landscape scenes in black on blue ground on the inside of case and cover and in the centre of the dial. Gilt hand. Movement with tangent screw regulator and silver index dial.
S. Kensington Museum. pp. 137, 153.

PLATE XXXV

are. The whole case, back and cover, is covered with a smooth layer of turquoise-blue enamel, and on this, little flowers are formed by specks of white enamel standing out in relief and picked out in pink, while the foliage is indicated by black painting on the blue enamel. The ribbon bow forming a pendant is also enamelled in blue, picked out in black. On the inside of the cover and in the centre of the dial are two beautifully executed scenes in black on a blue ground, and a third similar scene is on the inside of the case. The movement, of the fine workmanship characteristic of East, is in perfect condition.

It is interesting that there is another English watch, by Jacob Cornelius, with exactly the same type of ornament. This is illustrated on Plate XII in black-and-white, but the colours are the same as on the East watch. The central pattern on the back is practically identical on the two watches, but the centre of the dial of the second watch is decorated with cloisonné enamel, with some painting. The two watches belong to the middle of the seventeenth century or a little earlier. The small watch on Plate xxxv, 3 has work of the same type in the form of a wreath of flowers and foliage painted in white enamel on a ground of translucent blue enamel. The wreath is shaded in pink. The watch is by Pieter Visbach of The Hague, of a date soon after 1650.

Now come some examples of enamel work of the most elaborate form, where enamel in relief is combined with painting, and also with jewelling. The watch shown in two views on Plate xxxiv, 1 has a groundwork of black enamel, and on this flowers and leaves are formed in relief in opaque enamel of many colours, and each flower is shaded by painting. The cover of the watch (the lower view) has two rows of paste brilliants set round its edge and also a cluster in the centre. The contrast between these and the enamelling is somewhat lost in reproduction. Inside the cover is a river scene with house, painted in black on light blue enamel, and there is a scene of ruins inside the case. The centre of

PLATE XXXVI

1

French watch, with later movement, second half of seventeenth century. Gold case enamelled in high relief, with masks, flowers and foliage in white enamel painted with black markings. Set with diamonds in the centre and alternating with the masks. One-third larger than actual size.
Louvre. p. 141.

2

French watch by De Baufre, Paris, *c.* 1675. Gold case covered with translucent red enamel carrying a gold covering, pierced, chiselled and enamelled in white and green, in a radiating pattern of flowers and leaves, with painted markings. Set with diamonds in the centres of the flowers. Other watches by Pierre De Baufre or Peter Debaufre are on Plates XXVI, 3 and XLVIII, 2.
Cluny Museum. p. 141.

3

French or English watch, unsigned, *c.* 1600. Hexagonal case of smoke crystal without frames. Gold dial, champlevé and enamelled in several colours. A similar gold enamelled plate covers the top plate of the movement.
Louvre. p. 107.

4

French watch by Josias Joly, Paris, *c.* 1640. Crystal case in form of a Maltese cross, without frames. Gilt dial plate engraved with floral design. Another watch by Josias Joly or Jolly is on Plate XXXII, 2.
Louvre. pp. 103, 107.

5

French cross watch by C. Phelizot, Dijon, first quarter of seventeenth century. Crystal case and cover with gilt metal frames. Gilt dial plate engraved with female figure below and winged cherub above. Hand in form of an enamelled dove. Another watch by this maker is on Plate XVIII, 3.
Louvre. pp. 103, 111, 117.

PLATE XXXVI

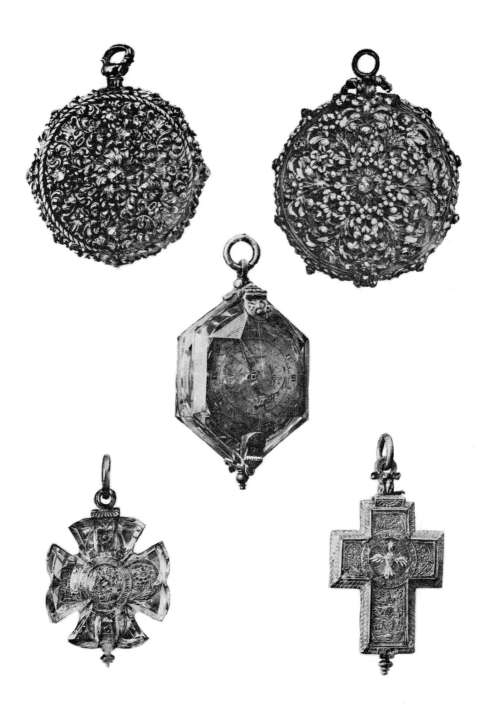

the dial has a landscape scene with figures painted in colours. The watch is by David Bouquet of London, who was admitted to the Blacksmiths' Company in 1628, was an original member of the Clockmakers' Company in 1632, and died in 1665. Its date is probably about 1650. There is a fine enamelled watch by him in the Palais du Cinquantenaire in Brussels, and several others are known.

On Plate xxxv, 4 is an exceptionally beautiful watch by Claude Pascal of The Hague, of about the same date, mid seventeenth century. Back and front are alike, pierced and formed with flowers and foliage in high relief, all enamelled with opaque enamels in rather subdued colours, and shaded by painting. Another beautiful piece of work is on the watch on Plate xxxvi, 1. This has, on a black enamel ground, masks, flowers and foliage in white enamel painted with black markings, with a central diamond and four diamonds alternating with the masks. The enamel and painting work is so fine and delicate that it could hardly be appreciated in a reproduction to scale, and the views of this and the adjoining watch are about one-third larger than actual size.

A watch equalling the last in the delicacy of its work is shown to the right of it. In this a gold case, covered with translucent red enamel, carries a gold covering pierced and chiselled in a radiating pattern of flowers and leaves, these being enamelled in white and green with painted markings, and diamonds are set in the centres of the larger flowers. The watch is by De Baufre of Paris, probably the Pierre De Baufre who was in Paris in 1675 and came to London before 1689, when he joined the Clockmakers' Company. In 1704 he became famous by joining with Facio in patenting jewelling in watch movements, and making the first jewelled watches. Other watches by him are illustrated on Plates xxvi, 3 and xlviii, 2.

German watches with this kind of enamel work of a high order are rare. One, in the Louvre, is shown on

141

Plate XXXII, 1.   A winged cupid, charmingly modelled in white enamel, holds a bow in one hand and an arrow in the other, and is surrounded by flowers and foliage in high relief.   The other side has the bust of a grotesque female figure in place of the cupid.   The maker is Johan Sigmund Schloer of Regensburg (Ratisbonne); two square watches by him are known, one in the Fränkel collection and one in the Carnegie Museum, Pittsburg. Case and movement both show fine work, and date probably from a little before 1650.

A later example of enamel is shown on Plate XXXV, 2. It is by Henri Collomby, a native of Geneva, who was in Basle in 1670 and in Hüningen 1679-99, where the watch was made.   Watches by him are in Munich and in the Mallett collection.   The work is quite good, but is not on the level of the preceding examples, and indicates the decline which set in towards the end of the seventeenth century.   After 1680 there are practically no examples of fine enamel work.

Painting on Enamel.—The general decline of art in the course of the seventeenth century is shown clearly in the paintings on enamel, the last form of enamel decoration.   The paintings of the first two decades, 1630 to 1650, are incomparably above any of later date, and those of the first decade are better than those of the second. They are very rare.   Perhaps the most perfect example in existence is the watch shown on the Frontispiece Plate.   The watch is in the British Museum, and is signed ' B. Foucher, Blois.'   This is, almost certainly, the first Blaise Foucher, who was a *compagnon* watchmaker at Blois in 1623, was a master in 1631, and died in 1662. The subject, Theseus and Hippolyta, is treated in four scenes, on the outside and inside of the case and the outside and inside of the cover.   It is more common to find the main subject on the outside of the case and cover only and landscapes of minor importance on the insides.   This watch, moreover, has a feature which the Author has not found on any other; the four scenes

142

are repeated in miniature in six pictures on the curved edge of the watch, four being turned into six by subdividing two of the subjects. The legends of Theseus and Antiope and Hippolyta are so diverse that it is not easy to say what the scenes represent. Possibly the inside of the cover (top left) shows the first battle with the Amazons, the inside of the case and the outside of the cover Theseus falling in love with Antiope, Queen of the Amazons, and the outside of the case the second battle with the Amazons after Theseus had abandoned Antiope. The condition of both case and movement of the watch is perfect; its date is probably about 1635.

Another magnificent example of painting is on a watch by Goullens of Paris in the South Kensington Museum, reproduced on Plate XXXVII. The case has hinged covers back and front. On the outsides of the covers are scenes representing the Holy Family, and on the insides are portraits of Louis XIII. and Cardinal Richelieu. The dial has, within the white hour circle, a scene with ruins and figures, and round the curved edge of the case are scenes of the Flight into Egypt. The date attributed to the watch is about 1640. Another watch by Goullens, also with splendid enamel paintings, is in the National Museum, Stockholm.

On Plate LVI, 3 is illustrated in black and white a magnificent example of flower-painting in the Kunsthistorische Museum, Vienna. The watch is of particular interest because it bears, in all probability, the work of Christophe Morlière, the most famous painter of his day in Blois, and is the only example known. Morlière was born at Orléans in 1604, went to Blois in 1628, and died in 1643. He was goldsmith and engraver to the King's brother, and is known to have specialized in flower-painting. His signature does not appear on any painting, but, as the watch illustrated is signed by his brother-in-law Jacques Poëte, it is a fair assumption that the flower-painting is by him.

The two views on Plate XXXIV, 2 are of a Dutch

143

PLATE XXXVII

French watch by Goullens, Paris, *c.* 1640. Gold
case with painted enamels on all surfaces. The
front cover outside shows the Holy Family, and
the back cover the Virgin and Child ; the edge
has scenes of the flight into Egypt and the
slaughter of the innocents. The insides of the
covers have portraits of Louis XIII. and Cardinal
Richelieu. Seven.other watches by this maker
are known.
South Kensington Museum.   pp. 143, 148.

PLATE XXXVII

watch of about 1645, with paintings by Jean Toutin of Blois, the younger son of Jean Toutin who discovered the process of painting on enamel. The work is quite different in character from that on the earlier Blois watch by Foucher, but still is exquisitely done. The inside of the case and the dial are also painted with similar scenes, and the edge has six landscape scenes with ruins and figures. The Louvre has a watch-case with paintings also signed by J. Toutin ; some of the figures resemble those on this watch very closely.

A watch probably of slightly later date, on Plate XXXVIII, is by Nicholas Bernard of Paris, one of the signatories to the second series of Statutes of the Corporation of Paris in 1646. The paintings on the outside of the cover and the back probably represent Charity and Faith and Hope. The inside of the cover and the dial, with their landscape scenes, are shown on the right of the Plate. The edge is painted with six landscape scenes with figures. A small portrait bust, painted probably soon after 1650, is on the Dutch watch on Plate XXXV.

Coming to a later date, 1680-90, a marked change is found in the paintings. On Plate XXXIV, 4 is a watch with enamel signed by a famous painter, Huaud le puisné. Though the technique is perfect, the colours are hard and inclined to be garish. The case inside has a river scene with castle and figure, and within the hour ring on the dial is painted a seated woman with a basket of flowers.

Painters on Enamel.—The Huaud or Huaut family of enamellers started with Pierre, a master goldsmith of Geneva, who was working in 1635 and died 1680. He is known to have painted on enamel, but no work of his is extant. His eldest son, Pierre, has left several signed paintings, and watches with enamels by him are in the Louvre and Olivier collections. He was born in 1647 in Geneva, went to the Court of Brandenburg in 1685 and, after revisiting Geneva, returned to Germany

145

PLATE XXXVIII

1

Four views of a French watch by Nicolas Bernard, Paris, mid-seventeenth century. Gold case with painted enamel on all surfaces. On the outsides of the case and cover are figure scenes emblematic of Faith and Hope and of Charity. On the insides of the case and cover and in the centre of the dial are landscape scenes. The edge has six landscape scenes with figures. Nicolas Bernard, second of the name, was signatory to the Statutes of the Paris Corporation in 1646. Two other watches by him are known.
South Kensington Museum.   pp. 145, 148.

2 (Centre)

English watch by Simon Hackett, London, *c.* 1640. Gold case, with a small central scene on the back in painted enamel, of a man on horseback on a white ground ; surrounding this is a broad band of translucent orange enamel on a guilloché ground. The edge has hunting scenes in painted enamel. The bezel, also enamelled, has a snapped-in glass. The dial has in the centre a landscape scene with figures. Simon Hackett was a founder member of the Clockmakers' Company, and was master of it in 1646, 1647, and 1659. Three other watches by him are known.
South Kensington Museum.   p. 149.

146

PLATE XXXVIII

in 1689 and was appointed painter to the Elector of Brandenburg in 1691 ; he died about 1698. He did by far the best work of his family, signing 'Huaud l'aisné,' 'P. Huaud primogenitus,' 'P. Huaud P.G.,' with other variations. The second son, Jean Pierre, the painter of the watch just mentioned, was born in Geneva in 1655 and died in 1723. Most of his work was done in association with his younger brother Amy, who was born in 1657 and died in 1729. They were appointed painters to the Court of Prussia in 1686, and after this date their paintings were signed 'Les Frères Huaud,' 'Les deux frères Huaud' or 'Fratres Huault,' generally with the addition of their title, as 'peintres de son A.E. à Berlin,' 'p.d. V.A. fct à Berlin' or 'les jeunes.' Watches with paintings by them are fairly common, and examples are found in all the principal museums. Their work is frequently given too early a date ; it is fairly well established by Clouzot[1] that they did not sign as *Les frères* before 1686.

There are but few enamel painters of the seventeenth century who have signed work on watches. Besides the Blois enamellers mentioned, there are :—Pierre Bordier, who became a master about 1629 and enamelled a watch presented by the English Parliament to General Fairfax. Pierre Lignac, a pupil of the Toutins, born about 1624 and died 1684 ; he went to Sweden in 1645, and a watch enamelled by him is in Stockholm. Jean André of Geneva, a pupil of the first Pierre Huaud, born 1646 and died 1714 ; three watches by him are known, one in the Côte collection. Camille André, probably of the same family, enamelled a watch in the British Museum by Tompion. Jean Louis Durand of Geneva enamelled a watch in the Gélis collection towards the end of the century. Jean Mussard of Geneva, born 1681 and died 1754, enamelled several watches, one in the British Museum by Gribelin, of which the dial is shown on Plate L, 2.

[1] *Les Frères Huaud.* Paris, 1907.

Painted Enamel Dials.—The dials of watches with paintings on enamel always have a painted scene, generally a landscape of ruins and trees, with some water and figures. The hand is always gilt, with the centre engraved as a sunflower. Examples of this type of dial are on Plates XXXV, XXXVII and XXXVIII.

A dial with painting which dates, probably, from the earliest days of enamel painting, is that of the crystal cross watch on Plate XXIII. The painting of the emblems of the Passion is of the simplest character, as if the brush on the enamel had replaced the graver on the metal.

In later painted enamel watches a figure scene in the centre of the dial is more common. The square watch at the bottom of Plate XXVI, in the Cluny Museum, Paris, is a fine example. This watch is by Pierre De Baufre, the probable maker of the beautiful watches on Plates XXXVI, 2 and XLVIII, 2. The watch with paintings by Huaud le puisné on Plate XXXIV, 4 has, on its dial, a scene of a seated woman with a basket of flowers on her lap. An early type of enamel dial which is found occasionally is on the crystal watch in the centre of Plate L. The hour ring is white, with the figures painted in black, as in nearly all enamel dials; the centre is light blue with, at the rim, a lace-like tracery composed of black markings on a white ground. It is curious that the tracery pattern has 14 and not 12 divisions.

Enamel on Glass.—A most unusual type of enamel work for watches is shown on the watch on Plate XXXIII, 4. The case has a layer of translucent blue glass or enamel, about one-fifth of an inch thick, and sunk in this is a design of flowers and foliage in opaque enamel and translucent enamel backed with gold. It has been suggested that this is an example of *émail en résille sur verre*, in which a plate of glass is cut with a pattern and the sunken portions filled with enamel, generally with a *paillon* backing. The Author, however, after a close examination of the work, believes it to be an example of cloisonné enamel, and that a thick ground of translucent

148

blue enamel was built up, cloisons attached to the enamel, with *paillons*, and the whole enamelled with translucent blue outside the cloisons, and opaque and translucent enamel of different colours inside them. Whatever the method of construction, it is an interesting and rare type of watch-case. The example shown is in the South Kensington Museum and has 'Blois' engraved on the plate, without maker's name. A case without movement, almost exactly like it, is in the British Museum, and another, with the same character of work, in the Louvre. All three belong, probably, to the first quarter of the seventeenth century.

Examples of enamel work on glass or crystal are very rare. There is one in the Metropolitan Museum, New York, by J. Vernede of Agen, an octagonal crystal watch, with a floral design engraved in the crystal and filled with enamel. The watch belongs to the first quarter of the seventeenth century.

Basse-taille Enamel.—Basse-taille enamel on a ground of any size is rare in the seventeenth century. In watches it became fashionable at the end of the eighteenth century, when engine-turning was introduced, but it is found early in the seventeenth century on guilloché ground, a ground worked over with a round graver in little scoops. It is the precursor of engine-turning, which, in France, retains the name. An example of the work is seen on the watch in the centre of Plate XXXVIII, covered with translucent orange enamel. The small paintings in the centre and round the edge of the watch, though they belong to the good period, are far from the level of the French enamels that are illustrated. The watch is by Simon Hackett of London, an original member of the Clockmakers' Company and, in 1646, Master of the Company. The watch is of a date probably a little before the middle of the century. Similar work is sometimes found on dials. The agate watch on Plate XX, 5 is an example, though here almost all the enamel has cracked off, leaving only a patch outside the hour ring.

149

PLATE XXXIX

1

English watch by James Barton, London, 1771. Gold outer case with painted enamel portrait of John Harrison. James Barton was John Harrison's son-in-law, and made the watch the year after Harrison received the award for 'finding the Longitude.'
Webster coll.   p. 219.

2

Watch, unsigned, *c.* 1700. Silver case, repoussé and engraved with a hunting scene, surrounding an opening containing a representation of the Garden of Eden, with Adam and Eve in ivory, partly coloured, within a pierced and engraved silver frame.
Cluny Museum.   p. 152.

3

Movement of German watch, *c.* 1600, showing stackfreed and dumb-bell foliot.
British Museum.

4

English watch by Edward Bysse, London, first quarter of the seventeenth century. Silver case inlaid with niello in a chequer pattern. Bysse was a founder member of the Clockmakers' Company.
British Museum.   p. 151.

5

English watch by Thomas Sande, first quarter of the seventeenth century. Cast silver case with chequer pattern, alternate squares being sunk and hatched.
British Museum.   p. 125.

6

German striking watch, unsigned, late sixteenth century. Gilt metal case with pierced edge. Gilt engraved dial plate with sundial and folding stile, a dial on the right with the cardinal points, and a dial on the left relating the age and phases of the moon.
Cluny Museum.   p. 94.

PLATE XXXIX

Inlay.—Inlay work is rare in watches at any period, and is almost confined to niello, which is sometimes found on early watches before and after 1600. Niello is an old process, not uncommon in Byzantine work, and consists in inlaying silver with an alloy of silver, lead and copper, mixed with sulphur to produce sulphides of the metals. This alloy retains a black surface which contrasts well with the surrounding silver. The work is not strictly inlay, because the alloy is run into the sunken portions of the silver in a molten state. In town museums the silver blackens nearly to the colour of the inlay and gives the work a dull appearance.

The fritillary watch on the left of Plate xxxix is an example of niello work in a chequer pattern. The watch, in the British Museum, is by Edward Bysse, an original member of the Clockmakers' Company, and dates, probably, from the first quarter of the seventeenth century. The watch on its right has already been mentioned as being engraved work that may be intended to resemble niello.

Britten mentions an English watch with outer case of steel damascened with silver, of a date near the end of the seventeenth century; the illustration, however, shows the front of the watch and very little of the inlay work. The Author has never seen an early watch with damascene work.

Cases of Amber and Ivory.—So far, only two kinds of material have been used in the watches examined, metal and stone. Cases of other material are very rare. The two views at the bottom of Plate xxxii show a watch in a case of amber, in the Garnier collection in the Louvre. The block of amber, cut in the form of a poppy-head, carries an engraved and gilt edging attached by six gold wires running between the lobes and joined to the pendant, and the movement and cover are hinged to the edging. The dial is of silver, champlevé in a design including a snail and a dragon-fly, and enamelled in blue, green and yellow. It is a most attractive little watch, and, unfortunately, is not signed. It must date from early in the seventeenth century and is mentioned in the Louvre catalogue as German work. It is the only amber watch known.

Ivory watch-cases, with parts of the movement also of ivory, are not uncommon; in the Fitzwilliam Museum is one with a stackfreed movement largely made of ivory. But the Author has never seen one which appears really to belong to the seventeenth century. The end of the eighteenth century was a period when many things were made in ivory, and, among others, watch-cases and movements, and most of the ivory watches of early types date from this period.

The watch on Plate XXXIX, 2, though rather late for this chapter, may be mentioned here, because it has a most curious form of decoration in ivory and silver. Sunk in the back of the watch is a repoussé and engraved background representing the garden of Eden, and on this are figures of Adam and Eve in ivory, with their fig-leaves and the serpent and apple coloured. The scene is behind a silver frame, pierced and chiselled in foliage, with a bear, a tortoise, a snail and a dog. The watch-case is of silver, repoussé and engraved in a stag-hunting scene. It is in the Cluny Museum, Paris, and dates from about 1700.

Outer Cases.—Outer cases of watches offered a fresh field for decorative work because they had no need for the strength and rigidity of the case that had to carry the movement, and so could be made of materials unsuited to the main case.

The fragile watch, or the work of art it bore, obviously needed a case, either to keep it in when not in use or to protect it when worn in a pocket. The repoussé cross on Plate XXII has a wooden case covered with leather, too clumsy for wear. The pierced and enamelled watch on Plate XXXI, I has a plain case of thin silver, and the lower of the two centre watches on the same Plate has a thin gold case engraved with Biblical scenes. These two cases were clearly intended for use when the watch was worn. There is, though, a third type of case, intended for ornament and not for protection. An example of this is on the watch in the centre of Plate LVII, which has a perfectly plain case of blued steel fitting in the case of gold filigree. This is another way of arriving at the attractive combination of gold *à jour* work on a blue ground found in the square watch on the right of Plate XXVI.

The most usual decorative outer cases were of leather, studded with gold or silver, and tortoiseshell piqué silver. On Plate XLV are shown two of these cases, the lower of leather, dating from about 1670, and the upper an exceptionally fine one of piqué tortoiseshell, dating from about 1700. Another studded leather case of the late seventeenth century is on Plate XLVII. Shagreen, too, and fish-skins of different kinds were not uncommon.

Later, especially in the eighteenth century, the outer case came to be more an integral part of the watch than a protective covering for occasional use; and it was generally of the same metal as the main case. An early example is the fluted silver case of the watch at the top of Plate XLIX. Most of the fine repoussé work of the eighteenth century was done on gold outer cases, and then it was common to have a third case acting as a protective covering.

Pendants.—The sixteenth- and early seventeenth-century watch has a pendant with a hole from back to front. The pendant is generally a small knob, as in the two watches on the top of Plate XXVI. Often, and more especially in watches near the beginning of the century, the pendant is decorated, as in the cross watch on Plate XXXVI, 5 and the watches on Plates XIII, XVI and XVII.

The pendant knobs, however, being usually riveted to the case, are frequently loose and can turn so that the hole can face in any direction, but a fixed pendant, with hole from side to side, is extremely rare before 1650. The watch by East at the bottom of Plate XXXV, with quite a special form of pendant, is an example ; the watch, though, is about 1650.

Early in the second half of the century another form of pendant came in, but did not oust the old form till the end of the century. The watch at the top of Plate XII shows this form of pendant, with a ring pivoted to the pendant knob. Modifications of this pendant are seen in the small watch on Plate XXX and the enamel watch on Plate XXXVI, 1.

Watch-glasses.—It is uncertain when glass first began to be used in the front covers of watches, because it is impossible to say whether the glass found in a watch belongs to the date of the watch. The first glasses were made by blowing spheres and cutting circles out of them, and they can often be recognized as being portions of spheres and looking rather bulbous. Balet[1] says that glass was the rule about 1610, but, though it was, no doubt, used at that date, the Author inclines to the view that it was not common before 1630.

Rock-crystal was used from the beginning of the seventeenth century, and not always because it was transparent. The cutting on the rock-crystal cover of the watch of Plate XXIII quite prevents the time being seen without opening the cover. This watch shows the most usual way in early watches of fixing the crystal with small tags. Occasionally a separate ring was used as a means of holding the crystal, the ring having a double series of tags, one series being bent outwards inside the edge of the cover and the other series bent inwards over the crystal.

The fixing by tags was used well into the second half of the century, but before the middle it became more common to split the bezel (the frame holding the crystal or glass) at the hinge, so that, on removing the bezel, it could be sprung open enough to allow the crystal to be inserted in a groove. The split in the bezel is visible in the square watch on Plate XXVI, 1.

[1] *Führer durch die Uhrensammlung.* Stuttgart, 1913.

154

The modern watch glass is 'snapped in'; the bezel has a slightly undercut groove, and the glass can just be forced past the upper edge of the bezel and then falls with a snap into the undercut portion of the groove, in which it fits more freely. This method was introduced probably soon after the middle of the seventeenth century. The split bezel continued to the end of the century, but became unusual towards the end.

This concludes the great period of the decorated watch-case, embracing practically all the types of ornament found on later watches. Some types, such as the engraved work, gradually disappeared, while others, such as the repoussé work, became fashionable. These changes will be followed in Chapters IX. and X.

'I frown the while ; and perchance wind
up my watch, or play with some rich jewel.'
Twelfth Night.

CHAPTER VII

PENDULUM AND BALANCE SPRING

'Axis Circuli mobilis affixus in Centro Volutae ferreae.'

Solution of HUYGENS' *anagram disclosing his invention of the balance spring*, 1675.

IN 1656 Christiaan Huygens made accurate time-keeping possible for clocks by applying a pendulum to them,[1] and in 1675 he did the same for watches by inventing the spiral balance spring. In both cases there is some question of Huygens' priority. Galileo Galilei, according to a letter written by his pupil Viviani, described a clock with a pendulum to his son Vincenzo in 1641 and gave a drawing of it. Vincenzo began to make the clock in 1649, employing a mechanic Domenico Balestri, but owing to his death it was never finished, and the parts were sold by Vincenzo's widow. A clock made after the drawing can be seen working in the Science Museum at South Kensington.

An earlier claimant is Leonardo da Vinci. A number of his drawings, both in the Codice Atlantico and in the Ravaisson-Mollien edition of his sketch-books, show clocks of various kinds and detached bits of clockwork, and several of them have been supposed to show indications of pendulum clocks.[2] In only two, however, can the Author see a pendulum applied to a clock escapement. The drawings in Codice Atlantico, 257 recto, and Ravaisson-Mollien MSS. H, fol. 110 verso, both show

---

[1] The application was patented in Holland in 1657 and published in 1658 in a small pamphlet. The full publication was in Paris, 1673, under the title *Horologium Oscillatorium sive de motu pendulorum ad horologia aptato demonstrationes geometricae.* A translation of this work, with commentary, is published in Ostwald's *Klassiker*, No. 192. Leipzig, 1913.

[2] Codice Atlantico, fol. 60 verso, 257 recto a, and 378 recto. Ravaisson-Mollien MSS. B, fol. 20 recto and 54 recto, and MSS. H, fol. 110 verso.

156

an escape-wheel placed horizontally, with the teeth on its upper surface in the former and on its under surface in the latter; the wheel drives a pinion connected with, in one case, a rather vaguely sketched train of wheels and, in the other, what looks like a drum. Across the escape-wheel is a horizontally placed verge with pallets engaging the teeth, and from the verge depends a rod with a block at its lower end. There is little doubt that both of these indicate pendulums applied to verge escapements, presumably for the purpose of a clock. The date attributed to MSS. H is 1493-4, a century and a half before Galilei and Huygens.

Another claim is that of Jost Bodeker of Warburg, who, in 1587, made a clock for the Osnabrück Dom, which he fitted with the ordinary foliot and also with a device alternative to the foliot escapement. He left an obscure description of this, but there is little doubt that it was a conical pendulum, that is to say, a pendulum swinging, not to and fro in a plane, but so that its bob describes a circle and its rod a cone. Veltman, in a pamphlet entitled *Jost Bodeker von Wartbergh* [Warburg] *der Erfinder des Pendels nicht Galilei?*[1], quotes the description left by Jost Bodeker and gives him all the credit due to Huygens. This is quite unjustified. Bodeker would be entitled to great credit if he really did devise a successful conical pendulum clock, because it would have been an immense advance over the foliot clock. But nothing is known of the subsequent history of his clock; it is not even known whether the clock worked with the foliot or with the conical pendulum. A conical pendulum clock, too, is much inferior to a clock with ordinary pendulum; though used for driving astronomical telescopes because it gives a continuous motion, it has not been used for timekeeping except in rare instances. Bodeker, in all probability, made a great invention, but one not in any way comparable to Huygens.'[2]

[1] Wetzlar, 1917.
[2] Von Bassermann-Jordan, in his recent book *Alte Uhren und ihre Meister*

157

The invention has been claimed also for Justus Burgi, astronomer and clockmaker to the Landgrave Wilhelm IV. of Hessen from 1579 and to the Emperor Rudolph II. from 1603-22, on the ground that a clock made by him had been seen with a pendulum. In the absence of any evidence that the pendulum had not been added later, this claim need not be considered seriously.

Another claim, put forward by De Fleury, Archiviste de la Charente,[1] is based on the slender evidence of a letter from Carcavy to Huygens, dated 1659, as follows, in translation :—

As I went yesterday to get a clock made according to your invention, I found an honest man, M. de Boismorand by name, who assured me that he had had, a long time ago, a clock of the same kind, at any rate with a pendulum, which was made about 1615 or 1616 by a German, for the late Queen Dowager, Marie de Médicis, and was not taken by her by reason of her departure from Angoulême. . . .

Researches made it fairly certain that the German referred to was a Georgius Kloss who was in Angoulême in 1603. It may be noted that Carcavy did not even see the clock.

Questions of priority of invention are always difficult to decide, but in this case there is no doubt that Huygens could have obtained a patent, under to-day's patent laws, as being the first and true inventor of the ordinary pendulum applied to a clock. Leonardo da Vinci's and Galilei's drawings would not have been considered anticipations, because they were not published ; Huygens was the first to give the invention to the world.

It is fairly certain that Leonardo da Vinci conceived the idea of applying a pendulum to a clock, but, as he never pursued it, he cannot have realized the importance of the application. The quite small mechanical change

(Leipzig, 1926), has, with great ingenuity, drawn a clock based on Jost Bodeker's description. He refers to Veltman's pamphlet, with its claims, in strong language, and goes to the other extreme in refusing Bodeker the credit due to him. Veltman has done his hero a disservice in asking too much for him.

[1] *Bull. et Mém. de la Soc. Arch. de la Charente*, 1890-1.

needed to turn a foliot clock into a pendulum clock hardly constituted an invention, in the absence of any understanding of what the change meant.

Galilei probably had this understanding. He had discovered the approximate law of the pendulum, and his use of a free-swinging pendulum for his astronomical work, by counting its swings, shows that he realized it was the best timekeeper available. It was a logical step to connect it with clockwork to produce a convenient and continuously working timekeeper; in connecting it, too, he did not merely modify the existing form of clock, but devised an entirely different form of escapement.

These prior conceptions do not detract from Huygens' merit as the inventor of the pendulum clock. With no knowledge of what Galilei had done, he applied the pendulum to a clock, published and obtained a privilege for his invention, and exploited it commercially through the Rotterdam clockmaker, Salomon Koster. Within a few years it had ousted the foliot.

The Balance Spring.—Hooke's position in the invention of the balance spring is like Galilei's in that of the pendulum. Hooke's own notes on the subject are[1] :—

I applied myself to the improving of the pendulum for such [astronomical] purposes, and in the year 1656 or 1657 I tried a way to continue the motion of the pendulum, so much commended by Ricciolus in his Almagestum. I made some trials to this end, which I found to succeed to my wish.

The success of these made me further think of improving it for finding the Longitude and . . . quickly led me to the use of springs instead of gravity for the making a body vibrate in any position.

Hooke, about 1660, explained his invention to Boyle, Lord Brouncker and Sir Robert Moray, and

showed a pocket watch accommodated with a spring, applied to the Arbor of the Ballance to regulate the motion thereof; concealing the way I had for finding the longitude.

[1] *The Posthumous Works of Robert Hooke*, by Richard Waller. London, 1705.

159

He endeavoured to make an agreement for financing his invention with the three, but did not agree on the terms.

Five years later it became known that Huygens was having watches made with a spring applied to the balance, and Sir Robert Moray wrote to Oldenburg :—

You will be the first that knows when his [Huygens'] watches will be ready, and I will therefore expect from you an account of them, and if he imparts to you what he does, let me know it ; to that purpose you may ask him if he doth not apply a spring to the Arbor of the Ballance, and that will give him occasion to say somewhat to you ; if it be that, you may tell him what Hooke has done in that matter, and what he intends more.

A spring applied to the arbor of the balance can be only a spiral spring. Hooke, therefore, had the conception of a spiral balance spring some fifteen years before Huygens produced a watch with such a spring. One wonders why Hooke did not produce his watches, knowing the great importance of the invention, and knowing that Huygens was at work on the same lines. Two extracts from contemporary documents indicate a possible reason. Huygens, in 1675, wrote to Denis Papin, then in London, to keep an eye on the going of the watches that were being tried in London with balances of his invention, and Papin replied :—

Je n'ai pas plus veu M. Hooke et quand j'ay demandé des nouvelles de sa montre à M. Oldenbourg, il m'a dit . . . qu'elle ne paroistroit point.[1]

Oldenburg, in 1675, wrote [2] :—

'Tis certain, then, that the Describer of the Helioscope [Hooke] some years ago caused to be actually made some watches of this kind, yet without publishing to the world a description of it *in print* ; but it is as certain that none of these watches *succeeded*, nor that anything was done since to mend the invention, and to render it useful, that we know of until

[1] *La Vie et les Ouvrages de Denis Papin.* L. de la Saussaye. Paris and Blois, 1869.
[2] *Phil. Trans.* 118.

Monsieur Hugens, who is also a member of the Royal Society as well as of the Royal Academy at Paris, sent hither a letter dated January 30, 1674/75, acquainting us with an invention of his of very exact Pocket Watches, the nature and Contrivance of which he imparted to us (as he is wont to do other inventions of his) in an Anagram ; which he soon after, in a letter of February 20, 1674/75, explained to us by a full description.

Hooke replied vigorously to this statement by Oldenburg in a Postscript to his *Lampas* (1677), but the fact that he never showed a watch publicly makes it probable that Oldenburg was correct.

Another claimant to the invention of the balance spring was the Abbé de Hautefeuille, who contested Huygens' claim in a pamphlet *Factum touchant les Pendules de Poche*, published in Paris 1675, but the Académie des Sciences determined the question in favour of Huygens. It is probable that the Abbé de Hautefeuille used either a straight or a wavy length of steel spring in the same way as a bristle was used in the watch illustrated in Plate XVII, 1.

Hooke certainly was the first to have the conception. Huygens was the first to publish the invention fully to the world and to have watches made that were successful.

The Balance Spring and Timekeeping.—The two inventions of pendulum and balance spring amount to the same thing in essence; they were not mere improvements, but radical changes in the principles of clocks and watches. The foliot, by itself, had no timekeeping properties; it had to be connected with an escapement and driven by a weight or spring before any timekeeping resulted; a change in the weight or in the friction of the train affected the timekeeping of the clock as much as a change in the form or size of the foliot. The whole of the foliot clock took part in the timekeeping. The pendulum changed all that; it is a timekeeper by itself, and the most perfect timekeeper there is. It wants a clock mechanism connected with it for two purposes only, first to keep it swinging, secondly to count its swings.

The clock mechanism plays, or should play, no part in the timekeeping; no alteration in the weight or in the friction of the train should have any effect. The less the clock mechanism interferes with the pendulum, the better the timekeeping. In a clock recently installed in Greenwich Observatory, the pendulum swings entirely free of any connexion with the clock mechanism except for a brief instant once every half-minute; it is, perhaps, the best timekeeper in existence.

Exactly the same applies to the balance spring of a watch. A balance fitted with a spiral spring, if disconnected from the watch mechanism and set swinging, will oscillate at a definite rate; it wants the watch mechanism only to keep it swinging and to count the swings. Apart from improvements in the balance spring itself, progress in watches has been almost entirely in producing escapements which leave the balance as far as possible disconnected from the watch mechanism. With the lever escapement, which is fitted to nearly all modern watches, the balance has no connexion with the watch mechanism for about seven-eighths of its swing. With the chronometer escapement, the connexion is for even a shorter proportion.

In this respect the verge escapement was thoroughly bad; it never left the pendulum or balance free, and interfered so much with their natural motion as to vitiate their timekeeping properties. The pendulum and balance spring, therefore, when first applied to clocks and watches, were far from giving the results of which they were capable. Even so they effected a great improvement, and in one or two decades their use became general. Watchmakers, however, took a long time to realize that they had been given a new principle to work on, and even Berthoud, one of the foremost makers of his day, and one of the few who regarded his craft as a science, showed in his writings that he did not appreciate the full significance of the pendulum.

Isochronism.—Galileo, when making his observations

on the pendulum, had, of course, no accurate timekeeper, and he concluded — wrongly — that a pendulum was isochronous, that is to say, that a pendulum of given length made its swings, whether large or small, in the same period of time. The fact is that a large swing takes a longer time than a small swing. The difference is very small, far smaller than Galileo was able to measure. A pendulum which beats seconds when it swings through a very small arc of two degrees will take nearly three ten-thousandths of a second longer over a swing of ten degrees. This does not sound much, but it corresponds to a difference of nearly forty seconds in the daily rate of a clock.

Huygens found out mathematically this variation of period with arc, and devised a method of suspending the pendulum which made it isochronous. It is never used, because it introduces a greater error than that which it corrects. The error in isochronism is negligible in ordinary clocks and can be made negligible in accurate clocks, first by keeping the swing of the pendulum small, when a variation has very little effect, and secondly by making the variation small by keeping the driving force as constant as possible. It is curious to note that the part of Huygens' invention which is never used was the part of which he was particularly proud.

With a balance and spiral spring the position is different. A balance is isochronous if its swing satisfies certain conditions ; if they are not satisfied, the balance can be far from isochronous. With the verge escapement, it did not matter whether the balance was isochronous or not ; it was influenced too much by the escapement. When better escapements were introduced, watchmakers began the search for isochronism. It was far more important in a watch than in a pendulum clock, because in a watch the variations in the driving force, and, consequently, the variations in the swing of the balance, are far wider, and also because the want of isochronism can be so much greater in a balance than in a pendulum.

Empirical rules for obtaining an isochronous balance were formulated, more or less applicable to particular cases, but quite inapplicable generally. A few men—the great watchmakers Pierre Le Roy and Arnold in particular—obtained good results with experiment as their only guide; but it was not till 1861 that Phillips, an engineer who had nothing to do with watchmaking, published a memoir on the geometry of the balance spring, and laid down the condition to be satisfied to make the balance isochronous and also the way to satisfy it. The condition is very simple: the centre of gravity of the spring must lie on the axis of the balance. The spring then opens and closes symmetrically and exercises no side pressure on the balance. The way to satisfy this condition is to fix the inner and outer ends of the spring in certain relative positions and to shape the ends of the spring to certain curves. Phillips published a large number of suitable end curves in his memoir, and they have been republished many times since. With these curves before him, any watchmaker can fit a spring to a balance so as to make it isochronous, if—a big if—he possesses the skill requisite to bend the ends of the spring, which is, perhaps, only one-quarter of an inch in diameter, to the forms of one pair of Phillips' curves, and to find the spring, when bent, of the right length. It is not the job of an ordinary watchmaker; it is the job of a specialist—the springer.

Phillips' memoir, however, was on the balance spring only, not on the watch. Phillips dealt only with the geometry of the spring, not with a material spring; there is a difference, but it is very small. What is wanted is that the balance in the watch, with its escapement, should be isochronous, and this is a different thing. Generally, an isochronous balance, when fitted in a watch, is no longer isochronous. The action of the escapement on the balance and the action of the balance on the escapement affect the time of swing of the balance, and—this is the important point—affect it differently for large and small swings. The effect with the lever escapement of to-day is to make the watch go slow when the swing of the balance diminishes. Every owner of a cheap watch—that is to say, most people—have found this to be so. As a watch gets dirty and its oil dries up, more of the power of the mainspring is used up in friction of the train and less reaches the balance; consequently, the swing of the balance diminishes and the watch loses. The springer can compensate for this by altering the end curves of the spring from the Phillips curves, in a way that would make the balance swing more quickly when it swings less if it were free of the escapement. In this way, when combined with the escapement, it can be made isochronous. There is also an effect in the opposite direction, giving a partial compensation, when the spring is fitted to a balance compensated for temperature in the usual way. This type of balance is not a wheel but is formed of two flexible arms bent to circular form, and the effect of centrifugal force is to make the balance larger as the swing increases. The result is, that a balance fitted with an isochronous spring swings, on this account, more quickly as it swings less. The effect is more important in chronometers than in watches.

Phillips' memoir, though it does not tell a watchmaker how to adjust a watch, and did not pretend to, marks an epoch in the history of watchmaking, because it provided a solid foundation for the system of springing and adjusting watches and chronometers that now exists and produces results of wonderful accuracy. Arnold curved the ends of the cylindrical springs of his chronometers in a way that, at the time, was regarded as mysterious. He, in fact, discovered by experiment some of Phillips' end curves. He was granted a patent in 1782 which included these end curves.

Types of Balance Spring.—There are three main kinds of balance springs. First, the ordinary flat spiral that was used in all watches up to the nineteenth century.

The early springs, Plate XL, 2, were very short, some having only one or two turns; they gradually became longer, but, with the verge escapement, four or five turns was the usual length. The balance spring of to-day, No. 3, has about thirteen turns. Second, there is the cylindrical spiral, No. 1, which is used in all chronometers. It is the best form of spring and was fitted to some of the watches known as pocket-chronometers, but requires too much room for use in a modern watch. The third form of spring is now used in all good watches and in many cheap ones. It is called the *Breguet* or *overcoil* spring, No. 4, and is an ordinary flat spiral with its outer coil bent up and curved towards the centre over the other coils.

Flat spiral balance springs are fixed at their inner end to a *collet*, which is pressed on to the balance staff, and at their outer ends to a fixed *stud*. The collet and a stud are shown in Plate XL, 2, 3 and 4. The collet is a small ring of brass, which is split so that it can be sprung on to the balance staff; the end of the spring passes through a hole in the collet and is wedged in by a pin. The stud, in verge watches, was fixed to the top plate, and the spring lay immediately above the plate and below the balance. In modern watches, as in No. 3, the spring is above the balance, between it and the cock, and the stud is fixed to the cock.

In No. 2, the balance wheel, with three arms, is shown in dotted lines; it is above the parts shown in the drawing. In No. 3, the cock is shown removed from its position over the balance. The stud is square below, where the spring passes through it, and is often made triangular above, the triangular portion passing through a hole in the cock, which has a small screw to fix it. The triangular end and fixing screw are seen in the drawing of the cock.

Phillips, in his memoir, dealt mainly with the chronometer spring, and secondarily with the Breguet spring; he found that the ordinary flat spiral spring could not be

166

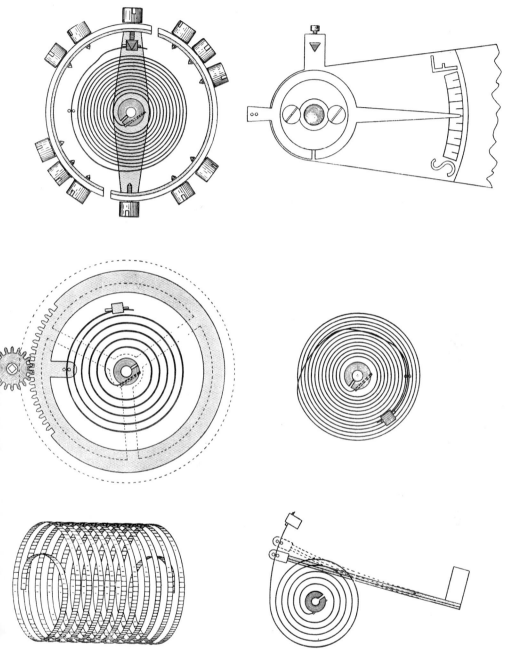

PLATE XL

BALANCE SPRINGS

made isochronous, except for very small swings. It is not, however, impossible to make it isochronous when fitted to a balance in a watch.[1] The flat spiral is necessarily unsatisfactory because, its outer coil being fixed to the stud, it cannot open and close, as the balance swings, on the side where it is fixed ; it has to open and close on the other side, with the result that it exercises a varying pressure sideways on the balance staff, and increases the friction in the place where friction is most harmful.

The Breguet spring, with its overcoil, can be made to satisfy Phillips' condition by properly shaping the overcoil, and then the spring opens and closes symmetrically all round, and exercises no side pressure on the balance staff. In a Breguet spring (Plate XL, 4), the inner end is attached to the collet in the same way as in the ordinary spring, but the outer coil is bent upwards, just before the point where it is seen crossing over the spiral coils. The curve which it follows is only one out of an infinite number of possible curves which satisfy the condition. The end of the overcoil curve is fixed to the stud, which is above the spiral coils. The difference in action of the two springs is easily seen in a watch. The ordinary flat spiral appears to bulge out on one side as it opens. The Breguet spring expands uniformly all round. But a watch repairer, who often knows nothing of springing, will sometimes make a Breguet spring bulge as much as any other.

Regulation.—When the balance spring came into use the watch was regulated, apparently from the first, by altering the effective length of the spring. The outer end of the spring was, as explained, fixed to a stud on the top plate, but a short distance from this the spring passed between two pins called *curb pins* (Plate XL, 2), spaced to allow only just easy passage of the spring, so that their

---

[1] This is not quite accurate ; it is impossible to make the balance isochronous *whatever be the cause of variation* in the swing of the balance ; it is possible only for a given cause—for instance, for varying power transmitted to the escape wheel.

position determined the effective length of the spring. The curb pins were fixed in a circularly curved plate which could be slid round the balance in a circular groove, so as to change the position of the pins. The shorter the effective length of the spring is made, the more quickly will the balance swing. Sometimes a pointer was fixed to the plate carrying the curb pins, so that it could be pushed round by the finger-nail, but, more commonly, the plate had teeth formed in it, as shown in the drawing, engaging with the teeth of a pinion turning in the top plate. A silver disk was generally fixed to the pinion marked with numbers, which had no meaning beyond the convention that, if the pinion were turned so that the number increased (as indicated by a pointer or through an opening), the watch went faster. In a few early cases the outer end of the spring was left straight, and the curb pins were moved along the straight portion by a screw device.

The spring is wound in a spiral until the outer half-turn, and this is bent to a circular form, so that the curb pins can move in their circular path without displacing the spring. The outer coil in No. 3 is first bent away from the other coils to give room for the curb pins, and is then bent to a circle. In the Breguet spring in No. 4, the curve of the overcoil ends in a circular portion round which the curb pins turn. Properly, a Breguet spring should have no regulating curb pins, because the curve of the overcoil is correct only when it is of one definite length, and any movement of the curb pins alters its length and partially destroys its effect. For this reason the highest grade of watch has no regulator, and can be timed only by means of the weights of its balance, screwing them in or out to make the watch go faster or slower. Such a watch is called a *rated* watch; the maker may deliver it with the statement that it has, say, a gaining rate of one minute a week, and its accuracy is shown in keeping to this *rate* and continuing to gain one minute a week, not in always showing the correct time.

168

In the more modern watch, the curb pins are fixed to the *index* or *regulator*, which is mounted on the upper part of the cock. The two pins alone are shown in the drawing of the balance (upper drawing of Plate XL, 3), and, in the drawing of the cock, their ends are seen on the projection from the index. The index is ring-shaped and springs on to a circular boss on the cock, round which it can turn stiffly to regulate the watch. The index for a Breguet spring is similar, but the curb pins and the stud have to be fixed closer to the centre of the balance.

To indicate the direction for regulation, the initial letters, either of Fast and Slow or of Avance and Retard, are engraved on the cock. Sometimes the language difficulty was solved by engraving a hare and a snail.

Temperature Compensation.—The timekeeping of a watch of 1700 was so poor that the effect of changes of temperature was quite negligible. Even in 1800 it was still negligible except for the highest class of watch, but, before this, the marine chronometer had reached a degree of accuracy which made the effect of temperature changes sensible, and called for some means of compensation. The marine chronometer is no more than a watch in which everything is sacrificed to accuracy. Size being one of the things sacrificed, the marine chronometer is not a pocket instrument, and its history is outside the range of this book. Moreover, since the publication of Commander Gould's splendid book on the subject,[1] there is nothing more to be said. The chronometer is mentioned here because the history of temperature compensation is part of the history of the chronometer.

The first step is to appreciate what is the effect of change of temperature on the going of an ordinary watch. There are three effects. A rise of temperature causes the metal of the balance to expand, making the balance larger. If the balance were of brass, this expansion would make the watch lose a little over one and a half seconds a day for a rise of one degree centigrade. It also causes the

[1] *The Marine Chronometer.* Rupert Gould. London, 1923.

metal of the spring to expand, which tends to make the spring stiffer. The effect of this, with a steel spring, would be to make the watch gain a little under one and a half seconds a day. The two effects of a rise of temperature, in expanding the two metals, balance one another very nearly—within about one-tenth of a second a day for the rise of one degree centigrade considered. The third effect is the important one. A rise of temperature produces a change in the metal of the spring which renders it less stiff. In engineering language, it diminishes its modulus of elasticity. The effect is a loss of nearly eleven seconds a day for a rise of one degree centigrade. This is quite a serious loss; it corresponds to a difference of two to three minutes a day between wearing a watch in the pocket and letting it lie on a table. A marine chronometer, without compensation for variations of this order, would have been of little use, even in the eighteenth century.

In 1714 the British Government offered 'a publick reward for such person or persons as shall discover the Longitude.' The scale of reward for determining a ship's longitude was :—

£10,000 for an accuracy of 1 degree
£15,000   ,,   ,,   ,,   ,, $\frac{2}{3}$,,
£20,000   ,,   ,,   ,,   ,, $\frac{1}{2}$,,

There are various possible ways of finding a ship's longitude, but the only practicable one is by a timekeeper, and the conditions of the reward meant that a time-keeper on a ship sailing from England to the West Indies must not lose or gain (on its rate) more than two minutes in the voyage. Clearly, such a timekeeper must be compensated for temperature, and, in fact, every serious attempt made to gain the reward was by compensated timekeepers.

John Harrison, born 1693, more than fulfilled the conditions in 1761, for his timekeeper No. 4 sailed in the *Deptford* from Spithead, and on arrival at Jamaica was found to have lost only five seconds—a truly marvellous achievement. Harrison possessed exceptional ingenuity, and the history of his timekeepers and of his struggles to obtain the money reward he had earned form two most interesting chapters in *The Marine Chronometer*.

Harrison's No. 1 and No. 2 timekeepers, made in 1735 and 1739, had devices for compensating the effect of temperature changes, but their balances were very different from a watch balance. His No. 3 was begun in 1740 and finished in 1757, and his No. 4 was finished in 1759. Both of these had compensation devices applied to the watch type of balance. In 1752, however, during the construction of Harrison's No. 3 timepiece, a famous watch and clockmaker, John Ellicott, produced a watch with a compensation device of similar type. Harrison and Ellicott, therefore, share the honour of first compensating a balance spring for temperature. They used the same method, of moving the regulating curb pins of the balance spring as the temperature varied, and they obtained the movement by what is known as a *bimetallic strip*. This is a long thin strip composed of a strip of brass and a strip of steel fixed together side by side. Brass expands more than steel for a given rise of temperature, so that a compound strip that is straight at one temperature has to bend at a higher temperature, the brass being on the outside of the curve, and, therefore, longer than the steel. Plate XL, 5 shows this device as arranged by Harrison. The bimetallic strip is shown in full lines for a mean temperature, and in dotted lines when curved at a lower temperature.

An inferior method, also making use of a bimetallic strip, was used by Breguet and other makers. One of the regulating curb pins was fixed and the other was connected to the end of a bimetallic strip, so that variations of temperature varied the distance between the curb pins. Plate XLI, 2 shows the arrangement; the regulating index, which is above the parts shown on the drawing, is in dotted lines; the inner curb pin is fixed to

171

the index, but the outer is a block fixed on the end of a bimetallic strip, which is bent back on itself and, at its far end, is fixed to the index. The spring as shown is not in contact with either pin, so that its effective length continues up to the stud. When the balance turns to expand the spring, it comes into contact with the outer curb pin, which then determines its length. The spring, therefore, varies in length as it expands and contracts, and the farther the curb pins are apart the longer is the time during which the spring has a longer effective length, and the slower is the rate of the watch. The device gives a compensation for changes of temperature, but no good regulation of a watch is possible if the spring has any free play between its curb pins.

The compensation method in use to-day was invented by Pierre Le Roy in 1766. Pierre Le Roy, born in 1717, was the greatest of French horologists. He produced a *montre marine* which was, in all essentials, the modern chronometer, and embodied in it a temperature compensation device acting on the balance wheel instead of on the spring. With a given balance spring, the time of swing of a balance depends on its mass and its radius. Increasing the mass of its rim without altering the radius, or increasing the radius without altering the mass of the rim, increases the time of swing. In shorter, but more abstruse, language, the time of swing is proportional to the square root of the moment of inertia of the balance.

A fall of temperature, which stiffens the balance spring and shortens the time of swing, can therefore be compensated by moving some of the mass of the balance outwards, so as to increase its radius. Le Roy's first method of doing this was to attach a pair of thermometers to the balance, their bulbs near the rim and their stems near the centre. A fall of temperature caused some of the mercury in the stems to retreat into the bulbs, thus moving some of the mass of the balance outwards. It was an excellent form of compensating device, but, of course, quite unsuited to watches. In the following year,

172

however, Le Roy produced the balance with rim composed of bimetallic strips, which now is the ordinary form of compensating balance. Plate XLI, 4 shows his balance, the dotted lines indicating the form it takes for a fall (rather an exaggerated fall) of temperature. A little later Le Roy attached weights at the four ends of the bimetallic strips, to increase the effect of their movement. Contemporary and later chronometer-makers made the same balance in many different forms.

Plate XL, 3 shows the form of compensating balance which has been standard in watches for many years. The rim of the balance is cut near the ends of the cross-arm, so that there are two long bimetallic strips instead of four short ones, as in Le Roy's balance. The weights are in the form of a number of screws, and there are spare screw-holes, so that any screw can be taken out and screwed into one of the spare holes. This is for adjusting the compensating effect of the balance. The movement of the bimetallic strip being greater towards its free end, the more weight there is near the free end the greater is the compensating effect of the balance. If, therefore, the watch be found to go slow with rise of temperature—that is, if the compensation be insufficient—a screw on one half of the rim is moved to a hole nearer to the free end, the corresponding change being made on the other arm to maintain balance. The effect of moving a screw that is near the free end is greater than the effect of moving one near the cross-arm, so that, by properly selecting the screw moved, an accurate adjustment of the compensating effect can be made.

A screw is inserted at each end of the cross-arm ; these have no effect on the compensation, but are used to time the watch. Screwing them outwards moves some of the mass of the balance to a larger radius and so makes the watch go slower. They generally have to be used to bring the watch back to time, after shifting a pair of screws on the rim, and, in a *rated* watch, they afford a means of regulation.

173

The balance is made by turning a disk of steel, casting a rim of brass round it, turning the whole to shape, cutting out the centre to leave the cross-arm, and, finally, making the two cuts in the rim. The method is due to Earnshaw, another of the early English chronometer-makers.

The compensation for temperature effected by the bimetallic strip, though good enough for all but the highest class of watch, is not perfect, and is not good enough for chronometers. Its defect is not a question of degree, but of principle. The stiffness of the balance spring varies with temperature according to a certain law ; the compensating effect of a bimetallic strip varies according to a different law. The consequence is that, while the compensation can be made exact for any two given temperatures, it is not exact for temperatures between the two or temperatures beyond them. This error in compensation is known as the *middle temperature error*, sometimes written *M.T. error*. The existence of this error, as inherent in compensation by a bimetallic balance, is generally supposed to have been discovered by Dent in 1833, but Gould has shown that Ulrich (1795-1875), a most ingenious English chronometer-maker, investigated the error in 1814. An immense number of devices have been invented to overcome the error by some means of auxiliary compensation, but those which are used in chronometers do no more than lessen the error within the temperature range in which chronometers are tested. The matter, until recently, belonged to chronometers rather than to watches, but a few years ago the problem of the M.T. error was solved by one of the brilliant researches of C. E. Guillaume on nickel-steel alloys, and now the finest watches are fitted with a balance which compensates without a M.T. error.

Nickel-steel Alloys.—In 1896, Dr. C. E. Guillaume, Director of the Bureau international des Poids et Mesures, started a series of researches on the properties of nickel-steel alloys ; they have already done much to further

174

accurate timekeeping, and promise, in the future, to change existing methods of compensation. The properties of these alloys undergo quite startling changes as the proportion of their constituents is varied. The property of expansion with rise of temperature will be taken as the first example. If the expansibility of steel be represented by 20, that of nickel is 13. Now, if alloys be made with a gradually increasing proportion of nickel, alloys of 5 per cent., 10 per cent., 15 per cent., 20 per cent. of nickel show successively a very gradually diminishing expansibility, just what would be expected from the lower expansibility of nickel. From this point the expansibility drops with extraordinary rapidity ; an alloy of 30 per cent. of nickel has an expansibility less than half that of steel and less than that of nickel, and an alloy of 36 per cent. of nickel has an expansibility of one-twentieth that of steel and far lower than that of any other metal. From this point, as the proportion of nickel is further increased, the expansibility rises rapidly to 10 and then very slowly to the 13 of pure nickel.

The alloy of steel with 36 per cent. of nickel has been christened *Invar*. Its expansion with rise of temperature is so small as to be negligible for many purposes, and is easily compensated or allowed for where great accuracy is required. It is now used for all standards of length and in the construction of many measuring instruments, and is always used (except in England) for the pendulums of good clocks. When used in place of steel in a bimetallic strip, the movement of the strip for a given change of temperature is tripled, and the electric advertising signs which light up intermittently are worked by a bimetallic strip of brass and invar.

When invar was first made it was subject to very minute changes in length in the course of years, but recently Dr. Guillaume has succeeded in making slight modifications that prevent this secular change. It is an interesting fact that invar can be treated mechanically so as to diminish its expansibility until, finally, it can be made to contract with a rise of temperature.

The next application of nickel-steel alloys concerns the middle temperature error. Most metals expand rather more rapidly than in proportion to the rise of temperature; that is to say, if a metal expands a certain amount for a rise of temperature of one degree, it will expand a little more than twice as much for a rise of two degrees. This can be expressed best by saying that it expands proportionately, plus a small extra amount which may be denoted by B.[1] Now, for brass and steel, and indeed for the other common metals, the extra amount B is much the same, even though the amount of the proportional expansion be very different. Consequently, when the two metals are combined in a bimetallic strip, the movement of which depends on the difference between the two expansions, the two extra amounts B, which are practically equal, cancel out, and the resulting movement is proportional to the rise of temperature. Also the compensating effect of the balance, due to the movement, is proportional to the rise of temperature. Now, the spring, in becoming more flexible as the temperature rises, behaves as do metals when they expand; that is, the increase in flexibility is proportional to the rise of temperature, plus a certain extra amount which may be denoted by C. This extra amount C is the cause of the middle temperature error. The compensating effect of the balance, which is proportional to the rise of temperature, cannot be made to compensate a change that is not proportional.

In 1899 Dr. Guillaume had the idea of searching for an alloy of nickel and steel for which the extra amount B was so much less than it was for brass that the difference between the two was equal to the extra amount C of the spring. The compensating effect and the change to be

---

[1] Those familiar with the expression for the length of a metal $1 + at + bt^2$, where t is the temperature and a and b constants, will recognize what is denoted by B as the term bt^2.

compensated would then follow the same law, and the former could be made to compensate the latter exactly. He found that, by varying the proportion of nickel in the alloy, he could change B from its value of, say, 7 for pure steel to 34 for an alloy of 28 per cent. of nickel and to zero for an alloy of 36 per cent. of nickel. Further increase in the proportion of nickel reduced B still further, making it negative. Dr. Guillaume finally adopted an alloy of 42 per cent. of nickel, for which B is 5 negative. When this is combined with brass the compensating effect of the balance follows very closely the law of variation of flexibility of the spring, and so the middle temperature error no longer exists.

For many years practically every foreign watch and chronometer submitted for trial at Kew and the foreign testing laboratories has been fitted with a *Guillaume balance*, or *balance intégral* as Guillaume has called it, and a foreign timekeeper has always received the highest marks. No English watch or chronometer with this balance appeared in the published lists until 1927. The alloy for the Guillaume balance has been christened Anibal (*a*cier au *ni*ckel pour *bal*anciers).[1]

Guillaume's third research was directed to the balance spring itself. He solved the problem of the compensation of pendulum clocks by his alloy invar, which needs little

---

[1] The graphical method gives the most clear explanation to those accustomed to it. In Plate XLI, 1 temperature is measured horizontally, and there is measured vertically, on an arbitrary scale, both the stiffness of the spring and the expansion of the metals. The curves for the expansion of steel and brass are drawn in full lines. If the expansion were proportional to the temperature, they would be straight lines. The upward curvature is exaggerated to make the effect more clear. The difference of the two curves is the straight line marked 'Steel and Brass Compensation.' The line has been drawn symmetrically on the other side of the horizontal axis to show its compensating effect on the curve of stiffness of the balance spring. It compensates exactly at $0°$ and at $31°$. The gap between the curves at $15°$ is the M.T. error, and there is also an error at temperatures beyond $31°$. By varying the amount of compensation, it can be made exact at any two desired temperatures, but between and beyond these there must be an error. The two dotted curves show the expansion of Guillaume's alloy of 42 per cent. of nickel, and the difference between this and the curve of expansion of brass. This last curve is similar to the curve of stiffness, so that compensation is exact at all temperatures.

or no compensation.   To do the same for the watch he had to find an alloy that maintained its stiffness constant at varying temperatures.   In respect to their stiffness, nickel-steel alloys vary even more strangely than they do in respect to expansion.   The gradually increasing addition of nickel to steel rapidly reduces the variation of stiffness with temperature, until, with from 30 per cent. to 45 per cent. of nickel, the variation is in the opposite direction—that is, the alloy becomes stiffer as the temperature rises.   With more than 45 per cent. of nickel it changes back again, and becomes more flexible with rise of temperature.   There is not, however, any alloy of nickel and steel which keeps its stiffness constant over any considerable range of temperature.

In 1913 Guillaume discovered that a certain alloy of steel, nickel and chromium maintained its stiffness very nearly constant over a large range of temperature.   This alloy he called *Elinvar* (Élasticité invariable).   A watch having a balance spring made of elinvar and a plain balance of brass varies so little with change of temperature that only watches that have been carefully compensated can do better.   The alloy proved troublesome to make and different samples behaved differently, but the manufacture has improved, and Guillaume, writing in 1924, stated that tens of millions of elinvar springs had been used in watches.   So far as the Author knows, no English watch has been made with an elinvar spring.

The advantage of the elinvar spring is in cheapening the watch.   The cost of the compensating balance is saved, and, more important, the cost of the labour in adjusting its compensation.   Elinvar has the disadvantage of being softer than a steel spring; so long as it is left alone in the watch this does not matter, but if a repairer treats an elinvar spring as he treats a steel spring he is liable to injure it.

For high-class watches some compensation is required, though, in comparison with a steel spring, the amount is very small.   Paul Ditisheim has brought out a form of

PLATE XLI

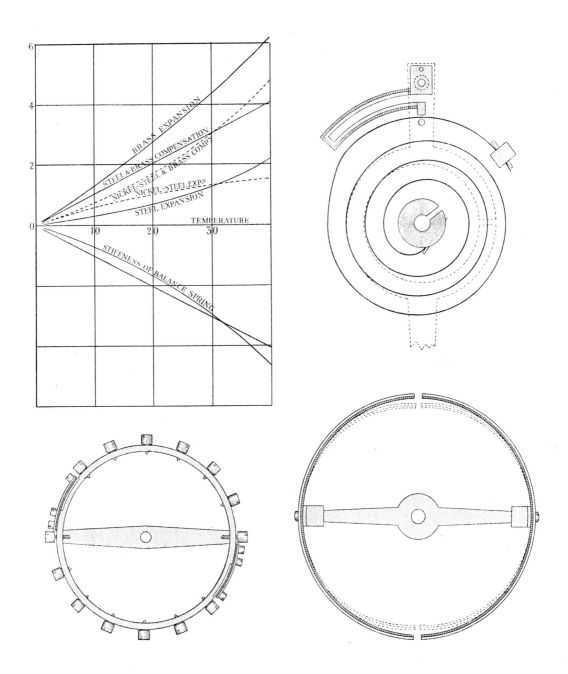

TEMPERATURE COMPENSATION

balance, illustrated in Plate XLI, 3, which he calls *Affix Elinvar*, because it has two minute bimetallic strips affixed to a solid rim. These provide the necessary small amount of compensation without losing the advantage of a rigid balance rim. The split, and therefore flexible, balance disturbs isochronism and increases the work of adjustment, and the return to a rigid balance is a great advance.

Dr. Guillaume's splendid work on the nickel-steel alloys has brought him the Nobel prize and has already been of immense service to the Swiss watchmaking industry. In England it has been entirely neglected; in fact, only a few of those interested in watchmaking appreciate what he has done.

CHAPTER VIII

THE LATER WATCH MOVEMENT

'Horologe entretenir,
Jeune dame à gré servir,
Vieille maison reparer,
C'est tousiours à recommencer.'

Before 1568.

A WATCH is a machine in which the motive power —the spring—has to drive the escapement through a train of gears, and it has generally a subsidiary train to drive a hand. The escape wheel, the last wheel of the train, has to turn some 3600 times as fast as the spring barrel, and the train, in doing this high multiplication of the speed of the spring barrel, absorbs in friction a large proportion of the power of the spring. The remainder of the power is also absorbed in friction, in the escapement and in the rapid motion of the balance in the air.

The size of the mainspring, therefore, depends entirely on the friction in the escapement and in the train, and so, to make the watch small—and this has always been the endeavour—the friction must be kept low. Friction, too, is always variable; it varies with the amount and temperature of the oil on the surfaces and with their wear, and any variation in the friction means a variation in the power reaching the escapement; this means variation in the timekeeping unless the balance is perfectly isochronous. For these reasons a reduction in the friction of the watch train has always been one of the principal aims of watchmakers.

Friction arises in the pivots of the wheel arbors and in the teeth of the wheels and pinions. The pivots are oiled, but the wheels and pinions are never oiled, even

180

though their friction would be less if they were covered with a film of oil. The reason is that they cannot be kept properly oiled ; any oil given to the teeth spreads and dries and leaves a sticky surface which collects dirt, and this leads to wear. A gear is always better without lubricant unless it can be run in a bath of lubricant. This makes it all the more important to keep down the friction between the teeth of wheels and pinions by other means.

Wheel and Pinion Teeth.—The friction between the teeth of a wheel and its pinion depends almost entirely on the form of the teeth. To-day the theory of tooth form is well understood, and, by making practice conform to theory, gear wheels can be cut which work together with almost negligible friction. The theory, though, is comparatively new. De la Hire dealt with the theory in 1694, and Camus, a great French mathematician, was the first to tackle the practical problem seriously, in 1733, but it was long after this before engineers and watch-makers helped their experience by knowledge. The editor of an English edition of Camus' work, published in 1842, asked a number of engineering and watchmaking firms on what basis they shaped their wheel teeth, and from one of the latter got the reply :—

In Lancashire they make the teeth of watch wheels of what is called bay-leaf pattern ; they are formed altogether by the eye of the workmen ; and they would stare at you for a simpleton to hear you talk about the epicycloidal curve.

Up to the middle of the nineteenth century, watch-makers gave their wheel teeth the shape they found to work best without knowing what that shape was, and the best makers, by the exercise of great skill, produced the theoretically correct shape quite as closely as any tools of the time could have produced it had they known what that shape was. Forming the teeth of wheels and pinions must have been a great art. Eighteenth-century books say little about it ; the only work on watch- and clock-making which deals with the subject at all closely is Vigniaux' *Horlogerie Pratique*,[1] and, by way of describing the shape of the tooth, he says it should be *de belle forme et solide.*

The method of forming the teeth of a wheel has been, until comparatively recently, to make, first, a number of saw- or file-cuts round the edge of the wheel, leaving rectangular teeth. In the earlier watches the teeth were marked out by hand on each wheel, and, occasionally, wheels are seen with the marks still visible. The inventories of the tools of a number of Blois watchmakers from 1617-38 which are given by Develle[2] always include several pairs of compasses, which, no doubt, were for marking out the teeth, and, apart from files, no other tool which could have been used for cutting the teeth. Later, wheel-cutting machines were used in which the wheel to be cut could be turned through the correct angle from one tooth to the next, and presented, in the right position for each notch, to a small circular file or saw. It is doubtful when this was first invented; Hooke devised one about 1675, and many were designed early in the eighteenth century. Probably wheel-cutting machines did not come into general use until the eighteenth century.

Once the rectangular teeth were formed by the saw-cuts, their tips were rounded off by files and by eye, giving them a *belle forme* or a bay-leaf shape. Some time after the middle of the eighteenth century *rounding-up* machines were devised for doing this, and in the nineteenth century a rounding-up machine was part of the equipment of most watchmakers, and is still an article of commerce.

Now, teeth are formed by a cutter which has the shape of the gap between two teeth. It is either formed of a single blade that is spun round at a very high speed and is called a fly-cutter, or is a circular disk with a number of cutting teeth on its edge. The fly-cutter is the older

[1] Toulouse, 1788.
[2] *Les Horlogers Blésois.* Blois, 1917.

tool—it was used side by side with the rounding-up machine through most of the nineteenth century—and does the better work, but it can cut well only one wheel at a time and so is unsuited to the twentieth century.

To get a multiplication of some 3600 from the spring barrel to the escape wheel with as few wheels as possible, each gear of a wheel and a pinion must be responsible for as high a multiplication as is practicable. A multiplication of eight in a single gear is quite usual in a watch, though an engineer would prefer to obtain it by two stages of gear, because the action of the teeth is better in a large than in a small pinion. In a modern watch pinions never have less than six leaves, and the greater the force on the pinion the more leaves it is given. Thus only the escape wheel pinion has as few as six leaves, while the pinion driven by the spring barrel never has less than ten, the two intermediate pinions generally having eight leaves. In a fine watch an extra two leaves are often given to each pinion.

Early watches, though with their more imperfectly formed teeth they should have used pinions with more leaves, actually had less leaves in the pinions, and pinions of five leaves were quite common. The ordinary eighteenth-century verge watch had, generally, all pinions of six leaves, though sometimes a pinion of five leaves on the escape wheel arbor. With the three-wheel train of the seventeenth century, however, pinions of five leaves were more common, and the crystal watch by East, illustrated on Plate xx, 1, has all its pinions of five leaves, making a train not quite worthy of the master. Progress in the watch train is reflected in the mainspring. The early watch, with its imperfectly formed teeth and low-numbered pinions, needed a large mainspring. The ingenious but badly made Waterbury watch had to have a mainspring eight feet long. The good modern watch has a mainspring which seems minute in comparison, yet ample power reaches its escapement.

Steel pinions continued to be filed out by hand long

183

after wheels were cut in a machine, the steel being difficult to cut with the early tools and impossible to cut with
a fly-cutter. In the first half of the eighteenth century,
however, the work of pinion-cutting was made easier by
the introduction of pinion wire, which was steel wire
drawn in the form of a long pinion with roughly formed
teeth. It was first made in Lancashire some time before
the middle of the century and supplied from there throughout Europe. There is an interesting manuscript in the
Archives Nationales in Paris,[1] from which it appears that
an English watchmaker, William Blakey, obtained in
1744 the exclusive privilege of making and selling pinion
steel in France. The grant of the privilege was supported by the Académie des Sciences on the ground of
the advantage to be derived from introducing the industry
into France, and because Blakey offered to sell it at
one-third less than the English steel. The result was
anticipated that the English would cease to be the
sole suppliers of all the watchmakers of Europe. Blakey
appears to have been successful in starting the industry,
because in 1755 there is another petition by him, stating
that he was making use of seven-elevenths of a mill for
making pinion and spring steel, and asking that the
remainder of the mill might be sold to him.

Pinion wire is still sold by all watch and clock
material dealers in a large number of sizes. A pinion
is made from it by cutting off a length equal to the
whole length of the arbor, turning off the leaves except
at the point where the pinion is required, and filing the
leaves to their correct form. Pinions are always hardened
and polished to reduce friction, but it is the hard pinion
and not the soft brass wheel that wears.

The wheel is generally fixed on to the pinion.
Plate XLII, 1 shows a pinion with its arbor running
between the two plates of the watch, with the central
portion of the wheel shown on the pinion. The tips of
the leaves of the pinions are turned away for a length a

[1] Carton F/12/1325/A.

little more than the thickness of the wheel, and the wheel is then pressed on to the stumps of the leaves. The stumps, which just project, are spread slightly into the metal of the wheel by hammering.

Pivots and Oil-sinks.—The bearings of the moving parts of a watch are just beginning to be investigated. Some experimental work on them has been done in Switzerland in recent years, and the last (1926) report of the National Physical Laboratory at Kew announces the start of a research. Bearings in engineering work have been the subject of a great deal of investigation, and, apart from size, they appear to be the same as watch bearings—a steel shaft running round in a hole, with some oil interposed. In reality the conditions are entirely different. A bearing in, for instance, a motor-car engine has to be tight; that is to say, the shaft has to fit its hole so closely that there is room only for a film of oil between the two, and the first essential in the bearing is that there should be no wear in it to destroy its tightness. The friction in the bearing is of minor importance, because only a very small proportion of the power of the engine is wasted in the friction of the bearings. In a watch, on the other hand, all the power of the engine, *i.e.* the mainspring, is wasted in friction and a considerable proportion of it in the friction of the bearings. Here the first essential is that the friction should be small; wear is of minor importance, and is of importance mainly because it roughens the surfaces of the bearing and increases the friction. A watch pivot is made with a great deal of play, and, within limits, the play does no harm.

In an engineering bearing the size is determined mainly by the pressure on the bearing, which must be kept down to a certain value to avoid wear. The size of the bearing has very little effect on the friction, which depends mainly on the total pressure on the bearing. In a watch, however, the forces are so small that there is an appreciable friction in moving the pivot in the viscous oil, especially in the more quickly moving parts, the escape wheel and the balance. This friction increases rapidly as the size of the bearing is increased, so, in watches, the bearings are made as small as possible, their . size being determined solely by the necessary strength of the pivot. The extreme limit of fineness is often expressed by 'as fine as a hair,' but escape wheel pivots are finer than many human hairs.

Then there is the question of lubrication. In engineering bearings provision is made for a continual supply of oil. In watches a small fraction of a drop of oil is supposed to last a bearing for three years, and often, though at the expense of the watch, is made to last for five to ten years. It does not really last so long; in five years no oil is left, but a good watch, with a reserve of power, will go on working without any oil. It is not, however, so good a watch afterwards.

Oil disappears from the pivots from three causes—evaporation, spreading and chemical change. All are avoided to some extent by using a suitable kind of oil. If a drop of mineral oil be put on a brass plate it will disappear as a drop in a few days, having spread itself as a film over the plate. A drop of some vegetable and fish oils, however, will remain as a drop for a long time, though all oils have a tendency to spread. The spreading tendency is combated by giving the bearings suitable shapes, relying on the characteristics which oils and other liquids possess of reluctance to turn a sharp corner and reluctance to leave a narrow space. A tumbler can be filled with water more than full—that is, the water can bulge above the edge of the tumbler without flowing over the edge, and the sharper the edge the more it can be made to bulge. This characteristic is made use of in the *oil-sink* of watch bearings, which is the cup formed in the watch plate to hold and retain the oil. Referring again to Plate XLII, 1, the two ends of the arbor are turned down to shafts of small diameter called pivots, and these turn in holes in the watch plates.

On the outsides of the plates the holes are opened out into cups or sinks, which act as reservoirs for oil, and these sinks are always made with a sharp edge to prevent the oil spreading from the sink over the plate. On the insides of the plates there are no sinks, but here the reluctance of oil to leave a narrow space is relied on to prevent spreading. Where the arbor is reduced in diameter to form the pivot there is a shoulder, and the oil tends to keep in the narrow space between the shoulder and the inner surface of the plate.

The retention of oil at the pivots is a question of tendencies. All oils have a tendency to spread over surfaces, but proper shaping of the pivot holes and arbors brings to bear a counter-tendency resisting the spreading. If the oil is mineral oil or if the surfaces are greasy, the counter-tendency is of no avail. With suitable oils and clean surfaces it is of some avail, but of how much is not yet known. An interesting discovery has been made recently permitting the use of mineral oil, which has the advantage over ordinary watch oils of not congealing till quite a low temperature is reached. M. Woog found that if watch plates and arbors were covered with a thin film of stearic acid, mineral oil spread as little as the best watch oil and could then be employed in chronometers subjected to cold in Arctic expeditions or at high altitudes.

Little attention was paid to the lubrication of watch pivots till well into the eighteenth century. Sully made covered oil reservoirs in 1715, and the Author has seen an original oil-sink in a watch by Quare, of about the same date, but oil-sinks do not appear as a regular feature till about the middle of the century. An absurd arrangement for supplying oil to a clock is described by Leutmann in 1717;[1] channels are cut in the plate which, with connecting tubes, lead the oil from a funnel at the top past all the pivot holes to a reservoir at the bottom; there is, however, no indication in the book that the author knew the value of an oil-sink.

[1] *Vollständige Nachricht von den Uhren.* Halle.

In all seventeenth-century watches and clocks, the pivots ran in holes drilled through the plates without any opening out. In the early German watches with iron plates, the pivots ran in holes in the iron. These holes are generally found bushed with brass plugs, which are almost certainly later repairs. Brass is a better metal for the pivot to run in than iron, but it is improbable that this was discovered before brass plates became general—that is, before 1600.

Jewels.—The first step to improve watch bearings was taken by the Swiss geometrician and optician Facio (or Fatio) de Duillier, who had settled in London. In 1704 he, together with the eminent watch- and clock-maker Peter Debaufre[1] and Thomas Debaufre, obtained a patent for using pierced rubies as pivot holes, and it is said that the first jewelled watch made by Debaufre was worn by Isaac Newton. It was, though, a long time before the invention came into general use. English makers were for some time the only users, partly no doubt because the method of cutting and piercing the stones was kept secret. The granting of a patent was not, at that time, conditional on a full disclosure of the invention, and Facio and Debaufre's patent refers merely to the use of precious stones.

Watch jewels were not prepared as a regular industry till the able mechanician Ingold studied the methods of production about 1825 and introduced the industry in Chaux-de-Fonds. About the middle of the nineteenth century, the industry of preparing and setting jewels was well established, and jewelling became the regular practice in watches.

Figs. 2 and 3 of Plate XLII show the end of an arbor with its pivot in a jewel fixed in a watch plate or cock. In Fig. 2 the jewel is set directly in the plate. The jewel itself has a flat side facing the arbor, with a bevelled edge; from this extends a rounded surface leading to a

---

[1] Debaufre was French, but established in London. In the patent his name is spelt Debanfre, probably in error; an alternative form of the name is de Baufré.

PLATE XLII

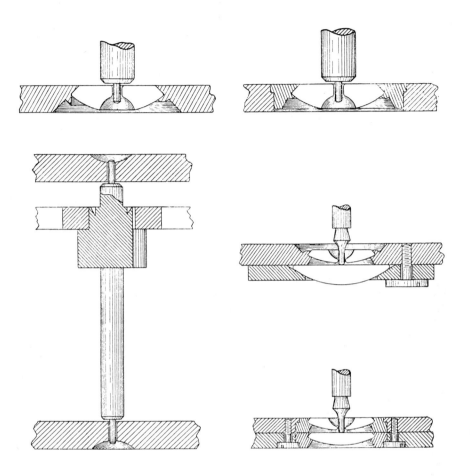

PIVOTS AND JEWELS

very narrow flat surface on the opposite side, and within this is the oil-sink. The jewel is set in the plate in different ways. In the way shown in Fig. 2, an opening is cut in the plate as indicated on the left-hand side of the jewel, having next to the inside of the plate a bevelled seat, on which the bevelled edge of the jewel rests. A narrow fillet of metal is left below the bevelled seat, and, when the jewel has been pressed home into its seat, this fillet is turned down against the rounded surface of the jewel as indicated on the right-hand side of the jewel.

Frequently, especially in Swiss watches, the jewel is put in from the other side of the plate, a seat being formed for the rounded surface. Then a sharp V-groove is cut round the hole on the inside of the plate and the fillet so formed is turned down on to the bevelled edge.

Fig. 3 shows the method employed in higher-grade watches, the jewel being in a separate setting which is pressed into a hole in the watch plate.

The pivots of the balance are given a different form from those of the other wheels of the watch train, the form being designed to give greater strength and less friction. The balance moves more quickly than any other part of the watch, so friction at its pivots is especially harmful. At the same time the balance is heavy, and a fine pivot is therefore more liable to break as the result of a fall. Figs. 4 and 5 show the shape of the balance pivot. It is made tapering, ending in a short cylindrical pivot, and has no shoulder. In the arbors of the train wheels, the shoulders are relied on to limit the endwise movement of the arbor, and, when the watch is lying on its back or face, the weight of the wheel and arbor is taken on the lower shoulder, which, consequently, rubs against the inner surface of the plate or jewel. The friction of this is avoided in the balance pivot by giving it *end-stones*. Outside the pivot jewel and almost touching it is a flat stone against which the end of the pivot rests, and the end of the pivot is rounded so that the

189

contact between pivot and end-stone is at only a minute surface. The two end-stones, one at each end of the arbor, keep this in position so that only the short cylindrical portions of the pivots enter the jewel holes, and these holes are made not quite cylindrical but smaller at the centre, so that there is only a small area of contact between the pivot and the walls of the hole. Such small areas of contact are possible, without leading to wear, only with a hard steel pivot and a still harder stone. A comparison of Figs. 3 and 4 shows how much smaller is the area of rubbing contact in a balance pivot than in a train pivot. In lower-grade watches and in most of the older watches, the end-stone is pressed against the watch plate by a brass plate held to the watch plate by a screw, as shown in Fig. 4. In higher-grade watches the construction of Fig. 5 is usual, both jewel and end-stones being in loose settings held in place by the heads of two or three screws. In Fig. 5 the end-stone is shown in a separate plate, but frequently the jewel setting and then the end-stone setting are pressed into a single hole in the watch plate or cock.

The construction of the balance pivots with end supports instead of shoulders on the arbor was employed before the use of jewels for end-stones became general, and early in the eighteenth century, instead of the end-stone, a small hard steel plate called a *coqueret* was fixed by a screw on the top of the cock. These end-plates, though of very hard steel, are generally found with a pit worn by the end of the pivot, but wear on a good end-stone is rarely seen. In the earlier high-grade watches, diamonds were generally used as end-stones, and are still used in marine chronometers for their heavy balances.

It is not uncommon in seventeenth-century and later watches to see a large stone in the centre of the cock, put there solely for ornament, though it has all the appearance of an end-stone. One of these prevented Facio and Debaufre from obtaining an extension of the period of their patent. The Clockmakers' Company, in opposing

190

the petition for a period longer than the normal fourteen years, produced a watch by Ignatius Huggerford with a stone in its cock, and this appears to have been accepted at its face value. Only later was it found not to be an end-stone at all.

The stones used in watches are ruby, sapphire and garnet. There is little to choose between the ruby and sapphire, but a great difference between these and the garnet, which is not nearly so hard or so strong. Jewels of garnet are far cheaper than those of ruby or sapphire, owing mainly to their being easier to prepare, and they are used in the great majority of watches. Rubies and sapphires are now made synthetically by fusion of alum with colouring matter in the oxy-hydrogen blowpipe. The product is a real not an imitation stone, and is rather better for watch jewels than the naturally formed stone. It is generally termed a *scientific* ruby or sapphire, distinguishing it from the *reconstituted* stone made by fusing together small fragments of natural stone.

Jewels are prepared by cutting and drilling with diamond powder impregnated in copper and steel wheels and steel wires. The stones are cut to size by saws consisting of copper wheels with diamond powder, and are sometimes turned to shape by a diamond tool. The holes are drilled by fine steel wires turning at a very high speed and supplied with diamond powder. Polishing is done by finer powder held in tin or wooden tools. A large number of different operations go to the preparation of a jewel, nearly all done in automatic machines by the same process of grinding with diamond powder.

The difficulty in preparing jewels is to ensure the hole being central and perpendicular to the faces. A method has been introduced recently to get over this difficulty, consisting in setting the jewel in a brass plug, which is then turned true to the hole in the jewel. In this way errors in the hole are corrected, because the hole is necessarily true to the outside of the plug, by which the position of the jewel in the watch is determined.

191

Watches are frequently described as 7-jewel, 11-jewel, 13-jewel, etc., watches. In a 7-jewel watch, the jewels are 2 balance pivot jewels, 2 end-stones, 2 lever pallets of jewel and 1 'ruby' pin on the roller of the balance staff, and only the very cheapest watches have less than this. Better watches have jewels for the pivots of lever, escape wheel and fourth and third wheels. The maximum number of jewels for an ordinary watch is 23, when the lever and escape wheel have end-stones, and the centre wheel and barrel have jewels for their pivots.

Another cause of loss of power lies in the intermittent motion of the watch. The whole train is stopped and started again four to five times a second, and every stop and every start means increase of pressure between the teeth and at the pivots, and, consequently, increase of friction. The effect increases so rapidly with the speed of the moving part that it is only in the escape wheel and lever (in a lever watch) that it is important. It is to minimize the pressures due to stopping and starting that these parts are made as light as is consistent with strength.

Types of Watch Movement.—The series of drawings in Plates XLIII and XLIV show the complete watch in its five main types from the earliest watch to the nineteenth-century watch. The trains have been drawn spread out into a straight line, not as they are arranged in the watch, so that all the wheels may be visible. The scale of the drawings has been increased in the later watches, making use of the full size of the plate so as to show the details more clearly.

These five types of watch should be regarded, not so much as showing the watch prevalent at different periods, but as containing the different characteristic features of watches from 1550 to 1850. Up to the nineteenth century it is unusual to find two watches alike, and a study of these types will add greatly to the interest of watch collecting by leading to an appreciation of the variations in the mechanism of watches. The great majority of old

192

PLATE XLIII

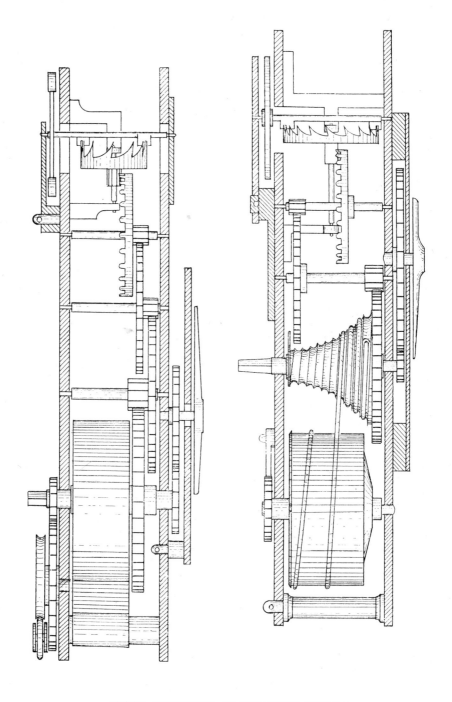

WATCH MOVEMENTS AT DIFFERENT PERIODS

PLATE XLIV

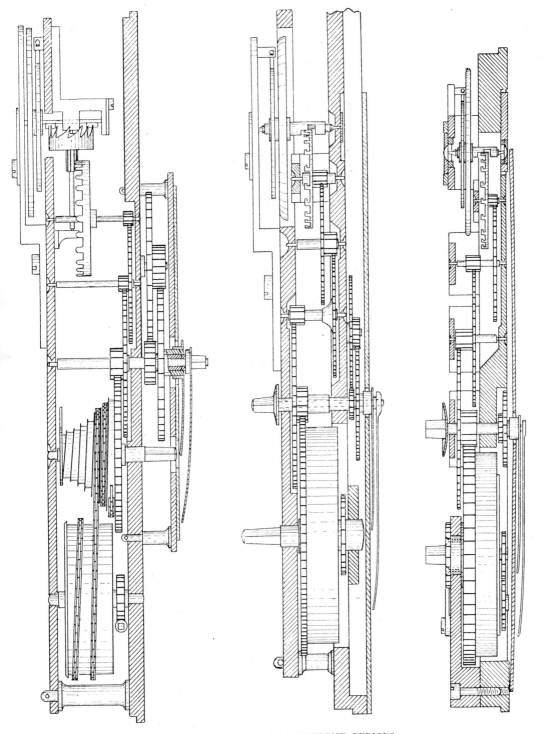

WATCH MOVEMENTS AT DIFFERENT PERIODS

watches are uninteresting externally. A far greater proportion are interesting if the insides as well as the outsides are examined.

Fig. 1 of Plate XLIII is the German stackfreed watch. The mainspring has no barrel, its outer end being bent round a pillar. The upper end of the mainspring arbor has a pinion which drives the stackfreed wheel, and the lower end drives the hand through a pair of toothed wheels. These are contained in the space between the bottom plate of the watch and an auxiliary dial plate, the visible dial, when ornamented, being sometimes a separate plate attached to the dial plate. The train consists of two intermediate wheels and pinions and the crown or contrate wheel, which drives the escape wheel. The verge, with its foliot above the top plate, has its upper pivot in a small cock and its lower pivot either in the bottom plate itself or in a separate plate fixed to the bottom plate, as shown. Winding is done on the mainspring arbor itself. This type of watch generally went for twenty-seven hours with three and a-quarter turns of the mainspring.

Fig. 2 shows the type of the early French and English watch with fuzee and gut band. The mainspring arbor is held by a ratchet and ratchet wheel above the top plate, and this was the only means of regulation. The hand is driven by a pinion on the fuzee arbor and a wheel, both contained between bottom plate and dial plate, as in the German watch. Between the fuzee and the crown wheel is only one intermediate wheel, and the watch goes for only about fourteen hours with three to three and a-half turns of the mainspring. The struggle of the early makers of fuzee watches was to make the watch go long enough. The fuzee watch has the same number of arbors as the stackfreed watch, but goes generally only half as long. This is because the multiplication ratio between spring barrel and fuzee is much less than that between the wheel on the mainspring arbor and its pinion. The fuzee shown has nine turns of its groove, so that it can only make nine turns to the three or three and a-half turns of the mainspring, a multiplication of three or less. The wheel and pinion of the stackfreed watch can easily have a multiplication of eight, or two and a-half times as much. The fuzee watch, therefore, has to have a higher multiplication in the rest of its train to go even half as long. For this reason the escape wheel was generally larger in diameter, as shown, and its bracket was frequently fixed to both the plates.

Great variations are found in the trains of early seventeenth-century watches, but not in the number of wheels; it is seldom that an extra wheel and pinion is used. The variations are in the number of turns of the fuzee, and in the teeth of the wheels and pinions and escape wheel. Watches going for twenty-four hours are found without an extra wheel, but with high fuzees of thirteen or even seventeen turns, making a very thick watch. The crystal watch by East (Plate xx, 1) is an example of a watch going for a little over twenty-four hours without an extra wheel and with a fuzee of only eleven turns, but the necessary multiplication is attained by the bad practice of using pinions of five leaves throughout. The numbers of teeth are: fuzee 54, intermediate wheel 48, contrate wheel 40, escape wheel 15, giving 273,715 swings of the balance at one winding. An example of a watch with a train at the other extreme is the beautiful crystal watch by Nouwen, No. 2 of the same Plate. This has an extra wheel in its train, and yet goes for only about sixteen hours. The fuzee has only six turns, and the pinions are of six leaves with one of eight leaves on the escape wheel. The teeth in the wheels are: fuzee 48, two intermediate wheels 36 and 28, contrate wheel 28, and escape wheel 17, giving only 159,936 swings to one winding. These two examples give an idea of the diversity in watch trains of the early seventeenth century.

The verge in French and English watches always had a wheel foliot or balance, never a dumb-bell. The earlier cocks were in two parts, as shown, one part riveted to the plate and the other pinned to it. Watches are rare without a screw, but up to 1620 it is common to find

194

only one screw, acting as a pivot to the ratchet. As screws came more into use, the two-part cock was replaced by a one-part cock fixed to the plate with a screw.

Fig. 1 of Plate XLIV shows the early eighteenth-century watch with balance spring and two hands. Here there is the extra wheel in the train enabling the watch to go for about thirty hours with fewer turns in the fuzee, and a smaller escape wheel. The mainspring arbor is held by a wheel and tangent screw placed between the barrel and the bottom plate. This began to replace the ratchet in 1620, though ratchets are found much later. The tangent screw was generally on the top plate in seventeenth-century watches, but occasionally both it and the ratchet are found below the barrel early in the century.

The essential feature of the train is that the arbor driven by the fuzee carries the minute hand. It is therefore in the centre of the watch, and its wheel is called the *centre wheel*. The arbor has a long extension which is seen just projecting beyond the set-hands square ; on this is slipped a pinion, called the *cannon pinion*, having a projecting sleeve on which the minute hand is fixed. The cannon pinion is held to the arbor of the centre wheel only by friction, so that it can be turned round on it to set the hands. The hour hand is fixed to a sleeve which can turn freely on the sleeve of the cannon pinion, and the toothed wheel immediately below the cannon pinion is fixed to this sleeve. In the drawing, the part between the minute hand and this wheel is shown in section, and the centre wheel arbor, the cannon pinion sleeve and the hour hand on its sleeve are visible.

The hour hand is turned at one-twelfth the speed of the minute hand by the wheel and pinion on the right, which turn on a stud fixed in the bottom plate. The cannon pinion turns the wheel, and the pinion fixed to the wheel turns the wheel to which the hour hand is fixed. These four wheels and pinions constitute what is termed the *motion-work*.

195

The winding square of the fuzee arbor is shown in a hole in the dial, but it was often at the other end of the fuzee, where it was always in the earlier seventeenth-century watches.

The escape wheel was generally small in diameter, sometimes very small. The balance cock is in one piece, English cocks having a large foot held by steady pins and a single screw, while French and Swiss cocks have two small feet, each held by a screw. Dutch cocks were like the French, but with more extended feet. The balance spring is below the balance, fixed to the top plate, and the balance is considerably larger. The pivot holes are shown with oil-sinks, though these became usual only in the latter half of the century.

In the first half of the eighteenth century came an important change in the mounting of the escape wheel. In Fig. 1 of Plate XLIV the escape wheel is pivoted on the right in a block extending from the bracket that supports the verge. Julien Le Roy, about 1740, gave this block its final form by constructing it separate from the bracket, forming it on the end of a piece which could slide on the bracket to and from the observer looking at the drawing. The slide could be worked by turning a screw by a key, and by its means the action of the escapement could be adjusted without dismounting the watch. The screw was not usual in English watches, but the slide was of real advantage, and soon became general.

Fig. 2 shows the cylinder watch of the earlier type. It is often called the horizontal watch in distinction from the verge or vertical watch. The reduction in thickness is apparent. There is no fuzee requiring a large distance between the plates, and the mainspring is changed to one of less height but greater diameter. English makers, however, gave up the fuzee reluctantly, and cylinder watches are found with fuzees. The balance is arranged to occupy less space by sinking it in a hole in the top plate or, as in the English three-quarter-plate watch, in the space left by cutting away a segment of the plate.

196

An essential feature is the shaping of the two plates. They are thicker than before, and space is obtained where required by cutting depressions called *sinks*. Also the bottom plate has a rim which leaves the space for the motion-work and does away with the need for an auxiliary dial plate; the enamel dial is supported directly on this rim. In order to allow more space for the spring barrel, a large hole into which it can pass is cut in the bottom plate, and its lower pivot runs in a separate bridge piece fixed on the under side of the plate. Since the mainspring is wound by turning its arbor, a ratchet wheel, placed beneath the barrel, is needed to retain it.

Winding is from the back of the watch, and hand-setting also is arranged to be done at the back by drilling a hole through the length of the centre wheel arbor and passing a pin through it. The upper end of the pin has a square for a key, and the lower end takes the cannon pinion and the minute hand. The pin is shown in the drawing in dotted lines. It is tight enough in the arbor to be driven by it, but is capable of turning in it for setting the hands. The balance spring is fixed in the modern way, to a stud depending from the cock.

The names given to the different wheels in English, French and German are, starting with the barrel :—

Great wheel, Roue de barillet, Federhausrad.
Centre wheel, Grand roue moyenne, Minutenrad.
Third wheel, Petite roue moyenne, Zwischenrad.
Fourth wheel, Roue de champ, Sekundenrad.
Escape wheel, Roue d'échappement, Gangrad.

Fig. 3 shows the Lepine type of cylinder watch, which is still thinner. Here there is no top plate, but only a very thick bottom plate, and all the upper pivots are supported in cocks or bridges held by screws to the bottom plate. Instead of having a rim, space is found for the motion-work in a sink on the under side of the plate. The wheel and pinion of the motion-work, not seen in the drawing, must be imagined behind the wheel and pinion on the centre arbor. The appearance of the movement is well shown in the watch on Plate LVI, an early nineteenth-century watch in which each bar and cock is enamelled.

Another and audacious change, to save space in thickness, was to hold the arbor of the spring barrel at one end only. The ratchet wheel was fixed to the arbor by three screws (shown in dotted lines in the drawing), and the arbor was therefore held to the bar by the ratchet wheel above and a shoulder of large diameter below. In the earlier Lepine watches the teeth have almost a ratchet form, supposed to give greater strength ; these teeth, however, were difficult to make and were soon abandoned.

'Clocks being things in themselves so useful and excellent, that no production of Art whatsoever doth surpass them (especially those that are truly and well made), yet are extraordinarily subject to give dissatisfaction to those that own them, which happeneth from two Causes ; the one from the Workman's unskilfulness and unfaithfulness in making them, and the other is from the owner's unskilfulness in keeping and managing them.'
Horological Dialogues. JOHN SMITH, 1675.

CHAPTER IX

WATCH-CASES, 1675-1725

'Senza piedi a girar sono costretto ;
    Voglion, ch' io parli ; eppur non ho la bocca ;
    Se tardo ad affrettarmi, son costretto ;
    E se troppo mi affretto, ognun tarocca.
Se troppo m' incammino, e non aspetto,
    Cento maledizioni ognun mi scocca ;
    E dopo avermi tanto maledetto,
    Dice, che son bugiardo, e cosa sciocca.
Se vigor più non ho, nè più s' accorda
    Al moto il passo, condannar mi sento ;
    M' aprono il petto, e poi mi dan la Corda.
Ma se mi muovo regolato, e attento,
    Benchè niun più mi guidi, e più mi muova,
    Mi pone in tasca, e prigionier divento.'

THE half-century 1675-1725 is one of the most interesting periods in the history of watches. It does not show the glorious enamels of the earlier period or the little works of art from the point of the graver, but it produced watches in immense variety, many of good design and fine craftsmanship as well as some of the ugliest ever perpetrated, and it is of especial interest to those who study the movement. It was, too, the period of the supremacy of the English watch, a supremacy so complete that no other watch was thought to be worth having.

The advent of the balance spring in 1675 influenced not only the movement but also the case; the watch began to be of some real use as a timekeeper and became something more than a bit of jewellery. By 1700 a minute hand was fairly common, and this brought about a radical change in the dial, minutes being shown on a special band with large figures, as if in pride that they

PLATE XLV

1

English watch by Fromanteel, London, *c.* 1700. Plain silver case. Tortoiseshell outer case with silver inlay. Champlevé engraved silver dial with sun and moon hour indicator, minute and seconds hands. The maker is probably Abraham, apprenticed in 1662, the fourth Fromanteel who worked in London.
Mallett coll. pp. 153, 212.

2

English striking watch by John Ebsworth, London, *c.* 1690. Silver case, engraved with birds, squirrel, fruit and foliage. Champlevé silver dial with circle of minutes. Two hands. Ebsworth was apprenticed in 1657, and was master of the Clockmakers' Company in 1697.
Mallett coll. p. 201.

3

English watch by Henricus Harpur, London, late seventeenth century. Plain silver case. Leather outer case studded with silver. Silver champlevé dial with figure plaques at odd angles. Henry Harper was apprenticed in 1657 and is known until 1708. A clock and several watches by him are known.
Mallett coll. pp. 153, 203.

PLATE XLV

had become things of account. A little after the balance spring, repeating mechanism was invented, an addition that now, except to the blind, is only a plaything, but was of real value when any light but daylight was scarce, and matches were unknown.

One result of regarding the watch as a timekeeper was that it became larger. It was made to go for twenty-six or twenty-eight hours instead of for fourteen or sixteen, and this meant including an extra wheel in the train. Besides this, it began to be recognized that bigger movements made for better timekeeping, and this is as true with the tools of to-day as it was with the primitive tools of 1700; the wrist-watch cannot compete as a timekeeper with a pocket-watch of good size.

Watches became circular; oval and form watches are found only very rarely.

Engraved Work.—The same types of decoration as in the earlier period are found. The piercing of cases had to continue, because it was needed for all striking and repeating watches, and the pierced work was engraved as before. The English striking watch in the centre of Plate XLV is a good example of this work of about 1690.

The engraving of scenes or landscapes on case or dial had been given up before 1675, and on cases engraving was limited to designs of flowers and foliage combined generally with figures of birds and animals. The design was nearly always on the larger scale of the watch on Plate XLVI, 1, with less conventional flowers than in the earlier period. A fine bit of engraving, signed by the artist Martin, is seen on the gold watch dated 1683, on Plate XLVII, 1, comprising, on a ground of foliage, a lion, a dog, a bear, an eagle and a serpent. The watch is by Thomas Tompion, the most celebrated of all watch- and clock-makers, and one of the two who are buried in Westminster Abbey. He was born in 1638 and died in 1713, and was the first to recognize the value of the balance spring and use it in watches.

Engraving, however, found its chief scope on the dial

201

PLATE XLVI

1

Swiss calendar watch by J. Sermand, Geneva, *c.* 1640. Silver case engraved on back with sunflowers, tiger lilies, daffodils, iris and carnations. Upper dial showing days of the month, small dials showing week-days and age and phases of the moon. Bezel with glass. Eight other watches by Jaques Sermand are known.
Mallett coll.   p. 201.

2

English calendar watch by W. Semor, York, *c.* 1630. Silver covers and side band with gilt metal edging. Circular glass in front cover. Outer case of plain silver.
Mallett coll.   p. 101.

3

French alarum watch by Josias Jenti, Paris, *c.* 1640. Gold case, pierced and enamelled in turquoise and white. Alarum disk pierced and engraved. Movement very thin, under one-quarter inch over the plates.
Mallett coll.   pp. 115, 122, 135.

PLATE XLVI

of this period. The silver watch on Plate XLVII, 3 is a good example of the dial for a watch with one hand. The hour figures are engraved on plaques standing up from a ground sunk by the graver; the plaques and the inner band with hour and half-hour marks are polished and the ground is matt. Outside the hour figures is a narrow gilt band that turns and indicates the day of the month by a short pointer on an outer silver band, also with polished plaques on a matt and sunken ground. Another champlevé silver dial of about the same date is on the watch on Plate XLV, 3; it is not the only example of a dial with oddly distributed figure plaques. The outer case of the watch, of leather studded with silver, is shown on its right. A champlevé dial showing minutes is on the watch on Plate XLVIII, 1, which dates from about 1725.

Lapidary's Work.—Watch-cases of crystal, agate or other stone were made only very rarely after 1675; an example is a gold watch in an outer case of crystal in the South Kensington Museum. Lapidary work was confined to stones set in cases which were nearly always of gold. The outer case on Plate LI, 1 is an example dating from about 1700, composed of carnelians set in chased gold.

A most interesting and unusual watch is in the centre of Plate XLVIII; the gold case is overlaid with plaques of mother-of-pearl, on which are set sprays of flowers, with butterflies, formed of diamonds, emeralds and rubies, many of the stones being cut to the form of the flower or butterfly. Here also the outer is the decorated case, the inner being of plain gold with hall-mark for 1722. The watch is by Peter Debaufre of London, already mentioned as the Paris maker of the watches on Plates XXVI, 3 and XXXVI, 2.

Repoussé Work.—Chased and repoussé work was more common after 1675, but it was only towards the end of the period now under discussion that it became the principal form of decoration for inner and, more generally, outer cases.

PLATE XLVII

1

English watch by Thomas Tompion, London, 1683. Gold case with engraving containing a lion, a dog, a bear, an eagle and a serpent, emblems of strength and cunning. Border of birds, figures and foliage. Signed by the engraver Martin. Thomas Tompion, born 1638, died 1713, was one of the greatest clock- and watchmakers of the world.
Mallett coll. p. 201.

2

Jacobite watch by Robert Moore, London, *c.* 1720. Gold outer case with central portrait bust of Charles I., flanked by angels' heads, with palm and laurel branches and surmounted by the martyr's crown with star points. Medallions with portraits of Charles II., James II., Queen Anne and James the elder Pretender. The bezel has panels with an oak tree, a rose and thistle with serpent, a lion and a rising star. Engraved gold inner case. Gold dial. Striking movement.
Mallett coll. pp. 205, 215.

3

English watch by Edward Hampton, London, late seventeenth century. Plain silver case. Silver champlevé dial with day-of-the-month circle. Leather outer case, studded silver.
Mallett coll. pp. 153, 203, 213.

PLATE XLVII

An early example is the watch at the bottom of Plate
XLVIII, which has both case and cover repoussé in a
manner strikingly different from that of the mid eighteenth-century work seen in the watches on Plates xxv
and LI. The watch is by Philibert Dagonneau of
Grenoble, who, unless there were two of the same name,
worked from 1629 to 1700. The dial is particularly
interesting in showing an attempt to indicate minutes
with a single hand. It is divided into six hours, marked
with roman figures I to VI and with arabic figures
7 to 12 superposed on the roman figures; half-hours
are marked by diamonds and quarter-hours by points
from the outer band, while a separate band outside this
has marks at the half-quarters. Outside this again is a
broad band with two-minute divisions and figures 20,
40, 60 between the hours. Again outside is a turning
ring with pointer and a day-of-the-month circle. This is
the only watch known to the Author with a minute band
adapted to be read by an hour hand, but the six-hour
division of the dial is not unknown. There is another
watch of about 1700 in the Webster collection, by Thomas
Shepheard of London, with the six-hour division, but the
two sets of figures are both roman, on separate bands.
Britten illustrates a watch by Tompion with only the
figures I to VI, and no subdivisions beyond the quarter-
hours.

A later example, of about 1720, but still quite
different in character from the mid eighteeenth-century
work, is the striking watch on the right of Plate XLVII.
It is a Jacobite watch, with portrait bust of Charles I.,
flanked by angels' heads, palm and laurel branches, and
surmounted by a martyr's crown with star points. Round
this central design are four medallion portraits of Charles
II., James II., Queen Anne and James the elder Pretender,
with pierced and engraved decoration between them.
The bezel has similar pierced and engraved work, with,
on panels, an oak tree, a rose and thistle with entwined
serpent, a lion and a rising star. The view shown is of

PLATE XLVIII

1

English musical watch by John Archambo, London, *c.* 1740, with carillon of five bells. Silver pierced and engraved case. Silver champlevé dial. A similar watch is in the Olivier collection. Bracket and long-case clocks by this maker are known.
Webster coll.   pp. 203, 213.

2

English watch by Peter Debaufre, London, dated 1722. Outer case of mother-of-pearl, set with diamonds, emeralds and rubies, cut to form flowers and butterflies. Inner case of plain gold. Peter Debaufre or Pierre De Baufre was in Paris in 1675 and in London in 1689. He patented jewelling for watches with Facio in 1704. Nine other watches and a clock by him are known, two of which are on Plates XXVI, 3 and XXXVI, 2.
Mallett coll.   p. 203.

3

French watch by Philibert Dagonneau, Grenoble, late seventeenth century. Silver gilt repoussé case. Scene of Samson carrying away the gates of Gaza on the back, and of his killing a lion on the cover. Silver champlevé six-hour dial with arabic figures 7-12 combined with roman figures I-VI. Single hand reading on a minute circle.
Webster coll.   p. 205.

206

PLATE XLVIII

the outer case, the inner having a band of pierced and engraved ornament.

Three other examples of repoussé work are on Plate XLIX. The watch, by Quare, at the bottom has a band of military emblems in repoussé between the hour and minute bands, and that by Fromanteel at the top has the lower part of its dial plate decorated in repoussé. The back of the silver outer case of this watch, shown below, has already been mentioned. The watch by Quare dates from a little after 1700, and the other from a little before.

Cast and chiselled cases were not made after 1675; repoussé work, which produces a result similar to, though easily distinguishable from, casting and chiselling, and in a much lighter case, took its place.

Enamel.—Enamel, apart from painting on enamel, was very little used on cases during this period. The inner case of the watch by Fromanteel, just mentioned, is an example of champlevé work filled with translucent red enamel which belongs more to about 1650 than 1690, to which date the watch must be attributed. Enamel work of this kind was most unusual after 1675; the little enamelling there was is more of the type on the watch by Collomby on Plate XXXV, already mentioned.

Dials.—On dials, however, enamel was used to a considerable extent, especially on French and Swiss watches. For a period in the neighbourhood of 1700 the favourite form of dial was a gilt metal plate with enamel plaques and bands for the figures and divisions. The watch on Plate L, 1 shows the type in all its ugliness, with a single hand graceless enough to be appropriate. The figures on the plaques are blue. The back cover is a bezel with glass, disclosing the top plate with a very large balance covered with a painted enamel portrait. The watch is not quite spherical, the thickness being a little less than the diameter. A later example, of about 1725, shown on its right, has an enamel minute band and painted landscape in the centre. This watch shows the type at its best. On the back is an enamel painting of the Roman

207

PLATE XLIX

1a   **1b**

English watch by Fromanteel, London, *c.* 1690.   Silver case champlevé
in foliage pattern filled with translucent red enamel.   Silver dial repoussé
and engraved with wandering hour figure.   Fuzee winds both ways.   The
maker is probably Abraham, the maker of the watch on Plate XLV, 1.
Webster coll.   pp. 153, 207, 209.

2

English watch by Daniel Quare, London,
c. 1700.   Plain silver case.   Tortoiseshell
outer case piqué silver.   Silver dial,
repoussé in military emblems.   The
hour circle turns so that the single hand
shows hours and minutes.   Daniel Quare,
born 1649 and died 1724, was one of the
most famous English makers of clocks
and watches.
Webster coll.   pp. 207, 211.

1c

Silver outer case, repoussé in
flutes, of the watch by Fromanteel.

PLATE XLIX

Charity signed by Jean Mussard, a well-known painter of Geneva.

The enamel plaque dial was occasionally retained even when the all-enamel dial became common, towards 1725, by raising the dial in the form of plaques, sometimes outlined with a fine black line and sometimes indicated only by the raising. The result was always ugly.

In England this type of dial was never used, and the champlevé metal dial was the standard form until enamel dials came into use.

The plain white enamel dial was introduced first in France and Switzerland, a little before 1700, and appeared in England about 1710, but it was not at all common before 1725.

Painting on enamel disappeared from Blois and went to Paris and Geneva, the latter becoming its permanent home. The principal artists of this period were mentioned in Chapter VI.

Hour and Minute Indicators.—The introduction of the minute hand gave rise to some interesting forms of dials during this period. The attempt to indicate minutes by dividing the dial into six hours has been described, but there are only isolated instances of this. The wandering hour-figure watch, however, was common enough at the end of the seventeenth century to be regarded as a recognized type. The watch by Fromanteel at the top of Plate XLIX shows the device. The minutes are marked on a semicircular band forming the outer edge of a slot in the dial plate. In this slot travels a circle with the hour figure which serves to indicate the hour and point to the minutes; the time on the dial shown is 3 hours 33½ minutes. When the circle with III reaches 60 minutes, a circle with IIII appears at 0 minutes and in turn travels round the slot. The quarters are marked on the inner edge of the slot. The circle is really a hole in a lower rotating dial plate, and the hour figure showing through the hole is on a small disk below this plate and

PLATE L

1

French watch by Dufour, Paris,
c. 1700. Gilt metal case with
glass back. . Gilt dial with large
enamel figure plaques. Single
steel hand. Very large balance
covered by enamel portrait.
British Museum.   p. 207.

2

French watch by Nicolas Gribelin, Paris,
c. 1700. Painted enamel case signed
Mussard. Gilt dial with central painting,
enamel figure plaques and enamel minute
circle. Two hands. Gribelin was born
in 1633 and died in 1715. Several
watches and clocks by him are known.
British Museum.   p. 214.

3

French watch by Charles Bobinet, Paris, mid
seventeenth century. Twelve-lobed crystal case
and cover in gilt metal frames. Enamel dial,
with gilt border, light blue centre with lace-like
edging, formed by black markings on white
ground. Silver hand, set paste brilliants. Six
other watches by Bobinet are known.
British Museum.   p. 148.

4

Swiss watch of the type known
as 'Montre Chinoise,' made for
China at Fleurier. Silver case.
Centre sweep seconds with
Chinese duplex escapement.
Bottom plate engine-turned;
cocks, bridges and barrel en-
graved. *c.* 1840.   p. 235.

5

English watch, unsigned, *c.* 1760. Outer
gold case repoussé with two figures of
children in white coral, and other portions
of the design in mother-of-pearl, lapis-
lazuli and horn. Gold inner case. Dial
of white enamel with figure in white coral
in centre and gold sun.
Cluny Museum.   p. 221.

PLATE L

pivoted to it. There are two holes in the rotating dial plate opposite each other, with a small disk under each, one disk bearing the odd numbers and the other the even. When the hole with III showing disappears after reaching 60 minutes, it passes under the fixed dial to reach o minutes after one hour, and, in the passage, the disk is given a partial turn to bring the next number, V, under the hole. During the next hour this travels round the slot, in turn disappearing and later giving place to VII. Meanwhile the disk under the other hole has been going through a similar course during the intermediate even hours. The Fromanteels were a family of clockmakers of Dutch origin, the first known being Ahasuerus, who was free of the Blacksmiths' Company in 1630. Seven of the family are known, all having been unruly members of the Clockmakers' Company. One of them, a celebrated maker, appears to have been the first to make pendulum clocks in England, under Huygens' instructions; the maker of this watch was probably Abraham. Its inner and outer cases have already been mentioned.

An ingenious method of indicating hours and minutes by a single hand is adopted on the watch by Quare, illustrated on the same Plate. The single hand is a minute hand, reaching to the minute band and going round once an hour. The hour figures are on a central disk which makes eleven-twelfths of a turn in the hour, and the hand serves also as an hour hand indicating on this disk. The time shown is 25 minutes past 5; when, after an hour, the hand has made a complete turn, the central disk will have made one-twelfth of a turn less than a complete turn, and the hand will then be nearly half-way between VI and VII, making the time 25 minutes past 6. This device is found only in a few watches. Daniel Quare, born 1649 and died 1724, was a contemporary of Tompion and in horology second only to him. He was one of the first to connect the hour and minute hands of watches so that the hour hand turned when setting the minute hand.

Another device for showing the hours is on a watch by Fromanteel illustrated at the top of Plate XLV. It has an outer minute band and a minute hand; instead of an hour hand there is a central disk turning once in 24 hours under the dial plate; a sun is seen engraved on this disk, and serves as a pointer to the hour figures arranged from VI to VI on a semicircular band. The time shown is 37 minutes past 3. When the sun has reached VI, on the right, at 6 P.M., a moon, engraved on the same plate opposite to the sun, takes its place as a pointer at VI on the left and acts as the hour indicator from 6 P.M. to 6 A.M. The watch, therefore, tells the owner whether it is day or night, and, as no other advantage of the device is apparent, it is surprising that this type of dial became quite common.

A remarkable feature of this watch is the seconds hand on a dial in the present-day position. The watch dates from about 1700, and it is almost certainly the earliest known watch with a seconds hand and dial on the main dial, though the Marryat collection has a watch some thirty years earlier, by John Fitter of Battersea, illustrated in Britten, with a seconds hand on a dial on the top plate of the movement. This latter watch has a minute hand, and, instead of an hour hand, the centre of the dial, engraved with a figure of Time, turns to show the hour.

A curious division of the minute band into 144 is found on two French watches of about 1700 in the British Museum. The Author can offer no explanation for this division.

'Pendulum' Watches.—The pendulum made so great a revolution in clocks in the last quarter of the seventeenth century that it was used in watches as what would now be called an advertising point. The balance was brought to a position just under the dial, and two small disks were fixed near the rim at opposite points; one of these appeared in a circular slot in the dial, oscillating back and forth like a pendulum bob. Watches

212

with this device were known as Pendulum watches, and the term, no doubt, served to invest them, in the eyes of the public, with some of the virtue of the pendulum clock. In reality, ease of examination and regulation were sacrificed by putting the balance under the dial, with no compensating advantage, and the bad practice was abandoned for the harmless practice of giving a pendulum bob appearance to the balance when in its normal position in the top plate. This gave rise to a special form of balance cock which came to be the common form in Dutch watches during most of the eighteenth century ; one half of the circular cock had a circular slot through which the 'pendulum bob' could be seen, and the other half was solid, with an engraving and motto.

The hour figures lengthen during this period, the XII soon becoming about twice as high as it is wide. The watch at the bottom of Plate XLVII shows the usual shape of hour figure. When minute figures were introduced they were large and still the hour figures were long, with the result that the two sets of figures and the division bands used up most of the dial, leaving only a small central space. The watch at the top of Plate XLVIII shows this type of dial, though not in the exaggerated form sometimes found. The date of this watch is about 1725, and by then there was a tendency for both hour and minute figures to be smaller. The small central space was generally sunk below the level of the dial, often sufficiently to allow a short hour hand to turn inside it. Later in the period the centre was usually repoussé in a design with two panels for the maker's name and place.

The white enamel dial, when it started, had the large minute and hour figures of the champlevé dial. Towards the end of the period the arched minute band was introduced, and is seen on an enamel dial on Plate LI. With both enamel and champlevé dials the arched band became standard on Dutch watches and on English watches made for the Dutch market.

213

In this period started the practice of winding watches from the dial, a hole being cut in the dial, generally with no attempt to suit the position of the hole to the figures. The enamel plaque dial on Plate L, 2 shows the winding hole. The practice became general in France, but was not so common in England.

Repeating mechanism was first applied to watches in 1687 by Barlow and Quare, but repeating watches before 1700 are very rare, and do not become common before the end of the period. Cases of repeating watches are, of course, pierced, and have a long pendant stem, the pendant being pressed in to make the movement repeat.

The form of pendant on the watches of Plate XLVII became standard towards the end of the period, but a plain knob with hole and ring, as in the French watches at the top of Plate L, was common before 1700 and is occasionally found afterwards. The hole in the knob can face either way, but is more usually as in the modern watch.

The method of holding the movement in the case by hinging it at the XII and fastening it by a spring catch at the VI became general about 1675. The catch can be neat as in the watch by Hampton at the bottom of Plate XLVII, or clumsy as in the watches at the top of Plate L. This chapter can fitly conclude with the instructions on closing a watch movement in its case given by J. G. Leutmann, a preacher in Dabrun, who, in 1717-32, wrote the excellent treatise on watches and clocks referred to in Chapter V. :—

'Wenn du die Uhr zumachest, und in das Gehäuse drückest, so thue es nicht mit dem Finger, den der Schmutz leget sich bey der 6ten Stunde in das Ziffer-Blatt, und bekommt daselbst einen unsaubern Fleck, sondern thue es mit dem Nagel am Finger, der schmutzet nicht.'

CHAPTER X

WATCH-CASES FROM 1725

'O d' Anglia nata su l' estreme Rive,
　　Machinetta gentile, onde l' eterna
　　Virtù matrice misurando alterna
　　L' Ore diurne, e della Luce prive;

　　　.　　　.　　　.　　　.

　Deh fra tante, che t' escono dal seno,
　　Machinetta gentile, un' Ora sola;
　　Segna un' Ora per me felice almeno.'
　　　　　　　　　　Padua, 1778.

THIS period begins with the Rococo style of
Louis xv., well exemplified in the repoussé work
which was then the principal form of decoration
in watch-cases. High relief, giving bright contrast of
light and shade, in an asymmetric design characterizes
the work. The three repoussé watches of Plates XLVII,
LI and XXV may be compared; the first, of a date about
1720, is a symmetric design in low relief; the second,
of about 1730, has an asymmetric design, but in a
symmetric frame, and is in higher relief with sharp
changes of relief, giving strong contrasts; the third, of
about 1750, has an asymmetric frame and very high
relief. This last watch, signed on the movement
J. Grantham, London, and on the dial Faver, London,
is an example of the high repoussé work mentioned in
Chapter VI. in which the relief is beyond the capacity of
a single plate of gold, and the work is therefore composed
of several pieces, separately repoussé and united by
solder.

In England repoussé was by far the most common
decorative work for watches, and a great deal of inferior
work is found, especially on the cheaper silver watches.

PLATE LI

1

Outer case of English watch, *c.* 1700. Carnelians set in chased gold.
S. Kensington Museum. p. 203.

2

German watch, unsigned, *c.* 1600. Gilt metal case of lenticular form.
Kunsthistorische Museum, Vienna. p. 61.

3

Diminutive English watch by Richard Crayle, London, *c.* 1630. Plain rounded silver case. Key shown below. Richard Crayle was born in 1600 and died in 1671.
S. Kensington Museum. p. 101.

4

Dutch watch by Gerret Bramer, Amsterdam, *c.* 1730. Gold outer case repoussé, signed H. Manly. Enamel dial with arched minute band, set diamonds between hour figures. Silver hands set diamonds.
S. Kensington Museum. pp. 119, 213, 215.

5

Outer case of watch, *c.* 1780. Gold, enamelled with figure in grisaille on a dark chocolate ground, in frame of gold and white enamel, surrounded by blue translucent enamel with gold and white enamel diamonds and quatrefoils.
S. Kensington Museum. p. 219.

6

English watch by James Upjohn & Co., London, 1778. Gold outer case, enamelled with figure scene in grisaille on a dark chocolate ground, in frame of a narrow band of red translucent enamel and a band of leaf ornament in gold and white enamel, surrounded by a broad band of translucent blue enamel, with green enamel on the edge.
S. Kensington Museum. p. 219.

PLATE LI

Paintings on enamel were employed less, whereas in France the painting was as common a decoration as the repoussé work and later became more common.

The great majority of the paintings on enamel are of little merit, and especially after the middle of the century are bad. Fine work is rare; an example is the picture of Danaë and the shower of gold on the watch on Plate XXXI, 6, by the great French maker Julien Le Roy. It belongs to a date probably a little before the middle of the century, when bright and clear colours were still used. About 1750 there was a tendency towards softer tints, and the paintings are often dull in colour and at the same time have a glassy appearance from a thick covering of translucent glaze.

In England, painting on enamel revived with the start of the Battersea factory about 1750, where a new process was worked, introduced by the engraver Ravenet. In printing phraseology, it was an 'offset' process, the colour being taken off an engraved metal plate on paper and transferred to the enamel surface. The factory lasted only until 1756, but the work was carried on in other factories, at Bilston in Staffordshire and elsewhere. The watch-case on Plate XXXIV, 5 is an enamel of the Battersea type, if not from the actual factory; it resembles work attributed to a group of workmen established on the Chelsea side of the river. It is, though, doubtful whether the offset process of the Battersea factory was applied to the curved surface of watch-cases.

Another English enamel of later date is on the magnificent watch on Plate LII, by William Hughes of London, dating from near the end of the century. The watch was taken from the bedroom of the Emperor of China at the sacking of the Summer Palace in Pekin.

Referring again to the watch by Julien Le Roy on Plate XXXI, 6, it will be noticed that the enamel is bordered by a rim of gold, instead of extending to the edge of the case as in seventeenth-century watches. Later in the century the gold case encroached more and

217

PLATE LII

English musical automata watch by William
Hughes, London, end of the eighteenth century.
The watch is 6·9 inches in diameter, nearly twice
the size of the illustration. Gilt outer case,
pierced and engraved and set with an English
enamel. Bezel set with diamond and ruby
pastes. Carillon of six bells. The watch plays
a tune at each hour, and figures pass over the
bridge over a waterfall composed of twisted glass
rods which, in turning, give an appearance of
flowing water. The watch was taken from the
bedroom of the Emperor at the sacking of the
Summer Palace, Pekin.
Webster coll.   pp. 217, 227.

PLATE LII

more on the enamel, the gold being repoussé and forming a frame with the asymmetric curves of the period, and, when the classic revival brought symmetry back, the enamel painting became a panel, often oval, surrounded by decorative work of many different kinds and sometimes set in a frame of precious stones.

A fine example of enamel painting of 1771 is the portrait bust of John Harrison on the watch on Plate XXXIX, 1. This watch was made by Harrison's son-in-law, James Barton, the year after Harrison received the Government award for 'finding the Longitude.'

Two examples of paintings in the later style in oval frames are at the bottom of Plate LI. That on the right is on a watch by James Upjohn & Co. of London, with hall-mark of 1778-9. The figure scene is in grisaille on a dark chocolate ground; its frame is a narrow band of red translucent enamel and a band of leaf ornament in gold and white enamel. Then comes a broad band of translucent blue enamel, and the edge of the watch is decorated with green enamel. On the left is an outer case only, with similar figure scene in a frame of gold and white enamel, surrounded by blue translucent enamel, with gold and white enamel, diamonds and quatrefoils. At the bottom, right, of Plate XXXI, 7 is a finely executed monochrome panel in the centre of a mass of the deep royal blue translucent enamel that was much in vogue about 1785. The watch is by Pierre Gregson, clockmaker to Louis XVI. A little later there came into fashion enamels called *à l'aurore*, which had a pinkish tinge, and were generally unattractive.

Four-colour Gold.—Soon after the middle of the eighteenth century the form of decoration known as four-colour gold (*or à quatre couleurs*) was introduced in France. Gold, variously alloyed to have yellow, reddish, silvery and greenish tints, was soldered on to a gold plate and worked by chisel and graver. The Swiss watch on Plate XXXI, 3 is a good example of this work, with the addition of rubies and turquoises set in the gold.

WATCHES

The watch dates from the early years of the nineteenth century, when four-colour gold work was fashionable.

A much earlier example, about 1780, is on the magnificent watch in the centre of Plate xxv. The sprays of flowers are in four-colour gold, and they, with the garlands of diamonds, are on a ground of translucent orange enamel, in turn on a gold guilloché (by handwork) ground; the pendant ring is set with diamonds, and the pendant push-piece and case knobs are of diamond. This watch, by Vauché (also spelt Vaucher and Vauchez) of Paris, belongs to the period when France had worked her way up in watchmaking to a position not far short of England's pinnacle, while in decorative work she was far ahead.

As soon as the Paris watchmakers had inspired their public with sufficient confidence to make it no longer *de rigueur* to wear an English watch, their watches, enriched with the fine work of the French goldsmiths and Swiss enamellers, came into fashion with great rapidity. Their elegance and richness appealed more to the French taste than the heavier and plainer English watch, and, though for timekeeping alone England remained supreme, the French decorated watch was the predominant watch of the second half of the eighteenth century.

It is a favourite period for collectors, because watches are plentiful and are very decorative, but it is full of pitfalls for the inexperienced. The great majority of watches lack the artistic merit that gives beauty to the rich decoration, and the result is mere gaudiness. The further result was shown at a recent sale in Germany of a collection of French watches of this time; a large proportion fetched prices which could have been little in excess of the scrap value of the materials. A watch such as that by Vauché in the centre of Plate xxv, which is very richly decorated and yet remains tasteful, is far from common. Another example of an attractive and richly decorated watch is on Plate LIII, 4, by the same maker, this time spelling his name Vauchez. These two watches are in the Smart collection in the Fitzwilliam Museum, Cambridge, one of the few museum collections of late eighteenth-century watches that has been made with discrimination. It contains also a number of interesting early watches, of which several are illustrated here. English makers of this period produced a plainer watch than the French, and a plain gold watch in a plain gold outer case was quite common and, when the outer case was well formed, looked neat. Repoussé work continued to the end of the century but became less common and enamelling became more common, and the richly decorated watch was produced, as in France, but it is even rarer to find one of real merit. The great English makers, Ellicott, Mudge, Arnold and Earnshaw, devoted themselves to the improvement of timekeeping, but makers of the second rank, such as Ilbury, Jefferies and Jones, Markwick Markham, George Prior, specialized in highly decorated watches, especially in watches for India, which by enamel and stones were made as barbarically gaudy as possible. Where real stones were too costly, imitation stones took their place, because stones in profusion appeared essential. M. Alfred Chapuis wrote an excellent monograph on the subject of the Indian watch, which was published with several plates in colour by the *Journal Suisse d'Horlogerie* in July 1920.

The example of English decoration on Plate L, 5 is interesting as showing some originality in choice and treatment of materials. The cherubs are of white coral and other portions of the design are of mother-of-pearl, lapis-lazuli, and horn, all set in the repoussé gold work characteristic of the last and worst stage of the Rococo.

Astronomical Watches.—One English maker, George Margetts, specialized in astronomical and calendar watches during the last quarter of the eighteenth century. Plate LVII, 1 shows the dial of an astronomical watch, of which several by him and all similar are known. The small central dial with two hands is the watch proper. Below this is an oval steel plate to which

221

PLATE LIII

1

Swiss automata repeating watch, unsigned, early nineteenth century. When the watch repeats, the two children strike the bells, the boy turns the wheel and the grinder moves the tool to and from the grinding wheel.
Fitzwilliam Museum.   p. 227.

2

Swiss astronomical watch by Marc Fabry Pinault, Geneva, 1759. Plain gold inner case. Outer case of bloodstone, not illustrated. Gold champlevé dial. Centre seconds with nib for stopping the balance. Indicates days of week and month, age and phase of moon, the sign of the zodiac and the number of days in the month. On the right the opening varies in size to show the instants of sunrise and sunset.
Fitzwilliam Museum.   p. 223.

3

Watch-key of mother-of-pearl, with portrait in relief of Corneille.
Fitzwilliam Museum.

4

French watch by Vauchez, Paris, *c.* 1790. Outer open-backed case of gold, enamelled red, not illustrated. Inner gold case enamelled on back in mauve, green, red and blue floral devices, with small diamonds and four-colour gold ornament, surrounding a band of translucent enamel on an engine-turned ground. Bezel with circle of diamonds.
Fitzwilliam Museum.
pp. 220, 224.

5

French watch by Lepine, Paris, *c.* 1800. Gold case, back engine-turned in 'barley-corns' under translucent grey enamel, and set pearls. Gold dial. Jean Antoine Lepine, born in 1720 and died in 1814, an eminent maker, introduced the 'Lepine' calibre, enabling watches to be made thin. See Plate LVI, 1.
Fitzwilliam Museum.   p. 224.

6

Ring watch, set diamonds, early nineteenth century.
Fitzwilliam Museum.   p. 227.

PLATE LIII

is attached the moon hand on the left, and below this again is a gilt disk to which the sun hand is attached. The end of the steel plate where the hand is attached is engraved 'High water,' and indicates the time of high tide. The moon hand shows the position of the moon in the heavens and its age on the gilt disk. The whole dial below the gilt disk makes one turn in a sidereal day, while the gilt disk with the sun hand makes a turn in twenty-four hours. The sun hand therefore travels over the dial once a year and indicates the month, day of the month, sign of the zodiac and the sun's declination. The gold cage, which is attached to the time dial, is stationary, and the moving dial below it shows the part of the heavens visible at any time of the year. Margetts was free of the Clockmakers' Company in 1779 and was working till past the end of the century. He was a fine maker, if not quite in the first rank.

Another interesting astronomical watch of 1759 is the Swiss watch shown on Plate LIII, 2. It is a very early example of a centre second stop-watch, having a nib for stopping the balance. In the two sector-shaped openings above and below the centre of the dial are shown the day of the week and of the month, the sign of the zodiac, the number of days in the month and the age of the moon. On the left is the ordinary moon dial, showing the phase of the moon, and on the right is an uncommon device for showing the time of sunset and sunrise; a sun rotates round the small dial once in twenty-four hours, being exposed to view during the day and hidden during the night; two blued steel plates move in and out of the aperture through which the sun is seen, according to the season of the year shortening or lengthening the time during which the sun is visible. The watch is shown without its outer case, which is of bloodstone with gold mounts and a diamond press button.

Engine-turning.—At the end of the eighteenth century there came into vogue the mechanical form of the old guilloché, known in France by the same name but in English by the term 'engine-turning.' It is seen, under translucent enamel, on three of the watches illustrated, those at the bottom of Plate LIII and the blue enamel watch on Plate XXXI, 7. Engine-turning is of particular interest because it has now become so fashionable that almost every one carries about an example of engine-turning, on a cigarette-case, or vanity-box or pencil-case. And this mechanical form of decoration, with its pleasant play of light and shade, is far better than the commercial art decoration which is almost the only alternative.

As few people know anything of the methods of engine-turning, and as old examples in the variety of the present day do not exist, the Author has prepared the samples of engine-turning on Plate LIV, executed on a much bigger scale than is usual, to show better the individual cuts. All the six patterns on the Plate are formed by repetitions of the single wavy cut shown on the central block.

The piece of work to be engine-turned is mounted on the head of the engine-turning lathe, so that it can be rotated; at the same time, the whole head is caused to oscillate, following the contour of a rosette which is the basis of a pattern. The combined rotation and oscillation causes a fixed tool to make the wavy cut shown. In the top pattern, successive smaller wavy cuts are made, with the cut moved each time half a wave round, so that the outward curves of the first cut face the inward curves of the second cut, leaving between them the barleycorn-shaped projections which give the pattern its name. The watch on Plate LIII, 5 has the barleycorn pattern. The pattern on the right is made by cuts decreasing in size, but without moving the cut round. This is the pattern on the watches on Plates XXXI, 7 and LIII, 4, only in the watches the rosette is cusped instead of being wavy. The pattern on the left is produced in the same way except that the cut is gradually shifted downwards. In the pattern at the bottom, the cut is moved round at each

PLATE LIV

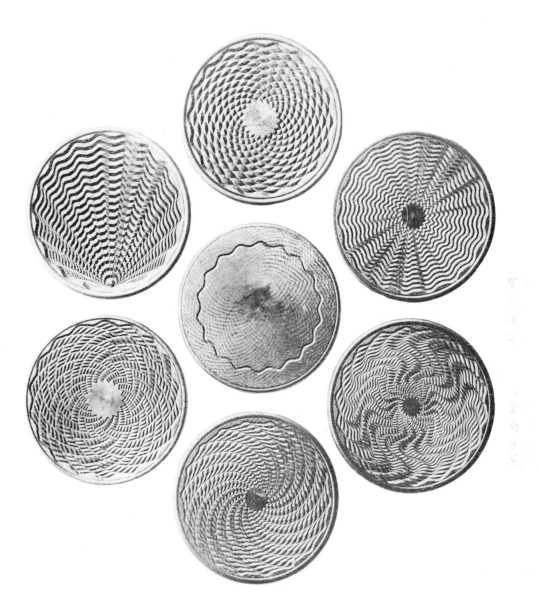

EXAMPLES OF ENGINE-TURNING

successive cut, but only about one-quarter as far as is necessary to give the barleycorn effect. In the lower pattern on the left, the cut is moved round as before for six cuts and then is moved round in the opposite direction for a further six cuts; then again moved in the first direction, and so on. This type of pattern is known as *flinquets*. A variant is the lower pattern on the right, where the direction of moving round the cut is changed gradually instead of suddenly.

Many other patterns, with just as much apparent diversity, can be produced from the same rosette giving the one wavy line, and, as every engine-turning lathe is provided with rosettes giving many different forms of waved and cusped lines, the diversity of pattern possible is quite extraordinary. Engine-turning is done on cigarette-cases, pencil-cases, etc., in straight instead of circular wavy lines by a device which converts the rotary motion of the lathe into an up-and-down motion of the work.

The inventor of engine-turning is unknown. François Guerint of Geneva has often been credited with it, but engine-turning was practised as part of the turner's art in 1670, over a century before he was born. It did not, though, appear on watch-cases before about 1770 and is rare before 1790.

In the Olivier collection is an interesting example of a stone case cut in a 'barleycorn' pattern, giving the appearance of engine-turning. It was done, no doubt, by grinding grooves by means of a tubular tool, the 'barleycorn' pattern being produced equally well, if the surface be flat, by a series of eccentric circular cuts.

Form Watches.—The period before and after 1800 saw the revival of form watches, and the introduction of musical and automata watches, painted dials and pearl decoration. Form watches are found in immense variety in the early years of the nineteenth century, nearly all of Swiss make. Plate LV shows a cross watch of blue enamel set with pearls. Above is a basket of flowers, set with

PLATE LV

1

Swiss watch, unsigned, mid nineteenth century. Gold case in form of a basket of flowers, enamelled in colours and set pearls. The flower portion hinges open to disclose the dial.
Fitzwilliam Museum. p. 225.

2

Swiss watch by Jaques Patron, Geneva, *c.* 1785. Gold case in form of mandoline. Front enamelled light blue with gold decoration and gold strings. Back enamelled in gores, alternately light and dark blue.
Fitzwilliam Museum. p. 226.

3

Cross with watch in centre, unsigned, probably Swiss. Blue translucent enamel on gold, with pearls.
Fitzwilliam Museum. p. 225.

4

Silver watch - key with female head and death's-head back to back.
Fitzwilliam Museum.

5

Swiss watch, unsigned, early nineteenth century. Gold case set pearls and rubies. Key shown above.
Fitzwilliam Museum. p. 227.

6

Swiss watch by Bautte et Moynier, Geneva, early nineteenth century. Gold case set pearls and olivines.
Fitzwilliam Museum. p. 227.

PLATE LV

pearls with an enamel painting of flowers; the flower part hinges open to disclose the watch face. To the right is a mandoline in coloured enamel.

On Plate LVI is a lyre watch of gold set with pearls, and above is a bracelet watch with a diamond-studded balance showing through the opening above the dial. These two are in the South Kensington Museum. On Plate LIII is a ring watch of ordinary form with diamond-studded bezel. Marquise ring watches similar to the bracelet watch just mentioned are not uncommon.

Pearl decoration became almost a mania for a short time after 1800. At the bottom of Plate LV are two watches which show the lengths to which it could be carried. The watch on the right is set with olivines, and is by Bautte et Moynier of Geneva; the other is set with rubies, and its key is shown above it. There are over 1500 pearls and 90 stones in each watch.

At the top of Plate LIII is an automata repeating watch of a type that was made in Switzerland in considerable number about 1800 and after. In many examples the gilt engraved plate carrying the moving figures shows inferior work, and the watch illustrated is unusually well executed. When the watch is made to repeat, the two cherubs hit the bells with their hammers, while, below, the boy turns the wheel for the grinder, who moves the tool down to the grinding wheel and up again. The narrow annular dial, as in the watch illustrated, is the most usual form on automata watches, but some have a small circular dial under the pendant, and the rest of the space is devoted to the gilt plate with automata figures.

Automata were often added to musical watches, as in the watch on Plate LII already mentioned as having belonged to the Emperor of China. A tune is played at each hour, and during the music the waterfall appears to flow and figures pass over the bridge.

Two watches with painted scenes on the dial are shown on Plate LVI, that on the right being English by J. Bradford of Liverpool, with hall-mark of 1815, and

227

PLATE LVI

1

Swiss watch, unsigned, first half of nineteenth century. Enamelled cocks, showing Lepine calibre.
S. Kensington Museum.
pp. 221, 229.

2

Bracelet watch, French or Swiss, early nineteenth century, with diamond-studded balance showing above the dial.
S. Kensington Museum.
p. 227.

3

French watch by Jacques Poëte of Blois, *c.* 1640. Gold case enamelled with flower paintings, probably by Christophe Morlière of Blois, brother-in-law of Poëte.
Kunsthistorische
Museum, Vienna.
pp. 131, 143.

4

Swiss watch, unsigned, early nineteenth century. Gold case champlevé and filled with black and white enamel.
S. Kensington Museum.
p. 229.

5

Dutch watch with fictitious English name and London hall-mark of 1773-4. Painted enamel dial.
S. Kensington Museum. p. 227.

6

English watch by J. Bradford, Liverpool, 1815. Silver case. Painted enamel dial.
S. Kensington Museum. p. 227.

7

Swiss watch in form of a lyre, early nineteenth century. Gold case, set pearls, enamelled light blue.
S. Kensington Museum.
p. 227.

PLATE LVI

that on the left Dutch with London hall-mark of 1773 and the name of an imaginary London maker. The paintings are always crude and generally take a seaport as the subject. In France painted dials came into fashion at the time of the Revolution, and M. Roblot made a large collection of watches and dials bearing revolutionary scenes, which were shown at the Paris Exhibition of 1900. They are of historical interest in illustrating practically every incident of the Revolution, but artistically or horologically they are without any merit.

In the first quarter of the nineteenth century there was a revival of champlevé engraving with the ground filled in with black wax or coloured enamels. The early seventeenth-century example of this work is on Plate XXIV, 5; the nineteenth-century example on Plate LVI, 4.

On the same Plate is a watch with glass back and the cocks of the Lepine-type movement enamelled white with fine black markings. Enamelling of the movement in colour was practised at Fleurier in some of the more richly decorated watches for the Chinese market.

Plate LVII contains reproductions of two watches by the most famous of later makers, Abraham Louis Breguet, who worked from about 1780 to 1823. The characteristic of Breguet's watches was extreme simplicity in the case, and, at the time when the fine watch was always richly decorated with stones, pearls and enamel, he offered his watches as timekeepers, generally with no form of decoration, and rarely with any but the simplest decorative work. In this he followed the practice of the contemporary fine English makers, but he did what they have never succeeded in doing from that time to the present day, he produced a watch that was perfectly plain and yet beautiful, not beautiful as a bit of goldsmith's or enameller's work, but purely as a watch, beautiful because all the parts—hands, dial, figures—were perfectly adapted to their function, and harmonized together in a way that made the whole aspect singularly pleasing to the eye. The watch on Plate LVII, 4 is a typical Breguet repeating

229

PLATE LVII

1

English watch by George Margetts, London, late eighteenth century. Gold case with astronomical dial, the outer dial turning once in a sidereal day, while the hand with sun indicates the month, the day of the month, the sign of the zodiac and the sun's declination. The gold cage shows the part of the heavens visible. Outside the inner time dial is a ring showing the tides. *British Museum.* p. 221.

2

German watch by Johann Christoph Ehrhardt, Augsburg, *c.* 1740. Vernis Martin case. White enamelled dial covered with a pierced and chiselled gold plate. Semicircular minute band with fly-back hand, the hour figure appearing in the hole at the top. Quarters are shown in the slot below and the day of the month in the opening on the left. *British Museum.* p. 232.

3

English watch by Benjamin Hill, London, mid-seventeenth century. Blued steel inner case. Outer case of filigree gold. Gold dial engraved with village scene in centre. Benjamin Hill was free of the Clockmakers Company in 1640, was master of it in 1657, and died 1670. Three other watches by him are known. *British Museum.* p. 153.

4

French repeating watch by Abraham Louis Breguet, early nineteenth century. Gold case, silver engine-turned dial.

p. 229.

5

'Souscription' watch by Abraham Louis Breguet, early nineteenth century. Silver case, with gold edge. Secret signature on enamel of dial under the 12. Movement has ruby cylinder and parachute. *British Museum.* p. 229.

230

PLATE LVII

watch with silver dial; it is thin, even for a repeating watch of the present day, and is less than half the thickness of the contemporary English watch. A Breguet watch made after 1800 is quite a fair timekeeper, and Mr. E. V. Lucas, the owner of the watch illustrated, uses it regularly and finds it a more satisfying possession than any watch made to-day.

The watch shown to the right of it is a Breguet *Souscription* watch, supposed to have been made in lots of half a dozen or so when sufficient orders, with a quarter of the price paid in advance, had been obtained. They sold at 600 fr. in a silver case with gold edge, and about 1000 fr. in a gold case, and were very cheap in comparison with Breguet's ordinary watches, though 1000 fr. in 1820 must be equivalent to about £100 now. The white enamel dial has only an hour hand, which is extended in a very fine point to the outer five-minute divisions; it was therefore quite easy to read the time to within one or two minutes. The watch is far from cheap in its movement; it has a ruby cylinder of the type described in the chapter on Escapements, and parachutes; it winds from the square in the centre of the dial.

Immediately under the XII it is just possible to discern something marring the enamel surface. This is revealed by a lens as Breguet's secret signature, with the number of the watch scratched on the enamel by a diamond point operated by a pantograph. In the watch illustrated it is unusually plain; in some cases a strong lens will show it only if the light falls on it at the right angle. Breguet was driven to this secret signature by the mass of Swiss watches bearing his name. To-day there exist many more forged Breguets than real Breguets.

Two other types of watch issued by Breguet were the *perpétuelle* and the *touche* watches. The former had an oscillating mass, like that of a pedometer, which moved up and down as the wearer walked, and wound up the

231

watch, and the latter had an hour hand turning outside the case and fitting closely to it, so that the watch could be worn without fear of the hand catching in the dress; feeling knobs, as in the sixteenth-century watches, enabled the time to be read by feeling the position of the hand.

Porcelain cases were not uncommon during this period. They were either set in a narrow frame of gold or were partially covered with gold repoussé work. The porcelain had to be fairly thick for the sake of strength, and the case tended to be clumsy; it is rare to find a really attractive case of porcelain.

The type of lacquer painting devised by Robert Martin, and known as *Vernis Martin*, is common on French clocks but is rarely found on a watch-case. It is not well suited to the small scale of a watch. Martin was appointed *vernisseur* to Louis xv. in 1733.

Paintings covered with a thin layer of transparent horn are common in the second half of the century. They never have any artistic merit, and are found only on inferior watches.

The white enamel dial, introduced about 1700, began to be common at the start of this period, and became the standard type of dial in the second half of the century. The champlevé metal dial became less common after the middle of the century, and died out after 1775. At the end of the century, metal dials with engine-turned centres were introduced and were popular during the first half of the nineteenth century.

The large minute figures took most of the century to disappear altogether, but after 1750 both minute and hour figures were usually much smaller, and the minute figures began to be confined to the quarter-hours before final disappearance.

The odd ways of showing hours and minutes which were popular in the last period were almost entirely given up after 1725, but the fly-back type of hand is found in different forms. On Plate LVII, 2 is a watch with

232

fly-back minute hand, which indicates on the semi-circular minute band, and flies back to 0 as soon as it reaches 60. The hour figure appears in the central opening at the top, while quarters appear in the circular slot above the centre; the day of the month appears in the opening on the left. The back of the case is decorated with the *Vernis Martin* mentioned above. After 1800 the minutes or hours or sometimes both were occasionally shown as figures in an opening, a system now being revived in Swiss watches, and about the same time Breguet and others made the hour hand flip from one hour to the next, an innovation that proved thoroughly unsatisfactory.

The pendants of Plate XLVII gradually changed to the type of that at the bottom of Plate LI, the ring sometimes being a very flat oval. About 1800 the lower part of the stem was often rectangular and enamelled. After 1800 a plain spherical knob with an inserted ring—the pendant of the late seventeenth century—became usual, as in the Breguet watches on Plate XLVII and the champlevé engraved watch on Plate XLIX. The oval pivoted ring, however, remained in use.

> ' L'une avance, l'autre retarde ;
> Quand près de vous je dois venir,
> A la première je regarde ;
> A l'autre, quand je dois sortir.'
> *Quatrain by a poet wearing two watches.*

CHAPTER XI

THE CHINESE WATCH AND THE CHEAP WATCH

'Every puny clerk can carry
The time of day in his pocket.'
Antipodes, a Comedy. 1638.

THE Chinese watch is a watch made for, not by, the Chinese. From the end of the seventeenth century the Chinese took a keen interest in clocks and watches, and even made some endeavour to make them themselves. In this they were unsuccessful, but their interest had the result of establishing a flourishing industry, centred at Fleurier in Switzerland and devoted to producing the particular type of watch that found favour in China. The history of this interesting byway in watchmaking was quite neglected until M. Alfred Chapuis wrote his splendid monograph, *La Montre Chinoise*,[1] to which the Author is indebted for the following notes.

At the end of the eighteenth century certain English and Swiss makers had established a considerable business in the supply of watches to China. These were watches of ordinary type, preferably rather gaudy with enamels, stones and pearls; the only peculiarity was that they were sold to the Chinese in pairs. Then, during the first quarter of the nineteenth century, there developed gradually a Chinese type, with decoration of the movement as the principal feature. Chapuis thinks it probable that it was started by Ilbury (Ilbéry) of London and copied by Bovet of Fleurier.

[1] Neuchâtel, *c.* 1920.

234

By the middle of the century the plain watch had reached a fairly definite type (Plate L, 4), with all the cocks, bridges and barrel engraved in the peculiar style seen. The visible portions of the plate were either engine-turned, as in the example illustrated, or engraved in the same style. The parts of the movement were arranged to please the Chinese eye, sometimes symmetrically and sometimes with the edges of cocks and bridges cut in festoons, and the whole was protected by an inner glass cover. All steel parts were highly polished and the screw-heads blued, and the jewels chosen of bright colour. The watch nearly always had a centre-seconds hand, and the special form of duplex escapement described in Chapter XIII. was generally used to give jump seconds. In the *de luxe* watch, in enamelled case, often set with pearls, the movement also was sometimes enamelled.

The real Chinese watch—made by a Chinaman—is extremely rare. An example, dating from the beginning of the eighteenth century, in the Gélis collection, is illustrated in M. Chapuis' book.

The Cheap Watch.—The Waterbury watch is generally regarded as the first cheap watch, no doubt because it became so notorious in its short life. It was not the first. cheap watch, though it sold more cheaply than any previous watch. There was little merit in its cheapness, because it was made so badly. It went, in spite of its defects, because it had a mainspring of inordinate length (eight feet) which turned round the wheels by brute force. The owner had to acquire the habit of winding the watch up whenever his hands were not otherwise occupied. Its one merit was an exceedingly clever design.

The watch that was really the first cheap watch was a thoroughly sound timepiece, and it is unfortunate that the name of its originator—Roskopf—has become associated with the cheap and nasty in Swiss watches. Roskopf himself made only what was good.

Georges Frédéric Roskopf was born at Niederweiler in Baden in 1813, and served his apprenticeship at

Chaux-de-Fonds, and until about 1865 worked as a master watchmaker, producing only higher-grade watches. During the last ten years of this period his dreams of a poor man's watch had been crystallizing into a reality. The watch was to sell for 20 francs, and yet was to be as good and durable a timekeeper as a watch then costing four times as much.

In 1865 Roskopf began to make up experimental watches. In the type of watch that he finally adopted, economy of work was secured mainly as a result of the design. The escapement was a lever, but of the pin type. This type was invented by Louis Perron of Besançon, but was not generally known, and it is probable that Roskopf reinvented it. The escapement was carried by a special plate capable of adjustment in position in the watch. This enabled the escapement to be made independently of the watch, and made its *planting*, or the positioning of its parts, easier.

The centre wheel was omitted, allowing the use of a large spring barrel of more than half the diameter of the watch, and the minute-work driving the hands was worked from the spring arbor, as in the old German stackfreed watches. Winding was done at the pendant, but without a ratchet, so that the winding knob could not turn backwards, and the hands were set, as in a clock, by pushing them round with the finger. Finally, high finish was omitted where it served only to improve the appearance of the movement.

The first watches were produced in 1867, and had an immediate success. The foremost makers and merchants in different countries gave large orders, Breguet of Paris continually complaining that Roskopf would not fill more than half his orders. Louis Favre, one of the first makers of Switzerland, wrote in 1869 :—

All these watches are going marvellously and with an imperturbable regularity. The chronometers and watches *de luxe* are liable to stop ; yours go always, as if their life were eternal, as if they were going on for ever. They are almost too good.

236

Since patent rights did not then exist in Switzerland, Roskopf soon had imitators, and in nearly all cases the design was imitated but not the high quality. At the present day, watches of Roskopf type with modifications on the original design, but always on its broad lines, are sold by the million, some good, the majority bad. The Author has bought one for half a crown, a new watch and at ordinary retail but pre-duty price. It is a better timekeeper than a verge watch by John Ellicott, in exceptionally good condition, which, in 1765, must have cost about 100 guineas.

CHAPTER XII

HISTORY OF WATCHMAKING

'A woman that is like a Germane Cloake,
Still a repairing ; ever out of frame,
And never going a right, being a watch ;
But being watcht, that it may still goe right.'

Love's Labour's Lost.

IN the early sixteenth century, Nürnberg and Augsburg were the only places which can be regarded as centres of clockmaking, and they were centres only in the limited sense that there are more table clocks of this period originating from Nürnberg and Augsburg than from any other town. It was natural that the fine work of the small clock should find its home where the only work in any way resembling it—the work of the locksmith and gunsmith—was most developed. As far as is known, watchmaking was started in Nürnberg by Peter Henlein about 1510. No other maker of the first half of the sixteenth century is known, though perhaps Caspar Werner, who died in 1545, made watches; Dopplmayr says that he made *kleine Uhren*. Hans Gruber, too, of whose work several examples exist, and Matthäus Buschmann of Augsburg, may have made watches shortly before the middle of the century.

The second half of the century, however, saw a rapid development, and watch- and clock-making then became a definite industry of the two towns. The first makers were locksmiths (*Kleinschlösser*), and the Nürnberg Archives refer to Peter Henlein throughout his life as a locksmith ; only in the notice of his death in 1542 is he called an *Vhrmacher*.

238

The industry was not incorporated as a guild till 1565, when three makers, Esias Vogel, Hanns Praun and Marx Steppinger petitioned for mastership in watch and clockmaking. A difficulty in language arises here; the German words used at the time for watch- and clock-makers were *Grossuhrmacher*, meaning turret clockmaker, and *Kleinuhrmacher*, meaning a maker of watches and small clocks; there is no distinguishing word for a watch corresponding to the modern word *Taschenuhr*. The three makers are described as Kleinuhrmacher, and the Nürnberg *Rat* set them an essay consisting of a striking and calendar table clock and a watch, to be made within a year, as follows :—

Two timepieces, the first a standing piece, 6 inches high, $4\frac{1}{2}$ broad and $2\frac{1}{2}$ deep in its iron case. Its movement of wheels and pinions to show good craftsmanship and to strike the four quarters and the hours; on one side it shall show the 24 hours of sun and moonshine during the day and night, indicating the quarters as well as the hours; on the other side shall be the calendar and the planets with the length of day. The other piece shall be of small size, such as one wears hanging at the neck; the movement shall strike up to 12 and have an alarum.

The description of the table clock applies well to the tower-shaped clocks of the late sixteenth century, of which examples are found in the British and South Kensington Museums. For later members of the craft the essays imposed were rather more severe, and it was a condition that the applicant for mastership should himself make the brass case with the cover over the bells, making use of no pattern, but cutting the decoration free-hand and without assistance. The time allowed was reduced to eight months.

With essays of such difficulty, the craft of watch- and clock-making must have been of a higher order than that of the locksmiths, but nevertheless it had not reached the status of the older craft even in 1629, because it was then laid down that any one who made his essay as a locksmith could work either as a locksmith or a clockmaker, but that if his essay was in clockwork he could not do locksmith work. Paul von Stetten[1] says that in Augsburg locksmiths, gunmakers and others had the right to make large and small clocks, but that after 1500 (the actual date is not given) the watch- and clockmakers became a special craft. The earliest clockmakers' guild known—and only the fact of its existence is known—is that of Annaberg in Saxony in 1543. An account is given in the *Allgemeines Journal der Uhrmacherkunst*[2] of a document of 1605 found in the Annaberg archives, in which the statutes of the guild of clockmakers of 1543 were renewed after their destruction by fire. The town of Annaberg and its district are unknown as a centre for clockmaking, and the existence of an early guild there shows how incomplete is our knowledge of early clockmaking.

Blois must be regarded as a little behind Nürnberg in starting the industry, because no watchmaker so early as Peter Henlein is known. Watchmaking, however, developed there with extraordinary rapidity, the presence at Blois of the Courts of François i., Charles ix. and Henry iii. fostering a craft so well suited to a luxurious age. The Abbé Develle has written an excellent monograph, now very scarce, on the watchmakers of Blois,[3] which gives the best picture that exists of early watchmaking in all its aspects. The famous Julien Coudray, if he was a watchmaker, is the first known ; before him, to the end of the fifteenth century, there were at Blois only locksmiths and *horlogers en grand volume* or turret-clock makers. Julien Coudray was clockmaker to Louis xii. and François i., and figures in the royal accounts from 1504 to 1529. The two orloges he made for the king in 1518 have already been mentioned, and the probability of

---

[1] *Kunst- Gewerb- und Handwerks Geschichte der Reichs-Stadt Augsburg.* Augsburg, 1779.

[2] Quoted by Speckhart in his edition of Saunier's book, *Die Geschichte der Zeitmesskunst.* Bautzen, 1903.

[3] *Les Horlogers Blésois au XVI. et XVII. siècle.* Blois, 1913 and 1917.

their being watches discussed ; no others from his hand are known, but there are several records of his work on public clocks.

In the time of François I. (1515-47), Blois had three or four watchmaking shops, but no trace of their work remains. In the reign of Henri II. (1547-59), seven workshops were added ; by 1589 there were twenty-eight in all, and by 1610 there were sixty-three. From 1600 to 1650 was the high-water mark of the industry. Evelyn, in his visit in 1644, writes :—

Blois is a town where the language is exactly spoken ; the inhabitants very courteous ; the air is so good that it is the ordinary nursery of the King's children. The people are so ingenious, that, for goldsmith's work and watches, no place in France affords the like.

After 1660 watchmaking began to decline, so much so that, from 1676 to 1682, only one maker was received in the guild as master. The watchmakers were incorporated into a guild in 1597, with statutes much the same as the earlier statutes of the Paris clockmakers. In fact, the more important conditions of the guilds in France, Germany and England are very similar ; they settled the term of apprenticeship, six to eight years, and the number of apprentices allowed to a master. At Blois a second apprentice could be bound only after the first had served four years. All guilds allowed special privileges to the sons of masters, and this, no doubt, accounted for the many cases of families embracing watchmaking as their craft for generation after generation. At Blois there is the striking instance of thirteen watchmakers of the Cuper family from 1556 to 1700, and even at the beginning of the nineteenth century there was a Cuper still at the craft.

Masters had to work in open shop on the street (*en boutique ouverte sur la voie publique*); many works on horology have reproduced the woodcut in Jost Amman's *Stände und Handwerker* of 1568, showing such an open shop with a counter giving on the street. Masters could take as assistants *compagnons* who had completed their apprenticeship but lacked the capital required to start as masters. In later times, though, it was not uncommon for an apprentice, after serving his time, to travel from master to master in different countries, serving as a *compagnon*, to gain a wider experience than was offered in his native town.

In Paris a guild was formed at an earlier date than at Blois, in 1544,[1] when seven masters petitioned François I. for corporate rights. The statutes, confirmed by Louis XIV. in 1646, provided for a maximum number of seventy-two masters. Of all the watch and clock corporations, that of Paris was the most exclusive. The sum payable by an apprentice on becoming a master was so high—amounting to the equivalent of several hundred pounds of present-day money—that few could afford it unless they were sons of masters, and the apprentice without private means could only work for some master as a *compagnon*.

The history of the Paris corporation will probably remain unknown, because its minute-books, which were kept in the Hôtel de Ville with those of the other corporations, were burnt by the Communards in 1871. Searches instituted by the Author in the Bibliothèque Nationale and among the Archives of Paris and the Departement de la Seine, though fruitful for the eighteenth century, gave a scanty yield of earlier date, and very little can be discovered about the sixteenth- and seventeenth-century members of the corporation beyond a few who signed petitions and left their record on watches.

The only existing document of real value is the *Grant Livre Jaulne: Création et erection du mestier d'orlogeur*, dated 1547 (Arch. Nat., Y. 6[5]). This contains the original statutes of 1544 of the Corporation, and also

---

[1] A date of 1483 has been given to the first statutes by l'Abbé Jaubert and Savary, but René de Lespinasse in *Les Métiers de Paris*, though often quoting Savary, says that the first statutes were in 1544, and there is no evidence of a guild before this. The date of 1483 is probably an error for 1583, when the statutes were confirmed.

a list of the twenty-two clockmakers who, in accordance with the statutes, had submitted their essays. None of them is known by any work. The essay of each is briefly described, but in a handwriting of at least fifty years later. Nearly all are *orloges,* and five are *sans contrepoix.* A few examples are :—

Une orloge a sonnerie sans contrepoix a six pans a deux haulteurs. Dedans quatre mois. Vn reueil matin sans contre-poix a six pans de grandeur tres petite dedans trois moys.

These were probably hexagonal table clocks.

Vne monstre faicte en façon d'heures dedans deux mois.

This must have been a book watch.

Vne orloge sonnante dedans un cristal dedans quatre moys. Vne monstre platte assez grande quy marche vingt six heures dedans deux moys.

The striking clock in a cristal is puzzling ; the last must have been a watch, or its going for twenty-six hours would not have been mentioned.

The names of the Court clockmakers are preserved, starting with Julien Coudray of Blois. They were of two grades—Officiers de la Chambre du Roy, acting as valets de chambre, with the duty of winding and regulating the king's clocks and watches, and members of another grade who were lodged at the Louvre and enjoyed special privileges, such as exemption from visits of the officials of the corporation. Exemption from control was, too, a privilege of a considerable number of streets and precincts of Paris, the old domains of abbeys and princes, so that the Paris corporation must have had greater difficulty in controlling the industry than the Clockmakers' Company in London, which enjoyed full power over the city.

Besides Blois and Paris, Rouen is the only town in which watchmaking became an industry of any importance, but its life was no longer than at Blois. At Autun, the family of Cusin became famous for their watches through the work of Noel Cusin. Lyons, Angoulême, Grenoble and Sedan were producing watches about 1600, but towards the end of the seventeenth century, after the decline of the industry at Blois, Paris remained the one centre of watchmaking in France.

The first record of any united action by the London clockmakers was a petition to the king in 1622 by sixteen clockmakers, said to be all those who were householders in London. It was entitled :—

The agreevaunces of the Clockmakers Cittizens and inhabitantes in London.

They were

much agreeved both in theire estates credittes and trading through the multiplicitie of Forreiners usinge theire profession in London . . . whereby their Arte is not onelie by the badd workmanshipp of Straingers disgraced, but they disinhabled to make sale of theire comodities at such rates as they maie reasonablie live by. For that divers straingers . . . offer their workes to sale, which (for the most parte) being not serviceable (the parties buying the same for the outwarde shew which comonlie is beautifull) are much deceaved in the true value, which rests in the inworke onelie. . . . Where by through the buyers unskilfulness and the fugetivenes of the sellers dyvers persons of worth have bine utterlie deceaved of their money by Straingers under cullor of faire wordes and promises.

The final request is :—

That you wilbe pleased (and the rather for that the lawes of all forreine partes being that noe Englishman or other strainger shall worke there excepte under a Master of the same Nation where he shalbe then residente) That the like course maie be heere taken.

The petition concludes with a list of 'the Knowne Straingers of the same Arte dwelling in and about London.' There are twenty-four names, including those of apprentices and servants ; they indicate generally a

French origin, and several are the same as those of makers in Blois.

The clockmakers may have had real 'agreevaunces' through the bad workmanship of some foreigners, but, judging by examples of the work of Englishmen and foreigners, the latter's work, generally, was the better. Not till the time of Edward East, whose name does not appear before 1630, is there extant a watch which can compare with that of the Flemish Michael Nouwen for perfection of finish in the movement and decoration.

There are no more records of the clockmakers till 1627, when their petition against the foreign makers was renewed through the Blacksmiths' Company, to which several of them belonged, but again there is no trace of any result. In the next year the clockmakers discussed a proposal for incorporation with the Blacksmiths' Company, but the negotiations failed, and in 1630 a petition for incorporation in a separate company was presented. This was granted in 1631, and the statutes gave the long-sought redress for the grievances against the foreigners by providing that a foreigner had to be accepted by a Court of the Company before he could exercise his profession in London. The list of subscribers at the incorporation has fifty-seven names, including two of the foreigners mentioned in the petition of 1622. It is improbable, therefore, that the sixteen signatories of this petition included, as alleged, all the English clockmakers in London.

The Master, Wardens and Fellowship of the Art or Mystery of Clockmaking of the City of London held its first Court in 1632, and effectively controlled the craft in the City for over a century. In the eighteenth century, their power, in common with that of the other Companies, weakened, and finally vanished, though, at the present day, they are one of the few Companies which retain an active interest in their craft. Their minute-books constitute an unbroken record of their proceedings, written in a continually varying, but always beautiful, script, perfectly preserved and full of interest. The Author is greatly indebted to the Court and Secretary for the facilities given him for examining the minute-books, and for the permission to take from them the names of makers embodied in the list annexed to the book. The detailed history of the Company, with the statutes and the principal items of interest in the proceedings, was published in 1881.[1] The Company's library and a magnificent collection of clocks and watches are housed at the Guildhall and are accessible to the public.

The Clockmakers' Company appears to have been the only guild in this craft to sanction the taking of female apprentices; the practice started in 1715, and a considerable number of girls were bound as apprentices. At first they were bound only to their fathers or to a master and his wife, but later records show less regard for the proprieties, and girls were bound to masters without mention of any wife. Only very few women, however, were admitted to the Company, though widows of masters were permitted to carry on their late husbands' businesses. There are, however, two or three instances of apprentices being bound to women. The statutes of Paris and Blois gave the same privilege to widows, but no sanction for female apprentices. The watches that exist bearing names of women must therefore be assumed, in general, to have been issued by widows in charge of a business and not to be the work of craftswomen.

Guilds were formed in Scotland, Sweden, Denmark and Switzerland, though in Holland, where the industry was of considerable extent, the clockmakers were never incorporated,[2] at any rate in Amsterdam.

In Scotland the clockmakers were never separated from the Hammermen, who were incorporated in the principal towns, and in the seventeenth century the

---

[1] *Some Account of the Worshipful Company of Clockmakers of the City of London.* Atkins and Overall. Privately printed. London.

[2] *Onder de minderin, zyn 'er ook eenigen, die in geene byzondere Gilden begreepen zyn; gelyk de Horologiemaakers . . .* Jan Wagenaar. Amsterdam, 1765.

essay for mastership included locksmith's work.　John Smith's admirable book on the Scottish clockmakers [1] gives a good insight into the customs of the Hammermen ; an account of the Essay of Andrew Brown in 1675, who became a maker of much repute, is as follows :—

The quilk day, in presence of the Deacon and brethren, compeared Andrew Brown, Knokmaker, sometime prentice to Humphrey Milne, knokmaker, burgess of Edinburgh, and presented his essay, to wit, ane knok with a watch larum and ane lock upon the door, which was found to be a well wrought ane essay, able to serve His Majesty's leigis and yairfor they admitit and received him amongst them in his airt and trade of knokmaking.

Later, however, the lock was omitted, and clockmakers could obtain their freedom by work of their proper trade.

There is no record of watches being made in Scotland till Paul Roumieu, the fine maker of Rouen, settled in Edinburgh in 1677.　David Ramsay, clockmaker to James VI. of Scotland and I. of England, was born, probably, in Dundee, went to France, and later settled in London.　The fine watch illustrated in Plate XVII, 2 is by him, but, though he may have learnt clockmaking in Scotland, it is almost certain that his skill in watchmaking was acquired in France.

In Sweden the early clockmakers were, as elsewhere, admitted to the corporation of the Smiths,[2] and in 1622 their essay for master was prescribed in an ordinance of the Smiths' guild to be a large clock, striking the hours on two bells and showing the seven planets and the rising and setting of the moon.　They separated from the Smiths and formed their own guild in 1695, when the essay was a repeating table clock or a watch in the English or French style.　Sidenbladh illustrates a watch of 1700 made by Johan Wideman, who was the first master (Elderman) of the guild.

In Denmark also the early clockmakers were incor-

---

[1] *Old Scottish Clockmakers.*　Edinburgh, 1921.
[2] *Urmakare i Sverige under aldre tider.*　Elis Sidenbladh.　Stockholm, 1918.

porated with the Smiths' guild, and, so long as their work consisted of the smithy work needed for church clocks, appeared to be contented to remain a part of this guild. With the advent of house clocks, with their finer work and the decorative work on their cases, the clockmakers felt that they were becoming artists and no longer had anything in common with the Smiths, but their number was so small that, for many decades, they were unable to obtain royal assent to their incorporation as a separate body, though in 1661 and 1681 they did attain some measure of independence. In 1755 thirteen clockmakers of Copenhagen, probably all there were in the city, made a petition to the king which, in its recitation of grievances against the foreign workmen and their wares, was singularly like the petition of the London clockmakers of 1622. Their request for a separate guild, renewed in the same petition, was at last granted, and the guild formed in 1755 continues to this day.

Bering Liisberg gives a full history of the guild in his book on the history of clocks and of Danish makers.[1] The Danish royal family took great interest in clocks and appointed many craftsmen as Court clockmakers. The list of these from 1547 is given; many were foreigners, French refugees, Germans and some Swiss, and the introduction of watchmaking into Denmark was no doubt due to them.

The Danish clockmakers were not successful either in maintaining the authority of their guild or in keeping abreast of the times in developing their craft, and the country was without any outstanding figure in horology until 1801. Then Urban Jürgensen returned from his studies in London and Paris with Arnold and Breguet, and in Copenhagen started the work on watches and chronometers which made him one of the most eminent men of his day.

There is no doubt that France started watchmaking in Switzerland by her persecution of the Protestants;

[1] *Urmagere og Ure i Danmark.* Copenhagen, 1908.

248

started it at the expense of her own industry, and failed, in spite of strenuous efforts, to re-establish it on a scale comparable with that of Switzerland.

Watchmakers appear, as a body, to have inclined towards the Protestant religion, and so, just as they were multiplying in France and developing a craft which gave promise of becoming one of the most important industries of the country, they were driven out by the series of persecutions of the second half of the sixteenth century and the seventeenth century. Geneva was the natural house of refuge. As Protestants, they were received there with open arms and given every privilege. The town, formerly a flourishing merchant centre, had fallen on bad times, and was practically without industry. Craftsmen were therefore welcome and found an open field for their work. St. Bartholomew's night in 1572 brought an influx of refugees which filled the town to overflowing, and a century later, when, in 1685, the Edict of Nantes was revoked, the new refugees had to seek their homes in other towns.

In 1550[1] Geneva lacked clockmakers to such an extent that the greatest difficulty was found in keeping the public clocks in order. By 1575 there were seventeen French clockmakers whose names are known, and from this nucleus the industry developed with remarkable rapidity, helped by the presence in the town of the allied craft of the old-established gold- and silver-smiths. There is no foundation for the common belief that Charles Cusin, a member of the family of makers at Autun, founded watchmaking in Geneva. He went there only in 1574, and was the last of the seventeen refugees mentioned. He acquired a considerable reputation by his ability, and this probably gained for him his title as founder of the industry, but he finished badly by

---

[1] For the following brief summary of watchmaking in Switzerland, the Author is largely indebted to the *Histoire Corporative de l'Horlogerie, de l'Orfèvrerie et des Industries annexes* (L. Babel: Geneva, 1916) and *Die Schweizeriche Uhrenindustrie* (A. Pfleghart: Leipzig, 1908).

disappearing in 1590, owing the town money advanced to him for repairing a clock.

In 1601 the makers obtained the right of incorporation, and made regulations admitting masters on unusually lenient conditions. An apprentice, after serving four years (in Paris the term was eight years) and working for one year as *compagnon*, could present his essay and become master at quite a small expense. The essay, too, presented no difficulties; it was an alarum watch to hang at the neck, and a square table clock *à deux hauteurs*, meaning, probably, a clock with striking movement. In 1673 the statutes were revised and made rather more stringent, especially in the admission of strangers to Geneva, and every precaution was taken to prevent work being done outside the town.

In its attitude towards women workers, however, the Geneva corporation was most intolerant; no concession was ever made, even to the widows of masters. In the second half of the seventeenth century, however, women managed to secure for themselves some accessory work, such as making fuzee chains and polishing, and gradually they enlarged the field, but it was only when the authority of the corporation began to wane, towards the end of the eighteenth century, that they were able to participate to any real extent in the manufacture of watch parts.

The end of the seventeenth century saw the beginning of the system that, ever since, has characterized the industry in Switzerland—the division of watchmaking into the two main parts of making the *ébauche* or *blanc* and of converting the *ébauche* into the finished movement. Until the beginning of the nineteenth century the *ébauche* contained only the roughest work; the plates, cocks, barrel and fuzee were roughly cut to form, but no wheels, pinions or any part of the escapement were made. Then came the *finissage*, which belied its name because it by no means finished the watch. The *finisseur's* principal work was to add the train of wheels and pinions to the *ébauche*, but at different times and in different places his

250

work comprised a variety of other jobs, leaving the *ébauche* more or less complete in its parts. Then the *repasseur* went over every part and turned the whole into a watch. As time went on, the *ébauche* included more and more of the work of *finissage* until it became known as a *finissage*, and then the *finissage* included more and more of the work of the *repasseur* until at the present time he has only to examine the parts, do a certain amount of fitting and polishing, send the brass parts to be gilt and then assemble the watch. In England, the *movement in grey* consisted of an *ébauche* with train of wheels and pinions, all more or less in the rough.

This gives only a very broad idea of the methods of watchmaking. Actually, a large number of independent specialized workers co-operated in the manufacture, the number increasing from the beginning of the nineteenth century onwards and then diminishing as more and more of the work was done by machines in the factory. The casemakers had their own corporation, while certain trades, such as spring-making, were outside the watch-makers' corporation but not themselves incorporated. Other trades remained in the corporation, but were so far recognized that their essays were in the type of work in which they specialized.

The development of the industry was far more rapid in Geneva than in any other country. In 1686 there were 100 masters; in 1716, 165; and in 1766, 800 masters with some 3000 other workers. It was, though, only the industry that developed; Geneva did practically nothing to further the craft. During the eighteenth century, while the great masters of London and, later, Paris were turning the watch into a real timekeeper and perfecting it by constant experiment, the Genevese could only follow in their footsteps and never led the way. While others followed the science they followed the practice, and by now have it so far ingrained in their nature that Geneva, with the neighbouring towns, is the watchmaking centre of the world, and the only country in which the skilled watchmaker is likely to survive.

The other watchmaking districts of Switzerland, stretching along the French frontier, north of Geneva, have not been mentioned because the industry developed there so much later. In the Vallée de Joux, watchmaking was started by French refugees after the revocation of the Edict of Nantes, but during the eighteenth century it developed largely in the form of *ébauches* supplied to the Geneva finishers. Farther north, in the district about Neuchâtel, La Chaux-de-Fonds, Le Locle and La Sagne, now an important centre, watchmaking is supposed to have been started in 1679 by Daniel Jean Richard, a native of La Sagne, who set himself to copy an English watch which came into his hands. The development was more in clockmaking, though large numbers of watches were produced and finished. Now the clockmaking has practically died out, while watch-making in factories continues on a large scale.

In Germany, the industry which started in Nürnberg and Augsburg with so much promise in the sixteenth century was killed by the Thirty Years' War, and found no chance to revive amid the disturbances that followed it. Ulm and several other towns had their corporations, but, after the middle of the seventeenth century, there was no place that can be regarded as a centre of watchmaking, and, until late in the eighteenth century, there is only one outstanding horologist in the history of German watch-making.

Italy, probably, was the birthplace of clocks and their principal home in the fourteenth century, and that was the end of Italian horology. An Italian clock or watch is a rarity, and the few watches bearing Italian names were quite likely made outside the country.

In Spain, watch- and clock-making never even started, and the names of only a few makers are known. Austria and Hungary produced a number of good makers, but no watchmaker of outstanding merit.

252

The beginnings of watchmaking in the different countries have now been traced, and an account will follow of its development as a craft.

By 1600 watchmaking had been well established in London, France and Germany. In London it developed rapidly, while in France and Germany it waned—in France because her craftsmen had been driven out by persecution; in Germany because it could not survive the long period of fighting. By 1700 London was the watchmaking centre of the world.

Up to 1675 the watch retained the mechanism it had at the start in France, except that it was given an extra wheel in the train to make it go for thirty hours. The construction naturally improved, cocks and pillars changed in form, and screws became common, but in principle there was no change. The great makers of the period were Michael Nouwen, *circa* 1600, David Ramsay, 1600-54, Edward East, 1610-73, Edward Barlow or Booth, 1636-1716, Fromanteel, *circa* 1630-60, Thomas Tompion, 1638-1713, and Daniel Quare, 1649-1724. During the latter half of the century there was no watchmaker in any other country who stood on the level of these men.

The year 1675 was the turning-point in the history of watchmaking. The decoration of the case was declining, but there started the series of inventions which turned what was little more than a bit of jewellery into a precision timekeeper. First, in 1675, came the balance spring, claimed in London by Hooke and in Paris by d'Hautefeuille—neither of them watchmakers—but first introduced as a spiral by Huygens. Thuret, a watchmaker in Paris, made the first watch there with a spiral spring in 1675, and in the same year Huygens writes to Denis Papin asking him to report on the watches being tried in London with the balance of his invention.

Tompion at once recognized the value of the invention, and all his watches have a spring, generally very short, of about two turns, and nearly all have two hands. In the same year he devised a modified form of verge escapement with a horizontal wheel and only one pallet, and, in conjunction with Booth (Barlow) and Houghton, patented an escapement which, from the vague description in the patent, must have been a kind of cylinder escapement.

In the next year Barlow invented repeating mechanism for clocks, and ten years later applied it to watches. It immediately became popular in England and France, and during the next century watchmakers were constantly modifying and improving the mechanism. A little later, Quare, who had successfully disputed with Barlow the application of repeating work to watches, connected hour and minute hands to the watch train in such a way that the hour hand was moved when the minute hand was set to time. In earlier watches with minute hands—and at that date a single hand was still the more common— the two hands were driven independently by the train, so that both had to be moved separately in setting to time. In clocks the device was introduced earlier.

Then came George Graham (1673-1751), the assistant, partner and successor of Tompion, who shares with him the honour of burial in Westminster Abbey. He was a Fellow of the Royal Society, and contributed many papers on horology. In clockwork he invented the mercury compensating pendulum and the dead-beat escapement, which remains one of the best escapements for clocks with seconds pendulums. In watchwork he invented the cylinder escapement in its present form about 1725, and introduced it into France by sending a watch to Julien Le Roy.

During the whole of the period under review, say from 1650 to 1720, England was pre-eminent in watchmaking. On the Continent there were makers capable of fine workmanship,but none that contributed to the development of watches or that gained the world-wide reputation of English makers. In Paris the craft was at a low ebb, and the beginning of the eighteenth century saw the first attempts in the country to revive the industry, and stop the large importation of watches by production at home.

254

Henry Sully, an Englishman born in 1680 and apprenticed to Charles Gretton in 1697, travelled in Holland, Germany and Austria from 1708 to 1715, and then went to Paris, where he settled. In 1717 he published his famous work *Règle artificielle du temps*, and gained so good a reputation that the Regent entrusted him in 1718 with the task of establishing a watch factory at Versailles, for which he obtained sixty craftsmen from England. After two years the factory failed, Sully having left it through difficulties with the management. A second factory was started by Sully at St. Germain-en-Laye in 1721, under the protection of the Duc de Noailles, and this failed also after a year. From these failures, however, dates the rise in French watchmaking, possibly because they awoke a new interest in the craft, while bringing craftsmen to Paris; possibly, though, the rise had nothing to do with the factories but was due to the work of the able makers who soon after appeared in Paris.

They were: Jean Baptiste Dutertre, master in 1735; P. Gaudron (1690-1730); Antoine Thiout (1692-1767); Jean André Lepaute (1720-87) and Julien Le Roy. Of these the greatest was Julien Le Roy, who, though not so eminent a horologist as his son Pierre, did more than any one to resuscitate the craft in France. He was born in 1686 and died in 1759. His reputation, soon after his death, may be judged from the following extract from the *Dictionnaire des Artistes* [1] :—

One knows that the English had acquired, by several discoveries, so great a reputation in horology, that they sent their watches to all parts of the known world, and that we ourselves had to get watches from them. Julien Le Roy had the honour of depriving them of this pre-eminence and of placing the watchmakers of France above those of all Europe. . . . His name is now engraved on most of the watches from Geneva in place of the names of Tompion and Graham with which they used to be embellished ; in fact, English watches are now quite given up.

[1] Bonafons, Abbé de Fontenai. Paris, 1776.

If the writer had praised Julien Le Roy less at the expense of the English, he would have been nearer to the truth. The English remained pre-eminent, even though the French reached a position but little below. The reputation of watches from the different countries towards the end of Julien Le Roy's life may be gathered from Zedler's *Universal Lexicon* of 1746 :—

The English watches are considered the best of all, especially the so-called repeating watches. After the English watches come the French, Augsburg, Nürnberg and Ulm watches. The Geneva watches are thought little of, because they are to be had so cheaply ; they are made in such quantities that one buys them in lots.

The same article says that Tompion watches are so famous that one can exchange an old Tompion for a new watch.

Julien Le Roy's chief work was in connexion with observatory and turret clocks, but in the design and beautiful workmanship of his watches he reached the standard of the finest English makers. He was the first to use the watch-case as a gong in place of a bell in repeating watches, which was a great step in bringing the watch to a more graceful form. As indicated in the extract from the *Dictionnaire des Artistes*, the Swiss forgeries of his name and the names of Tompion and Graham are so common that a watch engraved with one of these names is more likely than not to be the work of some one else.

The impetus given to French watchmaking by Julien Le Roy was maintained, and France produced a number of talented men and, for the rest of the century, shared equally with England in developing the chronometer and improving the watch. Antoine Thiout published in 1741 a *Traité d'Horlogerie Pratique* which is by far the best work written on the construction of watches and clocks. He showed much originality in the design of clocks and in modification of repeating mechanism. Enderlin,

256

probably one of the family of watch- and clock-makers of Basle, settled in Paris in 1736, and contributed several chapters to Thiout's book. Amant, who developed the pin-wheel escapement, Pierre de Rivaz, Jean Romilly, a Swiss, and Pierre Auguste Caron, were eminent makers of the middle of the century, the last disputing with Lepaute the invention of an escapement for clocks, and later giving up horology for the theatre and gaining even more renown as Beaumarchais, the author of *Le Barbier de Séville* and *Le Mariage de Figaro*. Jean Jodin, in 1754, published a *Traité des Échappements*, and Jean André Lepaute in 1767 his *Traité d'Horlogerie*, an excellent book, though not so complete as Thiout's. A little later was Antide Janvier, born 1751, whose *Manuel chronométrique* has passed through many editions and is a valuable book. He gained a great reputation for his complex planetary clocks. In England, at this period, there was John Ellicott, born 1706 and died 1772, who was a Fellow of the Royal Society and on its Council. He was the first watchmaker to use the cylinder escapement to any large extent, and made some with ruby cylinders. His workmanship was exceptionally fine. Christopher Pinchbeck, born 1670 and died 1732, has endowed the English language with a word denoting bad quality and falsity, derived from the pinchbeck gold which he invented. It was an alloy of zinc and copper, and was much used for watch-cases. He was a most able maker of watches and clocks, and specialized in musical and automata clocks.

Now comes the period of rapid development, with the 'Discovery of the Longitude' as the stimulus. This meant concentration on one thing only—accuracy of timekeeping. The adjuncts of watches, repeating and striking mechanism and calendar work, on which the great makers had, perhaps, wasted their time, had to be laid aside in producing a marine chronometer, and size and shape became of no importance. Sully had devoted the last days of his life to chronometers, but without success. John Harrison, born 1693 and died 1776, was the first to make a timepiece that went accurately enough to be useful as a marine chronometer, and gained the prize of £20,000 offered by the British Government. His fourth timepiece was not merely accurate enough to be useful, but, on its voyage to Jamaica, it showed the accuracy of a modern chronometer. This instrument in design and construction is certainly the greatest achievement in horology, and yet there is no device in it which has survived or has even been useful in later timepieces. The escapement used was a form of verge, and the device for temperature compensation was soon recognized as defective.

Harrison's success gave an impetus to the construction of chronometers, and all the great makers of the last quarter of the eighteenth century strove to attain his results with a chronometer of better design. The principal makers engaged were Thomas Mudge (1715-94), John Arnold (1736-99) and Thomas Earnshaw (1749-1829) in England, and Pierre Le Roy (1717-85), the son of Julien Le Roy, and Ferdinand Berthoud (1727-1807) in Paris. Mudge, about 1765, made the great invention of the lever escapement, now used in practically all watches, but left it to others to use. Arnold, Earnshaw and Le Roy, almost at the same time, invented the detent escapement, Le Roy's escapement being that of present-day chronometers. Le Roy, too, adopted the principle of modern temperature compensation, first by applying the compensating device to the balance instead of to the spring, and then by making the balance rim of bimetallic strip, so he may be regarded as the inventor of, substantially, the modern form of the marine chronometer. To John Arnold, however, belongs the credit of the helical balance spring of the chronometer. Mudge and Le Roy are the authors of the two essential parts of the modern watch—the lever escapement and the compensating balance.

258

After the failure of the two factories near Paris, abortive attempts were made to start factories for watches at Bourg-en-Bresse in 1765, at Salins in 1785 and at Lyons, but another factory that was started in Paris managed to exist from 1785 to 1790. In 1770, however, a colony of watchmakers settled down in Ferney, a small village close to Geneva but just over the frontier. The initiative lay with the watchmakers themselves, who left Geneva because the authorities at that time were making life difficult for those who were not burghers. Voltaire, who then had settled in Ferney, is often supposed to have founded the colony, but the only part he played was to help in marketing the watches. He devoted himself to this with great energy, writing to his immense circle of acquaintances, and frequently, after selling a watch, finding himself involved in a long, rather one-sided correspondence directed towards extracting payment. With this help the colony flourished, but at Voltaire's death in 1778 the market disappeared and the colonists gradually returned to Geneva, where meanwhile regulations had become less irksome for non-burghers.

The colony was associated with the name of Jean Antoine Lepine, an eminent horologist who was responsible for a radical change in the *calibre* or arrangement of the watch. Using the cylinder escapement, he introduced the thin watch, which, especially in France, became fashionable. He was born in 1720 at Gex, went to Paris in 1744, and became watchmaker to Louis xv. A letter from Voltaire says that Lepine, the king's watchmaker, had his establishment and workmen at Ferney. Members of his family worked at Ferney, and sold their watches through J. A. Lepine in Paris.

The Lepine calibre, described in Chapter VIII in reference to Plate XLIV, 3, began to come into general use about 1776. Towards the end of the century, Breguet introduced some modifications which, as in many of his designs, offered some advantages at the cost of difficulty in construction. Finally, there was evolved a calibre called *demi-Breguet*,[1] and this came into fairly general use. The Lepine calibre (the *demi-Breguet* calibre is now generally called Lepine) did not find favour in England. Its chief advantage was in giving a thinner watch, and the English makers refused to pander to the popular taste in this respect. Long before the Lepine calibre, French and especially Swiss makers had been reducing the thickness of their verge watches by making the escape wheel of very small diameter, and foreign writers often gibed at the thick English watches. The English followed the principle of making the parts of a size that gave the best results, and would not sacrifice good performance to appearance, and, when the cylinder escapement allowed a considerable reduction in thickness without sacrifice, they made the reduction, but would not admit a barrel with only one pivot, and retained the fuzee long after it had been abandoned on the Continent. In this they were right; at that time, with non-isochronous balance springs, a watch was a better timekeeper with a fuzee. The fuzee was finally given up in England only when keyless watches became general, because keyless work was troublesome to apply to a fuzee watch.

English watches of the nineteenth century were known as *full-plate, three-quarter-plate* and *half-plate*. In the full-plate watch there is a complete top plate, as in the old watch, the balance with its cock lying above it. In the three-quarter-plate a segment of the top plate is cut away, leaving a space in which the balance, with its cock, is sunk, so as not to project above the plate. The advantage of the bar or Lepine calibre in saving space and thickness is secured in the three-quarter-plate watch, and it was the usual form in the latter half of the nineteenth century. In the half-plate watch, more of the plate is cut away, to give room for a

---

[1] This had the spring barrel pivoted at one end only and the fourth wheel of the train and the escape wheel sunk in holes in the bottom plate and pivoted in a separate plate attached to this, under the dial.

cock for the fourth wheel.   This gives room for a larger balance, but the half-plate was not common.

The Swiss carried the thinning process too far and the English not far enough.   The French makers varied in their practice—Ferdinand Berthoud favoured a thick watch as strongly as any English maker—but there are many French watches of the period, of fine workmanship, which strike a happy mean.

In Germany, watchmaking showed some signs of recovery in the second half of the eighteenth century, but there was only one man of outstanding ability, and he is hardly known outside Germany.   This was Philipp Matthäus Hahn, a parson in Onstmettingen, Kornwestheim, and Echterdingen, all in Württemberg, born 1730 and died 1790.

Hahn was known mainly by a number of remarkable astronomical and calendar clocks, but a recent biography by Max Engelmann[1] has published the extent of his activities in watchmaking, and includes an interesting article by Hahn on the development of watches from the earliest to the cylinder watch.   Hahn made a considerable number of watches, nearly all with calendar motion, and many with repeating work, showing much individuality of design.   He studied the cylinder escapement, and his article tells how he convinced himself of its great superiority, when properly constructed, over the verge. This alone is evidence that he possessed a clearer insight than many more famous contemporaries.   Had he worked in London or Paris, instead of in small country towns, there is no doubt that his name would have ranked with those of Arnold and Le Roy.

In other countries, Holland, Sweden and Denmark, not a single man in the eighteenth century can be credited with any progress in the craft, although many were able, with fine workmanship, to follow in the path of the English and French makers.

Another attempt to establish in France a watch

[1] *Philipp Matthäus Hahn.*   Berlin, 1923.

factory to supply the needs of the country was made by the Revolutionary Government. Strangely enough, the initiative came from a Swiss, Laurent Megevand, a native of Le Locle, and a man of considerable ability. In 1790 he presented a memorandum to the Government pointing out that 120,000 watches were imported annually into France, and asking for subsidies to enable a watchmaking centre to be started in France. The Government acceded to this proposal in 1793, and accorded very favourable terms, the craftsmen being provided with free lodgings and workrooms, while money was advanced without interest. There was no actual factory, but each craftsman could work on his own account or for any master he might choose. Megevand and two colleagues, Trott father and son, were administrators, supplying the raw materials and placing the products on the market, while a committee acted as intermediary between the Government and the body of craftsmen. In the same year, Megevand brought to Besançon the first group of Swiss from La Chaux-de-Fonds, Le Locle and neighbouring towns, all men who, through their revolutionary sympathies, were in disfavour in their own country. By the end of 1794 the colony was 2500 strong, and, as a colony, it never exceeded this number. A report of January 1795 states that 25,000 watches had been made.

Thus started the present French watchmaking industry. The national idea was fostered by offering a prize of 100 livres to any craftsman who taught a French pupil of either sex satisfactorily, and by offering girls who completed their apprenticeship a prize of 500 livres. This was an ingenious scheme to encourage relations between craftsmen and their pupils, designed to fix the craftsmen in the country. Watches were marked with the revolutionary symbols between the letters F and N (Fabrique Nationale), with B (Besançon) below, and the cases were hall-marked on the pendant with the symbols and F S (Fidélité Sûrété).

Then trouble began. The colonists never settled

down. The Bisontins strongly objected to the inundation of their town by Swiss who were given every conceivable privilege, and nothing was done to make the colonists feel at home. Meanwhile, Switzerland was using every endeavour to entice them back and stop the competition. In 1796 the exodus began, incited by the commercial crisis following the fall of the assignats, and colonists could be induced to remain only by continued benefits offered by the Government. Still, the manufacture continued on a small scale, and in 1805, after a total of 181,500 watches had been produced, subsidies were stopped. The lowest ebb was reached in 1814, and then a fairly rapid recovery began. In 1820, 20,000 watches a year were being finished from *ébauches* made by Japy Frères, the still flourishing firm of Besançon, and in 1826 the number had risen to 60,000 with 2000 workers. Megevand, though he had striven vigorously for the success of the colony, had also speculated on his own account, and was unable to meet his engagements to the Government. He was made bankrupt, and died soon after in 1814.

While Megevand's proposals were being considered, the Convention, in 1792, included time-reckoning among its many reforms, and decided that the day-and-night periods should be divided into ten hours instead of twenty-four, and each of the new hours into ten tenths, and each tenth into ten hundredths of the hour. Conscientiously maintaining the decimal system, ten months were allowed for transforming all timekeepers, but before the time was up the Convention was over, and no more was heard of decimal time-reckoning. The calendar reform, after a few preliminary trials, survived fourteen years.

At the start of the Besancon industry there were in France two men most eminent in watchmaking, though in quite different branches—Abraham Louis Breguet, the last of the craftsmen of the old type, and Frédéric Japy, the first manufacturer of the present-day type.

263

Breguet was born at Neuchâtel in 1747 of Swiss parents, but from 1762, when he started his apprenticeship at Versailles, spent almost his whole life in Paris. He is claimed by the Swiss as a Swiss and by the French as a Frenchman. Breguet excelled in combining perfection in the mechanism with beauty in the form of the watch. His plainest watches—and the great majority had little embellishment—had a singularly graceful appearance, with dials designed to show the time as clearly as possible, and yet with figures and hands so well proportioned and so beautifully executed as to give them an elegance characteristic of their maker. The same combination is found in the movement—exquisite workmanship with a beauty of form which, perhaps, can be appreciated only by a mechanic. Moinet, a pupil of Breguet, in his *Traité d'Horlogerie*, says of him :—

feu Breguet avait un tact heureux pour la distribution gracieuse à l'œil des parties d'une composition mécanique.

Except in his 'subscription' watches, Breguet never, as far as is known, made two alike, either in form or in the movement. Each watch was an individual work of art. He revelled in difficulties ; the many complicated watches made in his workshop were full of them, while the plain watches show departure from normal design requiring workmen of exceptional ability.

Of his many inventions, one, the Breguet overcoil described in Chapter VII, is found in all good modern watches. Another, the *Tourbillon*, described in Chapter XVIII, has been often used and still appears in some precision watches, but it is extremely difficult to make, and improvements in regulation now render it of little benefit. The *Parachute*, which Breguet used in most of his watches, is a device in which the end stones of the balance are mounted on spring supports which can yield if the watch be dropped, and so save injury to the stone or pivot.

Breguet watches were all costly ; the cheapest were

264

his subscription watches, made several at a time for customers who paid one-quarter of the price in advance. He sold about 150 of these at a minimum price of 600 livres for a watch in a silver case. One in the Marryat collection in a gold case, with ruby cylinder and *parachute*, has its certificate showing a price of just under 1000 livres. The subscription watches had only one hand and a plain enamel dial, but the time could easily be seen to a few minutes. An average price for a watch was 2000 livres, which would be equivalent to about £200 of present-day money. He made a considerable number of *montres perpétuelles*, watches which were wound by movement of the body in walking.

Breguet's reputation among his contemporaries is indicated by John Arnold's remark to Urban Jürgensen, the eminent Danish horologist, when, after working under Breguet, he went to Arnold to learn the methods of the English makers :—

Vous avez travaillé avec Breguet, que croyez-vous avoir à apprendre de nous ? N'avez-vous pas travaillé avec l'artiste le plus distingué de l'Europe.[1]

The firm founded by Breguet continues to this day in Paris producing work of the highest grade and maintaining the charm of form characteristic of its founder.[2]

Breguet's contemporary, Frédéric Japy, was born at Beaucourt, near Belfort, in 1749, and died in 1812. After serving an apprenticeship at Le Locle, he started making *ébauches* in Beaucourt, and showed great ingenuity in devising special machines for the work. Thanks to these the factory grew rapidly, and, on Japy's retirement in 1806, was taken over by his sons under the style of Japy Frères. In 1865 it was turning out 500,000 *ébauches* a year, besides clock movements and other

---

[1] *Urbain Jürgensen*. Alfred Chapuis. Neuchâtel.
[2] The late Sir David Salomon, who collected Breguet watches, published in 1923 *Breguet*, containing illustrations of his watches and notes on Breguet.

articles, and remains the most important horological firm in France.

This was the start of the manufacture of the watch by special machine tools. From then on there was steady progress in machines and methods in Switzerland and France, and later in America and Germany. England made no attempt to manufacture watches until much later, and then it was too late. In 1800 she had lost her supremacy, even in the fine hand-made watch. John Arnold, with his contemporaries and successors, devoted themselves to marine chronometers, and gave England even a greater position for these than she had for watches in the days of Tompion, but the watch industry declined steadily and to-day it has practically vanished. Pitt's tax of 7s. 6d. for carrying a watch, imposed in 1797, was hard on a dying industry, but was not the disease that killed it. There were many fine watchmakers in the nineteenth century—James Ferguson Cole (1799 to 1880), who has been named the English Breguet, may be mentioned as a notable example; their watches, regarded as timekeepers, were on the whole the best obtainable, but they were expensive in comparison with the French and Swiss watches, and lacked their elegance.

About 1800 there came into prominence the great Danish maker Urban Jürgensen, a pupil of Houriet, an eminent maker of Le Locle, and then of Breguet, Berthoud and Arnold. He developed the watch factory started by his father first near and then in Copenhagen, but devoted himself more to chronometers, for which he established a great reputation. The firm survives as the *Chronométrie Jules Jürgensen* of Bienne in Switzerland, and is one of the foremost firms of Switzerland for high-grade watches.

Improvements in design during the nineteenth century are almost all due to Swiss. The lever escapement was developed by Moïze Pouzait of Geneva in 1786, and later by Antoine Tavan, who, though a native of France, lived in Geneva. Georges Leschot in 1835 studied it closely and declared it to be the escapement of the future; it was first manufactured in quantity in 1837 in Geneva by him and his colleague Antoine Lechaud. The chronograph was developed by Rieussec and Winnerl of Paris in the first quarter of the century, and then by Piguet and Adolphe Nicole of Geneva, who patented in 1862 the return-to-zero mechanism. Keyless mechanism is due mainly to Audemars, Lecoultre and Adrien Philippe. The discovery of elinvar and the alloy for the *balance intégrale* is due to Guillaume, a Swiss by birth, and it is in Switzerland that they have been utilized. Switzerland in the nineteenth century has played the part of England in the seventeenth and eighteenth centuries.

It is now time to consider America. A few watches were being made by hand about 1800, with the help of parts obtained from Europe, and a little later Luther Goddard made watches on a larger scale. The first machine-made watch appeared in 1838, produced by James and Henry Pitkin, but the factory proved a failure. This was the first of a long succession of failures that marked the development of American watchmaking. There were few successes, but they were great successes, built on the foundations of the failures.

Aaron Dennison was the first man in America to start watch manufacture on the present-day basis. Before him, and in Europe long after him, watch parts were made by machine roughly to size and were then fitted together by hand. Now parts are not fitted together. A part made by one machine in one year will adapt itself to another part made by another machine in the next year, without any fitting work. The parts are said to be interchangeable. This is secured by establishing a system of gauges and making each part to fit a gauge. If the gauges were accurate and the parts were made to fit the gauges accurately enough, then a watch could be made simply by picking one of each part out of the hopper into which the machine drops it, and putting the parts together. This is the ideal, and was the ideal which Dennison had in mind when he started manufacture in 1851. The ideal is never reached, but in some of the best modern factories it is nearly reached. In the early factories, hand fitting remained an important part of the manufacture, first because the system of manufacture to gauges had not been learnt, and secondly because the machine tools were far from perfect.

In watchwork of the present day there is no real distinction between machine-made and hand-made watches. All watches are to a large extent machine-made and all to some extent hand-made. The cheapest watches have little done by hand beyond assembly of the parts. The best have a considerable amount of handwork, even apart from the springing and adjusting, which in a high-grade watch entails much work by highly skilled men.

It is a general impression that a machine-made watch, or a machine-made anything else, is necessarily inferior to a similar thing made by hand. This is not true, but, in fact, the machine-made article is generally inferior. It can be made as well and accurate as is desired, but the cost grows rapidly as the accuracy is increased and a point is reached where it can be more cheaply made by hand.

Dennison, associated with Howard, Davis and Curtis, sold his first watches in 1853, the watches bearing the names, successively, of 'The Warren Manufacturing Company,' 'Samuel Curtis,' and 'The Boston Watch Company.' Next year the factory was moved to Waltham, and the watches were engraved 'Dennison, Howard and Davis.' At this time N. B. Sherwood joined the company and made a great name as a designer of machine tools for watchwork. In 1837, however, the company got into difficulties and sold its business to R. E. Robbins, who, after one or two changes, formed the American Watch Company in 1859 which, later, was known as the American Waltham Watch Company. This was the first great success in American watchmaking; it declared its first dividend in 1860, and has prospered ever since.

Meanwhile a Nashua Watch Company started, and

268

soon failed. Then Sherwood formed the Newark Watch Company in 1864, and this was taken over in 1870 by the Cornell Watch Company of Chicago. The company issued a considerable number of watches under a variety of names, but failed in 1874. It was then moved to San Francisco, and failed again in 1876. The United States Watch Company was started in 1864 at Marion, but failed in 1872; after reorganization as the Marion Watch Company it failed again two years later.

Then came another great success. The National Watch Company of Chicago was formed in 1864 and built a factory at Elgin, some way outside the city. It was successful from the start, and in 1874 changed its name to the Elgin National Watch Company. It remains one of the foremost factories in America.

Dennison, in 1864, organized the Tremont Watch Factory on the basis that certain parts, including the balance and escapement, were to be made in Zürich. The business was successful until the directors, against Dennison's advice, decided to make the whole watch in America in a new factory at Melrose. In 1868 the factory failed, and Dennison, who had resigned from it, arranged the purchase of the plant by the English Watch Company. Later, Dennison founded the existing Watch Case Company of Birmingham.

Another, now successful, company had a most chequered career. It started in 1864 as the Mozart Watch Company, making a three-wheeled watch invented by Mozart, but this was soon abandoned and the company, then called the New York Watch Company, made ordinary watches, moving in 1867 to Springfield, Mass. This was successful until 1875, when the factory closed and was reorganized; closed again in 1877 and reorganized again as the Hampden Watch Company. It is now the Dueber-Hampden Watch Company, with works at Canton, Ohio. Mozart, who left the Mozart Watch Company in 1866, started another company which, after several changes, ended in 1875.

Edward Howard, the early associate of Dennison, shared with him the honour of pioneer work in American watchmaking and played a greater part in developing the industry. After his initial failure, he started a company in Roxbury which, in 1861, became the Howard Clock and Watch Company. This, after some vicissitudes, separated into the existing Howard Clock Company at Roxbury and the E. Howard Watch Works at Waltham. The Howard watches, from the start, have had a high reputation for quality.

This account covers, very briefly, the history of the factories started in the 'sixties. Many more were formed in the 'seventies and 'eighties, but the survivors are few: the South Bend Watch Company of Indiana, the New York Standard Watch Company of Jersey City, the Illinois Watch Company of Springfield, Ill., and the Waterbury Clock Company. This last company purchased in 1922 the business of R. H. Ingersoll & Bros., who in 1914 had purchased the New England Watch Company, the successor of the famous Waterbury Watch Company. The Waterbury watch was designed by Buck in 1878 and put on the market in 1880. In eight years the output had reached the enormous figure of half a million a year.

The earlier factories had a curious habit of naming their different types and grades of watches after directors and managers of the factory. These watches are too modern for the ordinary collector, but yet possess some interest as early factory products, and a list of the names on watches, compiled mainly from Abbot's *Watch Factories of America* and the catalogue of the Paul Chamberlain collection of watches in the Chicago Art Museum, has been included in the list of watchmakers in the companion volume to this book. The name has been inserted under the heading of the name itself and also under that of the company that made it.

The idea of watch manufacture on the basis of interchangeable parts arose in Switzerland long before the days of Dennison. When the firm of Sandoz & Trott

270

of Besançon started a factory in Geneva in 1804, the *Comité de Mécanique* supported the enterprise in a report to the Government, pointing out the great advantages that would result from machine production to size in such a way that all parts were interchangeable. The idea was put into practice, but only in the manufacture of the *ébauche*, and no attempt appears to have been made to perform by machine the more skilled work of the *finisseur*, until Georges Leschot, of the firm of Vacheron & Constantin, organized, in 1840, a factory to produce the complete movement on an interchangeable basis. Their example was followed by Patek, Philippe et Cie and other firms, and there followed the greatest period of prosperity that Swiss watchmaking has ever known.

While America was struggling, with costly experiments, to reach the high ideal of watch manufacture which she had set for herself, Swiss watches were pouring into the country at a price that, in spite of the duty of 25 per cent., made competition by the inexperienced American factories very difficult. In the 'seventies the tide began to turn. The American factories made steady progress, while the Swiss thought more and more of price and less and less of quality. Though this was true of the bulk of the Swiss factories, yet the two already mentioned, with some others, maintained the high quality of their watches, and are still among the finest watch-making firms of the world. Switzerland was sending to America a few watches of the highest grade and a mass of watches of low quality. The American factories saw their opportunity of filling the gap with a good ordinary type of watch, and succeeded so well that the number of Swiss watches that entered America in 1876 was less than one-fifth of the number that entered in 1872.

The year 1876 was a turning-point in the history of Swiss watchmaking, which, from the prosperous years of 1850-55, had fallen on evil times. An exhibition was held in Philadelphia, and two Swiss watchmakers, E. Favre-Perret and Th. Gribi, visited it as representatives

271

of the watch industry; their report gave no hope of improvement in the American market. Favre-Perret, in a meeting at La Chaux-de-Fonds at the end of 1876, told the Swiss manufacturers some home truths about their methods in comparison with the American. His speech was published broadcast and bore fruit. It is perhaps the only instance of manufacturers listening to the voice of a critic. The whole industry set to work to reorganize itself, and with such good result that in six years the exports to America were trebled. From this time Switzerland has retained its position as the first watchmaking country of the world, producing the finest watches and the cheapest and all intermediate grades. Up to 1800 the Swiss had taken no part in developing the watch; now all progress, in theory and practice, starts in the Swiss watch. They have beaten the English in precision work and at least equalled the Americans in factory methods, and only the French, in a few watches, can rival them in the design and decoration of the case.

Last, and least, comes English watchmaking of the nineteenth century. An interesting description of the position of the industry at the very beginning of the century is given in Philipp Andreas Nemmich's account of his journey to the industrial centres in 1805 and 1806 [1] :—

French or Geneva watches were formerly imported in considerable number into England. Now they can be imported only secretly. They are, however, no longer much favoured; for the cheap ones are regarded as mere factory work, while the well-made and costly ones are esteemed less than the English. The Englishman marvels at the foreign artistic work, but always with a suspicious eye. There are, too, London firms who have watches made abroad engraved with 'London' and their own names, but they run the risk of being exposed, with loss of their reputation. Many of the inner parts of the watch come from Lancashire and are assembled in London; some parts also come

---

[1] 'Neueste Reise durch England, Schottland und Ireland, hauptsächlich in Bezug auf Produkte, Fabriken und Handlung,' quoted in the *Deutsche Uhrmacher Zeitung*, No. 2, 1926.

from Coventry, but are not considered so good.   Watch springs are made, as far as England is concerned, only in London, and are sent to Lancashire and elsewhere.   Abroad, the Geneva springs are preferred, but English makers will have none of them.   The wheel-work is cheaper in London, but not nearly so good as in Lancashire. . . . Cases are made best in London, and are sent to Coventry and Derby and even to Lancashire.

One can buy ordinary watches in London at three guineas in silver and seven in gold, and upwards.   Gold repeating watches are from eighteen guineas upwards.   Hunters cost five guineas in silver and twelve in gold.   Watchmakers of good repute in London are: Perigal & Duterrau; Geo. Jamison and others. . . .

Precision timekeepers are nowhere better or more perfectly made than in London.   The craftsman with the greatest reputation of all is J. R. Arnold; he sells no watch in silver case under 50 guineas, and his price in silver and gold cases rises to 120 guineas.   Brockbanks, not under 50 but not over 100 guineas; Earnshaw, from 40 to 100 guineas.   Barraud has a fixed price of 40 guineas.   John Grant from 30 to 60 guineas.   Grimaldi and some others belong to a lower class. . . . The district from Prescot to Liverpool, including both towns, is the centre of a special industry.   This consists in the manufacture of all sorts of watch tools and watch parts.   The small files made here are considered the best in the world; they are cut with the greatest accuracy and are of exceptionally good steel.   The wheel-cutting engine invented here is in great demand, and does splendid, clean work.   Pinion wire also was invented in Prescot; at first it was very expensive, but, as it was later drawn in London and sold at half the price, the Prescot makers have had to reduce their prices; it is now made principally at Park, near Liverpool. The assembling of watch parts and the finishing are done in Liverpool.

This account gives an excellent picture of watchmaking in England, while the industry was still flourishing, while it was in the transition stage between the individual work of the craftsman and the factory production, though still practically all handwork.   Contrast this with another account forty years later.   Aaron Dennison, in 1849, before starting his watch factory in America, made a tour of observation in the watchmaking districts of England; he writes as follows :—

273

I found that the matter had been correctly represented, but in carrying out their system, one-half of the truth had not been told. How that the party setting up as a manufacturer of watches bought his Lancashire movements—a conglomeration of rough materials—and gave them out to A, B, C and D to have them finished ; and how A, B, C and D gave out the different jobs of pivoting certain wheels of the train to E, certain other parts to F and the fuzee cutting to G. Dial-making, jeweling, gilding, motioning, etc., to others, down almost the entire length of the alphabet ; and how that, taking these various pieces of work to outside workpeople—who, if sober enough to be at their places, were likely to be engaged on some one's work who had been ahead of them, and how, under such circumstances, he would take the occasion to drop into a " pub " to drink and gossip, and, perhaps, unfit himself for work the remainder of the day. Finding things in this condition as a matter of course, my theory of Americans not finding any difficulty in competing with the English, especially if the inter-changeable system and manufacturing in large quantities was adopted, may be accepted as reasonable.[1]

This was at a time when Japy's *ébauche* machine factory was in full swing and after Georges Leschot and others in Switzerland had organized their factories on a sound footing.

An attempt made to start a machine factory on a basis comparable with that of the Swiss was made by P. F. Ingold, a native of Berne, in 1842. A man of great ability, he had designed a series of machine tools for watch manufacture, and he promoted the British Watch and Clock Company in London to build them and start watchmaking. The opposition of the trade in Clerkenwell and Coventry, however, killed the company before it could begin its work, and Ingold left for America and later returned to Switzerland.

In 1881, when watchmaking in England was at a very low ebb, Edward Rigg delivered the Cantor lectures before the Society of Arts on 'Watchmaking,' and surveyed the position of the industry in England in the

---

[1] *The Watch Factories of America.* H. G. Abbott. Chicago, 1888.

274

light of statistics he had collected. It is now possible to appreciate Rigg's masterly grasp of the position, the accuracy of his reasons for the decline of the industry, and the shrewdness of his recommendations for reviving it. What Favre-Perret's report on the Philadelphia Exhibition did for Switzerland five years before, Rigg's lectures did for England and did far better. Swiss makers took Favre-Perret's report to heart and set their houses in order. English makers appear to have taken no notice of Rigg, and their industry continued to decline. Rigg prophesied that the trade in the high-class watch would go the way of the trade in the medium-quality watch, and his prophecy has come true. At present there exist two watch factories, but their output is negligible.[1]

There is no reason why watchmaking should not flourish in England. On the handwork system there was a reason why competition with Switzerland was impossible; there, a large amount of home work used to be done by peasants in the mountain regions, at rates far below the rate of labour in England. Now, however, this class of labour has almost disappeared; the watch is a factory production, and its cost depends more on the machine-tool designer and the manager than on the rate of labour.

In machine-tool work England has always excelled. In the way it adapted itself to the production of munitions it proved its superiority. It could quite well compete with other countries in watch production, but the present lack of knowledge and experience would make it extremely difficult to organize a factory on a competitive basis. The probability is that, in a few decades, watchmaking and watchmakers will have disappeared from the country.

---

[1] In 1924, 4800 watches were made in England and 4,215,500 were imported.

CHAPTER XIII

WATCH ESCAPEMENTS

'Encores met li orlogiers à point
Le foliot qui ne cesse point
Ce fuisselet et toutes les brochettes :'
FROISSART. *Le Orloge amoureus.* (*c.* 1365.)

THE verge escapement was the first applied to clocks and watches, and it remained the only escapement for watches until about 1700. Then began a period of invention of escapements ; they were few at first, but from 1750 to 1850 the number was enormous. Charles Gros, in 1913, published a book[1] in which he described over 250 escapements, and at the end confesses—quite rightly—that his task is far from completed. The greater number of these escapements saw the light only because their inventors lacked an elementary knowledge of mechanics, but there are a great many that are perfectly sound in principle. Yet there are only two, the cylinder and the lever, that have stood the test of experience, and only two others, the virgule and the duplex (with its variant for Chinese watches), that enjoyed a short period of popularity. The chronometer escapement, though it has been applied to watches, will not be regarded here as a watch escapement ; a remarkably good history of its development is in Gould's *Marine Chronometer* already mentioned.

The cylinder escapement was invented about 1725 by George Graham, and is still made.[2] The lever escapement

---

[1] *Échappements d'Horloges et de Montres.* Paris, 1913.
[2] In 1695 a patent was granted to Barlow, Houghton and Tompion for a new

276

was invented by Mudge about 1755, and is now, except for a few cylinder watches, the only escapement used. Nevertheless, the verge continued to be the escapement principally used until the nineteenth century, and was quite common well into the century.

About 1800, some three-quarters of a century after it was invented, the cylinder was recognized by many, but not all, of the foremost makers as an escapement far superior to the verge. It was, too, three-quarters of a century after its invention before the lever was recognized as superior to the cylinder. These delays must not be attributed to the stupidity or conservatism of watch-makers. The craftsmen of 1800 were not equipped with the theoretical knowledge that is now so easily acquired, but they were very capable practicians, who judged their work by its results, and the new escapements did not give as good results as the old.

An escapement, apparently, is a simple mechanism. In reality its success depends on many factors—the pro-portions of the parts, the weight of the balance and length of the balance spring, the right materials for resisting wear, the forms that best retain oil at the working surfaces. There is, too, the all-important question of repair. A bad escapement familiar to the repairer can give better results than a good escapement which he does not understand. It is difficult, therefore, for a new escapement to replace an old. The old escapement has been brought to its point of perfection by years of trial and error; the new has all the faults of youth and competes at great disadvantage.

escapement, not illustrated, but described as follows: 'A new sort of watch or clock with the balance wheele or swing wheele either flatt or hollow, to worke within and crosse the center of the verge or axis of the ballance or pendulum, with a new sort of teeth made like tinterhooks, to move the ballance or pendulum withall, and the palletts of the axis or verge of the ballance or pendulum are to be circular, concave, and convex, or other teeth or palletts that will not goe but by the helpe of the spring to the ballance.' This has been regarded as the cylinder escapement, but, in the absence of more particulars of which the Author has no knowledge, the description, though applicable to the cylinder escapement, is too vague to prove the invention of this escapement by Barlow, Houghton and Tompion.

No attempt will be made to give a history of escapements. Gros' valuable book is a *catalogue raisonné*, and a real history remains to be written, but it would need a book to itself. In the following pages the cylinder and lever escapements will be described fully in their modern forms, and the virgule and duplex escapements briefly, and a few variants will be mentioned.

Cylinder Escapement.—The cylinder escapement is shown in perspective in Plate LVIII, and a series of diagrams illustrating its action are on Plate LIX. The escape wheel has its teeth standing on columns above the wheel itself. The cylinder in Plate LVIII is shown without the balance wheel, which must be imagined mounted on the cylindrical part below the upper pivot. The cylinder proper is, roughly, a semi-cylindrical tube with thin walls; at its lower end a portion is cut out, leaving a bit of tube only about one-quarter of the whole circumference. The teeth of the escape wheel pass through the axis of the cylinder, and their length allows them to have just free play inside the cylinder.

Turning now to Plate LIX, each diagram shows two or three teeth of the escape wheel, which turns in the direction in which the teeth are pointing. The shaded semicircle is the acting part of the cylinder, and turns under the swing of the balance in the directions shown by the arrows. In Fig. 1 the forward tooth is just moving clear of the cylinder, and the rearward tooth then falls on to the outer surface of the cylinder into the position of Fig. 2; the action between Figs. 1 and 2 is the *drop*. The balance continues its swing until the cylinder reaches the position of Fig. 3, the escape wheel remaining stationary or *locked*, with its tooth rubbing against the outer surface of the cylinder. The balance then swings back until the position of Fig. 4 is reached. This swing, out and back, of the balance is the *supplementary arc*; in the verge escapement, while the balance swings out on its supplementary arc, the escape wheel with all the watch train is turned backwards; here, on the

PLATE LVIII

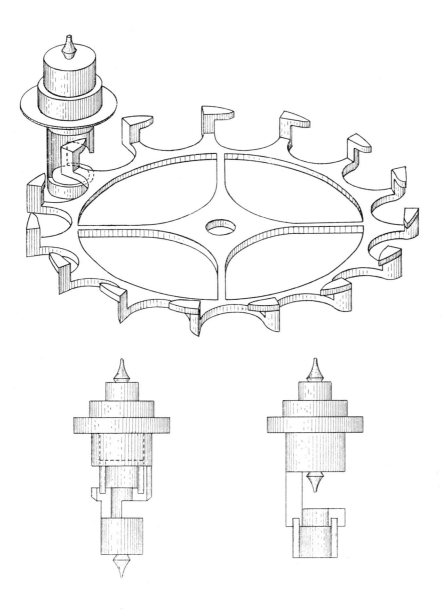

THE CYLINDER ESCAPEMENT

contrary, it remains stationary until, as in Fig. 4, the cylinder has turned enough to bring its edge to the point of the escape-wheel tooth.

The movement of the escape wheel from the position of Fig. 4 to that of Fig. 5 gives the *impulse*. Each tooth of the escape wheel slopes so that its radius is greater at the heel than at the toe, and the tooth, in pushing past the edge of the cylinder, gives the cylinder a partial turn which constitutes the impulse required to keep the balance swinging. The positions of Figs. 5, 6, 7 and 8 correspond to those of Figs. 1, 2, 3 and 4, the latter showing the action of a tooth on the outside of the cylinder and at its entering lip, while the former show it on the inside and at the leaving lip. Between the positions of Figs. 5 and 6 is the drop ; between those of Figs. 6 and 7 is the outward swing on the supplementary arc ; between those of Figs. 7 and 8 the back swing ; and between those of Figs. 8 and 9 the impulse given on the leaving lip. Fig. 9 is the same as Fig. 1, and so the action is complete.

In Fig. 7 it will be seen that the cylinder lies over the arm of the tooth ; it is to enable this position to be reached that the lower part of the cylinder is cut away, as already mentioned, leaving, as a support, only a bit of tube about one-quarter of the circumference ; this supporting bit is below the part of the cylinder against which the tooth rests in Fig. 7. The cylinder, then, is a very delicate part ; in a small watch it has the diameter of a pin of ordinary size. The pin must be imagined as a tube with thin walls, having at one point half and at another point three-quarters of its circumference cut away.

The cylinder is made as a tube of hard steel, highly polished inside and out ; the central portion is cut to the right shape, leaving a little more than a semi-cylinder, and then a plug is driven into each of the tubular ends. The ends of the plugs are formed as pivots, and the upper plug has a shoulder to take the balance wheel.

279

WATCHES

The cylinder escapement is called a *dead-beat* escapement, because the escape wheel, when locked by the cylinder, remains stationary during the supplementary arc. The verge is a *recoil* escapement, because the escape wheel is turned backwards by it. The cylinder, however, is not a *free* escapement, because the escape wheel always engages it; when not giving it impulse it is rubbing against either the inside or the outside circumference. The friction due to this rubbing was a valuable feature of the escapement in the days when the balance spring was far from isochronous, because it tended to keep the swing of the balance the same whatever the force on the escape wheel. If the force on the wheel diminished, either because the mainspring was nearly run down or because the oil had dried up, the impulse given to the cylinder and balance was less, tending to lessen the swing of the balance. At the same time, however, the pressure of the tooth on the cylinder was less, so there was less friction retarding the swing of the balance, and this compensated in some measure for the smaller impulse.

Wear was the chief defect of the old cylinders. The two lips of the cylinder are rubbed by the teeth of the escape wheel in giving the impulse, and their very small surface quickly wore away. The defect was to a great extent removed by the Swiss practice of making the wheel of hard steel. It may seem strange that a hard steel surface is worn more quickly when rubbed by a soft metal than by a hard; the fact is that the soft metal itself does not wear away the hard, but hard particles of grit get embedded in the soft metal and these do the damage. The hard metal resists the embedding of grit, and the rubbing of two clean surfaces leads to little wear when the pressure and speed are low. Breguet appears to have been the first to use a hard steel wheel about 1800, but the use of steel did not become general till long after this.

The wear of the cylinder was avoided in the finest watches by making it of ruby. The steel cylinder is a

280

PLATE LIX

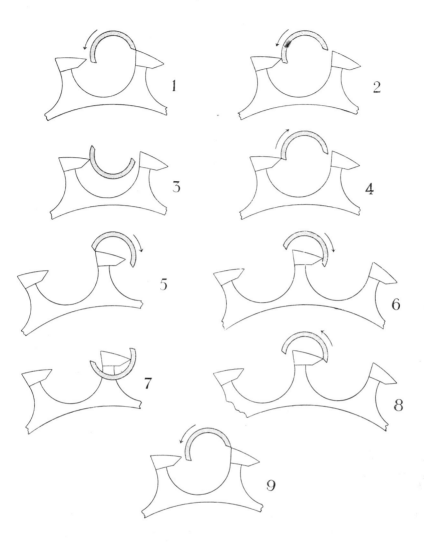

ACTION OF THE CYLINDER ESCAPEMENT

fragile thing but not difficult to make; the ruby cylinder is a triumph of craftsmanship. It is a built-up cylinder, having a framework of steel and a short semi-cylindrical piece of ruby. Fig. 2 of Plate LVIII shows the construction of the ordinary ruby cylinder. Starting from the lower end, there is the plug with its pivot fitting in the lower tubular part; above this is the cut-away portion which allows passage for the arm of the escape-wheel tooth; above this is a short semi-cylindrical part in which a groove is cut, and the semi-cylinder of ruby is fixed in this groove. The steel is continued up from this point in a very slender pillar, seen outside the right lip of the ruby; referring to Fig. 3 of Plate LIX, this pillar occupies the place between the point of the tooth and the lip of the cylinder close to it, so that it does not interfere with the tooth. The pillar joins the lower part to the upper tubular part, through which the ruby is dropped into its groove; it is held in place by the upper plug, which is cut as shown in dotted lines so as to form a groove for the upper end of the ruby.

Another form of ruby cylinder, shown in Fig. 3 of Plate LVIII, was generally used by Breguet. The ruby was fixed on to the end of the steel portion of the cylinder beyond the pivot, and, looking at the watch from beneath, the ruby is seen standing up without any support that is easily visible. The construction was not quite so fragile as the ordinary, but the minute space available for the lower pivot and its cock made it very difficult to make. The end of the cock with the pivot hole had to be smaller than the cylinder and supported on an arm narrow enough to allow the cylinder to make about three-quarters of a turn. Breguet used also a special form of pivot and a special form of cylinder wheel, but they were used only to a very small extent.

Virgule Escapement.—The virgule escapement, which is a modification of the cylinder escapement, is generally attributed to Lepaute, who describes in 1767 [1] a form of

---

[1] *Traité d'Horlogerie.* J. A. Lepaute. Paris, 1767.

escapement from which it may have been evolved, and speaks of his escapement as far superior to the cylinder. It is, however, more probable that the virgule escapement, which was largely used by Lepine, was devised by him in its ordinary form about 1780. The virgule escapement is shown in plan in Fig. 1, Plate LX; it may be regarded as a small cylinder with thick walls and one very long lip. The escape-wheel teeth stand up from their arms, as in the cylinder escape wheel, but are semi-circular pins, their front edges corresponding to the points of the teeth of the cylinder escape wheel. They lock first on the outside of the semi-cylindrical part and then drop into the central hole, which is just big enough to admit them, and lock on its inside surface. On escaping from this they come against the long curved tail, from which the escapement gets its name, and give the impulse in pushing past it.

The cylinder escapement gives two nearly equal impulses, one when the tooth pushes past the entering lip and one when it pushes past the leaving lip, but in the virgule escapement the impulse given by the tooth on entering is negligibly small, while the impulse on leaving, against the long tail, is large. The small segment of a circle shaded with cross lines represents a section of the minute column, which is all that can support the virgule and balance wheel.

In theory, the virgule is better than the cylinder escapement. The body of the virgule against which the teeth rub is smaller than that of the cylinder, and so the friction is less; at the same time the long tail enables impulse to be given to the balance with a more effective leverage. On the other hand, only one out of the two impulses is effective. The virgule escapement gave good results and was popular, especially in France, towards the end of the eighteenth century, but it was soon abandoned. It was more fragile and more difficult to make than the cylinder, and did not retain the oil so well.

282

PLATE LX

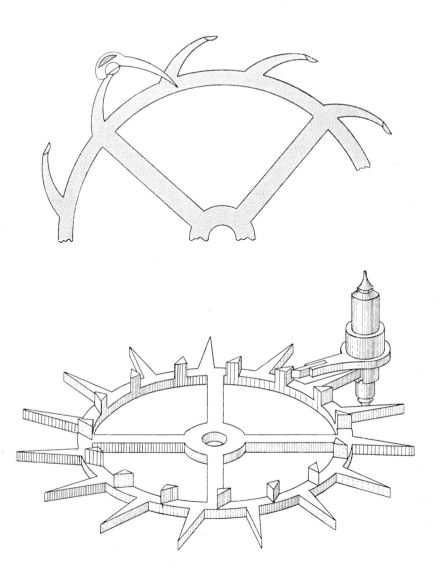

VIRGULE AND DUPLEX ESCAPEMENTS

Duplex Escapement.—It is difficult to determine either the inventor of the duplex escapement or the date when it was first made. Le Roy, about 1750, was the first to apply it to watches in anything like its ordinary form, though Dutertre made a clock escapement on the duplex principle at a much earlier date. Plate LX shows, in Fig. 2, a perspective view of the escapement. The idea underlying it is the same as in the virgule escapement—to secure an effective leverage for the impulse with slight friction while the escape wheel is locked. The escape wheel has two sets of teeth, one set of long, pointed teeth on the edge of the wheel and a set of triangular teeth standing up on the face of the wheel. The long, pointed teeth engage a cylindrical portion on the balance staff of very small diameter; this is called the *roller*, and the teeth rest against this while the escape wheel is locked. The triangular teeth engage a long arm, fitted to the balance staff just above the roller, and give impulse to the balance through it.

The roller has a small notch cut in it, just deep enough to admit the point of a tooth when opposite the centre of the roller; in the drawing a tooth is seen in the notch. Assuming the escape wheel to be turning clockwise and the balance staff counter-clockwise, the escape wheel can turn from the position shown because the notch enables the tooth to pass the roller. One of the triangular teeth, however, is seen bearing against the end of the impulse arm, and this tooth, as the escape wheel turns, gives the impulse. The wheel is then locked by the next long tooth coming against the roller, where it remains during the supplementary arc, or the swing of the balance out and back. On the back swing the impulse arm just misses the triangular tooth, and the notch in the roller passes under the tip of the locking tooth with a very slight jerk. Not until the next swing counter-clockwise does the notch come towards the tip of the tooth and allow it to enter and so pass the roller. The escapement, therefore, has only one impulse for the double swing out and back, and is called a *single-beat* escapement.

The duplex escapement requires very accurate workmanship, and is found mainly in high-grade watches. The roller then is of ruby, in the form of a tube pushed on to the balance staff and fixed with shellac, and a jewel pallet is fixed in the end of the impulse arm, as indicated in the drawing. Under these conditions the escapement gave excellent results and, for a time, about 1800 and later, was popular, especially in England. Its chief defect was that any wear in the pivots of the balance or escape wheel, allowing these to get too far apart, led to rapidly increasing wear and failure of the escapement.

It is curious that this escapement, which used to be restricted to the finest watches, was adopted for the cheapest watch of its day, the Waterbury watch. A little disk with a notch was the roller; a big disk with a notch was the impulse arm, and the escape wheel was stamped out of sheet brass with, alternately, long and short teeth, the long teeth being bent down below the short teeth.

A variant of this escapement is known as the Chinese Duplex, because it was common in watches made at Fleurier for the Chinese market. It was invented in 1830 by Charles Edward Jacot to give *sweep-seconds*, that is to say, a movement of the seconds hand, apparently, from one second mark to the next, which meant one tooth of the escape wheel passing per second. The escape wheel has only six locking and six impulse teeth, but the locking teeth are double, each ending in a fork. When the first prong of the fork passes the roller, the wheel is immediately locked again by the second prong, and only when this has passed does the whole tooth pass and enable an impulse to be given. In consequence the balance has only one impulse for two swings out and two back. The movement of the escape wheel from one prong to the other of a tooth is so small that it is hardly perceptible on the seconds hand.

284

PLATE LXI

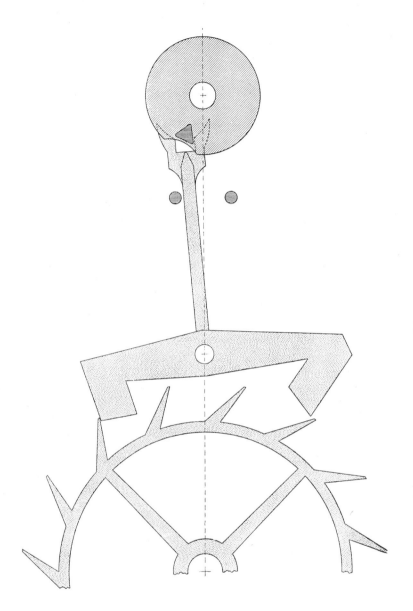

LEVER ESCAPEMENT—ENGLISH FORM

The Lever Escapement.—The lever escapement of modern watches was the first *free* escapement, that is to say, the first in which the balance was entirely free of any connexion with a part of the watch train, except at the moment when it unlocks the train and receives an impulse. The feature which distinguishes it from the escapements that have been described is the *lever*, which is a part intermediate between the balance and the escape wheel.

The escapement was invented by the great English maker Mudge, about 1755. A drawing of his escapement, taken from his son's book,[1] is given in Gould's *Marine Chronometer*. The modern form, exactly the same in principle, is shown in Plate LXI. The disk at the top of the drawing is on the balance staff, which must be imagined passing through the central hole and carrying the balance. The disk is called the *roller*. The *lever* is the three-armed piece, one arm ending in a *fork* and engaging a triangular pin on the roller, while the other two arms end in pallets engaging the teeth of the escape wheel. The resemblance of the lever to an anchor gives the escapement its name in French, *échappement à ancre*, and in German *Anker-Hemmung*. The lever is pivoted on an arbor passing through the hole between the two pallets. The two dark-shaded pins, one on each side of the forked arm of the lever, are *banking pins*, which limit the movement of the lever. The triangular dark-shaded pin in the roller is the *impulse pin*, sometimes called the *ruby pin*, because it is always made of jewel, except in the cheapest watches. It projects downwards from the under face of the roller and engages the fork, which lies below the roller. The fork proper is the rectangular notch at the end of the lever arm, but its prongs are continued in the form of two horns, which are safety devices playing no part in the normal working of the escapement.

---

[1] *A Description, with Plates, of the Timekeeper invented by the late Mr. Thomas Mudge.* London, 1799.

Turning now to Plate LXII, the six figures show the action of the escapement in successive stages, the arrows indicating the direction in which the escape wheel and balance turn. Starting with Fig. 4, the escape wheel is locked by a tooth resting on the *locking face* of the left-hand pallet. Meanwhile the balance is making a swing counter-clockwise, and the impulse pin has entered the fork of the lever and reached the right-hand prong. Further movement of the balance will move the lever from the position of Fig. 4 to that of Fig. 5. This movement of the lever has unlocked the escape wheel by drawing away the pallet, and the tooth is at the start of the end surface of the pallet, which is the *impulse face*. The inclination of the impulse face is such that the travel of the tooth along it from the position of Fig. 5 to that of Fig. 6 pushes the pallet outwards, and this gives the impulse, which is transmitted to the balance by the left-hand prong of the fork pushing the impulse pin to the right. The impulse pin, therefore, serves two purposes; first, by striking one side of the fork, it unlocks the escape wheel and then, by the other side of the fork striking it, it receives the impulse. During the impulse the lever is thrown over till it rests against the right-hand banking pin.

From Fig. 6 to Fig. 1 is the *drop*, the small free movement of the escape wheel from the position where one tooth leaves the impulse face of one pallet to that where another tooth drops on to the locking face of the other pallet. In Fig. 1, the balance is making its outward swing to the left and is entirely free of the lever. In Fig. 2, the lever and escape wheel meanwhile remaining stationary, the balance is on its back swing and the impulse pin is just entering the fork. In Fig. 3, the pin has unlocked the escape wheel and this is giving impulse by its tooth acting on the impulse face of the right-hand pallet. This throws the lever over till it rests against the left-hand banking pin as in Fig. 4, when the tooth has escaped from the impulse face and the other tooth

286

PLATE LXII

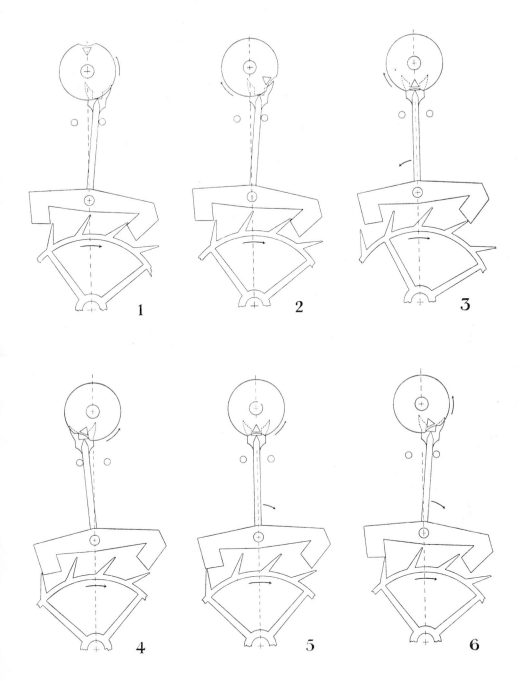

LEVER ESCAPEMENT ACTION

has dropped on to the locking face of the left-hand pallet. The cycle is then complete.

The balance is in its central position—with its spring unstrained—in Fig. 5, the impulse pin being then in the fork, facing the centre of the lever. From this position the balance swings from a half to three-quarters of a turn in each direction. During this swing the balance is connected with the watch train through the lever, only while passing from the position of Fig. 4 to that of Fig. 6. This is a small fraction of the whole swing, and during the remainder the balance is quite free.

There are two other points to be noticed in the lever escapement. Looking at Fig. 1, where the balance is free, a touch on the lever would move it over to rest against the other banking pin. The impulse pin then, on the return swing of the balance, would come against the outside of the fork and be stopped by it. To prevent any possibility of this happening, through a jerk given to the watch, a *safety finger* is provided. This is seen in Plates LXI and LXII as the pointed end of the lever arm which just reaches the gap of the fork. It is above the fork and on the same level as the roller and, in Fig. 1 of Plate LXII, is almost touching the edge of the roller, so that the slightest movement of the lever to the left brings the finger against the roller, which prevents any further movement. The lever can pass from its right-hand to its left-hand position only when the impulse pin is close to the fork, because at the impulse pin a rounded notch is cut out of the roller to give passage to the finger, as seen in Fig. 3.

The safety finger, however, introduces a possible defect in the escapement, because, if the lever, instead of resting against the banking pin, rested with the finger against the edge of the roller, the friction would interfere with the free swing of the balance. A reference to Plate LXI will show how easy it is for this to happen. Supposing the impulse pin to be moving out of the fork, a slight movement of the lever to the right, which might be due to a rebound from the banking pin, would allow the tooth of the escape wheel to slip off the locking face and reach the impulse face of the pallet; the escape wheel would then press the finger against the edge of the roller and cause considerable friction. Any tendency of the lever to leave the banking pin is counteracted by the *draw*, which consists in cutting the locking faces at such angles that the pressure of the tooth on them *draws* the lever towards one or other banking pin. Imagine a line drawn from the point of the tooth on the locking face to the centre of the lever; if the locking face were at right angles to this line the pressure of the tooth would have no effect in tending to move the lever in either direction. Actually, the face is at an angle of from 12 to 13 degrees within the right angle, with the result that the pressure of the tooth tends to make the locking face slide down the tooth and so keeps the lever against the banking pin and the safety finger out of contact with the roller. On the locking face of the other pallet the effect is obtained by making the angle greater than a right angle. The *draw* is an important addition to the lever escapement. Its invention is attributed by Gould to Josiah Emery, who died in 1793, but there is a watch of 1785 in the Guild-hall Museum by John Leroux which shows draw on the pallets, so that Emery's claim to the invention is not quite clear.

The horns of the fork form an additional safety device; just before the impulse pin enters the fork the safety finger is inoperative, because it can enter the notch in the edge of the roller. The horns then replace it, any movement of the lever being prevented as soon as the impulse pin reaches them.

Plate LXIII shows another form of the lever escapement, exactly the same in operation but different in construction. The escape wheel has the *club* teeth used generally by the Swiss in place of the pointed teeth which were used by the English when they made watches. The first contact with the impulse face is made by the heel of the

288

PLATE LXIII

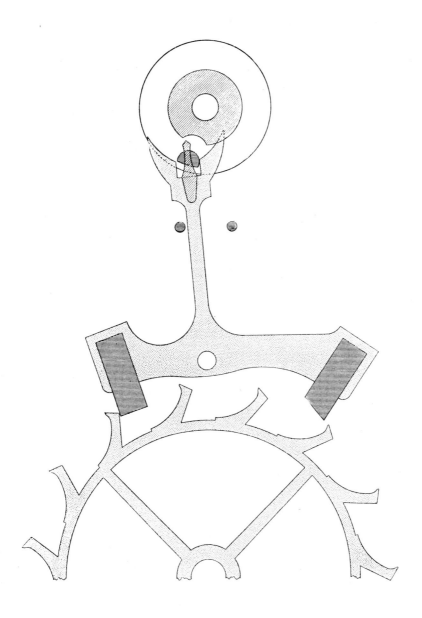

LEVER ESCAPEMENT—SWISS FORM

tooth and the last by the toe, the impulse face being partly on the pallet and partly on the tooth. The impulse faces on the pallets are therefore longer with the English form of escape wheel. The advantage of the pointed teeth is that the wheel can be made accurately circular; the disadvantage is that the *drop* must be larger than with club teeth, because the inclined form of the backs of the teeth prevents the pallet passing close behind a tooth.

The lever in Plate LXIII is shown with the jewelled pallets which practically all modern watches have; it is, though, now more usual for the jewels to be inserted in horizontal slots made in the plane of the lever instead of in the vertical slots shown. There is, too, another difference between the levers of Plates LXI and LXIII. In the former, the lever has equal impulses; that is, the distances from the centre of the lever to the centres of the impulse faces of the two pallets are equal, so that the impulses given on the two pallets are equal in their leverage. The result of this is that the locking face of the left-hand pallet is farther off the centre of the lever than that of the right-hand pallet. The lever of Plate LXIII has equidistant locking faces, with the result that the impulse given to the right-hand pallet acts at a greater leverage. The English form of escape wheel, which requires long impulse faces on the pallets, is generally used with a lever having equal impulses. With the club-tooth wheel both forms are used.

In Plate LXIII there is a *double roller* on the balance staff instead of the *single roller* of Plate LXI. The large roller (unshaded) carries the impulse pin and is below the horns of the fork. The small roller is above the horns and serves only to co-operate with the safety finger, which is seen passing over the impulse pin. The double roller is the better form, because the action of the safety finger on its roller is more secure the smaller the roller, whereas the action of the escapement is more secure the larger the roller carrying the impulse pin near

289

its edge. Watches of good quality generally have the double roller, though its greater security makes it even more important for the inferior watch, which, for the sake of cheapness, commonly has a single roller. The safety finger sometimes takes the form of a pin fixed upright in the lever and called a *guard-pin*.

Different forms of impulse pin are seen in the two Plates, and a third form, an ellipse, is now perhaps more common than either. The form is of no consequence provided that the pin has rounded edges to engage the sides of the fork and only a small projection towards the edge of the roller, so that the edge of the pin, when moving to hit the edge of one prong of the fork, can pass close to the horn on the other prong.

The lever in English watches frequently has a *straight-line* form, the arm with the fork being nearly in a line with the pallets. The difference between this and the anchor form is merely one of arrangement of the parts in the watch. In another form, which used to be common in Swiss watches, the anchor form of lever had two horns reaching from its centre over the escape wheel, one on each side of the escape wheel arbor. The arbor then was used as a single banking pin, the two horns resting against it alternately. The horns were made very light, so as to balance the forked arm of the lever. This balance of the lever, so that its centre of gravity is at its pivot, is of importance for two reasons: first, to avoid its being displaced by a jerk given to the watch; and second, to avoid the position of the watch affecting the escapement. Supposing the lever were out of balance in such a way that the arm with the fork tended to fall when horizontal, the escape wheel would have less work to do in moving the lever in one direction than in the other, and this difference would affect the timing of the watch.

A lever escapement with a third form of escape wheel was invented by Louis Perron of Besançon, and used by Roskopf in 1868 for the first cheap yet well-made watch ever produced, and is now used in all clocks of the

American alarum type. In this the pallets are pins, from which comes its name of the *pin-lever* escapement, while the wheel teeth have inclined ends which form the impulse faces. There are, then, three types of lever escapement—the English type with pointed teeth, in which the impulse faces are all on the pallets ; the pin-lever, in which they are all on the wheel teeth ; and the Swiss lever with club teeth, in which they are partly on the pallets and partly on the wheel teeth.

Mudge appeared to have no idea that, in the lever escapement, he had made perhaps the greatest invention in horology. He took little interest in it, and made only two or three watches with it. Soon after, he devoted himself to experiments on marine chronometers, using verge escapements of special form and beautiful construction. Yet marine chronometers are being made to-day with lever escapements differing only in details from Mudge's form. Emery and Margetts, two famous makers to whom Mudge showed his lever escapement, made a number of watches with it, improving the form in several respects, but, after their death in 1796 and 1804, for about a quarter of a century it was used only occasionally by a few makers, such as Breguet. Then it came to be recognized as the escapement for high-grade watches, though for all others the cylinder escapement held the field till the last quarter of the nineteenth century. It should, though, be borne in mind that, though collections have many specimens of cylinder watches dating from 1800 to 1825, and some of lever watches, the ordinary watch escapement remained the verge. The text-book of the period describes the cylinder watch as a novelty, sometimes condemning it, but makes no mention of the lever.

Each escapement, verge, cylinder and lever requires an appropriate length of balance spring. The verge swung with short arcs—half a turn of the balance was a good total swing, and a balance spring of from two to five turns was usual. The cylinder escapement, from its construction, did not permit a swing exceeding half a turn in each direction, or a total of one turn ; a spring of about eight turns was usual. The lever escapement balance can swing nearly a whole turn in each direction, and in a fully wound and freshly oiled watch the total swing often reaches a turn and three-quarters. This meant a further increase in the length of the spring, and thirteen or fourteen turns is now usual.

In the latter half of the nineteenth century there were endless discussions on the relative merits of the cylinder and lever escapements. They were necessarily endless, because the disputants never realized that the question was bound up with the isochronism of the balance spring. With a non-isochronous spring, the cylinder escapement often gave better timing because its friction kept the arc of the balance more constant. Only when the conditions of isochronism became known did the lever escapement find its true place as the escapement for all watches.

Ten years ago it might have been said that nothing better than the lever escapement was wanted or could be found. Now, however, the want of a better or at least a different escapement is felt. The lever escapement is far from satisfactory in the small wrist-watch, which to-day is the main watch of commerce. High-grade wrist-watches exist to which this does not apply, but very few people buy them, even when they pay a high price for a watch. The escapement is too small to make cheaply of proper form and, at the same time, with sufficient margin of safety in action, and the power of the minute main-spring is not enough to work it. If an escapement could be found which needed less accuracy in construction and would work with less power, it might be better for wrist-watches than the lever, even though inferior to it in principle.

CHAPTER XIV

ALARUM AND STRIKING MECHANISM

THE *New English Dictionary*, under 'Watch,' gives as the earliest use of the word in English, in 1440, *Wecche, of a clokke, meaning alarm, from watch, to awaken.* This leaves it quite obscure why a pocket timekeeper was called a watch, but it does indicate that the earliest watches had alarum mechanisms as an essential part. The early German watches had alarums, with few exceptions; about 1600, especially in French and English watches, the exceptions grew in number until they proved the rule.

The alarum mechanism is similar to the timekeeping or going mechanism; there is the same arrangement of mainspring and ratchet wheel and the same crown wheel and escape wheel, but the wheel turned by the mainspring turns the crown wheel directly instead of through an intermediate pinion and wheel. There is also a foliot, but this acts as a double hammer and strikes the bell when made to oscillate by the escape wheel. Normally, the hammer is prevented from oscillating by a finger, held by a catch in the path of the hammer, a spring tending to withdraw the finger and allow the hammer to oscillate. A projection, which was generally a pin on a thin disk turning with the hour hand (sometimes a notch in the disk), withdraws the catch as soon as it reaches the given hour and lets off the alarum. The disk, which is made springy, is pressed against the hour-hand wheel and held to it by friction, but it can be turned relatively to it for setting the alarum.

Two methods were used for setting, and in the late sixteenth and early seventeenth centuries were used concurrently. In one, probably but by no means certainly the earlier, the centre of the dial is occupied by a small dial, marked with the hour figures. This is turned by inserting a point in one of the holes provided, until the figure of the hour at which the alarum is to sound is below the hand of the watch (sometimes below the tail of the hand). The small dial is connected with the disk and pin, and moves this to the correct position on the hour-hand wheel.

In the other method, the hour hand is replaced by a similar small dial with a pointer fixed to its edge, the pointer projecting over the circle on which the hour figures of the watch are marked; the disk, with the pointer, turns to show the time. There is a small hand in the centre, pointing to a circle of hour figures marked on the disk, but in reverse order. To set the alarum, the small hand is turned to the desired hour figure on the disk.

Plate IX shows a watch with alarum on the former plan, and Plates XVI, 1 and XVII, 2 on the latter. There is no real difference between the two; the hour hand and dial of the former become respectively a dial with pointer and an alarum hand in the latter.

Hour-striking mechanism was not quite so common in early German watches as alarum mechanism, but it was rarely fitted without an alarum as well. The essay for master in Nürnberg included a watch with both alarum and hour-striking mechanisms.

The Earliest Striking Work. — The hour-striking mechanism fitted to the earliest German watches is shown in Plate LXIV, where the parts are drawn spread out, not as they are arranged in a watch. This mechanism differs somewhat from that of the French and English watches of about 1600 and later, and, so far as the Author knows, has never been described.

A portion of the edge of the bell is shown at A, and B is the hammer. There is a train of three wheels

PLATE LXIV

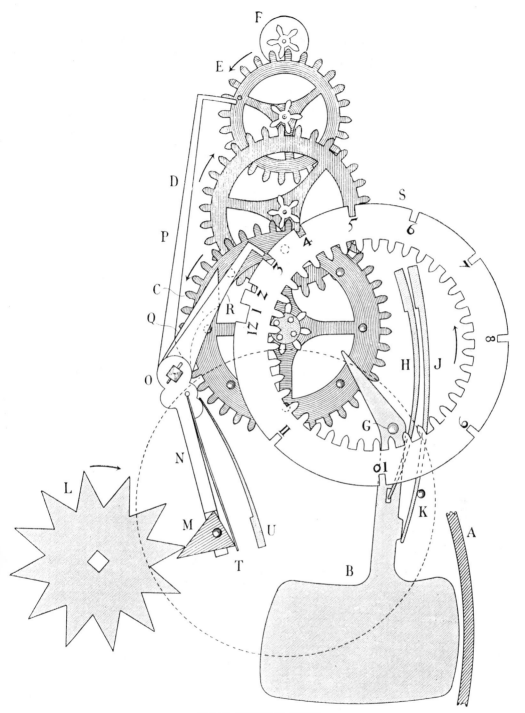

EARLY STRIKING WORK

and pinions, C, D and E, driving a final pinion F and turning in the direction of the arrows. This train is driven by a mainspring with ratchet wheel and large toothed wheel, precisely the same as that in the watch movement described in Chapter V with reference to Plate XIV; this large toothed wheel, which engages with the pinion of the wheel C, is merely indicated in the drawing by the dotted circle. There is no escapement, and the train is prevented from running too fast only by friction; since the final pinion F turns very quickly, its friction is considerable and mainly determines the rate at which the train runs. The wheel C has eight pins projecting from its face, and the hammer B, which is pivoted to the watch plate at G, has a tail which lies in the path of these pins. As the wheel turns, each pin in turn moves the tail of the hammer (to the right in the drawing), so lifting the hammer away from the bell, and, as the pin escapes from the tail, letting the hammer fall back to strike the bell. Two springs H and J regulate the motion of the hammer; the former hooks into a slot in the hammer and presses it towards the bell, and the pins have to move the hammer against this spring, which supplies power to the hammer for striking the bell. The other spring J acts as a stop to keep the hammer just out of contact with the bell. The contact of the hammer with the bell must be momentary only, otherwise the bell would give a buzzing note. The spring rests against a pin K fixed to the watch plate, and the hammer, in order to move the extra little distance to touch the bell, must bend the short and stiff bit of spring beyond the pin. The momentum of the hammer in swinging towards the bell is enough to do this and bring the hammer into contact with the bell, but the spring J immediately moves the hammer back out of contact with the bell, leaving the bell free to vibrate. This device for giving only a momentary contact between hammer and bell is used in all striking and repeating mechanism up to the present day.

Now comes the regulating mechanism, which starts the train at each hour and stops it after the right number of strokes has been made. The star-wheel L turns with the hour hand of the watch once in twelve hours. It has twelve rays, and the action of each ray on the finger M starts off the train. This finger is on the arm N, which is pivoted to the watch plate at O, and there are fixed to it three other arms P, Q and R. Each ray of the star-wheel, in passing the finger M, pushes it and its arm N to the right, and the three arms P, Q and R to the left. The arm P lies normally in the path of a pin on the wheel E and so prevents the train turning, but, when P is moved into the position shown in the drawing, its end is just clear of the pin and the train can start running. At the same time the arm R is moved, so that its bent end is withdrawn from the notch in the wheel S. This wheel is called the *count-wheel*, and it, with the arm R, determines the number of strokes made by the hammer. The count-wheel is only a ring that lies in an annular groove on the top of the watch plate, in which it can turn. The teeth on its inner edge engage with a pinion of four teeth on the arbor of the wheel C. This pinion has a different form from that of the ordinary pinion, but a form quite common in watches of the first two centuries where the pinion has to be on the end of the arbor. It consists of a flat disk on which are fixed four upright pins which act as teeth. The flat disk runs in a hole in the watch plate, its face being flush with the plate, and the pins are as long as the thickness of the wheel, so that no part of the pinion projects above the wheel. A similar type of pinion is common in American and Black Forest clocks, the teeth being pins fixed between two disks; such pinions are called *lantern pinions*, but they never have less than five teeth.

In the drawing, the top plate of the watch is omitted, but it must be imagined just level with the count-wheel and under the pins of its pinion and the arm R. The wheels and their pinions (including the ordinary pinion on the wheel C, seen below the count-wheel pinion) are between the two watch plates ; so also are the two arms P and Q and the hammer. The star-wheel and the arm N are below the bottom plate, on which the hour hand turns.

The arms P, Q and R being moved to the position shown, the train is released and the wheel C in turning brings a pin against the hammer tail to lift the hammer and strike one blow. By a device that will be explained later, the arm N is now no longer held to the right by the star-wheel, so that the arm P would now be free to fall into the path of the pin on the wheel E, to stop the train, but for the fact that the count-wheel has been turned through a small distance, enough to move the notch from under the end of the arm R. This prevents the train being stopped, and it continues to give strokes on the bell until the count-wheel has turned enough to bring the next notch under the end of the arm R. Then this arm can fall into the notch, and the arm P, moving with it, stops the train. The number of strokes given on the bell is thus determined by the distance between the notches on the edge of the count-wheel, the distance corresponding to so many pins on the wheel C. Four pins pass the hammer tail to strike four blows, while the count-wheel moves the distance to bring the notch marked 4 under the end of the arm R. The next notch, marked 5, is at a distance corresponding to five pins, the next six, and so on up to twelve, the notch for 12 and the following notch for 1 being combined into a single wide notch. In watches, as in the drawing, the notches are generally marked with the number of strokes completed when the arm R is in the notch.

It remains to explain how the finger M gets clear of the star-wheel, so that, after one stroke has been given, the arms P and R are free to move to the right. The finger M is pivoted on the end of the arm N, a spring T tending to keep it at right angles to the arm, while another and stiffer spring U presses the arm towards the star-wheel. When a ray of the star comes against the finger M, its first action is to turn the finger on its pivot into the position shown, where a corner of the finger has come against a shoulder on the arm N, and prevents the finger being turned any more. Further movement of the star-wheel then presses the arm N to the right and releases the striking train. Then the arm Q comes into play; the acting part of this lies under the arm R and is shown in dotted lines. It is in the path of the pins on the wheel C, and, as soon as the wheel turns, the arm Q is pushed to the left by the passage of a pin; this moves the arm N enough to the right to bring the finger M clear of the point of the ray of the star-wheel, and then the spring T can turn the finger into its normal position at right angles to the arm. The point of the finger is then on the other side of the ray, and, as soon as the arm Q is free of the pin, the arm N can move to the left, pushing the finger into the gap between two rays of the star-wheel, and the arm P can move to the right to stop the train whenever the arm R finds a notch into which it can fall.

The count-wheel, sunk in a groove in the top plate, can be seen on the movements illustrated on Plates IX, XVI and XXIX. In the two spherical watches on Plate VI it can be seen below the dials. On the upper of these two is the finger N, with its pivoted end M and its two springs.

Later Count-wheel Striking Work.—The striking mechanism of French and English watches and of the later German watches is shown on Plate LXV. All the German watches that the Author has seen with the earlier striking work are attributable to the sixteenth century, but by 1600 the work of Plate LXV was usual. The parts are arranged so far as possible in the same way as those of the earlier mechanism of Plate LXIV. The count-wheel, train of wheels and hammer are the same, except that the train has an extra wheel and pinion. The star-wheel L on the hour arbor of the watch acts to lift the arm M of the

PLATE LXV

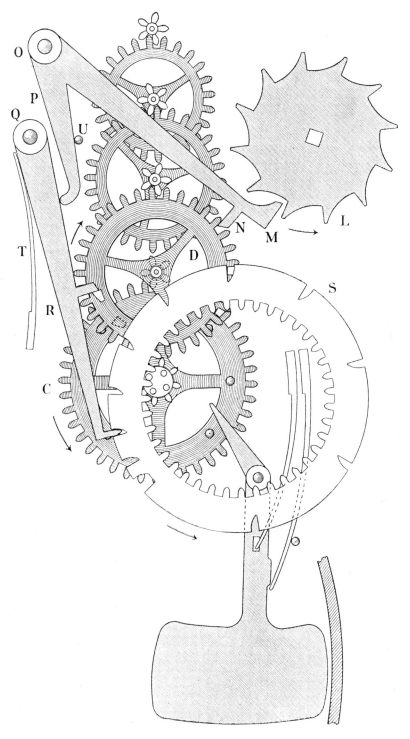

LATER STRIKING WORK

lever pivoted to the watch plate at O every hour, lifting it gradually and letting it fall suddenly ('lifting' being used in its technical sense of movement outward from the centre of the wheel). When the arm M is lifted, the other arm P of the lever lifts the arm R pivoted to the watch plate at Q, this arm and the lever being kept normally in the position shown by the spring T and the stop U.

The arms M and R each have a projecting tongue engaging stops on the wheel D; the tongue of R is shown in engagement with its stop, which is fixed above the wheel; the stop for the tongue N of the arm M is below the wheel and is shown in dotted lines close to the other stop. The arm R also has, at its end, a tongue which engages in the notches of the count-wheel S.[1]

As the watch approaches the hour, a ray of the star-wheel lifts the arm M and with it the arm R, and, at a certain time, generally a few minutes before the hour, the arm R has been lifted enough to bring its two tongues clear of the count-wheel and of the stop on the wheel D. The train is then free and begins to turn. The lifting of the arm M, however, has also brought its tongue N below the wheel D and into the path of the other stop on the wheel, and the train is stopped after the wheel D has made about half a turn. This preliminary motion of the train is known as the *warning*.

The train remains in this position until the ray of the star-wheel has moved enough to allow the arm M to fall behind it and so release the train again. The arm M, however, having fallen, no longer supports the arm R to keep its tongue clear of the stop on the wheel D, but the half-turn of this wheel has allowed the count-wheel to move enough to take the notch away from under the tongue on the end of the arm R, and this tongue, riding on the edge of the count-wheel, prevents the arm R falling and keeps its other tongue clear of the stop. The train, therefore, keeps on running and striking blows

---

[1] The count-wheel is also called the locking-plate, a bad name, because it does not lock the train.

corresponding in number to the distance along the edge of the count-wheel to the next notch; as soon as this comes under the end tongue of the arm R, the arm falls and the train is stopped by the stop on the upper side of the wheel D.

As far as the principle of the mechanism is concerned, the stop on the upper side of the wheel D is superfluous, the arm R and the notches on the count-wheel (if suitably shaped) being all that is needed to stop the train. In practice, however, the count-wheel turns slowly and with considerable force, and the pressure it would exert on the tongue would be so great that the star-wheel might be unable to lift the arm R out of the notch on account of the friction. The pressure exerted by the stop on the wheel D on the other tongue of the arm R is only about one-fortieth of that exerted by the count-wheel, and the friction opposing the lifting of the arm R is then negligible. It is an important point to observe, in adjusting the mechanism, that the train really is stopped by the stop on the wheel D, without there being any pressure exerted by the count-wheel on the tongue.

This mechanism is far simpler than the earlier one, and accurate striking is more easily secured by it. It is, in fact, the most simple and effective striking mechanism that has been devised. Its accuracy does not depend, as in the earlier mechanism, on the amount by which any one of the arms is lifted, but only on the spacing of the straight backs of the rays of the star-wheel.

This remained the standard striking work of watches until the eighteenth century, when, for high-grade watches, it was replaced by the rather more complex rack striking mechanism, invented by Barlow and applied to clocks about 1675. Rack striking work was designed to overcome the defect that the count-wheel has no connexion with the hour hand of the watch; if the watch be set forward three hours it will strike once, a number corresponding to the first hour passed, and subsequent striking will correspond to two hours behind the hour shown.

300

The watch, in setting, can be kept right with its striking only by waiting for each hour to strike as it is passed by the hour hand. The watch cannot be set back past an hour without making it strike wrongly. In the mechanism shown on Plate LXV the watch could not be set back at all, because the straight back of a ray of the star-wheel would butt against the end of the arm M, but provision is sometimes made for setting back by making this arm flexible and so shaping its end and the star-wheel rays that a ray can lift it and pass under it.

The train shown in Plate LXV has been copied from that in the magnificent watch by Jean Vallier, of about 1610, illustrated on Plate XI, the numbers of teeth in the wheels, pinions and count-wheel being those in the train of this watch.

In German watches the count-wheel varies very much in size and arrangement. At the end of the sixteenth century it was generally a ring sunk in an annular groove in the top of the top plate and close to the edge of the plate (see Plate IX). In a watch by Hans Gruber, of about 1575, in the South Kensington Museum, it is concentric with the bottom or pillar-plate and raised above it on three blocks, and is about three-quarters of the diameter of the plate. In the earlier spherical German and French watches on Plate VI, the count-wheel is in a similar position but smaller. Generally, in French and English watches the count-wheel is not sunk in a groove in the plate but is a disk fixed above a toothed wheel with external teeth, the disk and wheel turning on a pivot fixed to the top plate. A pierced and engraved gilt cover kept the disk and wheel in place (see Plate XI).

Rack Striking Work.—The rack striking mechanism, which became the standard form at the end of the eighteenth century, is shown on Plate LXVII as arranged in a watch, and on Plate LXVI in three positions, with the parts spread out for greater clearness ; the mechanism as arranged in the watch differs only in having an addition for striking quarters.

Referring to Fig. 1 of Plate LXVI, the disk A, with a single tooth, is turned once an hour by the watch movement in the direction of the arrow; the watch strikes when this tooth trips the arm B of the three-armed lever B, C, D. The gong E is a hardened steel wire which runs nearly all the way round the rim of the watch; only a short length of it is shown on the drawing. The hammer F is pressed towards the gong by the spring G and prevented from quite touching it by the stiff spring H. The hammer is operated by the star-wheel J, which turns in the direction of the arrow and presses back the hammer from its position of rest (Figs. 1 and 2) into the position in Fig. 3, and finally allows it to escape from the ray of the star-wheel. The star-wheel, which is fixed to the toothed wheel below it, is turned by a special mainspring and train of wheels, not shown on the drawing.

This part of the mechanism is similar to that of the old striking work, the star-wheel J taking the place of the pins on the toothed wheel of the old work. The essential difference between the two devices lies in the part that determines how many blows are to be struck— that is to say, how much the star-wheel has to turn when the train is released.

The arbor close to the letter K is part of the train of wheels driven by the mainspring. It carries three pieces: uppermost is a four-armed star which is the detent by which the train is stopped; below this is a kind of pinion with two teeth called *gathering pallets*, which engage with the teeth of the rack L; and below this is an ordinary pinion of eight leaves which drives the toothed wheel below the star-wheel J. One ray of the star-wheel corresponds (in its travel) with four teeth of the toothed wheel and therefore with half a turn of the arbor K, so that the hammer strikes one blow for every half-turn of this arbor.

Looking at Fig. 1, which shows the parts in their normal position when at rest, the rack L is pivoted to the watch plate at M, and a spring N tends to turn it

302

PLATE LXVI

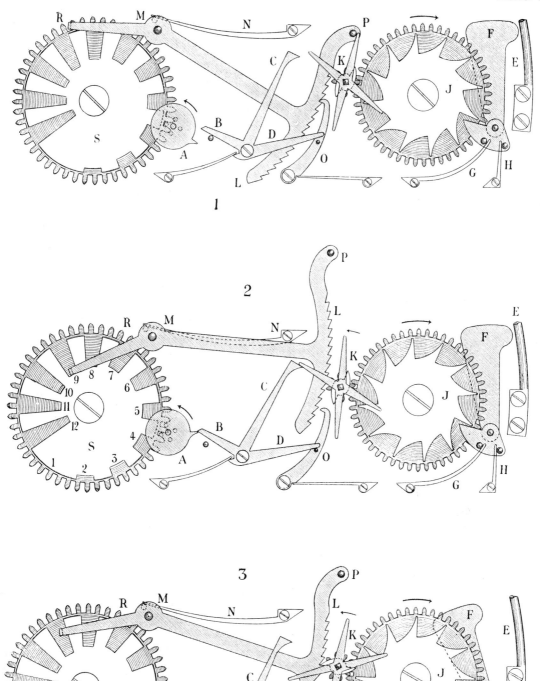

RACK STRIKING WORK—ACTION

into the position of Fig. 2, while a detent O, by engaging one of the teeth of the rack, prevents its turning. In this position of the rack, a pin P on it lies in the path of one arm of the four-armed star and thus stops the striking train.

Fig. 2 shows the parts in their positions after the warning, about a minute before the watch is due to strike. The tooth on the disc A has moved the arm B upwards (in the drawing), with the result that the arm D has come against a pin on the detent O and lifted the detent clear of the teeth of the rack. The rack then, being free to turn under the pressure of the spring N, has moved upwards as far as it could go. The pin P is therefore moved clear of the four-armed star and the striking train is released. It is released, though, only momentarily, because the third arm C of the three-armed lever B, C, D has moved into a position where it arrests an arm of the four-armed star. This star, then, as soon as it is free of the pin P and has begun to turn, is stopped by the arm C and the parts are again at rest, but in the position of Fig. 2.

Turning now to Fig. 3, the tooth on the disk A has passed the arm B, and the three-armed lever B, C, D has been brought back by its spring to its normal position against the stop. This finally releases the four-armed star and the striking train starts to run. At every half-turn of the arbor K the hammer strikes a blow; also one of the two gathering pallets engages a tooth on the rack L and moves it back, through a distance of one tooth, towards its position of Fig. 1. The action continues until the gathering pallets have moved far enough back to bring the pin P into the path of the four-armed star, when the train is stopped and the parts are back in their positions of Fig. 1.

The number of blows given by the hammer is then equal to the number of teeth through which the rack has to be moved to bring it back to normal position—that is to say, to the distance through which the rack moves when released from this position at the warning. This distance is determined by the count-wheel S and the tail R of the rack. The wheel S has a number of notches, and the tail R, which has a depending projection, can enter a notch until the projection comes against the bottom of the notch as in Fig. 2. The wheel S is fixed to the toothed wheel below it, and this is turned by the pinion composed of four pins shown in dotted lines below the disk A. One notch corresponds to four teeth of the wheel and therefore to one turn of the disk A or to one hour, so that at each succeeding hour the next deeper notch is presented to the tail R. The notches are numbered in Fig. 2 with their corresponding hours, and the movement permitted by each notch to the rack is over a corresponding number of teeth and consequently a corresponding number of blows are struck on the gong.

Against the figure 1 on the wheel there is no notch, but, as seen in Fig. 1, the tail R has a short distance to move before it comes against the edge of the wheel, and this distance corresponds to one tooth on the rack and provides for one stroke. The arrangement then can be made to strike one stroke at the half-hours, merely by adding another tooth to the disk A, opposite to the tooth shown. This tooth will release the train at the half-hours, and the tail R will then fall on to one of the projecting portions of the wheel S between the notches and will allow one stroke to be given.

If the mechanism had to strike only the hours, the projections of the wheel S would be cut away, leaving a piece with twelve steps like, and usually called, a *snail*. The projections have been drawn in to show how the half-hours can be struck, and also, by reference to Plate LXVII, how the quarters are struck.

The mechanism as actually arranged on the top plate of a watch (Plate LXVII) is not easy to follow, because the parts lie so much one over the other. Except for arrangement, however, it is exactly the same as that just described, with the addition of a few parts for striking

304

PLATE LXVII

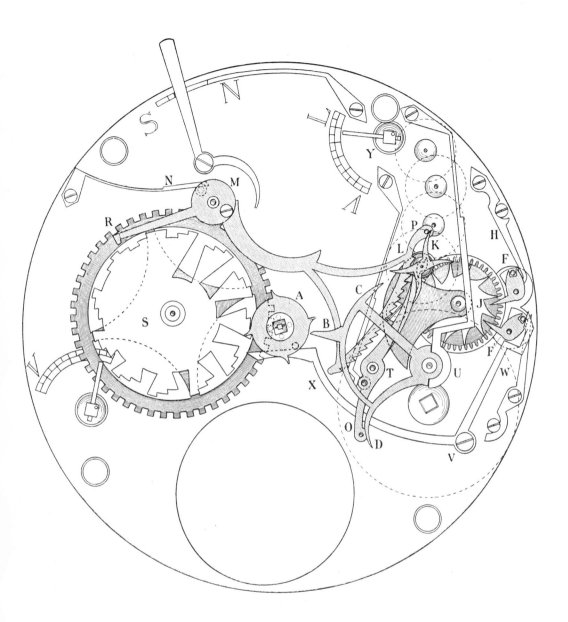

RACK STRIKING WORK

the quarters with two hammers on two gongs. Equivalent parts have the same reference letters as in Plate LXVI. The disk A has four teeth to release the mechanism at the hour and the three quarters. The three-armed lever B, C, D is very different in form, but its three arms do the same things in the two Plates, its arm D pressing the pin on the detent O to the left to move the other end of the detent (pivoted at T) to the right, out of engagement with the teeth of the rack. The curiously shaped spring U acts as both a spring and a stop for the three-armed lever, allowing it to turn in the wrong direction if the hands of the watch, with the disk A, are turned backwards. The actual hammer with its gong and spring are below the plate and not visible, but the part marked F operates the hammer by the pin seen in its forked end. The similar part marked F' is the hammer for striking the quarters. The wheel S and its toothed wheel are similar except that each projection has three steps; the highest corresponds to one stroke, giving the first quarter, the second to two and the third to three strokes. There is a provision to enable the two hammers to work and strike ting-tang at the quarters, but to put the second hammer out of operation at the hour. A lever, pivoted at V, has an arm W which, if moved to the left, presses the hammer F' back and retains it there. The arm is moved by a pin on the disk A which moves the other arm X of the lever downwards. The parts are in their position a short time after the hour has been struck, and the pin has allowed the arm X to return towards its normal position; when the hour is being struck, the pin has moved the arm X to its extreme downward position and has put the hammer F' out of action.

The mainspring barrel and the striking train are shown in dotted lines; the train ends in a pinion running in a pivot hole placed eccentrically on a circular plug Y, which has a pointer indicating on a scale marked V and L for 'Vite' and 'Lent.' Turning the plug Y moves the pinion more or less into engagement with the last wheel of the train, and thereby increases or lessens the friction and so regulates the speed of the train.

At the top is seen a lever movable between two letters S and N; these are used in all countries to mean 'Strike' and 'Silent'; they are said to be the initial letters of *Schlag* and *Nicht*, but there is no known reason why they should not be those of *Strike* and *Not*. The lever when moved to N bears against the screw-head seen on the boss of the rack L and prevents the rack moving when released.

The parts appear to be arranged in a most inconvenient way, but the drawing shows only the striking movement; on the other plate of the watch is a repeating train, and the parts of the top plate that appear vacant in the drawing are, in reality, occupied by pivot holes and other parts of the repeating and going movements.

The work of Plate LXVII dates from a little before 1800. Modern watches rarely have striking movements, and they were not common after the first quarter of the nineteenth century. This rack striking movement may be regarded as the most modern type in all essentials. It has the great advantage over the count-wheel type that the hands of the watch may be moved forwards or backwards without waiting for the striking, and the watch will always strike the next hour or quarter correctly.

CHAPTER XV

REPEATING AND MUSICAL WATCHES

'' T strikes ! One, two,
Three, four, five, six.   Enough, enough, dear watch,
Thy pulse hath beat enough.   Now sleep, and rest ;
Would thou couldst make the time to do so too ;
    I 'll wind thee up no more.'
                              BEN JONSON.   *Staple of News*, i. 1.

THE beginnings of repeating work in clocks and watches are well described by Derham in his *Artificial Clockmaker* of 1734 :—

These Clocks are a late Invention of one Mr. *Barlow*, of no longer standing than the Latter-end of King *Charles II.*, about the Year 1676. . . .

This Invention was practised chiefly, if not only, in larger Movements, till King *James II.*'s Reign : At which Time, it was transferred into Pocket-Clocks.   But there being some little contest concerning the Author hereof, I shall relate the bare Matter of Fact, leaving the Reader to his own Judgement.

About the Latter-end of King *James II.*'s Reign, Mr. *Barlow* (the ingenious inventor before mentioned) contrived to put his Invention into Pocket-watches ; and endeavoured (with the Lord Chief Justice *Allebone*, and some others) to get a Patent, for it.   And in order to it, he set Mr. *Tompion*, the Famous Artist, to work upon it : who accordingly made a Piece according to his Directions.

Mr. *Quare* (an ingenious Watchmaker in London) had some years before been thinking of the like Invention ; but not bringing it to Perfection, he laid by the Thoughts of it, until the Talk of Mr. *Barlow*'s Patent revived his former Thoughts ; which he then brought to Effect.   This being known among the Watchmakers, they all pressed him to endeavour to hinder Mr. *Barlow*'s Patent.   And accordingly Applications were made at Court,

307

and a Watch of each Invention, produced before the King and Council. The King upon Trial of each of them, was pleased to give the Preference to Mr. Quare's ; of which Notice was given soon after, in the Gazette.

The Difference between these two Inventions was, **Mr. *Barlow*'s** was made to Repeat by pushing in two Pieces on each side the Watch-box : One of which Repeated the Hour, the other the Quarter. Mr. Quare's was made to Repeat, by a Pin that Stuck out near the Pendant, which being thrust in (as now it is done by thrusting in the Pendant) did Repeat both the Hour, and Quarter, with the same thrust.

It would (I think) be very frivolous to speak of the various Contrivances, and Methods of Repeating work, and the Inventers of them ; and therefore I shall say nothing of them.

It appears from a minute of 12th October, 1688, in the Journal of the Clockmakers' Company, that it was by the 'diligence and endeavours of the Master and Wardens' that Barlow's application for a patent was rejected. The rejection is in the Privy Council Registers of 2nd March, 1687, as follows :—

Whereas on the 24th of February last his Majesty thought fit to appoint this day to hear the Master, Wardens and Assist-antes of the Fellowship of the Art or Mistery of Clockmaking of the City of London against Edward Barlow, in whose name a Patent is passing for the sole making and manageing all pulling Clocks and Watches usually called repeating Clocks. And both parties attending accordingly were called in and heard by their Counsel learned. His Majesty in Councill having fully Considered what was alleaged on either side, Is pleased to Order, and it is hereby Ordered that no Patent be granted to the said Edward Barlow or any others for the sole making and managing of pulling clocks and watches as aforesaid. The same being now made by severall Clockmakers. Whereof all persons concerned are to take due Notice.

No description of Barlow's and Quare's repeating work is extant, but Mr. Webster and Mr. Marryat lent the Author two early repeating watches by Tompion, Nos. 150 and 157, which must have been made soon after Barlow's and Quare's, and, in spite of Derham's suggestion of frivolity, a description of these will be given later with reference to a drawing of their mechanism in Plate LXX.

The electric light has made the repeating watch almost useless except to the blind, but in the eighteenth century and a great part of the nineteenth century repeating work was a most valuable addition to a watch. It was made by every maker of repute. Now only a very few firms in Switzerland make it, supplying the work for fitting in watches by other makers.

Before describing the special repeating mechanism of the early Tompion watches, the common form of the mechanism will be explained. Plate LXVIII shows a quarter repeating mechanism arranged so as to show the parts clearly. It is the type of mechanism used in watches almost through the eighteenth century, and is the same in principle as the modern repeating work.

Fig. 1 shows the parts in their normal, non-striking position; Fig. 2 in their position when the pendant of the watch has been pushed in to make it repeat, and Fig. 3 in their position when the last stroke of the quarter is about to be struck.

Repeating mechanisms, with rare exceptions, derive their power from a small mainspring that is wound up by the action of pushing in the pendant of the watch or moving a slide on the edge of the case. The amount by which the pendant is pushed in, and the mainspring wound up, depends on the hour to be struck, so that the mainspring does its work of striking in unwinding to its normal, unwound position.

The pendant of the watch acts on the point A of the lever which is pivoted to the watch plate at B. To the other end of the lever is attached a chain that passes round a pulley C and is wound round a small wheel fixed on the same arbor as the wheel D with twelve teeth. This arbor is that of the mainspring, which is not shown on the drawing; by pushing down the lever A B from the position of Fig. 1 to that of Fig. 2, the arbor is pulled round by the chain and the mainspring wound up.

309

The hour striking will be described first, without reference to the quarter striking. The hour arbor of the watch is at E and has on it an irregularly shaped plate carrying a small disk F (Figs. 2 and 3). This disk acts as a tooth to engage and turn the star-wheel; in Fig. 1 it is seen in engagement with one of the rays. Once an hour, therefore, the star-wheel is turned through a distance of one of its twelve rays, a spring-pressed detent G holding the star-wheel in correct position when it is not being turned (Figs. 2 and 3). To the star-wheel is fixed the *hour-snail*; this is below it, and the protruding parts are shaded dark, while the rest of its outline is shown in dotted lines. The hour-snail is a disk with twelve steps, at different radii, each step corresponding to an hour, the highest to one o'clock and the lowest to twelve. The tongue H of the lever A B is arranged to come against one of the steps of the hour-snail, which, therefore, limits the amount by which the lever can be pushed in, the amount by which the mainspring is wound up and the amount by which the wheel D is turned. In Fig. 2 the tongue is against the step corresponding to six o'clock.

The hammer which strikes on the gong is not shown in the drawing, but the pin by which it is worked is at J, and it is pivoted on the arbor K. On this arbor are two small levers L and M, one above the other; both act on the pin J to work the hammer, L for striking the quarters and M for striking the hour. In Fig. 2 one end of M is shown close to the pin J; the other end is a tooth engaging with the teeth of the wheel D. Looking at Fig. 2, when the lever A B is released the mainspring unwinds, turning the wheel D to the left; in its rotation, some of its teeth catch the tooth of the lever M, each tooth in succession turning it so as to move the hammer away from the gong and then releasing it to let the hammer strike a blow. The number of blows struck is determined by the number of the teeth of the wheel D which have been moved past the tooth of M in turning the wheel round; in Fig. 2 five teeth have been moved past

PLATE LXVIII

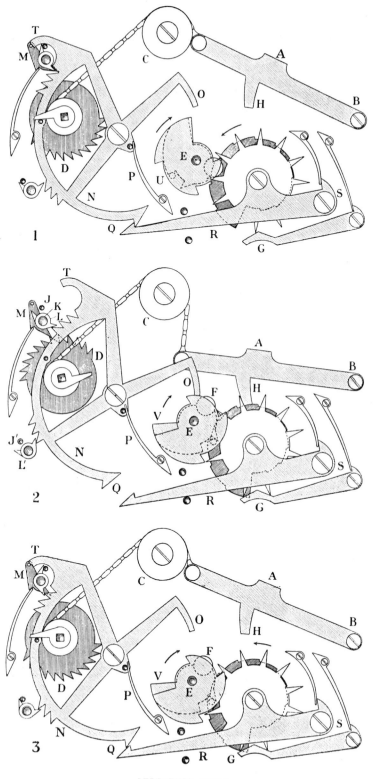

REPEATING WORK

the tooth (which is resting against the back of the sixth tooth), so that five strokes will be given as the wheel D turns back to its normal position.[1] The reason why the teeth of the wheel act, not directly on the hammer, but through the medium of the lever M, is that the teeth, in moving to the right past the tooth of M, must be able to turn it without affecting the hammer. It will be seen that the Tompion mechanism has a far less simple means of avoiding a backward movement of the hammer.

The number of strokes given by the hammer, then, depends on the number of teeth past the lever M, and this depends on the distance through which the lever A B is pressed, and this in turn is determined by the step of the hour-snail opposite the lever—that is to say, by the hour to be struck. The rate at which the mainspring unwinds is regulated by a train of wheels exactly as in the striking mechanism.

The quarter striking will now be described. The plate on the hour arbor E is the *quarter-snail*; it has four steps corresponding to the four quarters, the highest corresponding to no completed quarter and the lowest to three completed quarters. The steps of the quarter-snail determine the position of the *quarter-rack*, which is a semicircular piece N, with an arm and tongue O, arranged to come against the quarter-snail; in Fig. 2 the tongue O is shown against the step corresponding to two completed quarters. A spring P tends to turn the quarter-rack to the right; normally, the rack is held by the catches Q, but when released it turns as far as the quarter-snail allows, from the position of Fig. 1 to that of Fig. 2. The rack has two sets of three teeth, because it strikes ting-tang with two hammers on two gongs; one set of teeth works the hammer pin J through the lever L already mentioned, while the other set works the pin J' of the other hammer through the lever L'. In

---

[1] By an error in the drawing, five teeth instead of the six which should correspond to the step of the hour-snail against which the tongue H rests have been shown past the tooth of M.

Fig. 2 the rack has moved enough to bring two of each of its sets of three teeth past the levers L and L', so that, when the rack is brought back to its normal position, each hammer will strike two blows. The quarter-rack is brought back by the finger on the mainspring arbor. In Figs. 1 and 3 this finger is seen against a pin on the rack; starting from the position of Fig. 2, as the hour is struck, the finger, turning with the wheel D, approaches the pin, and, after the last stroke of the hour, reaches it and then pushes the quarter-rack back to its normal position. In Fig. 3 one quarter has been struck, and the last tooth on each of the sets of three teeth is just moving the hammers to strike the second quarter.

The earliest repeating mechanisms had the defect that the hour struck depended on how far the pendant was pushed in; if it was pushed in as far as it would go, the hour was struck correctly; if it was pushed not so far, a lesser number of strokes was given. To prevent this error, most repeating mechanisms have what is appropriately termed an *all-or-nothing* device, which provides for all the hour being struck if the pendant is pushed fully in, but for nothing to be struck if it is not. The star-wheel and hour-snail turn, not on a fixed pivot on the watch plate, but on a pivot on the arm R, pivoted to the watch plate at S, and ending in a hook which engages a hook on the quarter-rack at Q, and holds the rack in its normal position. A spring acting on the arm R tends to keep the hooks in engagement. When the lever A B is pressed in, its tongue H first comes in contact with the hour-snail, and then continued pressure moves the whole snail, with the arm R, through a very short distance up to a stop pin close to the letter R. This last movement disengages the hooks at Q and releases the quarter-rack. Consequently, if the pendant is not fully pushed in, the quarter-rack is not released and no quarters are struck. It remains to show how the hours are prevented from striking if the quarter-rack is not released. A projection T on the quarter-rack, when this is in its normal position,

312

as in Fig. 1, comes against a pin on the lever M, and moves this so far to the left that the tooth on the lever is turned out of the path of the teeth on the wheel D. This may be seen by comparing the positions of the lever M in Figs. 1 and 2. In this way the hour hammer is kept out of action until the quarter-rack is released by pushing the pendant fully in.

Now, there was another error to which repeating work was subject. In Fig. 1 the hour- and quarter-snails are shown in their positions just before the hour; the tongue H will come on step five of the hour-snail, and the tongue O will just miss the highest step of the quarter-snail and fall on the lowest step to strike three quarters. In a short time the disk F will have turned the star-wheel until the point of a ray has passed the angle on the detent G, and then this detent will give a quick turn to the star-wheel, bringing step six under the tongue H. The watch then, if made to repeat, will strike six, and at this moment, and not a second before, the tongue O must catch on the highest step of the quarter-snail; if it be late in doing so, the watch will strike six and three quarters instead of six and no quarters. It was found impracticable to make the parts work together so accurately as to prevent this error, so, to avoid it, a *surprise* piece was devised. Looking at Fig. 1, there is seen below the quarter-snail an irregularly shaped piece shown in dotted lines. This is the *surprise* piece. It is quite free to turn on the hour arbor E, but the amount it can turn is limited by a pin U fixed to the quarter-snail in a position where a slot is cut in the surprise piece; this can turn until one or other end of the slot comes against the pin U. As seen by the dotted lines, the surprise piece is smaller than the quarter-snail everywhere except at the end of the highest step, where this falls down to the lowest, and near this point the surprise piece has the same radius as the quarter-snail. When the pin U is at one end of the slot, as in Fig. 1, the surprise piece is entirely hidden by the quarter-snail, but when the

313

surprise piece is moved to bring the other end of its slot against the pin U, as in Figs. 2 and 3, a portion of it sticks out beyond the quarter-snail at V, so prolonging the length of the highest step of the quarter-snail.

Now the disk F, which acts to turn the star-wheel, is not fixed to the quarter-snail but to the surprise piece. Consequently, the disk F can exert pressure on the ray of the star-wheel only when the pin U is against the end of the slot in the surprise piece, as in Fig. 1, so that the hour arbor forces the surprise piece to turn with it. The act of turning the star-wheel then moves the surprise piece so that it is entirely hidden by the quarter-snail. When, however, the star-wheel has been turned enough to bring the point of its ray past the angle of the detent G, the spring pressure of the detent no longer acts against its turning, but forces it to turn quickly the remainder of its step. Meanwhile, the ray which is behind the disk F hits against it and turns it with the surprise piece till the other end of the slot comes against the pin U, thus making the surprise piece project at V beyond the highest step of the quarter-snail.

In this way the highest step of the quarter-snail is lengthened at the moment the hour-snail moves from one step to the next, thus making sure that the tongue O comes against the lengthened step to strike no quarters. In its simplicity and effectiveness the surprise piece is a beautiful device. Substitutes have been tried, but it remains the best and is used in all modern repeaters.

A variant of this mechanism is the half-quarter repeating work, in which a ting-tang is struck for every $7\frac{1}{2}$ minutes after the hour. The snail on the hour arbor is given eight steps instead of four, and the quarter-rack has two sets of seven teeth; otherwise the mechanism is the same.

A few changes have been made in the modern repeating work; the chain has been replaced by a rack, though this is really a reversion to the earliest type, and the all-or-nothing device with a movable star-wheel is no longer used. Otherwise, several makes of repeating mechanisms are practically the same as that described. Certain types, however, are different and simpler. Fig. 1 of Plate LXIX shows a form of modern quarter repeating work, and will serve to illustrate the rack which is used in all types. The large lever which is pivoted at B is pushed at A to operate the mechanism ; it is no longer the pendant which pushes on A, but a knob on the edge of the case at one side of the pendant ; this leaves the pendant free for the winding. Sometimes a slide, with a nick for the finger-nail, is used, but it actuates the same kind of lever.

The lever carries a rack C which engages a pinion, of which a few teeth are visible, on the mainspring arbor, so that pressing the lever at A winds up the spring, the extent of winding being determined, as in the old mechanism, by the tongue H on the lever coming against a step of the hour-snail. The mainspring arbor carries a portion of a wheel D with the twelve teeth for working the hammer lever L. This also is the same as in the old mechanism, and details of the hammer are omitted. Now, however, comes an essential difference : the teeth for striking the quarters are also on the wheel D instead of on a separate quarter-rack. There are the two sets of three teeth for striking ting-tang quarters, and the two hammer levers L and L ; the first set of three teeth follow the set of twelve hour teeth and work the same hammer L after a short interval; the other hammer L′ is farther away than the hammer L and just out of reach of these teeth, but the teeth of the second set of three teeth are longer and so work it.

The quarter-snail is, as before, on the hour arbor E and carries the surprise piece, which is not shown in the drawing. A lever F is pivoted on the stud of the hour-snail and star-wheel, and has a tongue G which is brought against the step of a quarter-snail by the spring J. This lever has on its end four long teeth, one of which is engaged by a pin K, which may be assumed to be fixed

315

to the wheel D, and therefore moves in a circular path indicated by the dotted line. In the position of the parts shown, the tongue G is on the third step down of the quarter-snail (to strike two quarters), and the pin K will engage with the third tooth as the wheel D turns to strike. As soon as it engages with the tooth it moves the lever F downwards (in the drawing) until the lever comes against the fixed pin M, when the whole mechanism is brought to a stop. The stoppage occurs (in the case considered) when two of the three teeth of each set have passed their hammers to strike two quarters. If the lowest step of the quarter-snail had been opposite the tongue G, the lever F would have been farther up (in the drawing), the pin K would have engaged the fourth instead of the third tooth, and so would have had a longer travel before the lever came against the stop, enabling the three teeth to strike quarters. The pin K is fixed, not on the wheel D, but on an arm pivoted to the wheel, and is held against a pin by a spring; this is merely to enable it to yield in coming out of the teeth on the lever F when the mainspring is being wound; during the striking it behaves as if it were fixed to the wheel.

This is a simpler mechanism than the old, but has no all-or-nothing device, the star-wheel being on a stud fixed to the watch plate. It will strike the wrong hour (but the right quarters) if the lever A B is not pushed fully home.

The modern form of all-or-nothing device is applied to mechanisms that have a separate quarter-rack, as in the old mechanism, and it acts in the same way, retaining the quarter-rack in its normal position in which a projection on the rack puts the hour hammer in an inoperative position. The device is shown in Fig. 2 of Plate LXIX, in which the lever and rack are almost the same as in Fig. 1, while the hook Q corresponds with the hook Q of Plate LXVIII, and engages the quarter-rack; this and the other parts have been omitted from the drawing. The tongue H, instead of being integral

316

PLATE LXIX

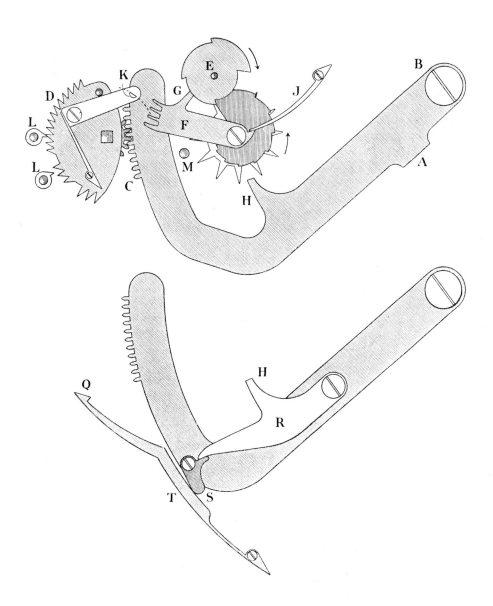

LATER REPEATING WORK

with the lever, is on a separate lever R pivoted to the main lever. The other end of the lever R bears against a small lever S, also pivoted on the main lever, and this bears against the circular part T of the spring that ends in the hook Q. While the main lever is being pushed to make the watch repeat, the small lever S moves freely along the circular part T, but, as soon as the tongue H comes against a step of the hour-snail, the pressure applied to the main lever is taken by the lever R, which in turn presses S outwards against T and so disengages the hook Q from the quarter-rack.

The rack, which was the first device used for winding the spring, appears to have been discarded on account of the difficulty of cutting the teeth well enough to work smoothly under the rather heavy pressure needed. The chain device was then more easy to construct, but gave a great deal of trouble from stretching and breaking. About 1800, when the art of tooth-cutting was better known, the rack returned to favour as a better and simpler device.

Any one who has followed the descriptions of the repeating mechanisms on Plates LXVIII and LXIX will be able to follow out the operation of almost any of the repeating works which have been and are being made. Apart, however, from the different forms of mechanisms, there are several types which differ in result. These can be best distinguished by setting out in tings and tangs (the sounds of the two hammers) how each type repeats at a given hour, taking as an example 43 minutes past 3 :—

    (1) Quarter repeater—
        ting, ting, ting . . . ting-tang, ting-tang.
    (2) Half-quarter repeater, 1st type—
        ting, ting, ting . . . ting-tang, ting-tang (5 times).
    (3) Half-quarter repeater, 2nd type—
        ting, ting, ting . . . ting-tang, ting-tang . . . ting.
    (4) Five-minute repeater, 1st type—
        ting, ting, ting . . . ting-tang, ting-tang . . .
        ting, ting.

(5) Five-minute repeater, 2nd type—

    ting, ting, ting . . . tang, tang, tang (8 times).

(6) Minute repeater—

    ting, ting, ting . . . ting-tang, ting-tang . . .
    tang-tang (13 times).

The half-quarter repeater that gave a *ting* after the quarters, if more than $7\frac{1}{2}$ minutes past the quarter, was not uncommon in the eighteenth century. Its mechanism was that of the old quarter repeater with, generally, a device similar to that of Plate LXIX for determining the quarters. The other types are comparatively modern except for a few early examples. The five-minute repeater of the first type is merely an extension of the half-quarter repeater, dividing the quarter into three instead of two. That of the second type is an extension of the quarter repeater, dividing the hour into twelve instead of four.

The minute repeater is considerably more complex. It has a quadruple minute-snail turning with the quarter-snail and an independent minute-rack. The quadruple minute-snail has to have a surprise piece to ensure accuracy; it is worked, not as is the quarter-snail surprise piece by the star-wheel, but by a spring arm which, at the right moment, presses it forward. The quarter surprise piece acts as a conseqence of the hour changing and requires no accuracy in adjustment; the minute surprise piece, however, does not act in consequence of the quarter changing, and its action depends on extreme accuracy in manufacture and adjustment. In the latest mechanisms the spring arm which works it is kept mainly out of action, and is put into action only when the repeating button is pressed. The whole mechanism is very delicate, and requires the accurate adjustment of one spring against another.

The earliest minute repeating mechanism known to the Author is in a German table clock in Mr. Percy Webster's collection, by Benedikt Fürstenfelder of Friedberg, near Augsburg, of about 1710, but the Author has never seen an eighteenth-century minute repeating watch. Thiout, in his *Traité de l'Horlogerie* of 1741, describes a minute repeating work, but says :—

although watches have been made on this principle . . . it is certain that they cannot be worth much, because a watch is not big enough to give this construction the requisite solidity.

The early Tompion repeating movement referred to at the beginning of the chapter is shown in Plate LXX. The quarter-snail is seen in the centre on the hour arbor of the watch. At the top is the hour-snail, partly covered by a star-wheel, which, however, does not correspond with the star-wheel in the later repeating work; its function is that of a surprise piece. At the bottom is the mainspring, which is below the plate, its arbor, with a pinion, being seen above the plate; on its arbor, but below the plate and shown in dotted lines, is a wheel with twelve teeth for striking the hour. On the right is the push-piece, pivoted above, with a rack engaging the pinion on the mainspring arbor. The finger that engages the hour-snail is pivoted to the push-piece and kept in the normal position by a spring. The very complex piece on the left is the quarter-rack; it is pivoted above and has the two sets of three teeth for striking ting-tang quarters below. Its finger for engaging the quarter-snail is pivoted to its under side and is shown in dotted lines; the tip of the finger just protrudes on the right. The finger is kept in normal position by a U-shaped spring. The two hammer levers for the quarters are at the bottom; that on the left is on an arbor which carries, below the plate, a lever for the hours, engaging the teeth of the hour-striking wheel. The hammers are fixed directly on the arbors that carry the levers, so that these cannot turn backwards to allow the teeth to pass when the mainspring is being wound up and when the quarter-rack is falling. To overcome this difficulty, the teeth of the quarter-rack are on a separate piece from the main pivoted part (shaded

319

differently in the drawing); this separate piece is so pivoted to the main part that it can turn upwardly and allow the teeth to ride over the points of the hammer levers. It is normally kept in its lower position by a flat spring (left unshaded) acting on its left upper corner. The left-hand sides of the hammer levers are bevelled and the right-hand sides of each tooth on the rack are bevelled below, so that as the rack falls to the right the pivoted piece rises, letting the teeth pass over the levers. A similar arrangement allows the teeth of the hour-striking wheel to pass the hammer lever, with the difference that the lever is pivoted as shown in dotted lines, so that it is forced down and allows the wheel teeth to pass over it. These devices are clumsy in comparison with the later device of making the hammer levers separate from the hammers, so that they can turn backwards independently of the hammer and allow the rack teeth to escape past them. The Author can discover no reason for the curious shape of the pivoted piece of the quarter-rack, with its two pivots at an angle with the main outline of the piece.

The quarter-rack is kept in its normal position, as shown, by a long, curved nose on the push-piece bearing against an arm on the quarter-rack to the right of its pivot. The nose and arm are seen in contact on the left-hand side of the star-wheel, most of the nose being under the star-wheel and snail and shown in dotted lines. When the push-piece is pressed in, the nose is lifted clear of the arm and the quarter-rack falls in the usual way (under the action of a spring which is not shown) till its finger abuts against the quarter-snail. After the hour has been struck, the nose meets the arm and turns it back to normal position, causing the rack to strike the quarters.

The hour arbor of the watch does not move the hour-snail in steps, as in all the later mechanisms, by means of a star-wheel; the snail is turned gradually by a gear consisting of a pinion of four pins (shown in dotted lines

320

PLATE LXX

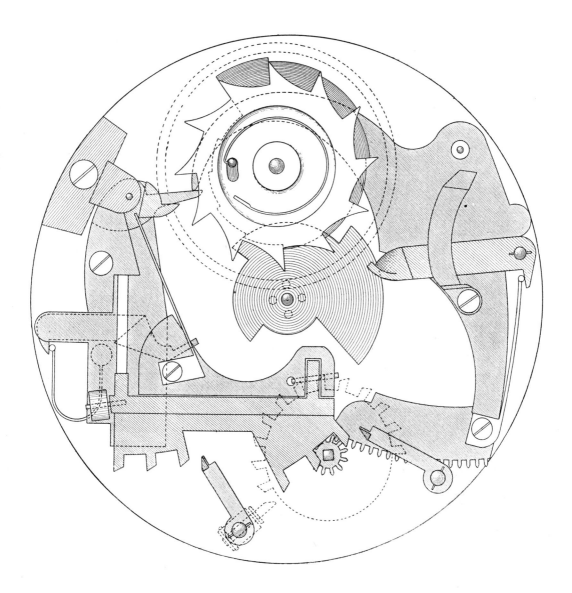

EARLY TOMPION REPEATING WORK

round the hour arbor) which engage a wheel of forty-eight teeth (indicated by two dotted circles) below the snail. The snail and star-wheel are fixed together, but not to the wheel; this drives them by means of a pin fixed to the wheel, which is seen protruding through a slot in the snail and star-wheel. The snail and star-wheel therefore are capable of a small movement relatively to the wheel, a spring normally keeping them in the position shown. This is part of the device for ensuring change of quarters with change of hours. The other part is a small nose-piece pivoted on the arbor of the quarter-rack above its arm (a different shading distinguishes this nose-piece). It is normally kept in the position shown by a spring, and is just clear of the rays of the star-wheel. When the rack falls, however, the tip enters the path of the rays and approaches a ray; in the position shown, if the rack fell on to the half-hour step of the quarter-snail, the nose-piece would move only about one-third of the distance towards the ray above it and would have no action at all, but, when the parts have moved into a position corresponding to a time a little before an hour, the star-wheel has turned so as to bring the ray close to the nose-piece and also the nose-piece moves farther, because the quarter-rack has farther to fall. The result is that the nose-piece pushes the star-wheel and snail back just before the finger on the push-piece reaches the hour-snail, and in so doing prevents the finger falling just over a step on the snail; prevents it therefore striking the next hour while the quarter-rack was striking the three-quarters of the previous hour. When the quarter-rack finger falls on the highest step of the quarter-snail it has only a very small movement, so that the nose-piece has no action in turning back the snail.

In the normal working of the mechanism there is no reason for the two fingers to be pivoted instead of fixed to the push-piece and quarter-rack. The Author attributes their pivoting to a lack of confidence in the mechanism. If the mainspring failed to return the parts

321

to their normal positions, the watch would stop at the next hour if the quarter finger were fixed, because the face of the high step on the quarter-snail would come against the finger. A pivoted finger would be pushed out of the way and so would avoid stopping the watch.

This mechanism is the more interesting because it was not an isolated or experimental design. The two Tompion watches examined are numbers 150 and 157, and their mechanisms are the same down to the smallest detail. The intervening watches may not have been repeaters, but the numbers show that for a certain period this was Tompion's type of repeating work.

Of the many variants of later repeating mechanisms, there is only one which was common enough and different enough from the others to call for special mention. Matthew Stogden early in the eighteenth century devised a work in which the parts were more compactly arranged. Moinet, in his treatise published in 1848,[1] says that the object was to leave room for the calendar mechanism which then was fashionable, and that the extra room taken by the parts in thickness was not considered an objection in the days of thick watches. Moinet speaks unfavourably of the mechanism, and quite rightly, but the Author has examined a watch by Moinet with repeating mechanism of this type and without calendar mechanism, though there is a day-of-the-month wheel placed over the repeating work. The watch was made probably ten to twenty years before the date of the book.

In Stogden's work, the quarter teeth are on the same disk as the hour teeth and all the quarter teeth always pass the hammer lever. This, however, is capable of sliding up and down on its arbor : in its up position it is engaged by the quarter teeth ; in its down position it is clear of them. The piece carrying the finger that engages the quarter-snail acts to depress the hammer lever as soon as the right number of quarters have been struck,

---

[1] *Nouveau Traité général d'Horlogerie.* M. L. Moinet. 2 vols. Paris, 1848.

so that any remaining quarter teeth pass over the lever. The quarter-snail has a shape the inverse of the ordinary —that is to say, the highest step determines the three-quarters and the lowest the no-quarters. The surprise, too, differs from the normal type and is a less pretty device; the whole quarter-snail has a free movement about the hour arbor, and is controlled by a spring so that, when the hour star-wheel jumps a step, the snail jumps forward also under the action of its spring.

The regulator for the train has undergone two changes. The earliest and nearly all the eighteenth-century watches depended on the friction of the train for the regulation of its speed and the rate of striking, just as did the striking watches. One pivot of the last pinion ran in a hole placed eccentrically in a plug, held by friction in the watch plate. Turning the plug brought the pinion more or less into engagement with the last wheel of the train and increased or diminished its friction.

About 1800, the last wheel of the train was replaced by an escapement, exactly like an alarum in which the hammer was reduced to a small weight. This simplified the mechanism, but made a disagreeable buzz. The latest form of regulator is a centrifugal governor, similar to the governors of gramophone motors. A pinion of the train has two weighted arms, pivoted so that they can swing outwards from the axis, but kept close to the axis by springs when the train is at rest. When the train runs, these arms swing out until their ends come into contact with a surrounding ring, against which they rub. This introduces friction, which increases as the speed increases and so tends to keep the speed constant. The device has the advantages of being more silent than the escapement and than the long quick-running train, and of giving better regulation.

The bell of all the early alarum, striking and repeating watches was no serious addition to the thick watches of the early eighteenth century and their predecessors, but was inadmissible in a thin watch. The difficulty was finally surmounted by Breguet, who in 1789 devised the wire gong. This was a hard steel wire, ending in a block which was screwed to the edge of the watch plate, the wire curling round the edge of the watch and occupying only very little space. Most repeaters had two of these and some three, generally with very little free play between them and the watch-case and the movement, and a gong, once bent, is difficult to restore to a form that passes clear of obstructions. Julien Le Roy, however, had omitted the bell about the middle of the century, letting the hammers beat against the edge of the case, to make a sufficient though a less attractive sound. Some watches were fitted with a gong and a *sourdine*. This was a small pin projecting from the edge of the case, which, when pressed in by the finger, received the blows of the hammer. The blows were then practically silent, but felt by the finger.

A modified form of push-piece which was much used by Breguet had the advantage that it did not project from the case. It had to be pulled out, then given a half-turn and then pushed in. It was never popular, because the watch could not be made to repeat by one hand stretched out of bed in the dark.

Musical Watches.—Musical watches before the end of the eighteenth century are very rare. A bell or gong was the only thing used for giving a musical note, and a set of gongs was bulky for use in a watch. A few watches with sets of from five to ten gongs were, however, made. The earliest known to the Author are two by John Archambo of London (1720-50)—one in Mr. Percy Webster's collection illustrated on Plate XLVIII, and the other, a similar watch, in M. Olivier's collection. Another, much later, about 1780, almost certainly by the famous mechanician Jaquet-Droz, is illustrated in Chapuis' *La Montre Chinoise*.

Musical mechanism became practical for watches only with the invention of the *comb*, the series of steel reeds

324

used in all musical boxes. Its inventor is not known with any certainty, but the earliest use of a comb known is in a clock by Antide Janvier of 1776, described by Chapuis. The reeds of the comb were, at first, operated by pins on a cylinder as in the ordinary musical box, and watches with this form of mechanism were made in Switzerland shortly before and after 1800, by Piguet and others. About 1810 the cylinder was replaced by a disk, giving an arrangement more difficult to make but more easily disposed in a watch. The disk has pins on its two surfaces which operate two sets of steel reeds with their ends bent down at right angles towards the disk. Each reed is a separate piece of steel, whereas the comb of the ordinary musical box with cylinder is a single block of steel which has been cut into reeds. The earlier combs of this type were, however, split up into groups of reeds or even separate single reeds. Chapuis attributes the invention of the disk to P. S. Meylan and I. D. Piguet, the famous makers of Geneva who specialized in elaborate watches for the East. Musical watches of about 1800 were generally arranged to play a tune at each hour, and also to play at will by moving a slide on the edge of the case.

> 'Complaisance is a gingerbread creature,
>   Used for shew, like a watch, by each spark ;
>   But truth is a golden repeater,
>   That sets a man right in the dark.'
>   *Inkle and Yarico.* COLMAN, 1787.

CHAPTER XVI

SECONDS HANDS AND CHRONOGRAPHS

' 'Tis with our judgements as our watches,
None go just alike yet each believes his own.'
                                        POPE.

THE first use of a seconds hand is on a watch by
John Fitter of Battersea, of about 1665, illustrated
in Britten and now in the Marryat collection.
The dial has a central minute hand, one of the earliest
known on watches, and the central portion of the dial is
a rotating disk with a figure of Time pointing to the hour.
The seconds hand is on the top plate of the movement,
indicating on a special small dial.

The earliest seconds hand in its normal position on
the dial appears to be on the watch by Fromanteel, illus-
trated on Plate XLV, 1, and described in Chapter IX.
This watch dates from about 1690, when Sir John
Floyer, the London physician, used a watch specially
made for showing seconds only, for counting the pulse.
He wrote a pamphlet in 1707 on *The Physician's Pulse
Watch*, which had a second edition in 1710.

The seconds hand became fairly common on long
case clocks towards the end of the seventeenth century,
but is seldom found on watches until the end of the
eighteenth century, and did not become common until
the verge escapement gave place to the cylinder.

When a watch is intended for accurate timing, the
seconds hand is a long central hand making use of the
full size of the dial, and the watch is then said to have
'centre-seconds.' To get the seconds hand in this
position, the train of the watch had to be rearranged

326

to bring the fourth wheel (the crown wheel in a verge watch) in the centre. The hours and minutes were then often shown on a small dial above or below the centre. The watch by William Hughes of about 1790 on Plate LII is an example of this arrangement, and that by Marc Fabry Pinault of 1759 on Plate LIII, 2 is an early example of centre-seconds hand with central hour and minute hands. In the latter arrangement the extra wheels required for the hour and minute hands introduced play, which gave the minute hand the appearance of being loose.

Thiout, who appears to have been the first to employ centre-seconds, discusses the various methods of showing seconds in his *Traité de l'Horlogerie* published in 1741, but the Author knows of no watch with centre-seconds hand so early as this.

Early in the nineteenth century a seconds hand going round once a second instead of once a minute was tried with the mistaken idea of getting greater accuracy. The Author has a watch by Martin, of about 1820, with small hour dial and centre-seconds hand and also a small dial with hand going round once a second in four jumps; the quick, jerky motion gives the watch a singularly busy appearance.

Many of these watches were stop-watches, having a nib projecting from the edge which could be moved to bring a finger against the balance to stop the whole watch. This is obviously an unsatisfactory form of stop-watch, because not only did the watch lose time when the stop device was used, but the watch took a little time to get under way, and this made the seconds recorded inaccurate.

To avoid these defects the 'independent seconds' were introduced, at the cost of considerable complication. The watch has an ordinary train, but the fourth wheel drives an extra pinion of six leaves. Then there is an entirely separate train, complete with mainspring barrel but without escapement, and the centre-seconds hand is fixed on the fourth wheel of this train. This wheel drives the pinion of a fifth wheel which drives a pinion carrying a finger called a 'flirt,' which engages with the leaves of the extra pinion in the other train. As the pinion turns, the flirt turns with it until it escapes from the leaf, when it flies round to be caught again on the next leaf of the pinion. It makes, in fact, about one-fortieth of a turn slowly and the remaining thirty-nine-fortieths very quickly. One turn of the flirt corresponds to a movement of the centre-seconds hand over one second, and the slow portion of its movement is so minute that it appears to jump from second to second, whence the name 'jump' or 'sweep' seconds. The arrangement is quite good, because the watch train has no extra work in driving the centre-seconds hand, but it makes an expensive watch and has the disadvantage that the seconds hand cannot be stopped to show a fraction of a second. It is stopped by means of a finger which is pushed into the path of the flirt just after this has left the leaf of the pinion.

In another method of stopping the seconds hand without stopping the watch, the first push on a knob stopped the hand and on a subsequent push the hand flew to the position it would have been in if it had never been stopped. The seconds hand was loose on its arbor and connected with it by a pinion and spring-pressed toothed sector; the mechanism is ingenious but complex to describe, and has hardly enough interest to warrant the trouble of following it. It was devised by Perrelet in 1827, but is generally attributed to Jacob, who made a number of watches on the system. Quite a different method which produced the same result was due to the celebrated Paris maker Winnerl (1799-1886), who applied it to two hands, thus producing the first split-seconds watch.

Before describing the modern system of independent seconds, reference will be made to variations of the method of obtaining sweep seconds, by using a balance

328

and escapement beating seconds or half-seconds instead of quarter or fifth-seconds. The most obvious way was to make the balance big enough to beat seconds. This was done fairly commonly about 1800, Edward Massey of London (1772-1852) being one of the principal makers to do it, producing watches with balances nearly as large as the top plate of the watch. Berthoud, the great Paris maker, was a partisan of large slow-swinging balances, and discusses their advantages in his *Essai sur l'Horlogerie* of 1763. Another way was to lengthen the time of swing of the balance by making it swing through two or three turns instead of about half a turn, the balance being far from isochronous for so big a difference of swing. A special form of verge escapement is used, and the balance is not on the verge but on a separate arbor driven by a large wheel on the verge. A balance driven in this way is known as a 'pirouette,' a term quite appropriate to the appearance of the balance when swinging.

The third method was common in what are known as Chinese watches, which are watches made in Switzerland, mostly at Fleurier, for the Chinese market. A special form of duplex escapement was used (described in Chapter X) with a balance beating quarter-seconds, and the seconds hand appears to jump whole seconds, though in reality it makes two jumps to the second, one large and the other small. The motion of the hand resembles that of the independent train watch, but the small motion is rather more apparent in the case of the Chinese watch.

The modern form of chronograph developed gradually, but there is little general interest in tracing its steps, and it will be described in its final form. The term 'chronograph' is misleading, because the watch has nothing graphic. Apparently the word has survived from an early form which was a true chronograph, the centre-seconds hand having a small ink reservoir at its tip which could be pressed momentarily on to the dial to make an ink dot.

Figs. 1, 2, and 3 of Plate LXXI show the mechanism

of the chronograph portion of a watch, which works as follows :—

On the first pressure on a knob, generally in the pendant, the centre-seconds hand starts from rest.

On the second pressure it stops.

On the third pressure it flies back to its resting position at 0 or 60 seconds.

The wheel A is mounted on the arbor of the fourth wheel of the watch, which is the wheel turning once a minute to which the ordinary seconds hand is attached. It is in its usual position near the bottom of the watch. The wheel B is in the centre of the watch, and the centre-seconds hand is attached to it. A third wheel C is pivoted in a carrier lever which is pivoted to the watch-plate at D. The three wheels A, B and C are really toothed wheels, but with teeth so fine that the wheels appear merely to have roughened edges. The wheel C is always in contact with wheel A and so is always turning. In positions 1 and 3 it is out of contact with wheel B, so that the centre-seconds hand is entirely independent of the watch movement, but in position 2 the carrier lever is moved so as to bring the wheel C into contact also with wheel B. The centre-seconds hand is then connected with the watch movement and turns. This is the position after the first pressure on the knob. The second pressure brings the parts into position 3; the wheel C is out of contact with the wheel B, so that the seconds hand is no longer turned by the watch, but also a brake is applied to the wheel B to ensure its stopping immediately. This brake is in the form of a spring E; it is seen in contact with B in position 3 and out of contact with it in positions 1 and 2. The third pressure has to make the wheel B turn so as to bring the seconds hand to zero. This is done by means of the heart-shaped piece, termed a heart-cam, on the wheel B, and the arm F, which is pressed towards the heart-cam by the spring G.

In position 3 the arm F is held back by a device

330

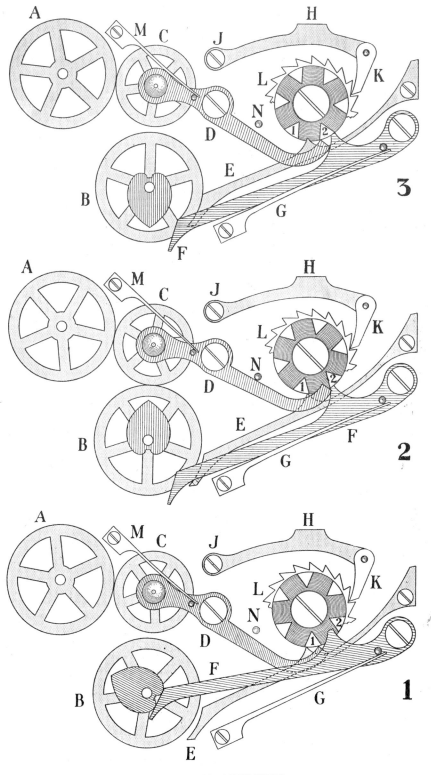

PLATE LXXI

CHRONOGRAPH MECHANISM

which will be described, but, assuming it to be released, the flat end of F is pressed against the sloping side of the heart-cam and pushes it away by turning it until it is suddenly brought up by the two lobes of the heart coming simultaneously against the flat end, as in position 1. The centre-seconds hand is then at zero. It remains to show how the carrier lever, the brake E and the arm F are operated at the proper times.

The knob of the watch presses at H on the arm which is pivoted to the watch plate at J. At the end of the arm is a pivoted piece K, known as a *pawl*, which engages the teeth of a ratchet wheel L pivoted to the watch plate. Pressing on H turns the wheel L a distance of one tooth in a clockwise direction. When the pressure is released the arm is brought back to its normal position by a spring, which is not shown in the drawing, and the pawl K slips back into the next tooth, so that a second pressure on H turns wheel L again, and so on. The teeth of the wheel L are broken away on the left-hand side so as not to confuse the drawing. Standing up from the face of L are six triangular (unshaded) projections ; L is called a *castle-ratchet* because these projections appear as castellations. There is one projection to every three teeth, so that after three pressures on H the wheel L has been turned through a distance corresponding to one castellation. Starting now with position 1, the brake E is held off the wheel B by a projecting point on its side coming against the outer face of the castellation marked 1. The carrier lever keeps the wheel C out of contact with B, because its end is against the same castellation. The spring M tends always to press the lever so as to bring C into contact with B. The arm F, which also has a projection on its side, has been able to move to the right because this projection enters the space between the two castellations 1 and 2.

Now the first pressure is given on H, and the wheel L is turned through one tooth. The first result is that castellation 2 comes against the projection on the arm F and moves the arm back until the projection rides on the face of the castellation as in position 2. This sets the wheel B free. At the same time the end of the carrier lever drops off castellation 1 into the space between 1 and 2, and the spring M then brings wheel C into contact with B and starts the seconds hand moving. The brake E is still held off the wheel B, because its projection is still against the castellation 1, at its other corner. Now the second pressure is given to H to turn wheel L another tooth forward into position 3. The arm F is still held back by castellation 2, but this castellation has pushed the end of the carrier lever outwards and brought wheel C out of contact with B, and the projection on the brake E has slipped off castellation 1, allowing the brake to come against the wheel B. The third pressure brings the parts back into position 1 (castellation 2 taking the place of castellation 1) and releases the arm F, which makes the seconds hand fly back to zero.

The great advantage of this arrangement is that, when the seconds hand is not in action, the watch train is entirely free of it. A stop N, generally made adjustable, allows the wheel C to come just into contact with wheel B without exerting pressure. In earlier types the end of the arm F has a rounded V instead of a flat end, the V entering the depression between the lobes of the heart.

The mechanism is difficult to make, but when properly made it works well and will register accurately to one-fifth of a second. A really fine chronograph is a very expensive watch.

There is a beautiful adjunct to a chronograph known by the bad term *split seconds*. The French *secondes rattrapantes* is a much better name. The watch has a subsidiary centre-seconds hand and a subsidiary press-knob. When the main knob is pressed the two hands start off together and move on as if they were one hand. Then when the subsidiary knob is pressed, the subsidiary hand stops, while the main hand continues. On a second pressure of the subsidiary knob the hand rejoins the

332

PLATE LXXII

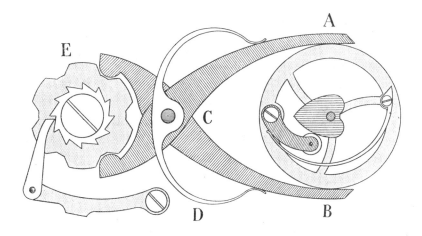

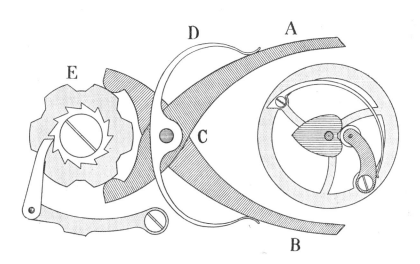

SPLIT SECONDS MECHANISM

main hand and they again move as one hand. If the main knob only be pressed, the two hands start, stop and fly back together as one hand.

The mechanism is shown in Figs. 1 and 2 of Plate LXXII. It is generally arranged on the other side of the watch to the ordinary chronograph mechanism. The heart-cam is fixed to the arbor of the main seconds hand ; the wheel below it carries the subsidiary seconds hand and turns freely on the shaft of the main seconds hand. In an actual watch, if the mechanism were on the pillar plate, below the dial, the heart-cam would be on the other side of the wheel and the wheel would be fixed on a tube surrounding the arbor of the main seconds hand, passing through the dial and carrying the subsidiary seconds hand.

On the wheel is pivoted an arm carrying a roller, made of jewel in good watches, and pressed against the heart-cam by the spring. This arm and roller act in the same way as the arm with a flat end in the chronograph mechanism just described, only here the heart-cam must be regarded as fixed, so that the roller tends to move the wheel into position 1 when the two hands are together. If the main hand (carrying the heart-cam) be started, stopped and allowed to fly back, the wheel with the subsidiary hand follows it in all its movements, the roller always remaining between the lobes of the heart. Now there are two arms A and B, pivoted at C to the watch plate, like a pair of scissors, and a spring D tends to close the arms on to the edge of the wheel as in position 2. In position 1 the arms are kept apart because their other ends ride on two projections on the wheel E pivoted to the watch plate. This wheel is turned by an arm and pawl operated by the subsidiary press-knob. When turned through a distance of one tooth of the ratchet wheel, into position 2, the arms of the pair of scissors are free to come together and press on the edge of the wheel. This stops the wheel and subsidiary hand, but the main hand can continue to turn,

333

though the heart-cam, in turning with it, moves the roller and its arm back and forth, as the roller rides over the heart-cam. The next pressure on the subsidiary knob moves the scissor arms apart and frees the wheel, whereupon the roller causes the wheel to turn until the roller again comes between the lobes of the heart and brings the subsidiary hand up to the main hand.

The scissor arms and their spring D are all free on their pivot, so that when the arms press on the wheel their two pressures counteract one another and cause no sideway pressure on the delicate wheel. To appreciate the delicacy of this mechanism, it should be realized that the wheel in an actual watch is about the size of the head of the screw of wheel E in the drawing.

CHAPTER XVII

KEYLESS WATCHES

'Hast Uhr und Wecker selbst gemacht
Und doch genommen nicht in Acht
Dass von Natur du gehst zum Grab,
Gleichwie die Uhr selbst läuffet ab.'
*Motto of picture of clockmaker's shop in the Dance of Death
by* MEGLINGER *on Lucerne Mühlenbrücke. c.* 1630.

KEYLESS watches did not become at all common
before the middle of the nineteenth century, and
it is difficult to understand why the nuisance of
a key was suffered for so long. Neither expense nor
difficulty could have stood in the way of keyless work,
because the costly and complex repetition work was
common enough in the eighteenth century.

The earliest mention of keyless, or rather self-winding,
watches is in Schwenter's *Delitiae Mathematicae et
Physicae*, published in Nürnberg in 1651 :—

In the four books which are called Les Conférences de Paris
du Bureau d'addresse, the following words appear among the
first hundred perpetual motions. Some one fastened close
against his skin a belt which, rising and falling as he breathed,
acted as a perpetual spring for a watch hanging from it, and by
this means there was no need to wind this watch. . . . What is
to be thought about this invention we leave to the judgement of
the competent reader.

The last sentence indicates that even Schwenter could
not quite believe in the breath winding.

Britten quotes an advertisement in the *London
Gazette* of 1686 about a watch having a spring wound
up without a key, and the Clockmakers' Company in 1712

335

opposed the application for a patent by John Hutchinson for a watch which, among other features, had 'a contrivance to wind up this, or any other Movement, without an aperture in the Case through which anything can pass to foul the movement.' A movement by Charles Goode of fourteen years before was produced, and acknowledged by Hutchinson to be similar, and the application was withdrawn. Then, about 1750, Caron (later Beaumarchais) made a watch in a ring for Mme. de Pompadour which was wound by means of a lever projecting from the case under the dial.

In all probability there were many other isolated instances of keyless winding mechanism in the eighteenth century, but they have left no records, and the Author has seen no keyless watch earlier than 1790.

The earliest device which, later, became at all common was the *Pedometer* type of self-winding. It was patented in England in 1780 by Louis Recordon, and is found in many watches by Breguet, called by him *montres perpétuelles*. A heavy mass, fixed on the end of a pivoted lever, is just supported by a spring and is jerked up and down by the motion of the body in walking. This up-and-down motion is used to wind the watch through a pawl on the lever engaging a ratchet wheel connected with the mainspring arbor.

Then, about 1790, began a series of winding devices worked by moving a knob at the pendant in and out, and known as *pump winding motions*. Lepine made some watches with pump action, and other makers from time to time patented forms of the device and produced a few watches; as late as 1860 it was used by the fine English maker Viner. The pendant knob was connected with the mainspring arbor either by a rack or chain, a ratchet wheel being interposed so that the mainspring arbor was turned only when the knob was pushed in, or, alternatively, only when it was pulled out. When the connexion was by chain, pulling out the knob wound up a light spring which served to coil the chain round the ratchet wheel when the knob was pushed in. Sometimes, when the connexion was by a rack, the knob had to be given a half or a quarter turn to make connexion with the rack before pumping action was given. All these devices replaced the key in winding only; as they had no means for setting the hands, they did not make the watch really keyless. It was not till about 1838 that hand setting, by turning the knob, was added to pump action winding, but the device had no success.

Keyless work by turning the pendant has generally been attributed to A. L. Breguet, but the present firm of Breguet tell the Author that they know of no watch by him with any kind of keyless device other than the pedometer watches, or *montres perpétuelles*. It is probable that in this A. L. Breguet has been confused with his grandson Louis Clément François Breguet, under whose ægis the house of Breguet et fils produced several really keyless watches soon after his father, Louis Antoine Breguet, retired in 1833. These watches resembled the modern watch in the external operation of the keyless work, but the mechanism was quite different. The knob in the pendant, when in its normal position, was engaged with the mainspring arbor, which could be wound by turning it; on pulling the knob out, it was brought out of engagement with the wheels connecting it with the mainspring arbor and into engagement with wheels connected with the hands. Very few watches appear to have been made on this system.

The first keyless watches made in any quantity as a regular type were by Louis Audemars of Brassus, in Switzerland, but the mechanism was not satisfactory. Then, in 1846, Nicole of London patented a type of keyless work applicable to either fuzee or going-barrel watches, and made a considerable number of watches fitted with it. In a fuzee watch the winding square of the fuzee turns with the watch train, and consequently the winding mechanism has to be normally out of engagement with it, so as to avoid giving the train more

337

friction to overcome. In a going-barrel watch, however, the mainspring arbor is stationary except in winding, so that the winding mechanism may remain normally in engagement with it.

In Nicole's device for fuzee watches, a wheel which could be turned by the pendant knob was between a wheel on the fuzee arbor and a wheel connected with the hands, and was normally kept out of contact with both wheels by a spring. On pressing the pendant knob in, the wheel turned by it was engaged with the wheel on the fuzee for winding, while on pulling it out the wheel was engaged with that connected with the hands. In his device for going-barrel watches, the pendant knob was permanently in engagement with a wheel connected with the mainspring arbor through a ratchet, so that, as in the modern watch, the pendant knob wound up the watch when turned one way and slipped freely round when turned the other way. Hand setting was done by moving a lever projecting through the edge of the watch-case, to bring a wheel connected with the hands into engagement with the ratchet-wheel. Turning the pendant then moved the hands, winding the watch at the same time if the hands were turned backward.

The two forms of keyless work that came into general use were the *rocking-bar* mechanism, invented in 1848 by Antoine Lecoultre, and the *shifting-sleeve* mechanism, produced by Audemars Frères about the same time, and invented independently soon after by Adrien Philippe, who later joined the existing firm of Patek, Philippe et Cie. Both these firms (Audemars Frères is now Audemars, Piguet et Cie) are among the Swiss makers of high-grade watches.

Fig. 1, Plate LXXIII, shows the upper part of a watch movement with the rocking-bar keyless work. The rod protruding up from the centre passes through the pendant of the case and ends in the serrated winding knob. Below, it ends in a pinion seen on edge in a slot in the watch plate. This pinion engages with a wheel

338

pivoted to the watch plate, the wheel engaging with two smaller wheels, one on each side, carried on the rocking-bar which turns about the same centre as the central wheel. The wheel on the left is shown engaged with a wheel on the mainspring arbor; the spring barrel is seen below it, shaded. In the position shown, turning the pendant knob winds up the spring; it turns also the small wheel on the right, but this turns idly. A light spring on the left tends to keep the rocking-bar in the position shown, and turning the winding knob to the right, *i.e.* turning the central wheel to the left, also tends to keep it there, because the teeth of the central wheel are then pressing the teeth of the left-hand wheel, and therefore also the rocking-bar, downwards. Turning the winding knob to the left, however, has the opposite effect, and tends to lift the rocking-bar so that the wheel on the left comes out of engagement with the winding wheel on the mainspring arbor; its teeth then slip over those of the winding wheel, thus allowing the winding knob to be turned to the left freely. The action is ingenious; so long as the teeth are in engagement some pressure can be applied by the winding knob, and this lifts them out of engagement; then, however, the small wheel being free, the pressure ceases, and the spring brings them back into engagement. The action feels like that of a ratchet-wheel but is actually quite different.

The small rod protruding from the edge of the movement on the right is the press-button for hand setting, found on most keyless watches of the last century. When this is pressed in by the finger-nail the rocking-bar is rocked to the right, bringing the wheel on the left out of engagement with the winding wheel and the wheel on the right into engagement with the wheel shown below, which is connected with the hands. When the rocking-bar is in this position, turning the winding knob moves the hands.

Figs. 2 and 3 show the shifting-sleeve keyless work There is a similar pinion on the rod of the winding knob,

339

which is permanently in engagement with the mainspring arbor through the two wheels which are below the plate and shown by dotted lines. The pinion, however, is not fixed to the rod, but can turn freely on it. The rod, the pinion and, below it, the shifting-sleeve are shown in Fig. 3 on the right-hand side, separated one from the other. The rod has a collar, and below this a cylindrical part, and below this a square part. The pinion lies on the cylindrical part and so can turn on it; the shifting-sleeve lies on the square part and so has to turn with the rod, though it can slide up and down; it has ratchet teeth above, which in Fig. 2 are shown in engagement with corresponding ratchet teeth on the pinion. In the centre of the shifting-sleeve is a groove in which lies the end of a curved bar supported on a spring; this tends to keep the ratchet teeth in engagement, in the position shown. Turning the winding knob to the left turns the shifting-sleeve, which, by the ratchet teeth, turns the pinion and winds up the watch. In turning the knob to the right, the ratchet teeth can slip, by the shifting-sleeve sliding downwards on its square against the pressure of the spring.

The hands are set by moving the shifting-sleeve downwards by the press-button, which bears on the curved bar. This brings the ratchet teeth out of engagement, so that the pinion is no longer turned by the winding knob, and, at the same time, brings the teeth on the lower end of the shifting-sleeve into engagement with the small toothed wheel which is connected with the hands.

Both these forms of keyless mechanism worked satisfactorily, but they required a finger-nail of sufficient length, and dust could enter the case past the press-button. The modern system avoids the use of a press-button for hand setting, and when well made is certainly the best. In cheap watches, though, the mechanism frequently gives trouble. There are innumerable forms of the device, and the one shown in Figs. 4 and 5 of

340

PLATE LXXIII

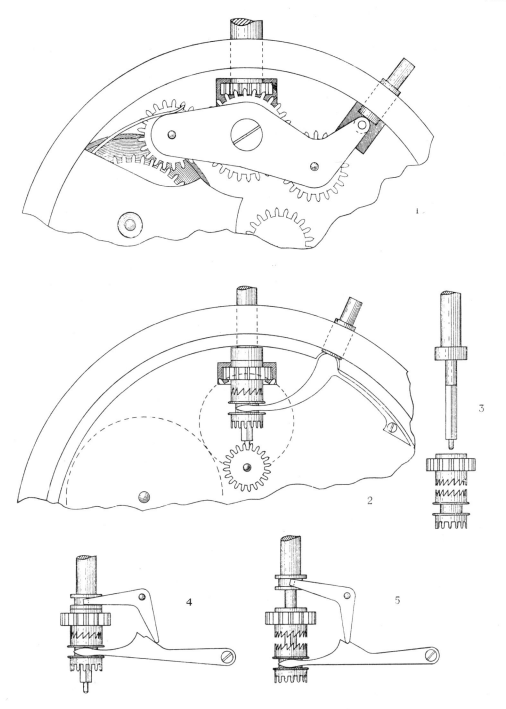

KEYLESS WORK

Plate LXXIII was selected because its action is particularly clear. It differs only in construction from the original form invented by Adrien Philippe.

The figures show the rod of the winding knob, the pinion and the shifting-sleeve apart from the watch movement, because they lie in it as in Fig. 2, and are substantially the same as in Fig. 3. There are the differences that the rod must have room to move upwards when the knob is pulled for hand setting, and that the collar on the rod has a groove in which the end of a lever engages.

In Fig. 4 the parts are in position for winding, and in Fig. 5 for hand setting. The upper lever is pivoted to the watch plate and its bent-down end engages the groove referred to. When the rod is pulled up, the upper lever is turned and its lower end presses the lower lever, together with the shifting-sleeve, downwards until it enters the nick in the lower lever, as in Fig. 5. The lower lever, which corresponds to the curved bar of Fig. 2, is kept normally in the position of Fig. 4 by a spring.

Sometimes the points of the teeth on the shifting-sleeve come against the points of the teeth of the wheel connected with the hands, and then pull on the winding knob is translated into pressure against this wheel. To avoid this, there is a form of the mechanism in which the upper lever does not act directly on the lower, but brings a spring to bear on it which overcomes the spring normally pressing it upward, and makes it move the sleeve down. The force acting on the sleeve is then determined by the spring, and is independent of how hard the knob is pulled.

CHAPTER XVIII

CALENDAR AND EQUATION WORK

ORDINARY calendar work allows for thirty-one days in the month, and the day-of-the-month dial has to be corrected at the end of the months with fewer days. Perpetual calendar work, which shows the day of the month correctly, even in leap year, is found in clocks in the first half of the eighteenth century, but, as far as the Author knows, was fitted in watches only in the second half, and then only very rarely. It is only the wonderful clock in Strasbourg Cathedral that keeps the calendar right over the centuries, omitting a leap year in 1900 and including it in 2000.

The lower diagram on Plate LXXIV shows the calendar work fitted in the watch by Jean Vallier of about 1610 illustrated on Plate XI. It is typical of the ordinary watch work, though in details many variants are found.

The pinion of 10 leaves marked HOUR is on the hour hand and drives the wheel of 40 teeth, which therefore turns once in two days. This carries two pinions, one of 8 leaves driving the wheel of 28 marked DAY OF WEEK, which therefore turns once a week, and one of 4 pins driving the wheel of 62 marked DAY OF MONTH, which therefore turns once in 31 days. A disk on this with a single tooth turns the star-wheel marked MONTHS through one ray at every turn or every month; the star-wheel, therefore, turns once a year and shows the months. The pinion of 4 pins also turns a moon wheel of 59 teeth. This is shown on the right, though actually it lies above the DAY OF MONTH wheel. It turns, therefore, once in

PLATE LXXIV

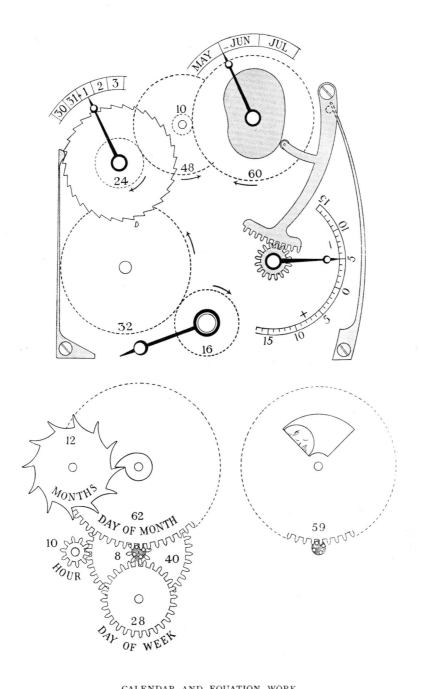

CALENDAR AND EQUATION WORK

$29\frac{1}{2}$ days, the approximate period of the moon's phases. It shows the age of the moon in days and also turns a disk with a moon below a fixed sector-shaped opening.

A different arrangement of calendar work is shown in the upper diagram, together with an equation-of-time work. The hand at the bottom of the diagram is the hour hand, and the wheel of 16 teeth on its arbor turns the wheel of 32 teeth once a day. A single tooth standing up from this wheel moves the wheel above it, with ratchet-like teeth, through one tooth daily. This wheel carries a hand indicating the day of the month, and it turns once a month. A wheel of 24 teeth attached to it turns a wheel of 48 teeth once in two months, and this, driving a wheel of 60 by a pinion of 10, turns the wheel once a year. Its arbor carries a hand showing the months, and also an irregularly-shaped piece called the *equation-cam*. This cam, as it turns, moves back and forth the shaded arm which is pivoted above and has teeth below; a projection from the arm carries a small roller which bears against the edge of the cam and is kept pressed against it by the spring on the right. This arm, in its back and forth motion, turns the pinion with which its teeth engage and moves the hand over the scale marked with a central 0 and extending to 15 on each side. This is the equation-of-time hand; in the position shown, the month and day-of-the-month hands indicate a date of June 1 and the equation-of-time hand indicates 5 on the side marked ' − ' (minus), meaning that 5 minutes must be subtracted from the time shown on a sundial to give mean solar time.

A similar device of a suitably-shaped cam moving an arm was used to give other irregularly varying indications, such as the length of the day throughout the year and the times of sunrise and sunset. These are even more rarely found in watches; the watch by Marc Fabry Pinault, illustrated on Plate LIII, 2, is an example. Berthoud, about the middle of the eighteenth century, fitted calendar and equation work to a watch without

343

giving the watch movement the extra work of driving it. He used the movement given to the fuzee-chain stop in winding to move a day-wheel one tooth forward. Watch-keys also have been made with calendar work operated by the action of winding.

CHAPTER XIX

THE TOURBILLON

THE Tourbillon is a device invented by A. L. Breguet in 1781 for avoiding some of the errors in time-keeping due to change of position of a watch. In ordinary use a watch is supposed to take up any one of five positions, known as pendant up, pendant right, pendant left, face up and face down, and in all observatory tests the rate of the watch is determined for each of these positions. Now, between the two positions of face up or down and the other three, when the watch is on edge, there is the essential difference that, in the former, the weight of the balance is supported by the end of its pivot resting on one of its end-stones, while in the latter it is supported by the sides of its pivots resting in its jewelled bearings. The friction in the latter case is generally more than in the former, and adjusters often have to equalize the friction in the two cases by flattening the ends of the pivots so as to increase the friction when the watch is face up or down.

As between the three positions when the watch is on edge, there are always differences in rate due to the balance wheel or lever not being accurately balanced. If one side of the balance be heavier than the other, it makes a difference whether the watch is held with the heavier side above, below or at one side.

The tourbillon avoids this form of position error by turning round the balance and escape wheel once a minute, so that the effect of one side of the balance being heavier is averaged out every minute. The device is

345

simple in principle but complex in practice—rather too complex to be described in a non-technical book were it not that a tourbillon watch by Breguet or one of his successors is regarded as a treasure, and it is better for the possessor to appreciate why it is a treasure.

Plate LXXV shows in section the part of a watch with a tourbillon. The drawing is not of an actual watch, the parts being given rather more space than they have in reality, to make the drawing more clear. Also jewels are omitted, though every tourbillon watch is jewelled.

The wheel A is the third wheel of the watch, that is, the wheel driven by the centre wheel, which turns once an hour. It drives the pinion B, which turns once per minute and carries on its arbor the whole of the tourbillon. This consists of a cage (indicated in the drawing by cross-hatching) having an upper plate C and a lower plate D, connected by pillars. The upper plate C carries a pivot running in the cock E, and this acts as the upper pivot of the arbor of the pinion B. The lower pivot is generally prolonged and carries a seconds hand. The tourbillon cage carries the balance wheel and the escape wheel. The balance wheel is pivoted centrally between the plates of the cage in the axis of the pinion B. The escape wheel F is pivoted above in a cock fixed to the upper side of the plate D; its pinion passes down through a hole in the plate, and the lower pivot is in a cock fixed to the under side of the plate. The escapement is shown as a lever, with the roller and pin on the balance staff, but with the lever itself omitted; this would be pivoted in the plate D and in a cock fixed to the plate. Actually, a tourbillon watch is generally given a chronometer escapement.

If the watch were not a tourbillon, the fourth wheel would be fixed on the arbor of the pinion B and would drive the escape wheel pinion. In the tourbillon, the fourth wheel G, which engages the escape wheel pinion, is fixed to the watch plate, the arbor of the pinion B passing freely

PLATE LXXV

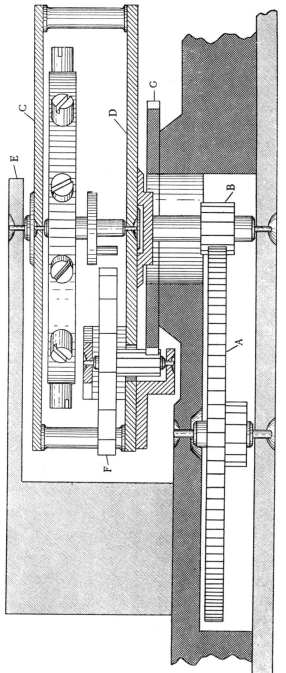

TOURBILLON

through a hole in the centre of the wheel. As the tourbillon cage turns, the escape wheel pinion rolls round the fixed wheel G, and in doing so is driven by it.

The difficulty in making a tourbillon lies in making the parts light enough and yet rigid enough. Unless the whole cage, with the escape wheel and its cocks, is very light, its quick intermittent motion produces so high pressures on the teeth and pivots that wear is rapid. On the other hand, the cage is part of the arbor of the pinion B, and if it is too flexible the timekeeping is subject to irregularities greater than the tourbillon is intended to cure. Though the top and bottom parts C and D of the cage have been referred to as plates, they are of very openwork construction, sometimes a narrow rim with three spokes. When it is realized that the actual size of the balance is little more than that of the roller on the balance staff in the drawing, and that all the pivots of the balance, escape wheel and lever must be jewelled, the extreme delicacy of the construction may be appreciated. Only the finest workmen are capable of producing a tourbillon watch which gives any advantage over an ordinary watch.

Different forms of construction have been evolved since Breguet's time, including one in which the arbor of the pinion B has its upper pivot below the tourbillon cage, so that this is supported only on the end of the protruding arbor.

Tourbillon watches are still made in Switzerland and at Glashütte in Germany, and appear in the watch trials at Kew and other observatories. The results indicate that the time and skill spent on the tourbillon might be better employed in perfecting an ordinary watch. But a fine tourbillon watch is a triumph of mechanical skill.

A different type of tourbillon was invented by Bonniksen of Coventry in 1892 and called by him a Karussell, the Swedish word for a merry-go-round. In this the need for great delicacy of construction is avoided by putting the fourth wheel in the rotating carriage, so

347

that this turns only once in $52\frac{1}{2}$ minutes. In observatory trials, in which the watch remains in one position for at least twenty-four hours, the Karussell avoids position errors just as well as the tourbillon. It is probable that, in wear, the longer time needed to average out the position errors would make no appreciable difference.

CHAPTER XX

THE CHRONOLOGY OF WATCHES

THIS chapter consists of a list, in chronological order, of the characteristics of watches at different periods, in respect of both case and movement. Such a list cannot be compiled with any accuracy of date, because practically every feature was introduced gradually, then became general or common, and, when transitory, gradually died out. Often, too, the locality has an influence on the date. Further, many features appeared in isolated cases long before they really came into use. For instance, it may fairly be said that seconds hands are not found on watches before 1750 and are not common before 1800; yet one is known of 1665 and another of 1690. For the sake of conciseness, therefore, statements are broad rather than strictly accurate, but references are made to the foregoing text, where the point is dealt with more fully, by page numbers in brackets.

The most important thing to remember in endeavouring to date a watch is that no one single feature should be relied on. What has just been said gives some reason for this; besides, there is the possibility of alterations having been made which may embrace anything from a change of screw to a change of the complete movement in the case. When several features of the case and its decoration and several of the movement all point to one date, then one can feel fairly sure that is the right date.

The same criterion of agreement between a number of features may serve to disclose a forgery. A forgery often looks wrong, for some indefinable reason; possibly it is that the eye is offended by incongruous features before the mind has analysed their incongruity.   Forgers, too, generally make mistakes in small details.   In one of the principal museums outside England is a fine watch with alarum, of the type in which the alarum disk acts as the hour hand ; the figures on the disk, however, are as on a watch dial.   Here the forger has confused the two types of alarum.

The innumerable forgeries of the names of the great makers, Tompion, Graham, Le Roy, Breguet, are in quite a different category.   Generally there was no attempt to imitate the work of the maker, and the forgery was confined to putting the great man's name on the small man's ordinary work, sometimes bad work, sometimes really good work.

Under the heading of 'Famous Makers' are the names of the more important watchmakers whose work is extant, excluding those eminent mainly in clock- and chronometer-making.

1510

Earliest record of watches made in Nürnberg by Peter Henlein (47).   They may have been of drum type or spherical.   Henlein made several spherical watches between 1520 and 1525 (52).

1518

Earliest record of watches made in France by Julien Coudray for François I. (63).

1550-1575

General.—Almost the only watches known are of the drum type, made in Nürnberg and Augsburg.   The earliest known French watch is spherical, dated 1551

350

(Plate VI).   Three other French watches are attributed to this period (65).

Famous Makers.—Hans Gruber, Nürnberg, 1552-1597. Jacques de la Garde, Blois, clockmaker to the King 1551-65.

Decoration.—Cases of German watches are of gilt brass, with cover pierced in a pattern having openings corresponding to the hour figures (56). Covers are generally hinged ; canister watches, with the cover pressed on, are very rare. Some watches are without cover. Except for chiselling on a few cast cases, decoration is confined to engraving of ornament.

Dials.—Dials of German watches are gilt brass plates with hour figures I-XII and generally 13-24, with feeling knobs ; sometimes with I-XII and I-XII and 1-24 inside. The roman figures are stumpy and in the arabic figures the 2's are like Z's. A narrow band is common between roman and arabic figures, divided into quarter-hours by lines or shading.

The centre of the dial is generally engraved with a sun of 12 rays, sometimes a pattern, very rarely scenes (94).

Hands.—Hands are of steel, rather heavy.

Movement.—The movement has iron wheels and iron plates ; brass plates may be found towards 1575 (80). Going time generally about 27 hours. Stackfreed and dumb-bell foliot. Mainsprings are generally without barrel and hooked to a pillar, but barrels may be found towards 1575. The verge is pivoted either in the bottom plate or in a piece attached to it. Pillars are nearly always square riveted to the top plate. The count wheel is annular, with internal teeth, and sunk in the top plate.

The spherical French watch has a fuzee, a wheel foliot, brass spring barrel and plates, and iron wheels. Striking or alarum mechanism usual, sometimes both. Striking mechanism is of the earliest type (294). Cock of S form, fixed by tenon and pin to very small foot riveted to plate.

351

Decoration in the movement is rare.

Screws which may be original generally found holding the stackfreed spring and cam.

1575-1600

General.—In Germany the drum type continues, but oval and octagonal shapes appear and become more common towards 1600 (60). Covers tend to become more domed and edges to bulge. Several book watches are known. Some watches in crystal cases and cross form may be of a date before 1600.

The few French watches known are oval with solid hinged covers and straight sides and with little decoration. Movements are not hinged to the cases.

English watches show both French and German influence in the case; there is no type.

Famous Makers.—Randolf Bull, 1590-1617, and Michael Nouwen, 1582-1613, in London. Paul Cuper, Blois, 1582-1618. Pierre Combret, Lyons, 1570-1622. Johan Georg Reinhold, Augsburg.

Decoration.—Engraving of ornament, rarely of figure scenes, and chiselling of cast cases. More profuse than in the previous period.

Dials.—Dials of German watches are of the same type as before, but sometimes have an incised pattern filled with translucent enamel. Silver dials are rare, and engraving of scenes is rare.

Dials of French watches are plain gilt plates, some with hour circles engraved on them, others with silver hour circles applied to them. The hour circle is always smaller than the dial would take, and the figures are always I-XII.

Hands.—Hands are of steel, with tail nearly as long as the pointer.

Movement.—The movement of German watches is of the same type as before, but brass plates become usual soon after 1575, and brass wheels are found and become

352

commoner towards 1600 (80). Iron wheels generally have four arms, and brass three. Stackfreed and dumb-bell foliot, but a fuzee and wheel foliot may possibly be found before 1600. Brass spring barrels become usual. Later type of striking mechanism found. Two or three screws probable. Pillars are square or round.

French watches have brass plates and wheels, fuzee with gut line and wheel foliot. Trains of three wheels going 14 to 16 hours. Ratchet regulator. No screws. Small oval pierced cock fixed by tenon and pin to foot of similar form. Pillars are round, with little decoration, and riveted to the bottom plate.

English watches follow French in the movement.

1600-1625

General.—German watches are most frequently oval or elongated octagons. Circular watches generally have bulging sides, but drum and regular octagon types continue. The egg type, oval with bulging sides and domed covers, belongs to this period. A great diversity of fancy forms, books, skulls, animals, buds, crosses (123); also crystal and stone cases. Gilt brass is usual, silver not common and gold very rare. Gold enamelled watches are known but are very rare.

French and Swiss watches appear in many forms (99); the long oval is most common, then the elongated octagon, and then circular, shell, cross (103), lobed and other forms (123). Gilt metal is usual, but silver is frequent and gold rare, though always used with enamel. Rock - crystal frequently used, and other stones occasionally (103).

English watches follow the French closely, but the long oval is not so common, the nearly circular oval and the octagon being commoner. A special type is found of plain silver, quite smooth without any break, generally with a small opening over the dial with crystal or glass.

353

Dutch watches are more of French than of German character, but there are exceptions.

Solid covers usual in metal case watches and crystal with crystal cases, but crystal covers are found with metal cases and, towards the end of the period, glass, set in a bezel by tags or in a split bezel.

Famous Makers.—Edmund Bull, London, 1610-1630. Nicholas I. Lemaindre, 1598-1652, Marc Girard, d. 1616, Pasquier Payras, d. 1632, Salomon Chesnon, 1572 - c. 1630, Loys Vautier, 1591-1638, Blois. Nicolas I. Bernard, Paris, c. 1600. Jean Vallier, Lyons, 1596-1649. Noel and Étienne Hubert, Rouen. Nicholas Rugendas, Augsburg, 1585 - 1658. Conrad Kreizer, c. 1600, Germany or Strasbourg. Jacques Sermand and J. Duboule, Geneva.

Decoration.—The period of the finest engraving work. Metal cases engraved all over with scenes and floral decorations (92). Chasing and repoussé work rare (117). Cast and chiselled cases occasionally found (119, 122). Niello work rare (151). Enamel mainly confined to champlevé work and simple in composition (131).

Dials.—Dials of German watches tend to lose the circle of arabic numbers and approach the French type of dial. Silver dials are more often found. Engraved scenes and decoration commoner. Champlevé enamel commoner.

Dials of French and English watches have small engraved or appliqué hour ring, and generally have landscape scenes inside hour ring and floral decoration with female and animal figures outside. A silver disk instead of a ring is less common (114). In alarum watches a pierced central disk on a blued steel ground is often found. The dial is usually enamelled when the case is enamelled. Hour figures stumpy, XII being as wide as high or wider (115).

Hands.—Hands are of steel, with tail nearly as long as pointer. Tailless hands uncommon (117).

354

Pendants.—The pendant knob has hole from back to front. Usually a small plain round knob, occasionally decorated (153).

Movement.—The movement of German watches usually with stackfreed and dumb-bell foliot, but fuzee is occasionally and wheel folio frequently found. Plates are always, and wheels generally, of brass. Later type of striking always used. There is usually some decoration by piercing and engraving of cocks, spring barrels, etc., but seldom much, and what there is is rarely good.

The movement of French and English watches remains the same. Trains of four wheels very rare, and watches going for 26 hours are rare. A tangent screw begins to replace the ratchet as regulator about 1620, but the ratchet continues. An indicating dial is found, but is not common till later. The baluster type of pillar is usual (Plate XXX, 1), but many forms are found ; the Egyptian type occasionally, and also spiral forms.

Decoration becomes more profuse and is generally very good.

The balance cock remains the same, but the part over the balance tends to increase in size. Towards 1625 the one-piece cock fixed with a screw becomes more common.

The ratchet nearly always has a screw as pivot. It is generally of gilt brass, pierced and engraved, with a pierced and engraved portion above and hiding the click (Plates XVI, 2 and XXI, 3). When a tangent screw was used, this had two bearing pieces of blued steel, each fixed by a screw and pierced in a very open design. Winding is by hinging out the movement, not through a hole in the case.

Decoration on the top plate itself, beyond the simple engraved wreath often found in English watches, is rare. Sometimes a band is engraved round the edge.

Dutch watches have no individual type. They are found with stackfreed but more often with fuzee. A dumb-bell foliot appears unknown.

Swiss watches are similar to French.

355

1625-1650

General.—German watches continue in the egg form, but tend towards the French and English forms.

French, English and Swiss watches continue in the same types, but the circular watch becomes more common and by the end of the period is the most common form. The type of circular watch with edges curved round from the back without break starts with this period. Form watches are more common.

Glasses become common, but metal covers continue.

Outer cases are introduced about 1640, generally of leather, piqué silver or gold, sometimes of silver or gold.

Famous Makers. — David Bouquet, 1632-65, Edward East, 1610-93, Edmund Gilpin, 1630-77, Robert Grinkin, 1609-60, Simon Hackett, 1632-64, David Ramsay, c. 1590 - c. 1654, London. Thomas Chamberlain, Chelmsford. Abraham Gribelin, 1589-1671, Nicolas II. Lemaindre, 1600-60, Blois. Jacques Barbaret, Nicolas II. Bernard, 1636-46, Josias Joly, 1609-40, J. Sermand, Paris. Timothée and Noel Hubert, Rouen. Johannes Buschmann, 1620-57, Andreas Stahl, Augsburg. Johan Sigmund Schloer, Regensburg. Hans Conrad Elchinger, Amsterdam. J. Silleman and Jacob Vibrandi or Wijbrandts, Leeuwarden. Henry Ester of unknown place.

Decoration.—Engraved work continues, but flower and foliage patterns on a larger scale and less conventional in form become usual later in the period.

Enamel work of all kinds develops, and this is the period of the finest work (125). Paintings on enamel start about 1630, the finest period being at the start; deterioration begins before 1650 (142). Paintings on enamel are always in circular watches with curved round edges and solid covers, scenes being painted on the outsides of case and cover and monochrome landscapes or, less commonly, coloured scenes on the insides.

Dials.—Dials continue as before, with a gilt engraved

356

dial plate and hour ring either engraved, or in silver and appliqué, as the most common type. The hour circle tends to become larger and, in the circular watches, was nearly the diameter of the dial plate, with only a narrow band of ornament outside. The later English circular watches often had a silver dial set in a narrow gilt rim. A day-of-the-month ring is often found on the outside of the dial, with indicator on a narrow gilt ring turning between it and the hour circle. Occasionally, the ring with figures turns and the indicator is fixed.

In enamelled watches the dial is generally gold, enamelled in champlevé.

In watches with painted enamels the dial has a painted scene in the centre and a white enamel hour ring. Figures remain stumpy, but towards 1650 the XII tends to become higher than it is wide.

Hands.—Hands remain as before, but the hand of painted enamel watches is invariably of gilt brass, generally with a sunflower centre.

Pendants.—Pendant knobs as before, with hole from back to front. Towards the end of the period they are occasionally found with hole in the other direction.

Movement.—The movement of French, English and Swiss watches is as before, but four-wheel trains going for 26 hours become more common and are usual at the end of the period. The fuzee chain was introduced commercially about 1625 by Gruet, a Swiss, and becomes common in watches towards 1650. A tangent screw is usual as regulator, but ratchets are still common. Indicating dials become more common.

The cock is generally in one piece with a single foot fixed by a screw, but a pinned-on cock in two pieces is still found, especially in English watches. The cock tends to leave the long oval form for the foot and the part over the balance, the latter becoming circular and covering the balance while the foot spreads outwardly. The long oval form, however, persists beyond 1650. Pillars are generally of baluster form or of the rectangular

357

Egyptian type, tapering downwards, but many forms are found.

Though the plates are generally without decoration, there are many examples with profuse decoration, either by engraving on the plate or by pierced and engraved plates applied to it. Decoration also appears between the plates in pierced and engraved spring barrels, pillars, screw-heads and the fuzee-stop support.

German movements become similar to the French and English, but examples of the stackfreed are found, even to the end of the period.

1650-1675

General.—The circular watch becomes general. Form watches are frequent but oval watches uncommon. Crystal and stone cases become less common. Outer cases usual for enamel watches.

Famous Makers. — Samuel Betts, Ahasuerus Fromanteel, Benjamin Hill, Henry Jones, 1654-95, Jean Rousseau, London. Solomon ii. Chesnon, Blois. Charles Bobinet, Balthazar and Gilles Martinot, Paris. Estienne Hubert, Rouen. Guillaume Nourisson, Lyons. Wilhelm Peffenhauser and David Buschmann, 1640-1712, Augsburg. Denis Bordier, 1629-1708, Geneva.

Decoration.—Decoration takes a great variety of forms, enamel of all kinds being frequent. The painted enamels of this period are good, though not equal to those of the earlier period.

The only type which can be said to be in any way typical of the period is the pierced and engraved silver watch, with rounded edges and bezel with glass. The design is generally of flowers and foliage on a large scale in naturalistic form ; figures and scenes are less common.

Dials.—Dials are found in great variety, mainly of the types of the earlier period. The champlevé type of dial is occasionally found towards 1675 (203). Figures are less stumpy, the XII being higher than it is wide.

358

Hands.—Hands remain as before, but tails tend to be shorter, and gilt and tailless hands are less rare.

Pendants.—Small spherical knob usual with hole either way, more commonly from front to back. The pivoted loop of the next period starts in this.

Movement.—Movements remain the same, generally, as in the previous period, but all watches go for 26 hours and have four-wheel trains. Fuzees all have chains, and the regulator is always a tangent screw.

French and English cocks become definitely distinguished towards the end of the period, the English and German having a single large foot with a single screw, while the French and Swiss have two small eyes opposite each other, each with a screw. Dutch cocks follow either the English or the French pattern, but in the latter case the eyes are larger and become feet, generally extending to the edge of the plate. The oval form is found in cocks with feet up to the end of the period, but the table is generally almost or quite circular, without rim, and the foot spreading. Pillars are of many types, as before; the tulip pillar begins to be popular.

1675-1700

General.—Any form but circular is very rare. Watches tend to become larger and thicker; the French watches of about 1700 are especially thick.

Outer cases become general for decorated watches. Leather, fish-skin, shagreen and tortoise-shell with gold and silver studs are all used; also filigree gold and silver.

Famous Makers.—Nathaniel Barrow, 1653-99, Peter Debaufre, 1675-1722 (also Paris), two Fromanteels, Charles Gretton, 1662-1733, Cornelius Herbert, 1660-1727, Daniel Quare, 1649-1724, Thomas Tompion, 1638-1713, London. Paul Roumieu, Edinburgh and Rouen. Isaac Thuret, Paris. Leonhard Burry, Basle. Jean

359

Choudens, Geneva.   Johannes Van Ceulen, The Hague.
Johan Wideman, Stockholm.

Decoration.—Engraved decoration becomes less
common, and chased and repoussé more common (203).
The use of coloured enamels is much less common, but
painting on enamel is more common.   From 1680 is the
period of the Huaud paintings (145).

Dials.—The minute hand was introduced.   It became
fairly common by 1700, but there were more watches
without it than with it.   Alternatives to two hands are
the sun and moon hour indicator, frequent in this period,
the wandering hour figure, commoner after 1700, and the
turning hour circle and the division of the dial into six
hours ; these last two are found only in isolated cases
(209).   'Pendulum' bobs with slot in the dial appear
towards 1700 (212).

The champlevé dial, in which the figures and divisions
are engraved on polished plaques standing up from a
matt ground, becomes the standard on English watches,
and is found on French watches (203).

The French dial from about 1690 was of gilt metal
with enamel hour plaques and division band ; when a
minute hand was used, the minute figures were either on
separate plaques or on an enamel band (207).   This form
is not found on English watches.

Hour figures become very long, the XII being about
twice as high as it is wide.   Minute figures, shown for
every five minutes, are also large, leaving only a small
central space in the dial (213).

Hands.—Generally of steel, more delicate.   The tail
begins to disappear, and by 1700 the tailless hand is
general.   Gilt pierced hands begin to appear towards
1700.

Pendants.—The pivoted loop becomes the most
common form, but the small spherical knob remains ; its
hole is more commonly from side to side (214).

Movement.—The balance spring was introduced in
1675 (159) ; most watches had one by 1700.   Springs at

360

first are very short, of one or two turns.   Balance wheels become larger when a spring is used, often very large.

Repeating mechanism applied to watches in 1687 by Barlow and Quare.   It is kept secret by English makers and does not appear in France till later.   Repeating watches before 1700 are rare.

The regulator, with a balance spring, is of varying forms, a sliding block moved by a screw or a plate turned either directly or by a pinion.   The tangent screw regulator on the mainspring arbor remains, but is more often between the plates.

Balance cocks are circular over the balance, completely covering it, and, especially towards 1700, have an external rim.   The foot, in English and German watches, spreads outwards to the edge of the plate, following the line of the edge.   The junction between the foot and the part over the balance remains very narrow, apparently retaining the form of the old pinned-on cock.   In French watches, the cocks have two very small eyes each with a screw, and towards 1700 painted enamel plaques, devoid of merit, are sometimes found on the cock over the balance.

All cocks are pierced and chiselled in a pattern symmetrical about a central line.   The tulip pillar is the favourite, but many other forms are found.

1700-1750

General.—Watches remain as before, circular, large and very thick, tending to become thinner and smaller towards the end of the period.

Outer cases are the general rule.   The inner case is usually plain, while the outer case receives the decoration.

Famous Makers.—Langley Bradley, a. 1687-1729, Charles Cabrier, father and son, John Champion, 1700-70, Daniel Delander, 1692-1730, John Ellicott, 1706-72, Ahasuerus Fromanteel, George Graham, 1673-1757, Benjamin Gray, David Lestourgeon, Christopher Pinchbeck, Quare and Horseman, Tompion (jun.) and E. Banger,

Joseph Williamson, 1686-1725, London.   J. B. Dutertre, Enderlin, P. Gaudron, Étienne Le Noir, Julien Le Roy, 1686-1759, Paris.   Albrecht Erb, Vienna.   Gerrett Paulus Braemar, Amsterdam.   Jean (le jeune) Van Ceule, The Hague.

Decoration.—The repoussé case becomes the principal form of decorated case, and continues to the end of the century (215).   It is commoner in English than in French watches, while enamel painting is commoner in French than in English.   The repoussé case has nearly always a figure scene in a frame of ornament, rocaille after 1730.   In the early part of the century the frame is symmetrical, but symmetry disappears in the Louis xv. period, towards 1750.

Enamel paintings, instead of reaching to the front edge of the case, have a metal frame, at first quite narrow, but later encroaching more and more on the enamel; the frame is then repoussé.   Enamels without frame or with narrow frame are, however, found (215).

Semi-precious stones, cornelian, agate, etc., are used set, often in large plaques, in repoussé or pierced and engraved metal.

Dials.—Minute hands become general, but single-hand watches, more especially French, are often found up to 1725.   The wandering hour figure is frequently found soon after 1700, but it and the other alternatives to two hands disappear before 1725.   'Pendulum' watches with bob showing under the dial are common soon after 1700, but soon disappear, the bob, however, remaining on the top plate and becoming the standard in Dutch watches. Fly-back minute hands are found in this period.

White enamel dials, introduced a little before 1700 in France and Switzerland, become common.   In England they appear later, but also become common towards 1750.   The French dial with enamel plaques continues till about 1725, and then disappears (207).   The champlevé dial remains the most common in England, and is also common in France.

362

Hour and minute figures are very large for some time after 1700, but both tend to become smaller. Dials with minute figures only at the quarters or without minute figures are rare before 1750 (213).

The minute band is sometimes arched between the minute figures. This is a Dutch fashion and is found on English watches for the Dutch market, for in Holland it became standard on enamel and champlevé dials after 1750.

Hands.—Two hands become general and tails disappear. In steel hands, the 'beetle type' with two loops on the hour hand becomes common; the minute hand is nearly always a 'poker' hand—that is, plain except for slight shaping. Gilt hands are commonly elaborately pierced, especially in Dutch watches, when the piercing is generally inferior.

Pendants.—Pendant rings always lie in the plane of the watch. The usual form is horseshoe-shaped, pivoted to a flattish knob, but an oval form becomes common towards 1750. The older small spherical knob with hole for the ring continues, but is rare.

Movement.—The balance spring becomes general, the number of turns of the spring increasing to four or five. The balance remains large, about half the diameter of the plate and often more.

Winding through holes in the dial becomes common, especially in French watches. Winding through the centre of the single hand is sometimes found, also in French watches.

Repeating watches become common, every maker of repute making them. Any other than quarter repeating rare before 1750. The Stogden work is introduced and used in England. Repeating work is always actuated by pressing in the pendant.

Jewelling invented by Facio and Debaufre in 1704. Jewels are confined to England and are very rare till 1720. They are confined to the balance, generally only as end stones. Many watches, however, have a jewel in

363

the centre of the cock which is ornamental only.   In the second quarter of the century jewels are not uncommon in English watches of the highest class, but are not found in French watches, though there is evidence of their use in France.   The coqueret is introduced.

Dust-caps are introduced about 1715, but are rare in the first quarter of the century.   Oil-sinks are found towards the end of the period, but are rare.

Any escapement but the verge is very rare.

Motion work, enabling the two hands to be set together, is used by Quare, but is found in clocks earlier.

English cocks always have an external rim; the foot follows the curve of the edge of the plate and also has a rim.   It is generally very broad and short, as in Plate XLVIII, 1.   Towards the end of the period it tends to get narrower, with sides more inclined, giving a wedge shape. Table and foot are pierced, but solid feet are found about the middle of the period and then become commoner. The decoration of the table springs from a mask or female head, more rarely a cherub or shell.

French cocks have larger eyes, giving the cock an oval appearance.   The design loses its symmetry about a central line.   Trellis-work designs are found.

Pillars of a baluster shape but of square section are often found, and also the tulip and Egyptian types; the latter frequently has foliage decoration above the tapering column.   Pillars composed entirely of foliage decoration are found, also octagonal pillars of a baluster shape.

1750-1800

General.—Any but circular watches rare until the end of the century, when form watches are introduced in great variety (225).   Watches become smaller and much thinner.   Automata and musical watches become popular in the last quarter of the century (227).   Repeating watches are common, repeating generally the quarter and often the half-quarter; any other form of repetition is

364

rare. Self-winding (pedometer) and keyless watches are introduced towards 1800, but are very rare. It is the period of richly-decorated and gaudy watches, with a tendency towards greater simplicity at the end. Breguet then introduced the perfectly plain and tasteful watch.

Famous Makers. — William Anthony, John Arnold, Charles Cabrier, Josiah Emery, John Grant, William Ilbury, John Leroux, James McCabe, George Margetts, Markwick Markham, Edward Massey, Thomas Mudge, Francis Perigal (three of the name from 1740-1824), George Prior, Isaac Rogers, James Tregent, Justin Vulliamy, London. Peter Litherland, Liverpool. Thomas Reid, Reid & Auld, Edinburgh. I. B. Baillon, Ferdinand Berthoud, A. L. Breguet, Pierre Gregson, J. F. Houriet, J. A. Lepine, Pierre Le Roy, Robert Robin, Jean Romilly, J. P. Tavernier, Daniel Vaucher or Vauchez, Paris. Leonard Bordier, Chevallier et Cie, Moise Constantin, Esquivillon Frères, H. L. Jaquet-Droz, Jaques Patron, Moise Pouzait, J. R. Soret, Philippe Terrot, Vaucher Frères, Geneva. Philipp M. Hahn, Echterdingen ; François Poncet, Dresden. Augustus Bourdillon, Stockholm. Samuel Ruel, Rotterdam.

Decoration.—Repoussé cases continue, but die out in the last quarter. Enamel painting is common, and many low-grade enamels are found. The enamel painting tends more and more to form only a part of the decoration, taking the form of plaques surrounded by repoussé work and later by four-colour gold ornament and borders of stones and pearls. In the last quarter of the century the enamel painting is often oval or lenticular, surrounded by translucent and opaque enamel decoration or other ornament.

Engine-turning was introduced on watches about 1770, though it had been used on turned works for over a century (223). From 1780 onwards it is often found covered with translucent enamel and is sometimes used as the background of an enamel painting. It is, though, always of the simplest kind. Engine-turning on plain

365

gold cases, giving 'barleycorns,' is found, but is not common.

Four-colour gold decoration is largely used towards the end of the century, sometimes combined with precious and semi-precious stones (219).

Pearl ornament becomes common at the end of the century.

Dials.—White enamel dials become standard, champlevé dials dying out about 1775.   Painted enamel dials become popular towards the end of the century, especially on cheap watches (227); the work is always bad.   In automata watches, most of the dial is taken up with a chased and engraved metal plate forming background for the figures, leaving either a narrow outer ring of white enamel or a small eccentric enamel dial (227).   Engine-turned metal dials are found, but are not common.

Minute and hour figures both become small and the minute figures disappear, but many exceptions are found. The arched minute band is standard in Dutch watches and watches for the Dutch market.

Centre and eccentric second hands, though found in isolated instances much earlier, appear in this period, but do not become at all common before 1800.

Hands.—The fine steel hand is the most common, the 'beetle' pattern with two loops giving place to the type with a single loop and to the spade type.   Pierced gilt hands continue and diamond-studded hands are often found.   Wavy hands are fashionable in France in the early years of the nineteenth century.

Pendants.—The oval ring pivoted to a flattish knob is usual.   Towards the end of the century the pendant stem is often rectangular.   Also a spherical knob is introduced with circular ring pivoted to it.

Movement.—There is a general endeavour to make the movement as thin as possible, more especially in France and Switzerland.   This leads to small escape wheels and short fuzees and the use of sinks and holes in the bottom plate (196).   The omission of the bell by

366

Julien Le Roy about 1750 and the introduction of the wire gong by Breguet in 1789 enabled repeating watches to be kept thin.   The adjustable potence (196), with screw in French watches, comes into general use at the beginning of the period (196).   Towards the end, Lepine introduced his calibre, using a cylinder escapement, without fuzee, and giving a much thinner watch (197); these watches are not common before 1800.   The cylinder is used frequently by the better makers in the last quarter of the century, in England always, and in France generally, with a fuzee.   Lever watches are found, but are rare.   Duplex escapements are fairly common among high-class watches about 1800.   The rack lever escapement was introduced by Peter Litherland in 1791, and it and the club-footed verge escapements are common in Lancashire watches.

Temperature compensation is introduced for chrono-meters, but is rare in watches (171).   The curb-pin form of compensation is occasionally found towards 1800 (171).

English balance cocks have feet that become narrower and narrower, and towards 1800 generally solid.   From 1800 the whole cock is generally solid.   Dutch cocks are generally solid with a semicircular slot ; often with a motto and a chiselled figure scene.

Cocks become smaller and the ornament inferior. Chiselling is generally omitted, leaving only flat piercing. The design is often symmetrical about the centre and, about 1800, is geometric.

In French cocks the eyes become smaller.

Towards 1800 Swiss cocks are found with pierced decoration of script forming the maker's name.

Cocks with decoration belonging to the first half of the century are found to the end of the century.   There is no type of pillar belonging particularly to this period, but towards the end there is a tendency towards a simpler circular form.

INDEX

References to pages in arabic and to plates in roman figures.

INDEX

INDEX

Dopplmayr, book on Nürnberg crafts-men, 48, 53, 60.
Dover Castle clock, 21, 24, 33. II, III, V.
Draw, in the lever escapement, 288.
Drecker, J., book on the theory of sun-dials, 14.
Drop, in escapement, definition of, 23.
Drum-type watches, 53, 60.
Dubié, enameller, 129.
Duboule, Jean Baptiste, watches, 114, 122. XXI.
Dueber-Hampden Watch Co., 269.
Dufour, watch by. L.
Du Jardin, Jehan, 65.
Dumb-bell foliot, 83.
Duplex escapement, description, 283. LX.
Durand, Jean Louis, enameller, 147.
Dutertre, Jean Baptiste, 255.
  and the duplex escapement, 283.

EARNSHAW, THOMAS, his method of making a bimetallic balance, 174.
  his work on chronometers, 258.
Earth's orbit, 2.
  rotation, constancy of, 7.
East, Edward, watches, 105, 137. XX, XXXV.
Ébauche, the rough watch movement, 250.
Ebsworth, John, watch by. XLV.
Ecliptic, 2.
Egg-shaped watches, 60.
Ehrhardt, Joh. Christoph, watch by. LVII.
Elgin National Watch Co., 269.
Elinvar, for balance-springs, 178.
Elizabeth, Queen, her watches, 69.
Ellicott, John, his work, 257.
  his temperature compensation device, 171.
Emery, Josiah, and the lever escape-ment, 288, 291.
Enamel, à l'aurore, 219.
  basse-taille, 149.
  champlevé and cloisonné, 133.
  decoration, kinds of, 127.
  dials, late, with paintings, 227. LVI.
  in relief, 135.
  Limoges, 128.
  on glass, 148.

Enamel—continued.
  painters of the 17th century, 147.
  painting in, 137.
  painting on, examples, 142, 217.
  painting on, process of, 129.
  royal blue translucent, 219.
Enamellers of Blois, 129.
Enamelling on early watches, 131.
  on watches about 1700, 207.
  process of, 127.
Encyclopédie, article on horology, 51.
Enderlin, 256.
End-stones for balance staff pivots and for ornament, 190.
Engine-turning, examples of, 223. XXXI, LIII, LIV.
  invention of, 225.
  process of, 224.
England, watchmaking in, 69, 272.
England's pre-eminence in watchmaking, 254.
English Watch Co., 269.
English watches, v. Watches, English.
Engraving and piercing, 92.
Engraving at Blois, 92.
  champlevé, late, 229. LVI.
  Italian, on watch, 93.
  line and champlevé, 92.
  on cross watches, 99, 103, 114.
  on early German watches, 94.
  on French and English watches, 95, 99, 201.
Epicycles, v. Dondi's clock, 37.
Equal hours, 11, 14.
Equation-cam, 343.
Equation of time, 7.
Equation-of-time work, 343. LXXIV.
Equinoxes, 3, 5, 6.
Escape-wheel, size of, at different periods, 196.
Escapement, as the characteristic of a clock, 20.
  cylinder, invention of, 254.
  dead-beat, 280.
  dead-beat, invention of, 254.
  duplex, description, 283. LX.
  free, 280, 285.
  lever, comparison of English and Swiss forms, 288.
  lever, description, 285. LXI, LXII, LXIII.
  lever, pin-lever form, 291.

373

INDEX

INDEX

INDEX